Spectres of the Self

Spectres of the Self is a fascinating study of the rich cultures surrounding the experience of seeing ghosts in England from the Enlightenment to the twentieth century. Shane McCorristine examines a vast range of primary and secondary sources, showing how ghosts, apparitions and hallucinations were imagined, experienced and debated from the pages of fiction to the case reports of the Society for Psychical Research. By analysing a broad range of themes from telepathy and ghost-hunting to the notion of dreaming while awake and the question of why ghosts wore clothes, Dr McCorristine reveals the sheer variety of ideas of ghost-seeing in English society and culture. He shows how the issue of ghosts remained dynamic despite the advance of science and secularism, and argues that the ghost ultimately represented a spectre of the self, a symbol of the psychological hauntedness of modern experience.

SHANE MCCORRISTINE is a postdoctoral fellow at Ludwig-Maximilians-Universität München and a visiting research fellow at the Institute of English Studies, University of London.

T0370784

Spectres of the Self: Thinking about Ghosts and Ghost-Seeing in England, 1750–1920

Shane McCorristine

CAMBRIDGE
UNIVERSITY PRESS

CAMBRIDGE
UNIVERSITY PRESS

Shaftesbury Road, Cambridge CB2 8EA, United Kingdom

One Liberty Plaza, 20th Floor, New York, NY 10006, USA

477 Williamstown Road, Port Melbourne, VIC 3207, Australia

314–321, 3rd Floor, Plot 3, Splendor Forum, Jasola District Centre, New Delhi – 110025, India

103 Penang Road, #05–06/07, Visioncrest Commercial, Singapore 238467

Cambridge University Press is part of Cambridge University Press & Assessment, a department of the University of Cambridge.

We share the University's mission to contribute to society through the pursuit of education, learning and research at the highest international levels of excellence.

www.cambridge.org
Information on this title: www.cambridge.org/9780521747967

© Shane McCorristine 2010

First published 2010

A catalogue record for this publication is available from the British Library

Library of Congress Cataloging-in-Publication data
McCorristine, Shane, 1983–
    Spectres of the self : thinking about ghosts and ghost-seeing in England, 1750–1920 / Shane McCorristine.
        p.   cm.
    ISBN 978-0-521-76798-9 (Hardback) – ISBN 978-0-521-74796-7 (pbk.)
    1. Ghosts–England–History.   2. Parapsychology.   I. Title.
    BF1472.G7M385 2010
    133.10942–dc22

                                                            2010020689

ISBN   978-0-521-76798-9   Hardback
ISBN   978-0-521-74796-7   Paperback

Contents

List of illustrations   *page* vii
Acknowledgements   viii
List of abbreviations   x

Introduction   1

I. **The dreams of the ghost-seers**   25

1. The haunted mind, 1750–1850   27
    Ghosts reformed   27
    The phantasmagoric dislocation   31
    The case of Nicolai   40
    The spectral illusions model   43
    Hallucinations and illusions in French psychiatry   52
    A Christmas Carol and 'The Haunted Mind'   61

2. Seeing is believing: hallucinations and ghost-seeing   66
    The dreams of the *Geistersehers*: Kant and Schopenhauer
        on ghost-seeing   66
    Hallucinations, spiritualism and pathology   75
    The clothes of ghosts   90

II. **A science of the soul**   101

3. Ghost-hunting in the Society for Psychical Research   103
    The Society for Psychical Research   103
    Ghost-hunting in the Society for Psychical Research   114
    The sociology of the psychical ghost story   127

4. Phantasms of the living and the dead   139
    Phantasms of the living   139
    Criticisms of *Phantasms of the Living*   162
    Phantasms of the dead   172
    A science of the soul?   182

5. The concept of hallucination in late Victorian psychology   192
    The concept of hallucination in the Society for Psychical Research   192
    The 'Report on the Census of Hallucinations'   194
    Dreaming while awake   202
    Some conclusions   210

Epilogue: towards 1920   218
Appendix   229

Bibliography   244
Index   271

Illustrations

1. *The Ghost Illusion*. Source: Jean-Eugène-Robert Houdin, *The Secrets of Stage Conjuring*, ed. and trans. Professor Hoffmann [Angelo John Lewis] (London, 1881). Courtesy of the University Library, Cambridge.   *page* 34

2. Francisco José de Goya y Lucientes, *El Sueño de la Razon Produce Monstruos* (1799). Courtesy of the Trustees of the British Museum.   38

3. Robert W. Buss, *Dickens' Dream* (1875). Courtesy of the Charles Dickens Museum.   64

4. George Cruikshank, *Alas, Poor Ghost!* Source: George Raymond, *The Life and Enterprises of Robert William Elliston, Comedian* (London, 1857). In author's collection.   94

5. Spirit photographs of deceased family members alongside Georgiana Houghton. Source: Miss [Georgiana] Houghton, *Chronicles of the Photographs of Spiritual Beings and Phenomena Invisible to the Material Eye: Interblended with Personal Narrative* (London, 1882). Courtesy of the University Library, Cambridge.   225

6. *Mrs Shaw and Mrs Coates' Daughter, Agnes Tweedale Simpson*. Source: James Coates, *Photographing the Invisible: Practical Studies in Spirit Photography, Spirit Portraiture, and Other Rare but Allied Phenomena* (London and Chicago, 1911). © the British Library Board. Shelfmark 08637.i.38.   226

Acknowledgements

I wish to acknowledge the support and funding I received from the Humanities Institute of Ireland: as an HII doctoral scholar, researching the PhD thesis from which this book came functioned as merely one element in a broader academic and social environment that was always stimulating and a pleasure to be a part of. I would therefore like to extend my thanks to Dr Marc Caball, Professor Anne Fuchs and Valerie Norton. I would like to thank my supervisor Dr David Kerr, my internal supervisor Dr Judith Devlin, and my external supervisor Professor Roger Luckhurst for offering interesting angles, problems and perspectives which influenced my research. The support of the staff in the School of History and Archives during my postgraduate years has always been appreciated: I would like especially to thank Kate Breslin, Professor Howard Clarke, Dr Declan Downey, Dr Elva Johnston, Dr Sue Schulze and Eiriol Townsend. For assistance in attending conferences in 2006, I wish to acknowledge the travel grant provided by the School of History and Archives and the graduate student travel grant provided by the College of Arts and Celtic Studies.

The staff and curators at the libraries I attended over the years have been very helpful. I would like to thank the staff of: the British Library, London; the National Library of Ireland, Dublin; the Society for Psychical Research, London; the College of Psychic Studies, London; the Harry Price Library at Senate House, London; the Wellcome Institute, London; the Wren Library, Trinity College, Cambridge; the University Library, Cambridge; Trinity College, Dublin (especially the staff at the Early Printed Books Department); the James Joyce Library, University College Dublin (especially Avril Patterson at the inter-library loan desk who went out of her way to source some of the more unusual books I requested). I wish to thank the anonymous readers at Cambridge University Press for offering such fruitful criticism of my original manuscript. Thanks are also due to Michael Watson, Helen Waterhouse and Joanna Garbutt at the Press, and Rebecca du Plessis, for expertly guiding me through the editing process.

Part of chapter 2 appeared in an earlier version in the *Paranormal Review* 44 (October 2007) and is reprinted with the permission of the editor. I also wish to acknowledge the Syndics of Cambridge University Library for permission to quote from the Society for Psychical Research Archive, and the Master and Fellows of Trinity College, Cambridge for permission to quote from the Henry Sidgwick Papers and the C.D. Broad Papers.

To my all friends and colleagues, I extend my appreciation for the years of laughs and the truly inter-disciplinary process we have shared: Joanne Banks, Rebecca Boyd, Fiachra Byrne, Corinna Connolly, Clara Cullen, Elizabeth Dawson, David Doyle, Mark Empey, Emily Mark FitzGerald, Vincent Gallagher, Tziovanis Georgakis, Fintan Hoey, Rania Kosmidou, Bill Mallon, Una Newell, Clare Ní Cholmáin, Niamh Ní Shiadhail, Diane Sabenacio Nititham, Laura O'Brien, Ross O'Connell, Jonathan O'Malley, Linda Shortt, Chiara Tedaldi, Karl Whitney and Ross Woods. Finally, this study would not have been possible were it not for the fantastic support of my relatives and family. To my parents Anne and Larry and my siblings Manus, Art and Anna Maria I extend a special word of gratitude.

Abbreviations

Light	*Light: A Journal Devoted to the Highest Interests of Humanity, Both Here and Hereafter* (1881–1883); *Light: A Journal of Psychical, Occult, and Mystical Research* (1883–)
JSPR	*Journal of the Society for Psychical Research*
PSPR	*Proceedings of the Society for Psychical Research*
SPR	Society for Psychical Research
Zoist	*The Zoist: A Journal of Cerebral Physiology and Mesmerism, and Their Application to Human Welfare*

Introduction

It is in one of Henry James's less well known short stories that the modern incarnation of the ghost as a representation of psychological haunting truly comes of age. 'The Friends of the Friends' (1896) illustrates so many of the facets of how ghost-seeing became something so psychologically ghostly in the nineteenth century that it can be considered a prime example of the underlying thesis of this study: that the ghosts which really haunt us today should be considered as spectres of the self, ghosts which are less real, and at the same time more real, than the type of traditional, restless ghosts that we read about in Homer's *Odyssey* or watch on popular television shows such as *Most Haunted*.

'The Friends of the Friends' relates the narrative of a lady who discovers that both her female friend and her fiancé have had a supernatural experience known to late-Victorian contemporaries as a 'crisis apparition'. In the case of the friend, we are told that she had a vision of her father's ghost while in a foreign town and soon received a telegram of confirmation that he had unexpectedly died in England, hundreds of miles away, at the exact moment of her experience. As for the fiancé, at a similar time, he had been studying in Oxford when,

> Coming back into his room while it was still distinct daylight, he found his mother standing there as if her eyes had been fixed on the door. He had had a letter from her that morning out of Wales, where she was staying with her father. At the sight of him, she smiled with extraordinary radiance and extended her arms to him, and then as he sprang forward and joyfully opened his own, she vanished from the place. He wrote to her that night, telling her what had happened; the letter had been carefully preserved. The next morning, he heard of her death.[1]

Touched by this curious coincidence, the lady resolves to arrange a meeting between these two ghost-seers. It is the bitter melancholy of James's story that such a meeting of minds never takes place, 'as meetings are commonly understood'.[2]

---

[1] Henry James, *Ghost Stories of Henry James* (Ware, 2001), p.154.
[2] *Ibid.*

1

Over the years, due to a series of accidents and bad luck, the friend and the fiancé somehow never manage to meet. For the lady, this situation becomes somewhat perverse given that she herself sees her fiancé daily and her friend frequently, and that both parties have expressed an interest in making each other's acquaintance. What makes the situation even more farcical is the fact that both of their 'sets' were strongly linked through friends of friends. The lady begins to suspect an inevitable train of events at work, linked to the shared supernatural perception of the non-friends:

> one couldn't help feeling that the joke had made the situation serious, had produced on the part of each a consciousness, an awkwardness, a positive dread of the last accident of all, the only one with any freshness left, the accident that *would* bring them together.[3]

On the one occasion when a definite rendezvous had been arranged, the lady sabotaged the meeting through a fit of jealousy, and yet, she notes a sense of relief in her friend at the news of the fiancé's non-appearance. That night, as the friend dies suddenly of a latent heart complaint, the fiancé finally sees her for the first time. He is shocked to learn of her death the next day for as he explains to the narrator, ' "I saw her living. I saw her to speak to her. I saw her as I see you now." '[4] As the couple drifts apart the lady realises that her fiancé is constantly visited by the ghost of her friend, with whom he is in love, an 'inconceivable communion'[5] which is seemingly consummated when the man takes his own life some years later.

Are we to take these two characters as doubles of each other, and their eventual meeting an integration of separate centres of self? As ghost-seers are they antipathetic in some sort of cosmic sense? Or is the author reflecting on the spectral nature of identity? What is certain, however, is that James's story echoes the experience of thousands of ordinary, sane and unimaginative people who saw ghosts and hallucinations in nineteenth-century Britain (as we shall see, one survey conducted a few years before James's story was published estimated the figure to be almost 10 per cent of the population). The type of ghosts which predominated were precisely the crisis-apparitions that appeared in 'The Friends of the Friends'; psychical phenomena that may or may not have been subjective hallucinations, but which affected people more than any ghost of popular culture, with its clanging chains and accusing glare, could ever do. This study is therefore concerned with the type of ghost

---

[3] *Ibid.*, p.157.   [4] *Ibid.*, p.164.   [5] *Ibid.*, p.174.

that modern investigators tended to be the most interested in – ghosts that were classified as purposeless, in that they rarely spoke, exhibited agency or requested action on their behalf. Yet it was this type of ghost which became the standard self-representation of the death of the other, a haunting development which James articulates. In the Victorian era, with a reliable postal service and telegraph system connecting the world, news of the death of loved ones could become swiftly known and the intervention of such epistolary confirmations of ghost-seeing served to further accentuate the uncanny nature of modern communication and notions of community. The instantaneous awareness of death that ghost-seeing provided points towards the existence of a ghost-haunted psyche which can supply us with a framework with which to understand why James's 'inconceivable communion' between ghosts and ghost-seers made sense to huge numbers of believers and witnesses in an age dominated by scepticism and loss of faith. At the same time, through looking at inter-related discourses, I want to show how interpreting ghosts as if they were 'the stuff of dreams' directly led to developments in our understanding of how this haunted mind manifested itself. Despite the fact that thinking about ghost-seeing embraced areas of psychological importance from psychopathology to dream-theory, this aspect of the history of ideas has been relatively neglected. Combining these varieties of ghost-seeing experience in one study, I hope that this approach has the cumulative effect of making space for the idea of a spectral self – a subjectivity that was conflicted, hemispheric and liable to hallucinations at any given moment; a mind that was haunted by death, by the past, by fixed ideas; a consciousness frightened by its own existence; and an emotional apparatus seemingly hard-wired to see apparitions of the dead.

'Neither the sun nor death can be looked at steadily.'[6]

Hélène Cixous notes: 'The Ghost is the fiction of our relationship to death, concretized by the specter in literature.'[7] *Spectres of the Self* focuses on and magnifies this relationship through an examination of several varieties of ghost-seeing experience between 1750 and 1920, primarily as exhibited in English culture but with forays into other Western contexts. However, such historical research is inherently problematic for the ghost is, as has been written about death, an 'incessantly receding,

---

[6] François de La Rochefoucauld, *Maxims*, trans. Leonard Tancock (Harmondsworth, 1959), p.40.
[7] Hélène Cixous, 'Fiction and Its Phantasms: A Reading of Freud's *Das Unheimliche* (The "Uncanny")', *New Literary History* 7:3 (1976), 542.

ungraspable signified, always pointing to other signifiers, other means of representing what finally is just absent'.[8] Even though death can be approached, it can never be experienced or authentically expressed by the living.[9] Ghost-seeing, however, is drenched in documentable experience and meaningful expressions of this experience, and this situation offers the historian of ideas unique opportunities to explore attitudes towards death, changing epistemological frameworks and the definitions of what is 'normal', 'scientific' or 'superstitious' in any given society. If we define death as that which is and yet cannot be experienced, then seeing ghosts may be looked upon as an experience in which the living come to encounter the haunting consciousness that they will some day die.

Trying to approach the cultural history of ghost-seeing is, as Daniel Cottom has noted of spiritualism, like 'trying to nail Jello to a tree'.[10] *Spectres of the Self* is therefore selective in its content: the approach I have taken bypasses the many plebeian, religious and occult varieties of ghost-seeing experience in favour of varieties primarily sourced in English bourgeois culture and connected to each other through ideas, themes and debates which made the ghost a dynamic figure in the modern age. The chief aim has been to present an interdisciplinary study that re-evaluates, reconstructs and re-interprets aspects of modern thinking about the ghostly 'other world' that was *at the same time* part of the haunted world of subjective experience.

In part, this study represents a critical development of general histories of the ghost which, with their broadly chronological outlook, failed to present ghost-seeing as an experience that was both dynamic in its representations and metaphorical in its ontologies.[11] Owen Davies's recent study *The Haunted: A Social History of Ghosts* (2007) is to be welcomed for changing this situation. Davies is most concerned with purposeful and memorial ghosts and makes impressive use of English

---

[8] Sarah Webster Goodwin and Elisabeth Bronfen, 'Introduction', in *Death and Representation*, ed. Sarah Webster Goodwin and Elisabeth Bronfen (Baltimore and London, 1993), p.4.

[9] For a cross-section of positions on the 'impossibility' of death see Sigmund Freud, *Civilization, Society and Religion: 'Group Psychology', 'Civilization and its Discontents' and Other Works*, ed. James Strachey (Harmondsworth, 1991), p.77; Michael Holland, ed., *The Blanchot Reader* (Oxford, 1995), p.315.

[10] Daniel Cottom, *Abyss of Reason: Cultural Movements, Revelations, and Betrayals* (Oxford, 1991), p.108.

[11] Ronald C. Finucane, *Ghosts: Appearances of the Dead and Cultural Transformation* (Amherst, 1996); Eric Maple, *The Realm of Ghosts* (London, 1964); P.G. Maxwell-Stuart, *Ghosts: A History of Phantoms, Ghouls, and Other Spirits of the Dead* (Stroud, 2006).

folklore and popular culture in his study.[12] In contradistinction, I wish to focus on the modern conception of the ghost as reflective of the haunted nature of the self, a conception that arose in the aftermath of the impact of the phantasmagoria in the late eighteenth century, and which was primarily approached in the psychiatry, psychology and psychical research of the nineteenth century. This study has also bene-fited from the boom in cultural studies of the supernatural, spiritualism and psychical research that, since Janet Oppenheim's path-breaking *The Other World: Spiritualism and Psychical Research in England, 1850–1914* (1985), have steadily built upon each other in a sophisticated manner at once attuned to the questions posed by psychological modernity and the uncertain place of the irrational and the occult in contemporary thought.[13] Finally, although like Marcellus this study passes on the 'hauntological' buck so to speak, no critical research dealing with ghosts and ghost-seeing can afford to be unaware of Jacques Derrida's *Specters of Marx* (1993), the intellectual reverberations of which are still being felt in cultural studies.[14] It is on the basis of this critical framework that the present study seeks to *grab* the figure of the ghost in a manner that has not hitherto been attempted. Such a project, how-ever, necessarily demands clear definitions.

---

[12] Owen Davies, *The Haunted: A Social History of Ghosts* (Basingstoke, 2007), p.132.

[13] Logie Barrow, *Independent Spirits: Spiritualism and English Plebeians, 1850–1910* (London, 1986); Diana Basham, *The Trial of Woman: Feminism and the Occult Sciences in Victorian Literature and Society* (Basingstoke, 1992); Gillian Bennett, *Traditions of Belief: Women and the Supernatural* (Harmondsworth, 1987); Peter Buse and Andrew Stott, eds, *Ghosts: Deconstruction, Psychoanalysis, History* (Basingstoke, 1999); Joy Dixon, *Divine Feminine: Theosophy and Feminism in England* (Baltimore and London, 2001); Roger Luckhurst, *The Invention of Telepathy, 1870–1901* (Oxford, 2002); Alex Owen, *The Place of Enchantment: British Occultism and the Culture of the Modern* (Chicago and London, 2004); Alex Owen, *The Darkened Room: Women, Power and Spiritualism in Late Nineteenth-century England* (London, 1989); Lynn L. Sharp, *Secular Spirituality: Reincarnation and Spiritism in Nineteenth-century France* (Lanham, 2006); Helen Sword, *Ghostwriting Modernism* (London and Ithaca, NY, 2002); Pamela Thurschwell, *Literature, Technology, and Magical Thinking, 1880–1920* (Cambridge, 2001); Marina Warner, *Phantasmagoria: Spirit Visions, Metaphors, and Media into the Twenty-first Century* (Oxford, 2006); Alison Winter, *Mesmerized: Powers of Mind in Victorian Britain* (Chicago and London, 1998). On the influence of Janet Oppenheim see Peter Mandler, Alex Owen, Seth Koven and Susan Pedersen, 'Cultural Histories of the Old and the New: Rereading the Work of Janet Oppenheim', *Victorian Studies* 41:1 (1997), 69–105.

[14] Jacques Derrida, *Specters of Marx: The State of the Debt, the Work of Mourning, and the New International*, trans. Peggy Kamuf (New York and London, 2006); Colin Davis, 'État Présent: Hauntology, Spectres and Phantoms', *French Studies* 59:3 (2005), 373–9; Michael Sprinker, ed., *Ghostly Demarcations: A Symposium on Jacques Derrida's 'Specters of Marx'* (London, 1999).

First a caveat: despite the ghost-grabbing intentions of this study, such tactile themes do not explicitly concern me (even more so Charles Dickens's very physical threat to shoot any 'ghost' he encountered).[15] It has been decided rather to observe from a critical distance (and via the framing media of commentators, sceptics and narrators) the representations of the ghost *seen* (or imagined to be seen). This decision has been made for several reasons. Firstly, this study demonstrates the strength of a particular sense-hierarchy – current in the nineteenth century, but firmly established by a train of thinkers stretching from John Locke back to Aristotle – that equated sight with knowledge, veracity and *evidence*, and which elevated the visual sense to the position of primary interpreter of the experienced world.[16] As James Joyce later put it: 'Ineluctable modality of the visible: at least that if no more, thought through my eyes ... Shut your eyes and see.'[17] Neither the advent of gaslight nor electric light could banish the ghost from the visual field for the ghost-sight had long been affirmed as being an *interior* visuality in both occultist and psychological discourses. For instance, the Swedish mystic Emanuel Swedenborg maintained that:

it is the interior vision which, through the eye, takes in those things which the eye sees, and not the eye itself, although it so appears. Hence also it may be seen, how much that man is involved in the fallacies of the senses, who believes

---

[15] See Charles Dickens, Hesba Stretton, George Augustus Sala *et al.*, *The Haunted House* (London, 2002), p.viii. Of course the threat of physical action could work both ways when it came to confronting ghosts in the nineteenth century. The magician Stuart Cumberland recorded one such dangerous episode: 'At Boston, in America, a leading light of the spiritistic cause, one Dr Bliss, drew a gun on me for interfering with the smooth working of one of the most fraudulent séances I have ever attended. In the course of a violent struggle one of my assailants had his skull cracked and I got a dislocated ankle. For some time I lay in bed under very kindly medical supervision with the dislocated ankle reposing in a pillow cradle, during which period the medium and his associates bombarded me with notes written in red ink, in which the early close of my earthly career was predicted. The final note contained the rough drawing of a coffin – studded with red nails, by the by – with the explanation that this was the sort of box in which alone I should leave my hotel.' Stuart Cumberland, *That Other World: Personal Experiences of Mystics and Their Mysticism* (London, 1918), p.79.
[16] See Marita Amm, 'Might and Magic, Lust and Language – The Eye as a Metaphor in Literature: Notes on the Hierarchy of the Senses', *Documenta Ophthalmologica* 101:3 (2000), 223–32; Stuart Clark, *Vanities of the Eye: Vision in Early Modern European Culture* (Oxford, 2007). See also Max Nordau's privileging of the 'distant senses'. Max Nordau, *Degeneration* (Lincoln, NE, and London, 1993), p.503. John Ruskin wrote that 'the greatest thing a human soul ever does in this world is to *see* something, and tell what it *saw* in a plain way ... To see clearly is poetry, prophecy, and religion, – all in one.' John Ruskin, *Modern Painters*: vol. III (Boston, MA, 1890), pp.330–1.
[17] James Joyce, *Ulysses*, ed. Danis Rose (London, 1998), p.37.

that it is the eye that sees, when yet it is the sight of his spirit, which is interior sight, that sees through the eye.[18]

While the German physician Johann Heinrich Jung-Stilling argued:

By the word 'vision', I understand an appearance which a person sees, without any real object being there: it therefore only exists in the imagination, and is consequently a mere dream, which is, however, regarded by him that has it, as reality. Yet visions distinguish themselves from common dreams, in this, that they are connected, and are like the reality; as also, that a person may have them waking.[19]

Secondly, the visual sense played a central role in the emergence of notions of modernity as a haunted project, a theme that has been stressed at length by many major studies in recent years.[20] By following this trend this study does not seek to pronounce a new interpretation of modernity, but rather to advance some arguments and historical examples that show how ghost-seeing is contiguous with the idea of a mind that is haunted by itself and a subjectivity that is ghost-ridden. It is intended that the topics and themes chosen will complement and converse with studies in the nineteenth-century imagination, and drive home my underlying argument of the spectral self as the true ghost in the modern age. One especially choice passage from a commentator on ghost-seeing in 1845 can perhaps help introduce the type of intellectual and metaphorical toolkit that I want to use:

The ghost which we see (the nightmare, for instance) is not without us, but within; yet not in our innermost, which were possession. Our own phantasy projects the apparition into the outer world, wherein it illudes us like a magic-lantern image (for which reason also, the ghost is before you, turn which way you will); but that which mockingly thus, as spectre, appears to us from without, has in reality its site in the medial (not the central) region of our being;

[18] Cited in George Bush, *Mesmer and Swedenborg: Or, the Relation of the Developments of Mesmerism to the Doctrines and Disclosures of Swedenborg*, 2nd edn (New York, 1847), p.112.
[19] Johann Heinrich Jung-Stilling, *Theory of Pneumatology, in Reply to the Question, What Ought to Be Believed or Disbelieved Concerning Presentiments, Visions, and Apparitions, According to Nature, Reason, and Scripture*, trans. Samuel Jackson (London, 1834), p.224.
[20] Constance Classen, *The Color of Angels: Cosmology, Gender and the Aesthetic Imagination* (London and New York, 1998); Jonathan Crary, *Suspensions of Perception: Attention, Spectacle and Modern Culture* (Cambridge, MA, and London, 2001); Jonathan Crary, *Techniques of the Observer: On Vision and Modernity in the Nineteenth Century* (Cambridge, MA, and London, 1990); Martin Jay, *Downcast Eyes: The Denigration of Vision in Twentieth-century French Thought* (Berkeley and London, 1993). See also Maggie Humm, *Modernist Women and Visual Cultures: Virginia Woolf, Vanessa Bell, Photography and Cinema* (Edinburgh, 2002); Catherine M. Soussloff, 'The Turn to Visual Culture: On Visual Culture and Techniques of the Observer', *Visual Anthropology Review* 12:1 (1996), 77–83.

and the phantasy, behind it, is a lamp, and the outward sense is as a glass before it, whereby its image is thrown out, and appears, huge and threatening, on the wall of the phenomenal.[21]

Finally, it is the underlying contention of this study that the human encounter with the ghost can be most fully examined through the rhetorical use of the visual sense: the ghostly world, the voices in this study declaim, was perceived 'through a glass, darkly'. While it would have been perhaps more apt to use the term 'ghost-feeling' in certain contexts, the sheer constitutive and rhetorical depth of the visualised imaginary gazumped any terminological rival to the over-arching descriptor 'ghost-seeing'.

The phenomenological facts of ghost-seeing, it should be borne in mind, have never really changed:[22] ghost-seeing experiences, on the contrary, constantly change due to their rootedness in certain socio-cultural environments that inform and map out how the existence of the supernatural world is framed, structured, dramatised, legitimised and de-legitimised, as the case may be.[23] I take the experience of ghosts to be a psychological phenomenon which constitutes, to use the concept of Wilhelm Dilthey, an incredibly rich *Kultursystem* that can be isolated in multiple overlapping, and sometimes clashing, contexts.[24] Pre-nineteenth-century varieties of ghost-seeing experience worthy of examination on this basis include the post-Reformation debates surrounding the issue of ghosts (interlaced with the interrogation of ghost-belief contained in William Shakespeare's *Hamlet*); Daniel Defoe's peculiar balancing-act of belief and scepticism played out in his supernatural trilogy *The Political History of the Devil* (1726), *A System of Magick* (1726) and *An Essay on the History and Reality of Apparitions* (1727); and the *spectacular* arrival of public/publicised ghost-seeing with the Cock Lane manifestations in London in 1762. While subjects such as these deserve, and continue to receive, significant scholarly attention, aside from Davies's breakthrough social history, the lack of an inter-disciplinary approach to ghost-seeing experience in the historical disciplines is noticeable. However, it should be stressed that the period under examination in this study facilitates the approach taken more so than any other, for the nineteenth century witnessed, to a quite remarkable degree, the disciplinary overlapping of

---

[21] Henry Ferris, 'Of the Nightmare', *Dublin University Magazine* 25 (1845), 40.

[22] See Michael Winkelman, 'Spirits as Human Nature and the Fundamental Structures of Consciousness', in *From Shaman to Scientist: Essays on Humanity's Search for Spirits*, ed. James Houran (Lanham, 2004), pp.59–96.

[23] See Geoffrey K. Nelson, *Spiritualism and Society* (London, 1969).

[24] H.A. Hodges, *The Philosophy of Wilhelm Dilthey* (London, 1952), p.177.

questions and problems – a situation that has come to characterise what it means to be 'modern'.[25] An oft-quoted example of this epistemological condition is the observation that William James wrote psychology texts like a novelist while his brother Henry James wrote novels like a psychologist.[26] Such a contemporary anecdote neatly encapsulates the disciplinary blending that was taking place in the human sciences as streams of influence and counter-influence created a situation where the ghost-seeing culture of the modern period could emerge simultaneously in a variety of locations. By taking a multi-sided view of the subject and placing contrasting experiences alongside each other this investigation merely mirrors developments that were taking place in the investigative culture of the time.

★ ★ ★

Modern spiritualism can be traced, by and large, to the dissemination and various adaptations of animal magnetism and mesmerism in the late eighteenth century.[27] As an Irish commentator put it: 'Magnetism (animal) is the charm, the "open sesame", at which the gates of the invisible world stand open.'[28] In 1788 the Société exégétique et philanthropique, a Swedenborgian society based in Stockholm, sought a rapprochement with the mesmerists of Strasbourg, on the basis that the somnambulist trances and spiritualism of the Swedenborgians could be accorded and synthesised with the discoveries of animal magnetism.[29] The origins of modern ghost-seeing as an *investigative* culture, however, can be traced back to the romantic psychology prevalent in German letters in the first decades of the nineteenth century.[30] It was in the

[25] See, for instance, the essays contained in Dorothy Ross, ed., *Modernist Impulses in the Human Sciences, 1870–1930* (Baltimore, 1994); Mark S. Micale, ed., *The Mind of Modernism: Medicine, Psychology, and the Cultural Arts in Europe and America, 1880–1940* (Stanford, 2004); Michael S. Roth, ed., *Rediscovering History: Culture, Politics, and the Psyche* (Stanford, 1994). See also Martin Halliwell, *Romantic Science and the Experience of Self: Transatlantic Crosscurrents from William James to Oliver Sacks* (Brookfield, 1999); Tim Armstrong, *Modernism: A Cultural History* (Cambridge, 2005), p.ix.
[26] See Eugene Taylor, 'Oh Those Fabulous James Boys!', *Psychology Today* 28:2 (1995), 58.
[27] In their turn, these phenomena drew much of their intellectual framework and pseudo-scientific impact from the occultist theories of the early modern period regarding sympathy, influence, magnetism, harmonial philosophy, fluidic transmission and so on. See Frank Podmore. *Modern Spiritualism: A History and Criticism*: vol. I (London, 1902), pp.44–50.
[28] Henry Ferris [pseud. 'Irys Herfner'], 'German Ghosts and Ghost-seers', *Dublin University Magazine* 17 (1841), 37.
[29] *Ibid.*, 76. See also Robert Darnton, *Mesmerism and the End of the Enlightenment in France* (Cambridge, MA, 1968), 67.
[30] Indeed, it was suggested that 'Germany and the ghost-world are geographically contiguous regions.' Ferris, 'German Ghosts and Ghost-seers', 36.

writings of Jung-Stilling, Justinus Kerner and E.T.A. Hoffmann among others that a specific discursive mode emerged which bridged the divide between medical philosophy and romantic poetics and allowed for the international transmission of a subject-network that was termed 'the Night Side of Nature' (from the German *Nachtseite*) – that is, the world of the unconscious, prophetic dreams, second-sight, ghost-seeing and the supernatural in general.[31] Kerner, a physician and lyrical poet, investigated a young ghost-seer named Friederike Hauffe from 1827 until her death in 1829 and sketched out the precincts of a dynamic 'inner life' made evident through magnetic sleep, or 'sleep-waking'. Kerner's account, *Die Seherin von Prevorst* (*The Seeress of Prevorst*) (1829) was hugely influential in formatting nineteenth-century ideas about the spirit-world and the ethereal body (*Nervengeist*) which may sometimes be seen by the living. Furthermore, the historian of psychology Henri Ellenberger later accorded Kerner a role in the 'discovery' of the unconscious, describing his investigations as 'a milestone in the history of dynamic psychiatry'.[32]

The English-language debt to this German romantic psycho-poetic tradition was made explicit with the translation of Kerner's work by the English authoress Catherine Crowe in 1845 and its subsequent dissemination in America, Britain and Ireland.[33] Crowe was a hugely important figure in the emergence of modern ghost-seeing culture chiefly because of her relentless calls for society to turn its attention to the unexplained phenomena in its midst and investigate them in an objective manner. Crowe's landmark book of 1848, *The Night Side of Nature; or Ghosts and Ghost-seers*, which went through sixteen editions in six years,[34] was a quasi-folkloric collection of supernatural narratives heavily drawn from German sources, rhetorically somewhere in between fact and fiction (or, as Neil Wilson terms it – 'faction')[35] and designed to bring to the notice of the public the *questionable* nature of ghost-seeing experience:

---

[31] On this see Uwe Henrik Peters, *Studies in German Romantic Psychiatry: Justinus Kerner as a Psychiatric Practitioner, E.T.A. Hoffmann as a Psychiatric Theorist* (London, 1990).

[32] Henri F. Ellenberger, *The Discovery of the Unconscious: The History and Evolution of Dynamic Psychiatry* (New York, 1970), p.79.

[33] This tradition had been notably present in the *Dublin University Magazine* where, between 1839 and 1851, Henry Ferris authored several articles and ghost stories with German settings and influences. See Richard Hayes, ' "The Night Side of Nature": Henry Ferris, Writing the Dark Gods of Silence', in *Literature and the Supernatural: Essays for the Maynooth Bicentenary*, ed. Brian Cosgrove (Dublin, 1995), pp.42–70.

[34] Robert Dale Owen, *Footfalls on the Boundary of Another World: With Narrative Illustrations* (London, 1860), p.4.

[35] Neil Wilson, *Shadows in the Attic: A Guide to British Supernatural Fiction, 1820–1950* (Boston Spa and London, 2000), p.164.

All I do hope to establish is, not a proof, but a presumption; and the conviction I desire to awaken in people's minds is, not that these things *are* so, but that they *may be* so, and that it is well worth our while to inquire whether they are or not.[36]

Crowe's impassioned pleas for this investigative approach were significant because they came before modern spiritualism, which emerged from the 'burned-over district' of north-eastern America later in that same revolutionary year of 1848, had reached British audiences.[37] These ghostly links between Germany, Ireland, Britain and America point to the existence of a broader cultural shift, in a state of crystallisation in the years 1847 and 1848, that is indicative of a *sympathetic* revolution in the West. Such a development was synchronically realised in literature and allowed the heroine of Charlotte Brontë's *Jane Eyre* (published in 1847) to state: 'Presentiments are strange things! and so are sympathies; and so are signs: and the three combined to make one mystery to which humanity has not yet found the key.'[38] This revolution in feeling was characterised by the establishment of new communication and communitarian networks that ventriloquised the tele-technological revolution of the Victorian age and thus *terrestrialised* the 'other world'.[39] For instance, a prominent journal in the early spiritualist movement was entitled the *Spiritual Telegraph* while the French spiritualist Allan Kardec recorded a message from a spirit which argued that the task of the medium ' "is that of an electric machine, which transmits telegraphic dispatches from one point of the earth to another far distant. So, when we wish to dictate a communication, we act on the medium as the telegraph operator on his instruments." '[40]

It was the clash between secular modernity (supported by orthodox science) and the palpable realities of the supernatural world that allowed spiritualists and ghost-seers to circumvent what Michel Foucault termed the 'blackmail' of the Enlightenment – the idea that 'you either accept the Enlightenment and remain within the tradition of its rationalism ... or else you criticize the Enlightenment and then try to escape from its principles of rationality'.[41] The 'Enlightenment-agnosticism' of ghost-seers, as it may be

[36] Catherine Crowe, *The Night Side of Nature; or, Ghosts and Ghost-seers* (London, 1850), pp.219–20.
[37] W.R. Cross, *The Burned-over District: The Social and Intellectual History of Enthusiastic Religion in Western New York, 1800–1850* (Ithaca, NY, 1950).
[38] Charlotte Brontë, *Jane Eyre*, ed. Margaret Smith (Oxford, 1980), p.222.
[39] According to Karl Marx 1848 was the year that revolutionary politics became ghostly. See Jann Matlock, 'Ghostly Politics', *Diacritics* 30:3 (2000), 53–71; José B. Monleon, '1848: The Assault on Reason', in *The Horror Reader*, ed. Ken Gelder (London and New York, 2000), pp.20–8.
[40] Allan Kardec, *Experimental Spiritism*, trans. Emma A. Wood (New York, 1970), p.292.
[41] Cited in Paul Rabinow, ed., *The Foucault Reader* (Harmondsworth, 1986), p.43.

termed, and the uncanny reflection of positivistic scientific practice in spiritualist discourses, found a particular mode of expression through the institutionalisation of public investigative cultures. The prescience of Crowe's call for a Baconian approach to supernatural phenomena was made evident by the institutionalisation of the 'will-to-investigate' in the spiritualist literature of the 1850s, a process that Crowe herself participated enthusiastically in.[42] Such an emergence was facilitated by the curious role-reversal that occurred in the wake of spiritualism as magicians and conjurers secularised and 'disenchanted' their own performances and took an extremely pro-active role in debunking and exposing mediums and psychics who claimed to be the conduits or possessors of supernatural powers – a radical-investigative, counter-obscurantist tradition that continues among magicians to this day.[43] The game of spiritualist investigation and anti-spiritualist investigation had been launched.

From the rapid success of the Fox sisters' séances and public demonstrations of the connection between the living and the dead in New York State from 1848, it became clear that the mantra of the age was, as one periodical declared, 'Show us our dead!'[44] It is hardly surprising that the do-it-yourself attitudes implicit in spiritualism and the popular spectacle of the séance, with private circles of mediums and interested parties being formed in all classes, incited a swift reaction from the English medical and the religious establishment and the chief 'deviant' science

---

[42] See the hints on investigating in G.W. Stone, *An Exposition of Views Respecting the Principal Facts, Causes, and Peculiarities Involved in Spirit Manifestations, together with Interesting Phenomenal Statements and Communications* (London, 1852), pp.103–4; Adin Ballou, *An Exposition of Views Respecting the Modern Spirit Manifestations: Together with Phenomenal Statements and Communications* (Liverpool, 1853), pp.46–7; Catherine Crowe, *Spiritualism, and the Age We Live In* (London, 1859), pp.iii–iv, 45; John S. Farmer, *How to Investigate Spiritualism* (London, 1883).

[43] James W. Cook, *The Arts of Deception: Playing with Fraud in the Age of Barnum* (Cambridge, MA, 2001); Simon During, *Modern Enchantments: The Cultural Power of Secular Magic* (Cambridge, MA, 2002); Peter Lamont, 'Spiritualism and a Mid-Victorian Crisis of Evidence', *The Historical Journal* 47:4 (2004), 903–6; Fred Nadis, *Wonder Shows: Performing Science, Magic, and Religion in America* (New Brunswick and London, 2005). For landmark works of anti-obscurantism by practising magicians see Cumberland, *That Other World*; Harry Houdini, *A Magician among the Spirits* (New York, 1924); James Randi, *Flim-Flam!: Psychics, ESP, Unicorns, and Other Delusions* (Buffalo, 1982). The lexical confusion that this situation created can be ascertained by the fact that Daniel Dunglas Home, one of history's most enigmatic mediums, turned gamekeeper and called for the debunking and exposure of fraudulent spiritualists in his controversial book *Lights and Shadows of Spiritualism* (1877). On the differences between conjurers and mediums/psychics see Peter Lamont and Richard Wiseman, *Magic in Theory: An Introduction to the Theoretical and Psychological Elements of Conjuring* (Bristol, 1999), pp.102–34.

[44] Cited in Ronald Pearsall, *The Table-Rappers: The Victorians and the Occult* (Stroud, 2004), p.57.

of the era – mesmerism. In an episode which touches upon many of the themes that this study examines, the *Zoist*, a prominent mesmerist/ phrenological periodical, gleefully reported in 1854 that Catherine Crowe had become insane following her encounter with spiritualism, running naked through the streets of Edinburgh, carrying a card case in one hand and a handkerchief in the other, apparently believing she was invisible.[45] While mesmerism had been suddenly forced into open com- petition with the rival pseudo-science of spiritualism, hostility from all quarters confirmed that spiritualist investigation had become an activity loaded with transgressive meaning: as Cottom put it: 'Spiritualism was suspect because it was thought to be wrong, but more importantly because it upset linguistic as well as other social and ideological rela- tions.'[46] Even though the scientific establishment rapidly declared spir- itualist investigations to be fallacious, the urge to see and know for one's own self proved irresistible to many, and for a large number of eminent and sceptical Victorian scientists, such as Michael Faraday and John Tyndall, judgement required investigation.[47] Given that Dickens also used the Crowe scandal as an example of the pathological potential in spiritualist investigations,[48] the impulses publicised (and enacted) by Crowe and other proponents of investigation dramatically affected the fictional representations of the ghost-seeing experience while at the same time initiated a form of cultural disembarrassment that the Society for Psychical Research (SPR) would later re-employ. Therefore it is impor- tant that, even though he criticised Crowe's investigative intentions, Dickens was himself fascinated by the supernatural and even allowed for the existence of an oneiric ghost-seeing perception:

---

[45] John Elliotson, 'More Insanity from Spirit-Rapping Fancies', *Zoist* 12 (1854–1855), 175. See also Antonio Melechi, *Servants of the Supernatural: The Night Side of the Victorian Mind* (London, 2008), p.174.

[46] Cottom, *Abyss of Reason*, p.18.

[47] Therefore the response of Thomas Huxley to the London Dialectical Society's call for scientific aid in their spiritualist investigations assumes counter-cultural significance: 'In the first place, I have no time for such an inquiry, which would involve much trouble and (unless it were unlike all inquiries of that kind I have known) much annoyance. In the second place, I take no interest in the subject.' Cited in *Report on Spiritualism, of the Committee of the London Dialectical Society, together with the Evidence, Oral and Written, and a Selection from the Correspondence* (London, 1873), p.229. Friedrich Engels praised this refusal to investigate, this *a priori* theoretical negation, as authentic empiricism. See Friedrich Engels, *Dialectics of Nature*, trans. Clemens Dutt (Moscow, 1954), p.61.

[48] See Madeline House, Graham Storey, Kathleen Tillotson and Angus Easson, eds, *The Letters of Charles Dickens*: vol. VII, *1853–1855* (Oxford, 1993), pp.285–6. Charles Baudelaire was struck by Crowe's notion of the 'constructive imagination' as distinguished from 'fancy'. See Charles Baudelaire, *Œuvres complètes II* (Paris, 1999), pp.623–4; G.T. Clapton, 'Baudelaire and Catherine Crowe', *Modern Language Review* 25:3 (1930), 286–305.

'I'll swear that I was not asleep', is very easily and conscientiously said; but there is a middle state between sleeping and waking, and which is not either, when impressions, though false, are extraordinarily strong, and when the individual not asleep, is, most distinctly, not awake.[49]

Such a transgressive attitude towards the supernatural draws attention to the accommodating, 'broad church' characteristics of the ghost-seeing culture of the Victorian period. Dickens was not alone in his disbelieving-yet-investigative attitude towards ghost-seeing: in her fiction, the sceptic Elizabeth Gaskell similarly assumed a 'half believing, half incredulous' attitude towards the phenomena of spiritualism.[50]

Had he lived longer, Dickens would undoubtedly have had something to say about the investigative enterprise of the London Dialectical Society (LDS), a short-lived society mostly made up of urban professionals and men of letters eager to pronounce upon topics they considered were wholly neglected. In 1869 the LDS formed committees and sub-committees and sent them into the field to investigate spiritualism, publishing a major report into spiritualism in 1871 which concluded, in a significantly circular manner, that 'the subject is worthy of more serious attention and careful investigation than it has hitherto received'.[51] This was not before, however, the existence of a new 'psychic force', capable of producing or inducing the physical phenomena of spiritualism (rappings, table-turning, levitation etc.) had been identified by LDS investigators. Such forces were 'in the air', it seemed. Edward Bulwer-Lytton, who participated in the LDS's enterprise, had arguably inaugurated the psychic detective genre of supernatural fiction with 'The Haunted and the Haunters' (1859), a popu-lar ghost story that dealt with precisely the same concerns about occult forces and the disembodied will that the LDS later identified. This link between the new committee-based ghost-seeing investigative culture and the literary explorations centred on the detection of supernatural forces may be taken as strong evidence that the blurring of the boundaries between eyewitness accounts and fictional stories led to a broader factional framing of ghost-seeing experiences as both were subsumed under the culturally parasitical definition/non-definition 'investigation'. For some, the factional aspects of spiritualism were indicative of cultural malaise and what William

---

[49] Charles Dickens, *Charles Dickens' Christmas Ghost Stories* (London, 1992), pp.249–50. On Dickens's relationship with spiritualism see Russell M. Goldfarb and Clare R. Goldfarb, *Spiritualism and Nineteenth-century Letters* (Rutherford, 1978), pp.94–6. On Dickens's use of phantasmagoric logic see Karen Petroski, ' "The Ghost of an Idea": Dickens's Uses of Phantasmagoria, 1842–44', *Dickens Quarterly* 16:2 (1999), 71–93.
[50] See Louise Henson, ' "Half Believing, Half Incredulous": Elizabeth Gaskell, Superstition and the Victorian Mind', *Nineteenth-century Contexts* 24:3 (2002), 251–69.
[51] *Report on Spiritualism*, p.6.

James later termed the 'will to believe'.[52] Robert Browning's imaginative strangulation of the medium Daniel Dunglas Home, as expressed in his vitriolic anti-spiritualist poem 'Mr. Sludge, "The Medium" ' (1864), functioned as an examination of how spiritualism appealed to the Victorians as mythopoetry: spiritualist practice was, as the exposed Sludge had it, 'Not lies – rather "what good people style untruth" ':

> It's fancying, fable-making, nonsense-work –
> What never meant to be so very bad –
> The knack of story-telling, brightening up
> Each old bit of fact that drops its shine.[53]

The increasing sophistication of experimental investigations into spiritualism, as shown in the well-documented encounter between the renowned chemist William Crookes and the medium Florence Cook, merely disguised and further sublimated what, to many contemporaries, were the fable-making impulses driving an intellectual climate that was increasingly loath to confront religious implications of evolutionary theory and the psychological fallout from the secularisation process.[54] Indeed, writing at the turn of the twentieth century, Carl Gustav Jung was of the opinion that spiritualism was a psychological compensation which necessarily arose during the zenith of scientific naturalism:

Rationalism and superstition are complementary. It is a psychological rule that the brighter the light, the blacker the shadow; in other words, the more rationalistic we are in our conscious minds, the more alive becomes the spectral world of the unconscious.[55]

Spiritualist investigations during the Victorian period have often been shown to have been therapeutic and edifying: what have long been neglected by researchers were the more base satisfactions, sense of playfulness, performance for performance's sake, and entertainment values that made factional ghost-seeing – from the pages of Crowe's *The Night Side of Nature* and W.T. Stead's bestselling *Real Ghost Stories* (1891) to the séance rooms of high-society London and lecture-halls

---

[52] See William James, *The Will to Believe: And Other Essays in Popular Psychology* (New York, 1898).

[53] Robert Browning, *Poetical Works, 1833–1864* (London, 1970), p.857.

[54] For the interactions between evolutionary theory and spiritualism see Malcolm Jay Kottler, 'Alfred Russel Wallace, the Origin of Man, and Spiritualism', *Isis* 65:2 (1974), 144–92; Peter Pels, 'Spirits of Modernity: Alfred Wallace, Edward Tylor, and the Visual Politics of Fact', in *Magic and Modernity: Interfaces of Revelation and Concealment*, ed. Birgit Meyer and Peter Pels (Stanford, 2003), pp.241–71. On secularisation see Owen Chadwick, *The Secularization of the European Mind in the Nineteenth Century* (Cambridge, 1975).

[55] Carl Gustav Jung, *Psychology and the Occult* (London, 1987), p.144.

of Lancashire – so culturally successful regardless of gender or class.[56] It is further noticeable that the physical phenomena of spiritualism went through progressive elaborations in the nineteenth century which brought the spirit-world closer to the investigator in terms of evidence: while in the early decades of the movement, séances generally featured rapping, table-turning and the appearance of 'spirit hands', from the 1860s and 1870s more sensational and palpable phenomena such as levitation, full-form materialisation, slate-writing, spirit photography and ectoplasm entered the repertoire of practising mediums.

The phenomena of spiritualism may have been, to use the words of one eyewitness, 'stranger than fiction', but this did not mean that fiction was unaffected by so topical a movement.[57] On the contrary, the evidential implications of spiritualist ghost-seeing contributed to a golden age for the genre of ghost fiction precisely on the basis of the *factional* fallout from modern spiritualism. Titles such as 'The Truth, the Whole Truth, and Nothing but the Truth', 'Reality or Delusion?' and 'Was It an Illusion?' attest to the fact that ghost stories, in their ideological attempt to relate truly, were contesting the same problems of testimony and hallucination that spiritualism encountered, only in a different frame of meaning.[58] Such cross-modal expressions contributed to what Peter Lamont has called a mid-Victorian 'crisis of evidence': this created what may be termed the 'factionality trap' as an operating mode of ghost-seeing experience expressing the liminal place of the ghost story in between fact and fiction, never to be definitively lodged in either mode of meaning. Yet

---

[56] In this regard the approaches of E.J. Clery and Daniel Herman are encouraging. See E.J. Clery, *The Rise of Supernatural Fiction, 1762–1800* (Cambridge, 1995); Daniel Herman, 'Whose Knocking? Spiritualism as Entertainment and Therapy in Nineteenth-century San Francisco', *American Nineteenth-century History* 7:3 (2006), 417–42. Tatiana Kontou observes: 'In both sensation novels and spiritualist practice, the question of theatrical performance is so profoundly ambiguous that it ultimately transcends any debate over its "natural" or "artificial" status. In fact, these spectral theatricals situate themselves at the very epicentre of the Victorian psyche. "Acting", whether we locate it in the domestic sphere, the séance or on the stage, becomes essential to our own (constantly developing) understanding of how to read and define Victorian personalities.' Tatiana Kontou, 'Ventriloquising the Dead: Representations of Victorian Spiritualism and Psychical Research in Selected Nineteenth- and Late Twentieth-century Fiction', DPhil thesis, 2006, University of Sussex, p.63. See also Nina Auerbach, *Private Theatricals: The Lives of the Victorians* (Cambridge, MA, and London, 1990). Erving Goffman has observed that 'a special kind of entertainment' occurs when a fabricated framework is questioned. Erving Goffman, *Frame Analysis: An Essay on the Organization of Experience* (Cambridge, MA, 1974), p.199.

[57] Robert Bell, 'Stranger than Fiction', *Cornhill Magazine* 2 (1860), 211–24. See Nicole Coffey, ' "Every Word of It Is True": The Cultural Significance of the Victorian Ghost Story', MA thesis, 2004, University of Manitoba, p.15.

[58] See Margaret L. Carter, *Specter or Delusion? The Supernatural in Gothic Fiction* (Ann Arbor and London, 1987), p.120.

this is not to say that the purely poetic framing of Victorian and Edwardian ghost stories by incredulous writers did not happen: Dickens is the perfect example of this. What is certain, however, is that even this poetic frame encountered the factionality trap – as if the signposting of the possible reality of the supernatural was a central constitutive factor in the autonomous ghost story: Samuel Taylor Coleridge characterised this attitude towards the supernatural as 'the willing suspension of disbelief for the moment, which constitutes poetic faith',[59] while recently Julian Wolfreys has examined 'the *experience of the undecidable*' with regard to Victorian supernatural literature.[60] Of this curious attitude Dorothy Scarborough wrote: 'The reader, as well as the writer, must put himself in the mental attitude of acceptance of the supernatural else the effect is lacking, for the ghostly thrill is incommunicable to those beyond the pale of at least temporary credulity.'[61] This situation contributed to the increasing psychological sophistication of ghost fiction, often pre-empting the themes and techniques of modernist aesthetics in its development.[62] As Michael Cox and R.A. Gilbert note, 'The relationship between veridical phenomena and imagined ghosts was a complex one. Fiction, for example, often posed as fact, and a range of narrative strategies was deployed to reinforce the masquerade.'[63] Perhaps the paradigmatic factional ghost story is Defoe's 'A True Relation of the Apparition of One Mrs. Veal' (1706) which in both its content and its literary history invites the reader to descend even more into the factionality trap. The narrative recounted the rather prosaic appearance of the ghostly Mrs Veal to her friend Mrs Bargrave, but debates over whether Defoe actually wrote it, whether he considered it fiction, whether he believed it, whether such an apparition was believable at all within Protestant theology, and

---

[59] Samuel Taylor Coleridge, *Biographia Literaria*: vol. II, ed. J. Shawcross (London, 1965), p.6.

[60] Julian Wolfreys, *Victorian Hauntings: Spectrality, Gothic, the Uncanny and Literature* (Basingstoke, 2002), p.xiv. Walter Scott noted 'that the person who professes himself most incredulous on the subject of marvellous stories, often ends his remarks by indulging the company with some well-attested anecdote, which it is difficult or impossible to account for on the narrator's own principles of absolute scepticism'. Walter Scott, 'Novels of Ernest Theodore Hoffmann', in *Critical and Miscellaneous Essays*: vol. II (Philadelphia, 1841), p.9. See also Glen Cavaliero, *The Supernatural and English Fiction* (Oxford, 1995), p.249.

[61] Cited in Coffey, ' "Every Word of It Is True" ', p.49.

[62] See, for example, Thomas Loe, 'The Strange Modernism of Le Fanu's "Green Tea" ', in *That Other World: The Supernatural and the Fantastic in Irish Literature and Its Contexts*: vol. I, ed. Bruce Stewart (Gerrards Cross, 1998), pp.293–306.

[63] Michael Cox and R.A. Gilbert, eds, *Victorian Ghost Stories: An Oxford Anthology* (Oxford, 1991), p.xvi.

whether the story was merely a sophisticated marketing ploy to advertise and sell copies of Charles Drelincourt's *The Christian's Defense against the Fears of Death* pointed – at the very birth of the novel and the modern English ghost story – to narrative strategies and cultural effects far in advance of its time.[64]

One of the central narrative strategies of the Victorian supernatural genre that can be traced to the factional attitude involved the rhetorical connection between the ghost story, forms of expression and bourgeois comfort. Witness the opening words of Joseph Sheridan Le Fanu's 'An Account of Some Strange Disturbances in Aungier Street' (1853):

It is not worth telling, this story of mine – at least, not worth writing. Told, indeed, as I have sometimes been called upon to tell it, to a circle of intelligent and eager faces, lighted up by a good after-dinner fire on a winter's evening, with a cold wind rising and wailing outside, and all snug and cosy within, it has gone off – though I say it, who should not – indifferent well. But it is a venture to do so as you would have me. Pen, ink, and paper are cold vehicles for the marvellous, and a 'reader' decidedly a more critical animal than a 'listener'. If, however, you can induce your friends to read it after nightfall, and when the fireside talk has run for a while on thrilling tales of shapeless terror; in short, if you will secure me the *mollia tempora fandi*, I will go to my work, and say my say, with better heart. Well, then, these conditions presupposed, I shall waste no more words, but tell you simply how it all happened.[65]

Here the implied reader/consumer of the ghost story is constructed by the teller through a shared environment conducive to intra-domestic connectivity – a form of *irrational* recreation, it may be said. It is at this point that the more material (and materialist) aspects of ghost-seeing enter the frame, for it is striking how quickly the ghost story became a staple of the typical Victorian Christmas and 'Englishness' in general: the desire to 'to make your flesh creep' became a seasonal market that

[64] James Walton, 'On the Attribution of "Mrs. Veal"', *Notes and Queries* 54:1 (2007), 60–2; George Starr, 'Why Defoe Probably Did not Write *The Apparition of Mrs. Veal*', *Eighteenth-century Fiction* 15:3–4 (2003), 421–50; Wolfreys, *Victorian Hauntings*, p.4; Sasha Handley, *Visions of an Unseen World: Ghost Beliefs and Ghost Stories in Eighteenth-century England* (London, 2007), pp.80–107. Leonard J. Davis argues that 'novels are framed works (even if they seem apparently unframed) whose attitude toward fact and fiction is constitutively ambivalent. The frame, context, and prestructure serve to place the narrative in a complex attitude toward "lived" experience – whether or not novels openly claim they are true, disavow particular authorship, or act as pseudoallegories. Verisimilitudinous writing or techniques of creating a pseudoreal textuality increase this complexity. In this sense, the novel is about reality, and at the same time is not about reality; the novel is a factual fiction which is both factual and fictitious.' Leonard J. Davis, *Factual Fictions: The Origins of the English Novel* (Philadelphia, 1996), p.212.
[65] Joseph Sheridan Le Fanu, *Best Ghost Stories* (Toronto, 1964), p.361.

was rarely ignored by the literary world.[66] Here the possibility of psychic forces fuelled literary market forces. This cultural codification can be traced to the burgeoning market for ghost fiction in middle-class periodicals such as *Dublin University Magazine, Macmillan's Magazine, Blackwood's Magazine* and especially Dickens's successive periodicals *Household Words* and *All the Year Round*: the importation and articulation of the 'night side of nature' in Victorian and Edwardian England was big business, comparable to today's strong association between the supernatural and the Halloween season.[67] The calendar, it was clear, was haunted by ghosts that returned annually to the world of the living and which were spiritually as well as materially lucrative. Here, as elsewhere, the factionality of ghost-seeing, with its ambivalent place in lived experience, came to be nostalgically lodged in the realm of myth, memory, and faded meaning. If, as Derrida seems to suggest, Hamlet's awareness that his 'time is out of joint' functions as a commentary on the haunted nature of modern subjectivity, then interpretations of ghost-seeing can offer valuable source material on how what constitutes 'the modern' comes to be adjoined and how individuals may 'learn to live finally' in a time and place occupied by spirits.[68]

* * *

Part I of this study argues that the notion that ghost-seeing was nothing more than a form of dreaming provided a gateway for successive investigations into the deceptions and impostures of mental life in the period from the Enlightenment to the mid-nineteenth century. The standardisation of this conceptual metaphor played a central role in the strength and success of the medical model within the hallucination discourse, using the cultural fascination with dream-production, and the sense of psychological uncertainty surrounding the dream-world, to deny the objective reality of supernatural apparitions. The origin of this dislocation was in the psychological culture of late eighteenth century

---

[66] This phrase occurs in Charles Dickens, *The Pickwick Papers* (Ware, 1993), p.104. In 'A Christmas Tree' (1850), Dickens wrote of Christmas time: 'There is probably a smell of roasted chestnuts and other good comfortable things all the time, for we are telling Winter Stories – Ghost Stories, or more shame for us – round the Christmas fire; and we have never stirred, except to draw a little nearer to it.' Charles Dickens, *Christmas Stories I* (London, 1967), p.14. On this see Elaine Ostry, *Social Dreaming: Dickens and the Fairy Tale* (New York and London, 2002), pp.79–104.

[67] Cox and Gilbert, eds, *Victorian Ghost Stories*, pp.xii–xiii. Crowe, it should be noted, published a collection entitled *Ghosts and Family Legends: A Volume for Christmas* (1859). For an interesting account of the business element of supernatural fiction see Gail Turley Houston, *From Dickens to Dracula: Gothic, Economics, and Victorian Fiction* (Cambridge, 2005).

[68] Derrida, *Specters of Marx*, pp.20–5.

Europe, and may be traced in particular to the metaphorics of the phantasmagoria which suggested that ghost-seeing experience could be both fallacious and veridical at the same time. The dominant spectral illusions model of ghost-seeing owed its discursive framework to a celebrated case of ghost-seeing which was published in *Nicholson's Journal* in 1803.[69] By suggesting a dramatic psychological connectedness between the spheres of dream and reality, the theory of 'spectral illusions', around 1800 to 1840, redefined the phenomenology of everyday life in British society. Following this, an analysis of the concept of hallucination in French psychiatry shows how the radical taxonomic innovations of Philippe Pinel and J.E.D. Esquirol influenced a new generation of psychiatrists and psychologists who, by the 1840s, were using the phenomena of hallucinations, illusions and hypnagogic illusions to map out the uncertain territory between dream and reality, a location that was synchronically being mapped out in ghost fiction.

That this metaphor operated as a cultural bridge is no more strongly evident than in the philosophical writings on ghost-seeing experience by Immanuel Kant and Arthur Schopenhauer, dealt with in chapter 2. Often neglected due to the British-centred orientation of most studies related to this topic, these writings offer critical perspectives on a range of issues that reflect and complement the more empirical bent of the Anglocentric world – in Kant's case the strange ambiguity of his position as a philosopher-as-dreamer, and in Schopenhauer's case as a proponent of a will-based system which allowed for the normativity of the ghost-seeing experience. Such metaphysical speculations were largely foreign to British, French and American psychiatrists and psychologists who believed the ghost-seeing reported by percipients, especially spiritualists, tended to be psychopathological in character. Once again, the dreaming/hallucinating analogy was employed, but unlike in the spectral illusions discourse, mid-century psychiatrists increasingly focused on the 'weak-willed' nature of ghost-seers. Such degenerationist themes also appeared in the pioneering anthropology of Edward B. Tylor who traced the origins of animism to ghost-seeing in the dream world. As anti-spiritualism abated somewhat towards the end of the century, the abnormal psychology of the sane, as investigated by Francis Galton, demonstrated that the general population had considerable hallucinatory capability – further problematising sceptical

---

[69] Christoph Friedrich Nicolai, 'A Memoir on the Appearance of Spectres or Phantoms Occasioned by Disease, with Psychological Remarks. Read by Nicolai to the Royal Society of Berlin, on the 28th of February, 1799', *Journal of Natural Philosophy, Chemistry and the Arts* 6 (1803), 161–79. See Appendix.

responses to the ghost-seeing experience. While the history of spiritualism, and sceptical reactions to it, have been cogently examined in
different contexts, untouched in most cultural-historical studies are the
basic perceptual beliefs and rationalisations of the ghost-seeing experience – the terrene and material issues that occupied a central place in
spiritualist writings, but which were vigorously countered by sceptics as
incongruous and absurd.[70] Seeking to redress this situation, chapter 2
takes the example of the clothes of ghosts – a topic which exercised
the minds of many throughout the nineteenth century and which was
explained by sceptics and anti-spiritualists chiefly through the concept
of hallucination.

Part II of this study focuses on the varieties of ghost-seeing experience
collected, described, and interpreted by the Society for Psychical
Research during the last two decades of the nineteenth century. This
early period in the SPR's history (1882–1903) has been widely recognised as being its most dynamic – a period when it boasted the talents of
psychical researchers producing landmark studies in a large number of
disciplines and discourses. Chapter 3 contextualises the work of the SPR
and covers the coming to fruition of an intense public interest in notions
of ghost-seeing and the possible scientific validity of the ghost-seeing
experience. The reasons why this period has been described as the 'era of
the "ghost hunter"' are demonstrated here.[71] Despite the prevalence of
such charged appellations as 'ghost hunters' or 'spookologists', the SPR
sought to play a normative role in late Victorian scientific community
and used scientific naturalism as its foil and its negative, as its starting
point and its destination.[72] Frederic W.H. Myers (1843–1901), an early
leader of the SPR, saw psychical research as a 'consultative scheme' and
assured the scientific community that the SPR 'far from aiming at any
paradoxical reversion of established scientific conclusions' conceived
itself 'to be working (however imperfectly) in the main track of [scientific]

---

[70] An important exception in this regard is the recent work of Steven Connor which has
attempted to trace a 'cultural phenomenology' of spiritualism that pays close attention
to the material practices of the séance-room. Steven Connor, 'The Machine in the
Ghost: Spiritualism, Technology and the "Direct Voice"', in Buse and Stott, eds, *Ghosts:
Deconstruction, Psychoanalysis, History*, p.206. See also Steven Connor, 'CP: or, a
Few Don'ts by a Cultural Phenomenologist', *Parallax* 5:2 (1999), 17–31.

[71] Christopher Evans, 'Parapsychology: A History of Research', in *The Oxford Companion
to the Mind*, ed. Richard L. Gregory and O.L. Zangwill (Oxford, 1987), p.584.

[72] 'Scientific naturalism' is the term used by Frank Miller Turner to label the scientific
movement which from the 1860s displayed strongly rationalist, positivist and naturalist
characteristics. See Frank Miller Turner, *Between Science and Religion: The Reaction to
Scientific Naturalism in Late Victorian England* (New Haven and London, 1974), p.11.

discovery'.[73] My aim in this chapter is to show how the SPR fought to establish itself as a professional, legitimate and scientific organisation through the figure of the ghost, or, as psychical researchers more often referred to it, the apparition or phantasm.

I then move on to an exploration of the SPR's ideas about ghost-seeing, a discourse which emerged in the midst of a cultural field dominated by notions of telepathy and other ghostly-communication formats. It is vital to my overall purpose to show how thinking about a new kind of ghost developed in conjunction with changing attitudes towards death, the tele-technological revolution, and modern methodological and epistemo-logical techniques. The major expression of this discourse, the SPR-authorised book *Phantasms of the Living* (1886), was balanced precariously between the twin pillars of religion and science: as a project it aimed to be scientifically valid and sought the approval of experi-mental psychology, yet at the same time it used the notion of the 'crisis apparition' to challenge the materialistic consensus of the post-Darwinian scientific community and offer evidence of man's spiritual nature. Rea-ding between the lines of *Phantasms*, so to speak, chapter 4 identifies and explores the concept of the 'community of sensation' through which the SPR moved beyond the pseudo-scientific idea of the mesmeric rapport and focused on statistically legitimate theories of intimacy based upon the architecture of psychical research. This concept, I argue, expressed the balancing act of *Phantasms* in such a way as to provoke a critical response which may be taken as the classic late Victorian rebuff of the scientific ghost.

Through an examination of the criticisms which *Phantasms* received, the SPR's theory of ghost-seeing, and the community of sensation which supported it, is shown to have been deemed unproven and unscientific by most commentators in the public sphere. Following various crises within the SPR, the experimental focus on the moment of death, on 'phantasms of the living', was gradually phased out in the 1890s as Myers, engrossed in his researches on the 'subliminal self', began to accept many of the spiritualist postulates concerning 'phantasms of the dead', eventually arguing in favour of the existence and survival of the human soul. It is thus my contention in this chapter that the years 1882 to 1903 – from the foundation of the SPR to the posthumous publication of Myers's magnum opus *Human Personality and Its Survival of Bodily Death* – formed the 'heroic' phase of English bourgeois investigations into the nature of ghost-seeing. That this heroic period in the history

---

[73] Edmund Gurney, Frederic W.H. Myers and Frank Podmore, *Phantasms of the Living*: vol. I (London, 1886), p.xxxvi.

of the SPR failed to scientise the ghost highlights the predetermined outcome of the enterprise, the spiritual impulses which drove the investigations, and the 'haunted' nature of scientific naturalism itself in the *fin-de-siècle* period, prey to the inner demons of religious doubt and the outer demons of what was termed 'pseudo-science'.

The role of the concept of hallucination in the Society for Psychical Research is dealt with in chapter 5. As with *Phantasms*, the analysis here highlights an SPR publication which aimed to persuade the scientific community that the ghost-seeing experience *could* be veridical. In this case the 'Report on the Census of Hallucinations' (1894) – the culmination of the SPR's engagement with statistical method – sought to promote the telepathic theory of ghost-seeing using the mechanisms of the contemporary hallucination discourse. However, the main response from the discipline of experimental psychology to this renewed epistemic assault was to argue, in compliance with the standardised metaphor, that ghost-seers were actually dreaming while awake. This chapter concludes with more explicit reasons for the failure of the SPR to convince the scientific world that ghost-seeing was a proven fact and not simply an expression traceable to the percipient dreaming while awake. Such an indeterminate conclusion, with discovery left dangling between the illusory dream-world and the scientific laboratory is, I would argue, a deliciously apt commentary on all efforts to seize ghosts in the modern age and a fate which, from the perspective of the early twenty-first century, seems destined to remain the case.

Part I

The dreams of the ghost-seers

1   The haunted mind, 1750–1850

Ghosts reformed

The ghost had a purpose and a place in medieval society. Its purpose was generally to return to the terrene world to urge sinners to repent, to request prayers be said for the benefit of the souls of the departed, or to counsel the living against specific courses of action in both everyday mundane affairs and in ecclesiastical disputes. In this, the repertoire of the ghost as *revenant* had remained relatively unchanged since the classical era.[1] Although medieval Christianity was notoriously vague in its demarcations between the natural and supernatural,[2] it was generally supposed that ghosts came from the non-terrestrial place called purgatory, although as one later commentator added, it was conceivable that disembodied souls could endure their purgatory 'among mountains or in waters, or in valleys, or in houses, and particularly are they attached to those spots where on earth they sinned and offended God'.[3] The phenomenon of being haunted, therefore, was not only a normal possibility in life, but the world of ghosts was remarkably well ordered, secured and explainable both doctrinally and logically. Richard A. Bowyer has argued that: 'While the modern "ghost" appears in a psychological vacuum, terrifyingly isolated from our normal, everyday experience, the medieval "ghost" or "spirit" appears as an integral part of an immense and ordered spiritual world.'[4]

---

[1] For a selection of cases from the classical period see Noel Taillepied, *A Treatise of Ghosts etc.*, trans. Montague Summers (London, 1933), pp.43–53; Daniel Ogden, *Magic, Witchcraft, and Ghosts in the Greek and Roman Worlds: A Sourcebook* (Oxford, 2002), pp.146–78; Sarah Iles Johnston, *Restless Dead: Encounters between the Living and the Dead in Ancient Greece* (Berkeley and London, 1999). For a categorisation of medieval types of ghost see Jean-Claude Schmitt, *Ghosts in the Middle Ages: The Living and the Dead in Medieval Society*, trans. Teresa Lavender Fagan (Chicago, 1998), pp.59–60.
[2] Robert Bartlett, *The Natural and the Supernatural in the Middle Ages* (Cambridge, 2008), p.26.
[3] Taillepied, *A Treatise of Ghosts*, p.148.
[4] Richard A. Bowyer, 'The Role of the Ghost Story in Medieval Christianity', in *The Folklore of Ghosts*, ed. Hilda R. Ellis Davidson and W.M.S. Russell (Cambridge, 1981), p.177. See also William A. Christian, Jr, *Apparitions in Late Medieval and Renaissance Spain* (Princeton, 1981).

The Reformation led to the collapse of this cosmic hierarchy by radically separating the living from the dead. Physically and psychologically, a distance emerged between the living and the dead as corpses began to be buried outside of towns and villages in Lutheran territories. Spiritually, a fundamental tenet of Lutheranism was the denigration of any vital communitarian link between the living, the dying and the dead.[5] As Martin Luther preached in a sermon of 1522:

> The summons of death comes to us all, and no one can die for another. Every one must fight his own battle with death by himself, alone. We can shout into each other's ears, but everyone must himself be prepared for the time of death: I will not be with you then, nor you with me.[6]

Although it is hazardous to over-simplify the quite complex cultural and psychological shifts which followed the Reformation in England, the basic consequences as far as the issue of ghosts goes can be sketched out. The doctrine of purgatory was denied by the reformers as a superstition which was (according to the Thirty-Nine Articles of 1563) 'repugnant to the word of God'.[7] Given that spiritual visitants could therefore only come from heaven or hell, Protestant ghost-seers were left in the position of having to rule out ghosts of the departed as an explanation and instead interpret their experiences as either angelic or demonic in source. It was in the context of the refutation of the doctrine of purgatory that reformers began to apply tentative forms of investigation to cases of ghost-seeing, usually with a view to exposing apparitions as the sinister doings of priests and monks. For the rest, one Swiss Protestant argued:

> If it be not a vayne persuasion proceeding through weakenesse of the senses through feare, or some suche like cause, or if it be not decyte of men, or some naturall thing ... it is either a good or evill Angell, or some other forewarning sent by God.[8]

Given that ghost-seeing in sixteenth-century England, or at least the cases considered most worthy of collection and dissemination, was explained as the intervention of malevolent spirits, it was inevitable that

---

[5] Craig M. Koslofsky, *The Reformation of the Dead: Death and Ritual in Early Modern Germany, 1450–1700* (Basingstoke, 2000), pp.2–3. See also Peter Marshall, *Beliefs and the Dead in Reformation England* (Oxford, 2002).

[6] Koslofsky, *The Reformation of the Dead*, p.3.

[7] E. Harold Browne, *An Exposition of the Thirty-nine Articles: Historical and Doctrinal*, 6th edn (London, 1864), p.492.

[8] Ludwig Lavater, *Of Ghosts and Spirits Walking by Night, 1572*, ed. J. Dover Wilson and May Yardley (Oxford, 1929), p.160.

the issue would become interlinked with demonology and witchcraft.[9] Reginald Scot's *The Discovery of Witchcraft* (1584), which had rubbished the claims of witch-hunters and attempted to exorcise England of belief in ghosts, was publically burnt by the hangman on the accession of James I in 1603, a monarch noted for his interest in witchcraft. Yet as belief in witchcraft began to decline steadily among elites in the Restoration period, and materialist philosophers turned their attention to the subject of ghosts, Protestant divines began to worry about the effect that scepticism would have on belief in the supernatural in general and Christian revelation in particular.

In 1588 a French Capuchin, Father Noel Taillepied, had viciously criticised the Protestant position on ghosts:

All those writers who have drunk of the muddy and stinking waters of the Lake of Geneva incline absolutely to deny apparitions and ghosts, and this lie they have brewed out of their superstitious hatred of Prayers of the Dead. You will continually find it stated in the books of these heretics and ignorant ethnic bigots that the spirits of the dead cannot and do not appear.[10]

Soon Protestants in their turn began to quake at the effect that free-thinking about ghosts had wrought upon religious belief.[11] Indeed, in Amsterdam the Calvinist minister Balthasar Bekker was removed from office in 1692 after adopting the new Cartesian mechanical philosophy in an effort to 'disenchant' the world of angels and demons.[12] At issue for Protestants was the so-called 'chain of connexion'[13] whereby scepticism about ghosts was seen as inevitably leading to scepticism towards Christian doctrine regarding the immortality of the soul. As Jo Bath and John Newton put it, 'Ghosts had been cast in the role of supporting the whole superstructure of the immaterial world, and the whole edifice of religion seemed to rest on the success of the perform-ance.'[14] It is from this tense background of claim and counter-claim,

---

[9] Gillian Bennett, 'Ghost and Witch in the Sixteenth and Seventeenth Centuries', *Folklore* 97:1 (1986), 3–14.

[10] Taillepied, *A Treatise of Ghosts*, pp.5–6.

[11] See Davies, *The Haunted*, pp.112–15.

[12] See Han van Ruler, 'Minds, Forms, and Spirits: The Nature of Cartesian Disenchantment', *Journal of the History of Ideas* 61:3 (2000), 381–95; G.J. Stronks, 'The Significance of Balthasar Bekker's *The Enchanted World*', in *Witchcraft in the Netherlands from the Fourteenth to the Twentieth Century*, ed. Marijke Gijswijt and Willem Frijhoff, trans. Rachel M.J. van der Wilden-Fall (Rotterdam, 1991), pp.149–56.

[13] Joseph Glanvill cited in Jo Bath and John Newton, ' "Sensible Proof of Spirits": Ghost Belief during the Later Seventeenth Century', *Folklore* 117:1 (2006), 5. On the spectre of atheism in this period see Michael Hunter, 'The Problem of "Atheism" in Early Modern England', *Transactions of the Royal Historical Society* 35 (1985), 135–57.

[14] Bath and Newton, ' "Sensible Proof of Spirits" ', 11.

where the very framework of religion was thought to hang in the balance, that Protestant divines drew back from an instinctual scepticism, thus allowing the impulse to investigate and to apply proto-scientific methods to slowly emerge. In his tract *Saducismus Triumphatus: or, Full and Plain Evidence Concerning Witches and Apparitions* (1681), Joseph Glanvill, a clergyman and prominent member of the Royal Society, urged that all investigators approach the question of supernatural agency with an open mind:

> Briefly then, *matters of fact* well proved ought not to be denied, because we cannot *conceive-how* they can be performed. Nor is it a reasonable method of inference, first to presume the thing *impossible*, and thence to conclude that the *fact* cannot be *proved*. On the contrary, we should judge of the *action* by the *evidence*, and not the *evidence* by the measures of our fancies about the *action*.[15]

It was this promotion of the tenets of experimental philosophy which allowed Glanvill to be praised centuries later by both spiritualists and psychical researchers as a pioneer – a Christian sceptic who argued for a rational belief in ghosts through investigation of the facts.[16]

Across the sectarian divide, theorists of ghost-seeing were in agreement about the huge range of ways that ghost-seeing could be naturally explained. However, while Catholic commentators had the luxury of falling back on both scriptural precedents and a dogma which generally legitimised the existence of ghosts as the souls of the dead, in Protestant cultural contexts thinkers were forced to pay much closer attention to the margins, so to speak, in order to weed out the mass of experiences caused by dreams, bodily distemper, sensory delusion, fraud, etc., before a ghost could be classified as an illusion or 'a spirit of health or goblin damn'd', as Hamlet succinctly put it.[17] Nevertheless, by the end of the seventeenth century there is evidence that ghosts as the souls of the departed started to become a theory that was compatible with Protestant theology.[18] At the same time, and in contrast to the situation

---

[15] Joseph Glanvill, *Saducismus Triumphatus: or, Full and Plain Evidence Concerning Witches and Apparitions*, 2nd edn (London, 1682), p.12.

[16] William H. Harrison, *Spirits before Our Eyes* (London, 1879), p.vi; H. Stanley Redgrove and I.M.L. Redgrove, *Joseph Glanvill and Psychical Research in the Seventeenth Century* (London, 1921).

[17] William Shakespeare, *The Complete Works of William Shakespeare* (London, 1966), p.951. Greenblatt notes that reformers paid special attention to the relations between purgatory and fantasy. Stephen Greenblatt, *Hamlet in Purgatory* (Princeton, 2001), p.35. For an in-depth analysis of a seventeenth-century haunting see Peter Marshall, *Mother Leakey and the Bishop: A Ghost Story* (Oxford, 2007).

[18] Jürgen Beyer, 'On the Transformation of Apparition Stories in Scandinavia and Germany, c.1350–1700', *Folklore* 110 (1999), 45; Maxwell-Stuart, *Ghosts*, p.126; Handley, *Visions of an Unseen World*, pp.43–5.

in the medieval period, aspects of visionary experience began to fall within the realm of psychopathology, that is to say, thinking about ghosts began to illuminate structural facets of the mind previously unexplored.[19] An important development, noted recently by Stuart Clark, was the employment of the analogy between melancholia and 'dreaming while awake' in seventeenth-century thinking about vision.[20] The progressive strengthening of these conflicting responses and the sheer spectrum of possible explanations kept ghost-seeing one of the most controversial and debated topics in England as the era of Enlightenment commenced. The lack of any definitive answers led Samuel Johnson, no stranger to investigating ghost stories, to famously remark in 1787:

It is wonderful that five thousand years have now elapsed since the creation of the world, and still it is undecided whether or not there has ever been an instance of the spirit of any person appearing after death. All argument is against it; but all belief is for it.[21]

The phantasmagoric dislocation

Central to the emergence of secular modernity was the systematic discrediting of credulity as a vulgar attribute and a consequent redefinition of supernatural experience as evidence of pathological imbalance.[22] The dialectic of the Enlightenment in eighteenth-century Western Europe radically altered interpretations of ghost-seeing by relocating the ghost from the external, objective and theologically structured world to the internal, subjective and psychologically haunted world of personal experience.[23] According to Daniel Defoe, a noted commentator on ghost-belief in the early eighteenth century:

CONSCIENCE, indeed, is a frightful Apparition itself, and I make no Question but it oftentimes haunts an oppressing Criminal into Restitution, and is a Ghost to him sleeping or waking: nor is it the least Testimony of an invisible World that

---

[19] On the lack of a psychological approach to ghost-seeing in medieval culture see Jerome Kroll and Bernard Bachrach, 'Visions and Psychopathology in the Middle Ages', *Journal of Nervous and Mental Disease* 170:1 (1982), 41–9.

[20] Stuart Clark, *Vanities of the Eye: Vision in Early Modern European Culture* (Oxford, 2007), pp.56–7.

[21] Cited in James Boswell, *The Life of Samuel Johnson*, ed. Christopher Hibbert (Harmondsworth, 1979), p.239.

[22] Lorraine Daston and Katharine Park, *Wonders and the Order of Nature, 1150–1750* (New York, 1998), pp.329–63.

[23] See Barbara Maria Stafford, *Body Criticism: Imaging the Unseen in Enlightenment Art and Medicine* (Cambridge, MA, and London, 1991), p.437; Theodore R. Sarbin and Joseph B. Juhasz, 'The Historical Background of the Concept of Hallucination', *History of the Behavioural Sciences* 3 (1967), 342–4.

there is such a Drummer as that in the Soul, that can beat an Allarm when he pleases, and so loud, as no other Noise can drown it, no Musick quiet it or make it hush, no Power silence it, no Mirth allay it, no Bribe corrupt it.[24]

In confirmation of this gradual psychologisation of the ghostly, from about the middle of the eighteenth century the figure of the ghost became placed under a medical and diagnostic model that considered it a 'hallucination', a term generally used pejoratively to designate a fallacious perception that impinged upon the mind and tricked the experiencing subject into seeing something that was not really there.[25] In his *Philosophical Dictionary* (1764) Voltaire expressed this new rationalist conception:

It is not at all uncommon for a person under strong emotion to see that which is not ... Fantastic visions are very frequent in hot fevers. This is not seeing in imagination; it is seeing in reality. The phantom exists to him who has the perception of it. If the gist of reason vouchsafed to the human machine were not at hand to correct these illusions, all heated imaginations would be in an almost continual transport, and it would be impossible to cure them.

It is especially in the middle state between sleeping and waking that an inflamed brain sees imaginary objects and hears sounds which nobody utters. Fear, love, grief, remorse are the painters who trace the pictures before unsettled imaginations. The eye which sees sparks in the night, when accidentally pressed in a certain direction, is but a faint image of the disorders of the brain.[26]

Yet rationalism casts its own shadow.

With the gradual eviction of the ghost from the world of objective reality the spectral sphere was now held to originate chiefly within the mind of the ghost-seer: one became a *victim* of the hallucination as well as its originator. This displacement of the ghost, and consequent intellectual reorientation of the figure, inaugurated a general transformation of writings on ghost-seeing which began to focus on the phenomenological perspective of the subject in order to reveal the fallacies of mental life and the dangers and irrationality of ghost-belief.[27] The pedagogical

[24] Daniel Defoe, *An Essay on the History and Reality of Apparitions etc.* (London, 1727), p.100.
[25] See German E. Berrios, 'On the Fantastic Apparitions of Vision by Johannes Müller', *History of Psychiatry* 16:2 (2005), 232. The medicalisation of the hallucination was contemporaneous with the medicalisation of the dream and indicative of a general shift towards the increased policing and monitoring of mental states considered irrational. See Lucia Dacome, ' "To What Purpose Does It Think?": Dreams, Sick Bodies and Confused Minds in the Age of Reason', *History of Psychiatry* 15:4 (2004), 395–416.
[26] Cited in Sarbin and Juhasz, 'Historical Background', 348.
[27] See for instance John Ferriar: 'I have looked, also, with much compassion, on the pitiful instruments of *sliding panels, trap-doors, back-stairs, wax-work figures, smugglers, robbers, coiners*, and all other vulgar machinery, which authors of tender consciences have employed, to avoid the imputation of belief in supernatural occurrences.' John Ferriar, *An Essay towards a Theory of Apparitions* (London, 1813), pp.vi–vii.

underpinnings of these new hallucination discourses were in tune with Enlightenment scepticism and the general contempt for the enthusiasm, credulity and superstition present in all orders of society. With the new habitation of ghosts, spectres and spirits in the mind of the percipient, the realm of psychological space itself became a deeply haunted and uncanny site. It is within this context that rationalist and sceptical arguments against the reality of the spectral world began to demonstrate the mutability of normal consciousness and the potential for the fluidity of psychical forms to constitute the content of supernatural phenomena.

In an incisive study Terry Castle has demonstrated how the 'invention of the uncanny' in the eighteenth century was inextricably linked to, and indeed shadowed, the culture of Enlightenment in Western Europe. Central to this development was the cognitive impact of the phantasmagoria, a perceptual paradox which appeared in Britain at the turn of the nineteenth century. The Scottish scientist David Brewster described the dramatic effects of Paul de Philipsthal's production, which was exhibited in London in 1801:

All the lights of the small theatre of exhibition were removed, except one hanging lamp, which could be drawn up so that its flame should be perfectly enveloped in a cylindrical chimney, or opake shade. In this gloomy and wavering light the curtain was drawn up, and presented to the spectator a cave or place exhibiting skeletons, and other figures of terror, in relief, and painted on the sides or walls. After a short interval the lamp was drawn up, and the audience were in total darkness, succeeded by thunder and lightning; which last appearance was formed by the magic lanthorn upon a thin cloth or screen, let down after the disappearance of the light, and consequently unknown to most of the spectators. These appearances were followed by figures of departed men, ghosts, skeletons, transmutations, &c. produced on the screen by the magic lanthorn on the other side, and moving their eyes, mouth, &c. by the well known contrivance of two or more sliders . . . Several figures of celebrated men were thus exhibited with some transformations; such as the head of Dr. Franklin being converted into a skull, and these were succeeded by phantoms, skeletons, and various terrific figures, which instead of seeming to recede and then vanish, were (by enlargement) made suddenly to advance; to the surprise and astonishment of the audience, and then disappear by seeming to sink into the ground.[28]

Castle noted how the pedagogical functions of spectre-shows, magic-lantern performances, and phantasmagorias were quickly undermined by this new kind of psychological superstition mediated through the

---

[28] William Nicholson, 'Narrative and Explanation of the Appearance of Phantoms and Other Figures in the Exhibition of the Phantasmagoria. With Remarks upon the Philosophical Use of Common Occurrences', *Journal of Natural Philosophy, Chemistry, and the Arts* 1 (1802), 148. See also David Brewster, *Letters on Natural Magic, Addressed to Sir Walter Scott, Bart*, 5th edn (London, 1842), pp.80–2.

Figure 1 *The Ghost Illusion*. Source: Jean-Eugène-Robert Houdin, *The Secrets of Stage Conjuring*, ed. and trans. Professor Hoffmann [Angelo John Lewis] (London, 1881). Courtesy of the University Library, Cambridge.

spectacle of ghost-seeing productions: 'Thus, even as it supposedly explained apparitions away, the spectral technology of the phantasmagoria mysteriously recreated the emotional aura of the supernatural. One knew ghosts did not exist, yet one saw them anyway, without knowing precisely how'[29] (see Figure 1). As described by contemporaries, the impact of the phantasmagoria was significant in terms of its re-codification of ghost-seeing as a spectacle which drew upon mental apparatus to explain its power. De Philipsthal himself declared:

I will not show you ghosts, because there are no such things; but I will produce before you enactments and images, which are imagined to be ghosts, in the dreams of the imagination or in the falsehoods of charlatans. I am neither priest nor magician. I do not wish to deceive you; but I will astonish you.[30]

[29] Terry Castle, *The Female Thermometer: Eighteenth-century Culture and the Invention of the Uncanny* (New York and Oxford, 1995), pp.143–4.
[30] Cited in Tom Gunning, 'Uncanny Reflections, Modern Illusions: Sighting the Modern Optical Uncanny', in *Uncanny Modernity: Cultural Theories, Modern Anxieties*, ed. Jo Collins and John Jervis (Basingstoke, 2008), p.75.

The cognitive dissonance and uncanny sensations unearthed by the phantasmagoria – the fact that the occult machinery of the process was both known and yet feared – spread quickly throughout a whole range of discourses. It is from this point of phantasmagoric dislocation that we can trace the origins of the new conception of the mind as a haunted entity, a transformation in our idea of consciousness which Castle describes as the ' "ghostifying" of mental space'.[31] In a letter of 1820 John Keats could write: 'I rest well and from last night do not remember any thing horrid in my dream, which is a capital symptom, for any organic derangement always occasions a Phantasmagoria.'[32] Also picking up on this *spectacular* psychological usage, in his preface to *The Blithedale Romance* (1852) Nathaniel Hawthorne mentioned 'a theatre, a little removed from the highway of ordinary travel, where the creatures of [the] brain may play their phantasmagorical antics'.[33] From this phantasmagoric conception of consciousness came the popular usage of the term 'haunted' in nineteenth-century letters. Laura Quinney has written about how William Wordsworth constructed the model of a mind that is haunted 'by parts of itself that have a quasi-autonomous stature: by thoughts, images, memoires and past selves. And it is also haunted, that is to say bestirred, at perceiving within it the presence of these alien forms.'[34] Among other innumerable examples, Hawthorne's 'The Haunted Mind' (1835), Dickens's 'The Haunted Man' (1848), and Le Fanu's *Haunted Lives* (1868) all express this same 'ghostification' of mental space. Yet I would suggest that it was in an unfinished novella of the late eighteenth century that the sinister psychological effects of ghost-seeing in the modern age were first extensively explored.

Friedrich von Schiller's *Der Geisterseher* (*The Ghost-seer*) (1789) should be considered a paradigmatic text for its use of the spectre-show as a potent psychological metaphor in gothic literature. The main protagonist in the novella, a German prince, is resident in Venice during the carnival season but is somewhat haunted by religious melancholy: 'Wrapped in his own visionary ideas, he was often a stranger to the world about him ... Though far from being weak, no man was more liable to be governed.'[35] Soon enough, the Prince is duped into seeing

[31] Castle, *The Female Thermometer*, p.142.
[32] John Keats, *The Major Works: Including Endymion, the Odes and Selected Letters*, ed. Elizabeth Cook (Oxford, 2001), p.528.
[33] Nathaniel Hawthorne, *The Blithedale Romance* (Harmondsworth, 1986), p.1.
[34] Laura Quinney, 'Wordsworth's Ghosts and the Model of the Mind', *European Romantic Review* 9:2 (1998), 293.
[35] Friedrich von Schiller, *Aesthetical and Philosophical Essays, the Ghost-seer, and the Sport of Destiny*: vol. V (Boston, MA, 1902), p.176.

the ghost of his dead friend during a conjuration séance directed by 'the Sicilian', a Cagliostro-type figure of ambiguous intentions. Despite the Sicilian's later confession of fraud, which detailed the ingenious ruses used in the whole performance (including ambient music, hired actors and the obligatory magic lantern), the Prince emerges from this episode psychologically damaged. Book II of *Der Geisterseher* shows the psychological consequences of what Schiller elsewhere termed *die Entgötterung der Natur* (the 'un-godding' of nature) as the Prince's whole mental space transformed into an uncanny and phantasmic stage where the ghosts of the past and the apparitions of lost love haunt unrelentingly. This reinforced the sense that, following the demystification provided by the Sicilian, the Prince's world has, paradoxically, become a spectralised and relentlessly haunted one:

The confessions of the Sicilian left a deeper impression upon his mind than they ought, considering the circumstances; and the small victory which his reason had thence gained over this weak imposture remarkably increased his reliance upon his own powers. The facility with which he had been able to unravel this deception appeared to have surprised him. Truth and error were not yet so accurately distinguished from each other in his mind but that he often mistook the arguments which were in favour of the one for those in favour of the other. Thence it arose that the same blow which destroyed his faith in wonders made the whole edifice of it totter. In this instance, he fell into the same error as an inexperienced man who has been deceived in love or friendship, because he happened to make a bad choice, and who denies the existence of these sensations, because he takes the occasional exceptions for distinguishing features. The unmasking of deception made even truth suspicious to him, because he had unfortunately discovered truth by false reasoning.[36]

Thus the conjuration scene in *Der Geisterseher* foregrounds, as we shall see in the following chapter, the Kantian moment when the investigator truly becomes a ghost-seer – one who faces the truth of mistruth, and the knowledge of the lack of secure knowledge.[37] In this context it is important to note that common to both gothic fiction and Kantian psychology was the assumption of a reactionary attitude toward 'the Other' of the irrational: as Hartmut Böhme and Gernot Böhme have noted: 'The reasonable person unlearns deportment with this Other and instead reacts to it with panic and dread.'[38]

[36] *Ibid.*, p.241.
[37] Liliane Weissberg, *Geistersprache: Philosophischer Literarischer Diskurs im Späten Achtzehnten Jahrhundert* (Würzburg, 1990), p.241.
[38] Hartmut Böhme and Gernot Böhme, 'The Battle of Reason with the Imagination', trans. Jane Kneller, in *What is Enlightenment? Eighteenth-century Answers and Twentieth-century Questions*, ed. James Schmidt (Berkeley, Los Angeles and London, 1996), p.437.

While concerns about the disturbing inability to distinguish between reality and unreality in everyday life occupied the literary imagination at the turn of the nineteenth century (especially in the fiction of E.T.A. Hoffmann), such preoccupations also demonstrated the incursion of the medical imagination into the arts, particularly through the staging of a borderland between waking and sleeping. The phantasmagoric sense of mental dislocation that has been described occurred perhaps most famously in Francisco de Goya's etching *El Sueño de la Razon Produce Monstruos*, which was conversant with contemporary medical writings on dreams, reveries and allied states (see Figure 2). This etching strongly envisions the fluidity of consciousness as the figments of a disordered imagination come to assume an external reality. Despite the invective of sceptical and anti-apparition tracts in the late eighteenth century, it seemed that in borderland mental states such as reverie, abstraction and slumber ghosts returned to haunt men assumed to be normal and sane by their contemporaries.

A prime example of the sense of psychological dissonance induced by the *investigation* of these states comes in the writings of Samuel Taylor Coleridge. Throughout his life Coleridge exhibited a deep interest in the subject of dreams and their relation to the phenomena of ghost-seeing, focusing on them as an example of what he famously called 'the willing suspension of disbelief', or the lack of volition and judgement which accompanies dreams and the dream-state.[39] Predictably then, Coleridge attacked the common-sense views of the associationists and 'Scotch Metapothecaries' on the subject of dreams and visions for belittling the significance, necessity and sublimity of dreams by excessively treating them under the physiologist/rationalist paradigm. As Jennifer Ford writes of this school:

They eliminated the potential to explore the perplexing physiologies of dreams and the ways in which dreaming mind and body are related. Dreams were not perceived by Locke and Hartley as divine phenomena, nor as windows into the psychological depths of the mind, nor as examples of its creative powers.[40]

More interested in psychosomatic theories of dreams, Coleridge was drawn towards investigating the medical aspects of the imagination and the origins of poetic creativity, thus representing the advent of a romanticist concern to chart the organic bases of higher states of being and the deep connections

---

[39] Coleridge, *Biographia Literaria*, p.6.
[40] Jennifer Ford, *Coleridge on Dreaming: Romanticism, Dreams and the Medical Imagination* (Cambridge, 1998), p.16.

Figure 2 Francisco José de Goya y Lucientes, *El Sueño de la Razon Produce Monstruos* (1799). Courtesy of the Trustees of the British Museum.

between the body and the mind.[41] Coleridge was known throughout the nineteenth century as a prototypical 'waking dreamer', and it was only within the context of the new hallucination paradigm that he could remark

---

[41] *Ibid.*, pp.1–8. Coleridge was particularly drawn to the dream theory of Andrew Baxter. See Samuel Taylor Coleridge, *The Notebooks of Samuel Taylor Coleridge*: vol. IV, *1819–1826*, ed. Kathleen Coburn and Merton Christensen (London, 1990), no.5360; Ford, *Coleridge on Dreaming*, pp.142–3.

that he did not believe in ghosts because '*I have seen far too many myself*'.[42] In a similarly paradoxical vein Coleridge also proposed that the very impossibility of proving visions 'amounts to a proof' that they occur.[43] For Coleridge, this circle could be squared by placing the phenomena of ghost-seeing within the genera of dreams and dreaming, as an experience physiologically rooted and somnial in nature.[44] Thus in *The Friend* (1809) Coleridge declared that he believed in the visions of Martin Luther, arguing that they were 'ocular spectra' which took place in a 'half-waking state' of abstraction which allowed Luther to have

a full view of the Room in which he was sitting, of his writing Table and all the Impressions of Study, as they really existed, and at the same time a brain-image of the Devil, vivid enough to have acquired apparent *Outness*, and a distance regulated by the proportion of its distinctness to that of the objects really impressed on the outward senses.[45]

The new internalised hallucination model solved an intellectual quandary: to admit to the reality of apparitions would be considered rank superstition among the educated classes, yet to totally deny the veracity of testimony and accuracy of the senses would be, as the physician John Ferriar wrote, 'the utmost tyranny of prejudice'.[46] One way of maintaining the ambiguity of these two positions – or the Coleridgean paradox – was to link visual hallucinations and hallucinatory phenomena with dreams and the dream-world.

Closely paralleling the strengthening medical model of hallucination, investigations into the phenomena of dreaming steadily rejected supernatural and spiritualist theories of divine, angelic or demonic influence in dreams: from being associated with the world of the soul, transcendence and death, the world of sleep and dreams became rooted in psychodynamic and materialist precepts, ultimately culminating in Sigmund Freud's epochal *The Interpretation of Dreams* (1899), which book-ended a century of investigation into somnial phenomena.[47]

---

[42] Patricia Adair entitles her book *The Waking Dream: A Study of Coleridge's Poetry*. This labelling was current within Victorian psychology and mental physiology. Indeed Coleridge himself described Luther and Swedenborg as waking dreamers. Samuel Taylor Coleridge, *The Friend*: vol. I, ed. Barbara E. Rooke (London, 1969), p.146.

[43] On doubleness, division and imagination in Coleridge's thought see Seamus Perry, *Coleridge and the Uses of Division* (Cambridge, 1999).

[44] Ford, *Coleridge on Dreaming*, p.93.

[45] Coleridge, *The Friend*, pp.139–40.   [46] Ferriar, *An Essay*, p.137.

[47] See Carleton Greene, *Death and Sleep: The Idea of Their Analogy Illustrated by Examples etc.* (London, 1904); Rhodri Hayward, 'Policing Dreams: History and the Moral Uses of the Unconscious', *History Workshop Journal* 49 (2000), 145. As late as 1913, the psychologist Frederick Van Eeden described the phenomenon of 'wrong waking up',

By insisting that external sensual influence could direct internal psychical processes, the new empirical and psychological theories of dreaming that emerged around 1800 maintained that the focus of speculation should remain on the internal subjective processes of the mind. Thus the notion of dreaming while awake – of misunderstanding the reality of the physiological and psychological signs presented to the mind – was a way of negotiating through the sense of uncanny dislocation triggered by the apparently real vision of an apparition. The belief that ghosts were 'the stuff of dreams' and that the spectral world was a naturalistic consequence of the dream-world consistently recurs as a form of re-enchantment in the writings on hallucinations by medical philosophers, scientists, alienists, psychical researchers and psychologists throughout the nineteenth century to the extent that dreaming while awake could become the standard sceptical response to ghost-seeing experience *and*, in the idealist philosophy of Arthur Schopenhauer, function as a valid description of *veridical* ghost-seeing. This referential continuity demonstrates, on one level, the conservative nomenclature of the psychological disciplines, but it also suggests that the dream/hallucination analogy expressed a kind of poetics of the mind that, in different contexts, both pathologised and privileged the notion of 'true dreaming'.

The case of Nicolai

In 1799 Christoph Friedrich Nicolai, a Berlin bookseller and philosopher of a sceptical disposition, read a paper to the Royal Society of Berlin entitled 'A Memoir on the Appearance of Spectres or Phantoms Occasioned by Disease, with Psychological Remarks' which, after its translation into English in Nicholson's *Journal of Natural Philosophy, Chemistry, and the Arts* in 1803, attained status as a paradigmatic case

---

i.e. waking up in the knowledge that one is still asleep, in resolutely theological terminology: 'As I said just now, however, the terror ends as soon as the demons are *seen*, – as soon as the sleeper realises that he must be the dupe of intelligences of a low moral order. I am prepared to hear myself accused of superstition, of reviving the dark errors of the Middle Ages. Well, I only try to tell the facts as clearly as possible and I cannot do it without using these terms and ideas ... Only I would maintain that it is not *my* mind that is responsible for all the horrors and errors of dream-life ... A truth, a deceit, a symbol, cannot be without some sort of thought and intention. To put it all down to "unconsciousness" is very convenient; but then I say that it is just as scientific to use the names Beelzebub, or Belial. I, for one, do not believe in "unconsciousness" any more than in Santa Claus.' Frederick Van Eeden, 'A Study of Dreams', *PSPR* 26 (1912–1913), 457–8. Freud's book – often presumed to have been published in 1900 – was in fact published in November 1899.

throughout the psychological literature of nineteenth-century Britain.[48] Following a diagnosis of 'violent giddiness' due to excessive study, Nicolai was accustomed to being bled twice a year by his physician. But Nicolai inadvertently missed his appointment in the second half of 1790, with intriguing results. One morning in February 1791, during a period of considerable stress and melancholy in his life, Nicolai saw the apparition of a deceased person in the presence of his wife, who, however, reported seeing nothing. This apparition haunted him for the duration of the day, and in the subsequent weeks the number of these ghostly figures began to increase. However Nicolai resolved to coolly use his powers of observation to study the phenomena and attempt, if he could, to trace their cause:

I observed these phenomena with great accuracy, and very often reflected on my previous thoughts, with a view to discover some law in the association of ideas, by which exactly these or other figures might present themselves to the imagination.[49]

When the apparitions began to speak to him, he resolved to allow himself to be bled by his physician, and leeches were applied to the anus one April morning. Almost immediately Nicolai began to note the acute link between his physiological condition and the spectacle of phantoms which haunted his sensual world: his awareness of the apparitions swarming around him in the surgical room gradually disappeared and by the afternoon of his bleeding the ghostly figures seemed to move more and more slowly, then became paler, and had finally dissolved into the air by the evening. Ruminating upon this very graphic illustration of the connection between bodily dis-equilibrium (in the form of disordered venereal circulation), the natural vivacity of the imagination, and the appearance of spectres in the visual sphere, Nicolai described it as a lesson for philosophers and sceptics to be both more credulous of accounts of ghost-seeing *and at the same time* less credulous of such phenomena which show

how far the human imagination can go in the external representation of pictures; it may also admonish those well-disposed persons not to ascribe to their visions any degree of reality, and still less to consider the effects of a disordered system, as proofs that they are haunted by spirits.[50]

[48] For Nicolai's life see Pamela E. Selwyn, *Everyday Life in the German Book Trade: Friedrich Nicolai as Bookseller and Publisher in the Age of Enlightenment, 1750–1810* (University Park, 2000). On his opposition to superstition and the occult see Böhme and Böhme, 'The Battle of Reason with the Imagination', p.435.
[49] Nicolai, 'A Memoir', 167.   [50] *Ibid.*, 173.

Modelling himself on the new breed of psychological investigators, Nicolai distinguished his response to the appearance of ghosts from those of the insane, the fanatical, the superstitious, or the lovers of the marvellous who would have readily imparted reality to these hallucinations, while he 'made them subservient to my observations, because I consider observation and reflection as the basis of all rational philosophy'.[51]

This decision by Nicolai not to ascribe any objective reality to his visions, not to *believe* in what he saw and what was presented to his senses proved a landmark test-case on the length to which practitioners of the new empirical psychology were prepared to go in the pursuit of knowledge of the internal and external worlds. In contemporary cultural terms it also demonstrated a courageous amount of faith in the powers of self-observation and the strength of the medical imagination to map out the gothic shadows of the psyche.[52] Nicolai's memoir provided medical philosophers with a lucid example of 'with what delusive facility the imagination can exhibit not only to deranged persons, but also to those who are in the perfect use of their senses, such forms as are scarcely to be distinguished from real objects'.[53] The notion that a person could dream while awake seemed like an uncanny contradiction in terms, yet it is clear that in Nicolai's narrative the sensual objects perceived by the ghost-seer were taken as the objects of the dream-world; valid and yet false. Nicolai reasoned 'as if' he were awake by discounting the phenomena in his sensual field and exercising the use of enlightened reason. In the hierarchies of sensibility 'common-sense' won out. Inaugurating the psychological investigation of visual hallucinations, the case demonstrated the startling potential for the blending of separate spheres of human experience previously considered inviolable and self-contained. Coming at the turn of the century, Nicolai's narrative highlighted the huge challenge which ghost-seeing would present to the empirical philosophies of the nineteenth century due to the fact that ghost-seers appealed directly to the evidence of their senses to support their claims of supernatural visitation – most frequently the evidence of the sense of sight, considered the most veridical human sense. The response to this evidential challenge from sceptics was to spectralise their thinking about the self even

---

[51] *Ibid.*, 176–7. Nicolai was satirised as the 'Proktophantasmist' in Goethe's *Faust* for his crusading rationalism. Johann Wolfgang von Goethe, *Faust* (London, 1970), pp.155–6.

[52] Nicolai's description of blood-letting as a method of curing ghost-seeing was followed throughout the nineteenth century. See for instance John Alderson, *An Essay on Apparitions, in Which Their Appearance Is Accounted for by Causes Wholly Independent of Preternatural Agency* (London, 1823), p.28.

[53] Nicolai, 'A Memoir', 164.

further, building upon the phantasmagoric dislocation of the end of the eighteenth century. Furthermore Nicolai's grounding of abnormal perception in the specific conditions of the subjective imagination raised disturbing questions about the subjective nature of human vision and the simultaneously atomised and permeable characteristics of human psychology. It is with this case, obsessively returned to throughout the nineteenth century, that the ghost-seer enters the modern age as a figure haunted by his own projections.

Mirroring Nicolai's development from the physical to the psychological, scholars have recently begun to shift attention from the ghost to the ghost-seer, from the object of wonder to the embedded and traceable cultural language of the percipient.[54] They have outlined how the Enlightenment ghost-busting project could be characterised as a double bind, for while debunking well-known fallacious perceptions and psychological delusions, progressive physiologists and medical philosophers radically 'undermined the Enlightenment imperative for absolute scientific objectivity by foregrounding the subjective nature of sensory perception, especially sight, and the ensuing uncertainties of all knowledge derived from empirical investigation'.[55] Furthermore, the dangers of evangelical scepticism came to be recognised with the new philosophical theories upon the nature of ghosts and spirits. These approaches, which began to focus on the (unconsciously) deceitful nature of human psychology, successfully challenged religious arguments of belief in the supernatural as an 'antidote against atheism'. It is in the spectral illusions discourse that these issues come to the fore.

The spectral illusions model

The translation of Nicolai's narrative into English in 1803 contributed greatly to the formation of a genre of rationalist, sceptical and avowedly anti-supernatural tracts, pamphlets and books which maintained an intellectual continuity and ideological consistency in the British medical imagination until the spread of spiritualism in the 1850s. Drawing upon the tradition of the sceptics who had attacked belief in witchcraft in the seventeenth and eighteenth centuries, these works rehearsed well-known cases of mass delusion and fallacious perception, often alarmingly dismantling any confidence in the capacity of the human mind to accurately

---

[54] See Castle, *The Female Thermometer*; Srdjan Smajic, 'The Trouble with Ghost-seeing: Vision, Ideology, and Genre in the Victorian Ghost Story', *English Literary History* 70:4 (2003), 1107–35.
[55] Smajic, 'The Trouble with Ghost-seeing', 1114.

interpret the world around it and to distinguish fact from fiction. Two of the most influential studies upon the nature and origin of hallucinations in the early nineteenth century centred their examination on the supposed sighting of apparitions and phantoms of the dead. In these works John Ferriar and Samuel Hibbert – both medical physicians – outlined the theory of spectral illusions – the argument that apparitions were to be traced to disorders and diseases of the human bodily apparatus, rather than to insanity, revelation or post-mortem haunting.

In *An Essay towards a Theory of Apparitions* (1813), the Manchester physician John Ferriar considered it a fact 'that the forms of dead, or absent persons have been seen, and their voices have been heard, by witnesses whose testimony is entitled to belief' and proposed to use the methods of physiology to explain these occurrences among persons classed as 'normal' and sane.[56] Basing his theory upon an optical paradigm of understanding, Ferriar believed that apparitions could be explained by what he termed a 'renewal of external impressions' through which a visual memory could be re-animated via the visual sense. Indeed, Ferriar extended the principle of a renewal of external impressions used to explain ghost-seeing to benign aesthetic states such dreaming and artistic composition, describing them as waking dreams because they were 'composed of the shreds and patches of past sensations' and while they could explain such phenomena as the appearance of ghost armies, the Spectre of the Broken, and the appearance of strange lights, the phenomenon could at the same time be taken as an 'idle amusement'.[57] As Ferriar's work illustrates, the capacity of the dreaming imagination to incorporate and define the nature of ghost-seeing was established by the increased categorisation and breakdown of formerly distinct psychological phenomena and an awareness of the multidimensional character of consciousness, even in sleep.[58] Such psychological developments soon elicited professional support.

Samuel Hibbert in *Sketches of the Philosophy of Apparitions; or, an Attempt to Trace Such Illusions to Their Physical Causes* (1824) enlarged

---

[56] Ferriar, *An Essay*, p.13.   [57] *Ibid.*, pp.19–20.

[58] Robert Macnish described dreaming as an incomplete form of sleep, a state of partial slumber 'and consists of a series of thoughts or feelings called into existence by certain powers of the mind, while the other mental powers which control these thoughts or feelings, are inactive'. Robert Macnish, *The Philosophy of Sleep* (Glasgow, 1830), p.51. In this context the drift towards a state of waking-dreaming becomes dependent merely on the forcefulness and power of the imagination when the reasoning power of the dreamer is deficient, and thus a faculty theorised as being based upon the activity of the moral will. This theme would become strongly apparent in the writings of the most prominent mid-Victorian psychiatrists – Henry Holland, Henry Maudsley and William B. Carpenter.

upon Ferriar's writings and outlined the similar thesis that '*apparitions are nothing more than ideas, or the recollected images of the mind, which have been rendered as vivid as actual impressions*'.[59] Agreeing with Ferriar that ghosts could be understood as waking dreams, Hibbert used analogies with the chemical world to illustrate the changeable nature of the individual's mental state, such as the intoxications of dangerous miasmas and the 'visionary world' induced by exposure to nitrous oxide.[60] A recurring reference-point in Hibbert's text was that the 'renovation of past feelings' through association to a certain level of intensity could produce apparitions in the mind of the percipient. These associations were initiated by objects actually present in the visual field of the percipient and used emotions such as hope, fear and resentment to transform the external object of perception into a sensual apparition. By thus outlining the 'morbific' origins of apparitions, Hibbert sought to explain some of the most basic, yet complex, features of ghost narratives: ghosts are pale and misty because the 'spectral idea' of colour does not equal in intensity the vividness of immediate sensation; the fact that ghost-seers report seeing hallucinations of both the living and the dead points to a psyche which does not distinguish between past memories and the feelings they contain; ghosts seem to always appear in contemporary garb because they are created in the mind of the contemporary percipient. Furthermore, ghosts are subjective because they are national, historically specific, and can reflect the political opinions of the day. Hibbert enthusiastically quoted the antiquarian Francis Grose in support of the latter idea: 'Dragging chains is not the fashion of English ghosts; chains and black vestments being chiefly the accoutrements of foreign spectres, seen in arbitrary governments: dead or alive, English spirits are free.'[61]

Through stressing the optical sense in their theories of spectral illusions, Ferriar and Hibbert supported those who argued that such visual phenomena had a peripheral origin in the brain. They stressed that people who experienced spectral illusions were neither insane nor ghost-seers, but merely peripherally affected by abnormal impressions

---

[59] Samuel Hibbert, *Sketches of a Philosophy of Apparitions; or, an Attempt to Trace Such Illusions to Their Physical Causes*, 2nd edn (Edinburgh, 1825), p.61. Hibbert's writings should be compared with John Hughlings-Jackson's descriptions of the 'dreamy state' in the last quarter of the nineteenth century. One of Hughlings-Jackson's patients reported his symptoms: 'The past is as if present, a blending of past ideas with present ... a peculiar train of ideas of the reminiscence of a former life, or rather, perhaps, of a former psychologic state.' Cited in R. Edward Hogan and Kitti Kaiboriboon, 'The "Dreamy State": John Hughlings-Jackson's Ideas of Epilepsy and Consciousness', *American Journal of Psychiatry* 160:10 (2003), 1741.
[60] Hibbert, *Sketches of a Philosophy*, p.69.
[61] Cited in Hibbert, *Sketches of a Philosophy*, p.221.

and could be treated by such down-to-earth methods as bleeding and the application of active purgatives. The secular implications of theories which anchored the supernatural in the venereal fluctuations of the body were easily detected by contemporaries.[62] One physician recorded the case of a gentleman from Silesia who was 'liable from time to time to a hemorrhoidal flux' and who was followed all over his house, and into bed, by a 'spectral company' which included his niece and her husband. Whereas in previous centuries such an episode would have elicited a variety of supernatural interpretations, in this case the prescription was more down to earth: 'Gentle laxatives; bathing of the feet; and afterwards a tincture of cinchona restored him to his usual state of health.'[63] It is clear that these physiological theories of visual hallucinations formed the basis for later psychological theories based upon the similarities between the phantasmagoric nature of the dream-world and the ghost-seeing experience, for by withdrawing the origins of ghosts from the supernatural world these theories laid responsibility for such marvels on the occult workings of the human mind. By the mid-century it was argued that it was in the 'shadowy border-land betwixt physiology proper and pure psychology that apparitions wander'[64] and the debate in English and French psychology became, not whether these perceptions were veridical or not, but whether they had a central or peripheral origin in the brain.[65]

A recurrent theme in the promotion of the theory of spectral illusions was the Enlightenment push to eradicate needless fears, terrors and superstition using the 'light of philosophy' to 'illustrate the dark visitors of the spectral and demoniacal world'.[66] This anti-superstition agenda generally came alongside an avowed interest in entertaining the reader with ridiculous situations that demonstrated the folly of ghost-belief. Some books, copious with examples of hoax, delusion and hysteria, were marketed as antidotes to ghost-belief and were

[62] See for instance the response to Hibbert by an anonymous critic, *Past Feelings Renovated; or, Ideas Occasioned by the Perusal of Dr. Hibbert's 'Philosophy of Apparitions' Written with the View of Countering Any Sentiments Approaching Materialism, Which That Work, However Unintentional on the Part of the Author, May Have a Tendency to Produce* (London, 1828).
[63] 'Case of Spectral Illusion from Suppressed Hemorrhöis', *Edinburgh Medical and Surgical Journal* 26 (1826), 216.
[64] Samuel Brown, 'Ghosts and Ghost-seers', *North British Review* 9 (1848), 397.
[65] See Edmund Gurney, 'Hallucinations', *Mind* 10:38 (1885), 168–71; Edmund Parish, *Hallucinations and Illusions: A Study in the Fallacies of Perception* (London, 1897).
[66] Robert Buchanan, *The Origin and Nature of Ghosts, Demons, and Spectral Illusions* (Manchester, 1840), p.3.

particularly aimed at eradicating 'slavish fear in the minds of children'.[67] William Chapman's *Nocturnal Travels; or, Walks in the Night. Being an Account of Ghosts, Apparitions, Hobgoblins, and Monsters* (1828) was a didactic tract for children designed to show how easily people may be terrified into believing their hallucinations and illusions were of supernatural origin. Chapman's text consisted of short anecdotes relating to instances of deception which supported the anti-apparition point of view simply through illustrating the psychological origins of ghost-seeing. A few examples from Chapman's tract demonstrate the shift in sensibility which had reoriented ghost-seeing as a laughable interpretation of reality:

Passing, one night, along a narrow path, I beheld something of mysterious size and shape, going before me, appearing to have two heads, and one of them considerably above the other; when, upon a nearer approach to it, I discovered it to be a man, with a large clock-case upon his shoulder.

A poor silly man, called Crazy Tom, once concealed himself in a hollow elm tree, and making a jabbering kind of noise as a person was passing that way at night, greatly alarmed him. By many persons poor Tom would have passed for a ghost; but this friend of mine satisfied himself, and discovered the innocent offender.

A woman and her daughter were greatly alarmed, on entering the church-yard, by the sight of some unknown object among the tombs, and retreated hastily back; when I met them, and engaged to investigate the matter. I proceeded to the awful place, and found that an old soldier had taken up a temporary abode there; and his red jacket and white cap had increased the terror which the situation inspired. He asked me the time of night, and the nearest way to the next town.[68]

J.H. Brown's *Spectropia; or, Surprising Spectral Illusions. Showing Ghosts Everywhere, and of Any Colour* (1864) is another good example of the popular anti-supernatural chapbooks designed for entertainment and education at home.[69] The reader of the book was instructed by Brown to stare for a while at a variety of ghostly illustrations with extremes of

---

[67] Mary Weightman, *The Friendly Monitor; or, Dialogues for Youth against the Fear of Ghosts, and Other Irrational Apprehensions etc.* (London, 1791), p.3.

[68] William Chapman, *Nocturnal Travels; or, Walks in the Night. Being an Account of Ghosts, Apparitions, Hobgoblins, and Monsters* (London, 1828), pp.7, 11, 12.

[69] This book was published in the midst of new spectral technology of Henry Dircks and John Henry Pepper which updated the phantasmagoria through new optical techniques. See Henry Dircks, *The Ghost! As Produced in the Spectre Drama, Popularly Illustrating the Marvellous Optical Illusions Obtained by the Apparatus Called the Dircksian Phantasmagoria etc.* (London, 1863); John Henry Pepper, *The True History of the Ghost; and all about Metempsychosis* (London, 1890); Geoffrey Lamb, *Victorian Magic* (London, 1976), pp.43–50; Frederick Burwick, 'Romantic Drama: From Optics to Illusion', in *Literature and Science: Theory & Practice*, ed. Stuart Peterfreund (Boston, MA, 1990), pp.167–208; Davies, *The Haunted*, pp.204–9. On 'rational recreation' see During, *Modern Enchantments*, p.87.

light and dark, and then direct their gaze at a white surface or sheet: 'the spectre will soon begin to make its appearance, increasing in intensity, and then gradually vanishing, to reappear and again vanish'.[70] This do-it-yourself ghost-seeing vividly brought home the point that the senses were easily deceived into seeing what is not there and that 'no so-called ghost has ever appeared, without its being referable either to mental or physiological deception'.[71] At the same time, as a form of home entertainment, this induced ghost-seeing represents the extent to which thinking about the supernatural could become re-enchanted so soon after its attempted disenchantment in the eighteenth century.

In *The Origin and Nature of Ghosts, Demons, and Spectral Illusions* (1840), Robert Buchanan attributed ghost-seeing to a disordered body or mind and to natural causes such as fraud or ignorance. However Buchanan especially isolated optical philosophy as conducive to investigating the reality of apparitions: 'The optic nerve is the channel by which the mind peruses the hand-writing of Nature on the retina, and through which it transfers to that material tablet its decisions and creations. The eye is consequently the principal seat of the supernatural.'[72] Using this concern for the visual aspect of ghost appearances Buchanan explained that in accounts of ghost-seeing, the ghost is always described as white and seen at night or in the dark because at this time objects or living beings could reflect more light than other objects around them, thus giving the illusion of a spectral presence. Furthermore it is during the night hours that the mental pictures and images of the mind are no longer restricted by external visible objects and through a state of mental abstraction the figments of the imagination can reach an intensity akin to that of visible objects.[73]

A typical post-Enlightenment instance of ghost-seeing is the case of 'Miss N.', as reported by the physician Robert Paterson. Representing the upsurge in the ghost-seeing accounts of the middle and upper classes sent to learned journals, Paterson assured the readers of the *Edinburgh Medical and Surgical Journal* that due to the unassailable respectability of the percipient 'the authenticity of the apparition is placed beyond the reach of question'.[74] Following a fever the lady in question was conva-lescing at home during a storm while her father was at church. As the storm progressively got worse, Miss N. began to suspect that her father

---

[70] J.H. Brown, *Spectropia; or, Surprising Spectral Illusions. Showing Ghosts Everywhere, and of any Colour* (London, 1864), p.4.
[71] *Ibid.*, p.7.
[72] Buchanan, *The Origin and Nature of Ghosts*, pp.6–7.   [73] *Ibid.*, pp.9, 39.
[74] Robert Paterson, 'An Account of Several Cases of Spectral Illusions, with Observations on the Phenomena and on the States of Bodily Indisposition in Which They Occur', *Edinburgh Medical and Surgical Journal* 59 (1843), 80.

had been killed and it was in this state of mind that she suddenly saw his ghost sitting in the chair by the fire. For thirty minutes the spectral illusion remained there, impervious to the lady's touch or attempts at communication: her father returned from church unharmed soon after. Explaining this case as due to either a disordered digestive system or congestion of the 'cerebral membranes',[75] Paterson went on to explicitly make the connection between the phenomena of these 'dreams or illusions' and their gradual transition from simple dreams to 'the ravings of insanity'.[76] It was cases such as these that David Brewster sought to interpret in his *Letters on Natural Magic* (1832) using the optical paradigm to explain how it was that sane people could 'see' ghosts and other supernatural phenomena. After a consultation with a lady who was haunted by apparitions, Brewster explained to her a technique which would distinguish a real ghost from a spectral illusion. He advised that

she might distinguish a genuine ghost existing externally, and seen as an external object, from one created by the mind, by merely pressing one eye or straining them both so as to see objects double; for in this case the external object or supposed apparition would invariably be doubled, while the impression on the retina created by the mind would remain single.[77]

Such advice – naturalistic in both method and implications – reflected the practical application the spectral illusions model could have for ghost-seers unsure of the veracity of their visions and further entrenched the place of the ghost within a psychologically haunted world. Another explanation for ghost-seeing, although not as prevalent as the various physiological theories, was the idea that extreme bereavement could leave one at risk of seeing the dead.[78] However, behind the debates over spectral illusions lay the uneasy worry that ghost-seeing could be a symptom of incipient insanity. Walter Scott, who in 1830 wrote that tales of ghosts and demonology were 'out of date at forty years and upwards', warned readers that despite the veracity of all the ghost-seers he had met, 'in such instances shades of mental aberration have afterwards occurred, which sufficiently accounted for the supposed apparitions'.[79] Perhaps even more worrying for ghost-seers, the Glasgow physician Robert Macnish stated that 'Spectral illusions constitute the great pathognomic sign of delirium tremens.'[80]

---

[75] *Ibid.*, 91.   [76] *Ibid.*, 94.   [77] Brewster, *Letters on Natural Magic*, pp.38–9.
[78] John Netten Radcliffe, *Fiends, Ghosts, and Sprites: Including an Account of the Origin and Nature of Belief in the Supernatural* (London, 1854), pp.161–2, 172–3.
[79] Walter Scott. *Letters on Demonology and Witchcraft.* (London, 1884), pp.320, 286.
[80] Robert Macnish, *The Philosophy of Sleep*, 3rd edn (Glasgow, 1845), p.307.

Despite some physicians equating ghost-seeing with insanity (which would recur in medical discourse with the advent of spiritualism), the fact that large numbers of respectable, bourgeois and trustworthy men continued to report their spectral illusions in the same rational manner as Nicolai heralded the psychologisation of supernatural perception in the sane. In his *Chapters on Mental Physiology* (1850) the highly influential physician-psychiatrist Henry Holland wrote of how easy it was for a sane person to experience spectral illusions, which

> while connected on the one side with dreaming, delusion, and insanity – are related on the other, by a series of gradations, with the most natural and healthy functions of the mind. From the recollected images of objects of sense, which the volition, rationally exercised, places before our consciousness for the purposes of thought, and which the reason duly separates from the realities around us; we have a gradual transition, under different states of the sensorium, to those spectral images of illusions which come unbidden to the mind; dominate alike over the senses and reason; and either by their intensity or duration, produce disorder in the intellectual functions, and in all the actions depending thereon.[81]

The continuum argument, advanced here by Holland, was the lasting legacy of the spectral illusions model in the later nineteenth century and radically altered the terms of the encounter between sceptics and believers in the public sphere. Of primary importance in this transformation of how issues of ghost-seeing were discussed by the medical profession was the fact that supernatural experience was being interpreted and re-imagined through the co-identity of dreams and hallucinations. For instance, in 1838 the German physiologist Johannes Müller wrote: 'Images seen in dreams, not the mere idea of things conceived in dreams, are phenomena of the same kind as the phantasms. For the images which remain before the eyes, when we awake are identical with the objects perceived in our dreams.'[82] Such radical ideas that connected the daytime imagination with night-time dreaming anticipated the neurophysiological revolution in theories of dreaming which followed the discovery of REM sleep in 1953.[83] Yet as this development led to deeper investigations into the workings of the mind – waking and

---

[81] Cited in Jenny Bourne Taylor and Sally Shuttleworth, eds, *Embodied Selves: An Anthology of Psychological Texts, 1830–1890* (Oxford and New York, 1998), p.109.

[82] Cited in Peretz Lavie and J. Allan Hobson, 'Origin of Dreams: Anticipation of Modern Theories in the Philosophy and Physiology of the Eighteenth and Nineteenth Centuries', *Psychological Bulletin* 100:2 (1986), 235. See also T. Forster, *Illustrations of the Atmospherical Origin of Epidemic Diseases, and of Its Relation to Their Predisponent Constitutional Causes, Exemplified by Historical Notices and Cases, and on the Twofold Means of Prevention, Mitigation, and Cure, and of the Powerful Influence of Change of Air, as a Principal Remedy*, 2nd edn (London, 1829), pp.72–4.

[83] See Lavie and Hobson, 'Origin of Dreams'.

sleeping – new difficulties and categories emerged demanding an increased nosological awareness and new systems of symptomatology to create some sort of coherence in the structuring of perceptual experience. By the mid-nineteenth century, therefore, there was an increasing awareness and propagation of the idea that the brain could go to remarkable lengths to 'trick' sceptics into ghost-belief, a state of mind which was not immune to satirical comment:

Your unbeliever on principle will not believe even his own senses. Let a ghost appear to him – he will relate the occurrence to his friends as a 'singular case of spectral illusion'. Let the ghost speak to him – he will tell you that 'the case was the more remarkable, inasmuch as the illusion extended itself to the sense of hearing'. Let it sit on him, squelch him, pinch, or pommel him black and blue – strong in unbelief, even this staggers him not: he has his 'congestion' to flee to, and his 'plastic power of phantasy', all very good as far as it goes, but which does not go far enough ... What *is* a ghost to do, to get himself believed in?[84]

As I have suggested before, the forceful arguments and anti-apparition philosophy behind the spectral illusion model could be considered as approaching anti-clericalism, or even materialism at times, in its hostility to accounts of ghosts, spirits and visions purporting to be real.[85] Thus preliminary remarks upon the assured religious beliefs of the author were common among the anti-apparition philosophers who were keen to annul any charges of atheism brought against them. For instance Ferriar's disclaimer read:

observe, however, that the following treatise is applicable, in its principles, to profane history, and to the delusions of individuals only. If any thing contained in the ensuing pages could be construed into the most indirect reference to theological discussions, the manuscript would have been committed, without mercy, to the flames.[86]

Despite such assurances, the perception that the anti-apparition project was a danger to public morality and the very foundations of theological belief never fully disappeared. Before the arrival of the modern spiritualist faith in Britain in the 1850s, the ghost-believing counter-discourse against the spectral illusions theory took the form of religious and biblical arguments in favour of the reality of ghosts and collections of tales by high-profile commentators designed to destroy 'Sadducean'

---

[84] Ferris, 'Of the Nightmare', 43.
[85] Expressing the views of many, T.M. Jarvis argued that the main reason that ghosts appear is to reinforce belief in the doctrine of immortality. T.M. Jarvis, *Accredited Ghost Stories* (London, 1823), p.12. See also Finucane, *Ghosts*, pp.153–71.
[86] Ferriar, *An Essay*, p.ix.

arguments. The alienists and medical philosophers arguing for the spectral illusions theory now faced one of the fundamental problems of nineteenth-century British psychiatric discourse: the socio-cultural necessity of allowing for a transcendental element in the workings of the mind, both conscious and unconscious. Just as in the SPR at the end of the century, reconciling science and faith was proving somewhat of an albatross for British psychiatrists, a situation markedly different in the French psychiatric discourses which were characterised by a relative freedom from the necessity for a constant avowal of religious certitude due to the changing political culture of the state.[87]

Hallucinations and illusions in French psychiatry

In 1813 Ferriar wrote, 'The peculiar disorder, which I have endeavoured to elucidate is termed generally HALLUCINATION, including all delusive impressions, from the wandering mote before the eye, to the tremendous spectre, which is equally destitute of existence.'[88] As the term 'hallucination' was held to cover a large range of psychological phenomena from false perception, to ghost-seeing, to outright delirium, it was clear that new definitions of perceptual disorders had to be outlined following the paradigmatic shift in early nineteenth-century psychiatry towards 'moral treatment' and classificatory consensus.[89] The increased knowledge about the nature of optical illusions and the potential of deception in the natural environment (such as the Spectre of the Broken and the Fata Morgana) led to increased knowledge about the differences between illusions, delusions, optical illusions and what were being isolated as 'hallucinations'.[90] Such nosological awareness reflected the scientific-rationalist drive to tutor the senses, in the

---

[87] See Janet Oppenheim, *'Shattered Nerves': Doctors, Patients, and Depression in Victorian England* (New York and Oxford, 1991), pp.12, 47; Jan Goldstein, *Console and Classify: The French Psychiatric Profession in the Nineteenth Century* (Chicago and London, 2001); Ian Dowbiggin, 'French Psychiatry and the Search for a Professional Identity: The Société Médico-Psychologique, 1840–1870', *Bulletin for the History of Medicine* 63:4 (1989), 331–55. On the paradox of Carpenter's efforts to keep a space for the soul in his psychiatry see Alan Willard Brown, *The Metaphysical Society: Victorian Minds in Crisis, 1869–1880* (New York, 1947), p.48. After meeting Charles Richet in 1885, Sidgwick complained: 'It is curious that he does not seem to have to face the kind of scornful opposition that we have to face in England from physiologists and physicians and their camp-followers in the press.' Arthur Sidgwick and Eleanor M. Sidgwick, *Henry Sidgwick: A Memoir* (London, 1906), p.427.

[88] Ferriar, *An Essay*, p.95.   [89] See Goldstein, *Console and Classify*, pp.64–119.

[90] On the Fata Morgana see Charles Wyllys Elliott, *Mysteries; or, Glimpses of the Supernatural* (New York, 1852), pp.271–3; Warner, *Phantasmagoria*, pp.95–103.

Baconian sense, and to discipline, to control and to regulate experience. As Steven Shapin writes:

Experience suitable for philosophical inference had to emerge from those sorts of people fit reliably and sincerely to have it, to report it, or, if it was not their own, to evaluate others' reports of experience. Undisciplined experience was of no use.[91]

The most organised and professional structuring of mental abnormalities in the early nineteenth century occurred in French psychiatric circles following the successful establishment of the moral treatment model – usually associated with Philippe Pinel and his *Idéologue* circle of alienists.[92] Central to the system of Pinel and his successors was the collection and deployment of data, statistics and inferential percentages as part of a wider, and politically astute, programme based upon new classifications of mental diseases and disorders.[93] Pinel explicitly opposed the use of purging and bleeding in cases of mental disorder, treatments which, as we have seen, were common among British physicians and alienists. A survey of the French hallucination debates therefore demonstrates the contrast between the exceptionally British spectral illusions model and the more politically, religiously and ideologically contested French psychiatric discourse.

The most influential of the nosological pronouncements in this discourse was Jean-Étienne-Dominique Esquirol's celebrated distinguishing of hallucinations and illusions in 1832. Esquirol, who had been patronised by Pinel in the early part of the century, wrote:

In *Hallucinations* everything happens in the brain (mind). The visionaries, the ecstatics, are people who suffer from hallucinations, dreamers while they are awake. The activity of the brain is so energetic that the visionary, the person hallucinating, ascribes a body and an actuality to images that the memory recalls without the intervention of senses. In *illusions* on the other hand, the sensibility of

---

[91] Steven Shapin, *The Scientific Revolution* (Chicago, 1996), p.94.
[92] Pinel wrote in 1801: 'The hope is well-justified of returning to society individuals who seem to be hopeless. Our most assiduous and unflagging attention is required toward that numerous group of psychiatric patients who are convalescing or are lucid between episodes, a group that must be placed in the separate ward of the hospice ... and subject to a kind of psychological treatment [*institution morale*] for the purpose of developing and strengthening their faculties of reason.' Cited in Edward Shorter, *A History of Psychiatry: From the Era of the Asylum to the Age of Prozac* (New York, 1997), p.12. On moral management in an English context see Roy Porter, *Madmen: A Social History of Madhouses, Mad-Doctors and Lunatics* (Stroud, 2006), pp.257–312; Michel Foucault, *Madness and Civilization: A History of Insanity in the Age of Reason*, trans. Richard Howard (London, 1989); Frank Mort, *Dangerous Sexualities: Medico-moral Politics in England since 1850*, 2nd edn (London and New York, 2000).
[93] Goldstein, *Console and Classify*, p.105.

the nervous extremities is excited; the senses are active, the present impressions call into action the reactions of the brain. This reaction being under the influence of ideas and passions which dominate the insane, these sick people are mistaken about the nature and cause of their present sensation.[94]

The designation of people who hallucinate as 'dreamers while they are awake' distinguishes them from the percipients of illusions of all types. In contrast to the spectral illusions theory which outlined a continuum from *normalised* vivid imagination to hallucinations, and which stressed the peripheral origins of the hallucinatory experience, Esquirol maintained that hallucinations were a symptom of madness, a pathological phenomenon with central origins, that is, in the brain of the percipient. Furthermore Esquirol opened up the concept of hallucination to all the sense modalities, and did not privilege the visual sense within this shift.[95] He estimated that out of a sample of 100 insane patients, 80 had experienced hallucinations.[96] Esquirol's much-consulted textbook *Des maladies mentales* (1838) – in Roy Porter's words 'the outstanding psychiatric statement of the age'[97] – linked instances of hallucinations with suicidal mania and monomania, and raised the issue of surprise, or the noted lack of surprise, among people who experienced hallucinations:

The hallucinated are sometimes conscious, as is the case also in a revery, that they are in a delirium without the power to disengage the mind. He who is in a revery, as well as he who has hallucinations, is never astonished nor surprised at the ideas or images which occupy his mind, whilst they would have excited the greatest wonder had the patient been fully aroused, or had he not been delirious.[98]

Thus hallucinations, as fallacious perceptions with no actual external percept to excite the mind, become part of the continuum of *abnormal*

---

[94] Cited in Kate Flint, *The Victorians and the Visual Imagination* (Cambridge, 2000), p.263. Esquirol had in 1817 written: 'A man ... who has the inward conviction of a presently perceived sensation at a moment when no external object capable of arousing this sensation is within the field of his senses, is in a state of hallucination. *He is a visionary.*' Cited in Tony James, *Dream, Creativity and Madness in Nineteenth-century France* (Oxford, 1995), p.70. Using different terminology, Jules Baillarger distinguished between the 'hallucination psycho-sensorielle' and the 'hallucination psychique'. See Raoul Mourgue, 'Étude-critique sur l'évolution des idées relatives à la nature des hallucinations vraies', doctoral thesis, Paris, 1919, p.17.
[95] See German E. Berrios, 'Tactile Hallucinations: Conceptual and Historical Aspects', *Journal of Neurology, Neurosurgery, and Psychiatry* 45:4 (1982), 285–93.
[96] Berrios, "On the Fantastic Apparitions of Vision", 237.
[97] Roy Porter, *The Greatest Benefit to Mankind: A Medical History of Humanity from Antiquity to the Present* (London, 1999), p.502.
[98] J.E.D. Esquirol, *Mental Maladies: A Treatise on Insanity*, trans. E.K. Hunt (New York and London, 1965), p.107.

states of consciousness ranging from reverie to madness where the subject projects the ideas and images of the memory and gives form to his imagination in real life, thus dreaming while fully awake.[99] As Henri Ey wrote, Esquirol's concept of hallucinations 'brought psychiatry nearer the hallucinated individual'.[100]

A prominent member of Esquirol's circle, Jules Baillarger, who was awarded the Prix de l'Académie in 1842 for a paper on the relationship between hallucinations and hypnagogic states, supported Esquirol's pathological analogy between dreams and hallucinations and outlined the inter-modal variety of hallucinations possible in the mental patient. For instance, Esquirol's notion of a central origin of hallucinations seemed to explain how the blind could have visual hallucinations and the deaf auditory hallucinations:

The most frequent and complicated hallucinations affect hearing; invisible interlocutors address the patient in the third person, so that he is the passive listener in a conversation; the number of voices varies, they come from all directions, and can even be heard only in one ear. Sometimes the voice is heard in the head, or throat, or chest; the insane-deaf is more prone to hear voices. Visual hallucinations are however easier to study and understand. Images vary a great deal in distinctness and duration and may occur during day or night, with eyes open or shut. The blind may also have visual hallucinations. In the case of smell and taste, hallucinations and illusions are difficult to separate, as are their intellectual and sensory components. Subjects with touch hallucinations often complain of insects crawling over their bodies. Genital hallucinations are more common in women. Hallucinations affecting all sense modalities are common in acute diseases, and their connection can be explained on the basis of the theory of association of ideas.[101]

Such a generic list of pathological hallucinations entrenched Esquirol's arguments in favour of a central origin. An alternative view of the matter came from Alexandre Brierre de Boismont, a Catholic alienist who had also worked within Esquirol's circle. In his influential study, *Des hallucinations, ou Histoire raisonnée des apparitions, des visions, des songes, de l'extase, du magnétisme et du somnambulisme* (1845), Brierre de Boismont broke with his mentor and emphasised the normality of hallucinations and their co-existence with sanity, regarding them as consistent with the due exercise of reason – an interpretation which

---

[99] *Ibid.*
[100] Cited in German E. Berrios, *The History of Mental Symptoms: Descriptive Psychopathology since the Nineteenth Century* (Cambridge, 1998), p.37.
[101] *Ibid.*, p.39.

allowed for the retrospective diagnosis of sanity upon many major religious and historical figures who reported hallucinations.[102] However, occupying a mid-way point between religion and rationalism, Brierre de Boismont also believed hallucinations to be epidemic phenomena, which were historically contagious. Citing cases of vampirism, ecstasy and visions observed during plague and social crisis, the work of Brierre de Boismont anticipated many elements of what would come to be known as 'crowd psychology' in the late nineteenth century.[103] In cases such as these, hallucinations were believed to have a moral cause traceable to states of mind such as panic and the ideas spread by charismatic propagandists of the supernatural realm. In this, as in most enthusiasms, Brierre de Boismont attributed the trans-historical reporting of hallucinations to the universal love of the marvellous:

The general desire to be fed with chimeras, which has given birth to the just observation: Man is ice for wisdom, and fire for falsehood – appears to us a fruitful source of hallucination. Having passed ten, fifteen, or twenty years in dreaming, it requires but a slight addition of color to deepen the tint, when the panorama stops at the favorite subject, and that which has caused the deepest impression. Sufficient attention has not been bestowed on this misty phantasmagoria in which we live.[104]

This fluid passage from the world of dreams to the world of hallucinations was represented through the metaphor of the photographic apparatus: Brierre de Boismont wrote that the person who hallucinates is someone who has 'daguerreotyped' the subject of their thoughts upon the external world. This would explain the conversion of indefinite objects into phantoms of the dead by people considered timid, superstitious and uneducated: much like Ferriar and Hibbert, Brierre de Boismont characterised apparitions as merely a category of ideation, albeit an intensification of normal thought-processes. As has been seen with Coleridge, Martin Luther's visions provided a good historical case for contemporary medical philosophers to illustrate the psychological

---

[102] On the intense and complicated debates on hallucinations which took place at the Société médico-psychologique in 1855 and 1856, see Berrios, *The History of Mental Symptoms*, p.40; James, *Dream, Creativity and Madness*, pp.147–50. These debates involved most of the major alienists and psychologists in France at the time including Boismont, Alfred Maury, Baillarger, Claude-François Michéa, Louis Peisse and Philippe Buchez.

[103] See also Charles Mackay, *Memoirs of Extraordinary Popular Delusions and the Madness of Crowds* (London, 1869).

[104] Alexandre Brierre de Boismont, *On Hallucinations: A History and Explanation of Apparitions, Visions, Dreams, Ecstasy, Magnetism, and Somnambulism* (Philadelphia, 1853), pp.286–7.

causes of hallucinations in the sane. Brierre de Boismont stressed that as Satan was a very real presence during the Reformation period, the visual apprehension of a figure who dominated the language, culture and career of someone such as Luther would not be incomprehensible.[105] In Brierre de Boismont's writings on hallucinations we thus witness the rather unlikely combination of Catholic beliefs, psychological acumen and socio-historical insights.

This conscious importation of the medical model of visionary experience into thinking about dreams and dreamy states initiated heated debates into the role of the will during dreaming and whether mentation during dreaming was to be considered pathological or not. It was through these concerns that mid-century French psychiatry began to investigate the workings of the unconscious, specifically in relation to the creations of the dream-world and its connection with illusions and hallucinations.[106] However it is interesting to note that the pioneers of the psychological study of dreams were not practising psychiatrists, but were two amateurs in the field; the librarian and scholar Alfred Maury and the oriental scholar Marie-Jean-Léon Marquis d'Hervey de Saint-Denys. Both kept a *nocturnal* (dream diary), and their texts on the nature of dreaming would form important sources to Freud's breakthrough work *The Interpretation of Dreams*.[107] Maury's *Le Sommeil et les rêves* (1861) demonstrated how the mind was able to construct – at amazing speed – detailed and vivid *illusions hypnagogiques*, further breaking down the boundaries between sleep and waking. In his most famous example, the 'guillotine dream', Maury dreamt that during the Reign of Terror he was condemned to death and led to the scaffold where he was to be guillotined:

---

[105] *Ibid.*, p.385.
[106] Jean-Jacques Grandville was a notable artistic precursor to these psychological debates. See Stefanie Heraeus, 'Artists and the Dream in Nineteenth-century Paris: Towards a Prehistory of Surrealism', trans. Deborah Laurie Cohen, *History Workshop Journal* 48 (1999), 151–68.
[107] See Jacqueline Carroy, 'Dreaming Scientists and Scientific Dreamers: Freud as a Reader of French Dream Literature', *Science in Context* 19:1 (2006), 24. See also Heraeus, 'Artists and the Dream in Nineteenth-century Paris', 157–8. In contrast to Maury's book, which was reissued and well known in the late nineteenth century, Hervey de Saint-Denys's work, while also well known, proved more difficult to acquire. Freud wrote: 'The most energetic opponent of those who seek to depreciate psychical functioning in dreams seems to me to be the Marquis d'Hervey de Saint-Denys, with whom Maury carried on a lively controversy, and whose book, in spite of all my efforts, I have not succeeded in procuring.' Sigmund Freud, *The Interpretation of Dreams*, ed. James Strachey (London, 1961), p.127. See also Ellenberger, *The Discovery of the Unconscious*, pp.304–11.

the blade fell; I felt my head separating from my body, I woke up racked by the deepest anguish, and felt the bedpost on my neck. It had suddenly come off and had fallen on my cervical vertebrae just like the guillotine blade.[108]

It was dream narratives such as this that convinced Maury that there could be a science and a system in dreams. Realising that the materials of the dream were rooted in the fluctuating associations of the conscious life, Maury stressed the automatic process behind dream construction, writing '[In dreams] I am an automaton, but an automaton which sees and hears.'[109]

It seemed as if the mind had the ability to automatically hallucinate narratives based upon the peripheral influences of the physical world and, given the specificity of Maury's French revolutionary nightmare, on the private workings of the unconscious. In *Les Rêves et les moyens de les diriger* (1867) – originally published anonymously – Hervey de Saint-Denys described his attempts at 'lucid dreaming' – the ability to be aware that one was dreaming while one was dreaming. Hervey de Saint-Denys considered this ability a psychological liberation through which the dreamer could explore the hidden and concealed reaches of the memory in 'vast subterranean passages in which the mind can never see more clearly than when the light from outside has been cut off'.[110] Hervey de Saint-Denys believed that in his researches he had made two major findings: first of all, he argued that there was no sleep without dreaming and that the mind dreamt in a continuous manner. This implied that the human mind was, in a sense, a dream-machine, capable of carrying forth the dreaming faculty through various states of consciousness:

Thus the passage from waking to sleep, from the thought of the man awake to the dream of the sleeping man, can take place gradually without any interruption in the chain of ideas – without, as it were, any intellectual hiatus between the two states. When the eyes of the body are closed on the real world, the eyes of the mind are opened to the world of fantasy and recollection.[111]

In sleep, as in waking life, there is a 'continuous reciprocal action between the physical and the moral or mental sides of our existence', and thus dreaming is differentiated from waking life only by the

---

[108] Cited in Carroy, 'Dreaming Scientists and Scientific Dreamers', 33. On Maury's politics see Ian Dowbiggin, 'Alfred Maury and the Politics of the Unconscious in Nineteenth-century France', *History of Psychiatry* 1:3 (1990), 255–87.
[109] Cited in Sophie Schwartz, 'A Historical Loop of One Hundred Years: Similarities between Nineteenth-century and Contemporary Dream Research', *Dreaming* 10:1 (2000), 62.
[110] Hervey de Saint-Denys, *Dreams and How to Guide Them*, trans. Nicholas Fry (London, 1982), p.72.
[111] *Ibid.*, p.46.

progressive vivacity of its imagery.[112] Secondly, Hervey de Saint-Denys argued that the will could guide the dream when the dreamer became aware that he was dreaming – aware of the 'true situation' he was in – an argument disputed by Maury, and later, Pierre Janet.[113] Hervey de Saint-Denys cited the example of his repeated attempts to commit suicide in his dreams: once, upon throwing himself from the top of a building, he was amazed to find that his memory, in an ingenious manner, had evaded the trap set and had fast-forwarded, as it were, to imagining the scene of a body on the ground:

> The imagination therefore can *create* in a dream, in the sense of producing visions not seen before. Admittedly these visions are formed by materials already contained in the dreamer's memory, but they are formed like the fortuitous combinations of pieces of glass in a kaleidoscope, or as a rational neologism is formed from already known word-roots.[114]

By actively engaging with their dream mechanisms and, in the case of Hervey de Saint-Denys, claiming to be able to guide and direct them, these positivistic 'scientific dreamers' located key aspects of their dream world in unconscious and hidden memories. In their pioneering *phenomenological* perspectives, which would prove a rich source for neurophysiological and cognitive developments in dream theory in the late twentieth century, waking life emerged as a liminal stage in an increasingly diffuse range of states of consciousness and contributed to the mediating concept of the waking-dream of the sane as an explanation for hallucinatory experience.[115] This notion of waking-dreams represented at once the argumentative field *and* the blind side of a rationalist psychology, rooted in the Enlightenment, which had aimed at bringing the workings of the mind and the soul to the light of reason and understanding. On the contrary, more and more commentators were writing about the essential hallucinatory nature of thought itself, and by extension, the idea of a spectral self.[116]

Maury's theories on dreams and hypnagogic illusions resonated throughout the hallucination debates at the Société médico-psychologique and influenced his acquaintance Hippolyte Taine in particular, despite their emphasis on the role of the will in the dreaming process. In his book *De l'intelligence* (1870), Taine urged that the individual be constantly

---

[112] *Ibid.*, pp.47, 49.   [113] *Ibid.*, p.20.   [114] *Ibid.*, p.93.
[115] Schwartz, 'A Historical Loop', 56.
[116] See Eliza Lynn Linton, 'Our Illusions', *Fortnightly Review* 49 (1891), 596–7; Stafford, *Body Criticism*, p.377.

aware of the invincible illusions, tricks and falsehoods of human consciousness. Like an eye with poor visual capabilities, he argued, consciousness must be magnified and en-lightened in order to make proper sense of the external world.[117] Taine particularly focused on the vagaries of sensation in his study and argued that in a hallucination situation the '*special reductive*' in the mind, that which contradicts and corrects the sensation, fails in its duty, allowing the brain to sense what is not actually there:

This is why solitude, silence, obscurity, the want of attention, all circumstances, in short, which suppress or diminish the corrective sensation, facilitate or provoke the hallucination; and reciprocally, company, light, conversation, aroused attention, all circumstances giving rise to, or augmenting, the corrective sensation, destroy or weaken the hallucination.[118]

Thus Taine particularly singled out Nicolai's strength of mind, praising his method of rectification, the acknowledgement that he was in fact ill, and the realisation that the phantoms surrounding him were merely dreamlike illusions not to be addressed or given supernatural significance. Yet in his study Taine came to the conclusion that the human mind was dominated by images, representations and ideas which have no external present reality, but are processed as if they do. Therefore he felt justified in characterising the hallucination as *the* basic fact of mental life, and the state of mind of a healthy percipient as a series of hallucinations which halt at a certain point – the inability of this halting mechanism characterising more morbid states of mind: Taine followed Brierre de Boismont and Maury in refusing to label hallucinations as general pathological symptoms. Thus 'external perception is an internal dream which proves to be in harmony with external things: and instead of calling a hallucination a false external perception, we must call external perception a *true* hallucination'.[119] Through this seemingly paradoxical statement – one which turned accepted approaches to the matter inside-out – Taine was merely echoing what had become a central trope in mid-century poetics, particularly in the booming literary genre of ghost stories which expressed the extent to which inner experience both constituted and constructed outer experience. As George Eliot pointed out in 1872, 'the division between within and without' was becoming increasingly harder to ascertain.[120]

[117] Hippolyte Taine, *On Intelligence*, trans. T.D. Haye (London, 1871), p.x.
[118] *Ibid.*, p.54.   [119] *Ibid.*, p.224.
[120] Cited in Owen, *The Darkened Room*, p.20.

A Christmas Carol and 'The Haunted Mind'

By the mid-nineteenth century there existed a widespread and democratic market for supernatural tales that shirked off compartmentalisation into a single discourse, entertainment network or episteme. According to Dickens, 'Ghost stories illustrating particular states of mind and processes of the imagination are common property, I always think – except in the manner of relating them.'[121] Ghost stories, whether told around a fire at Christmas time, conceived in the imagination of scores of the most accomplished Victorian authors and poets, or collected and collated in psychological and psychical journals, exerted a huge influence upon mid- and late-nineteenth-century fields of debate centred upon the reality of the sensual world and the extent to which scientific epistemology could accurately interpret the phe-nomenological reality reported by percipients throughout Britain. Two of the strongest examples of the poetic use of the concept of hallucin-ation, and in particular how this use involved an interrogation of the waking dream, were Dickens's *A Christmas Carol* (1843) and Hawthorne's 'The Haunted Mind' (1835).

Dickens's *A Christmas Carol* was an important literary representation of the many issues in the hallucination debates regarding the vagaries of human perception. Towards the end of the French psychiatric discourse that has been traced above, Taine had gone so far as to ascribe to external objective perception the metaphor of the hallucination – a situation in which the world itself becomes a phantasmagorical dream – further breaking down notions of outside and inside. Dickens echoed this devel-opment through an interrogation of the dissonance experienced by the ghost-seer at the uncertainty of knowing whether the senses are to be trusted in their interpretation of reality.[122] The opening words of *A Christmas Carol* (the 'Marley's Ghost' section) read:

[121] Cited in Louise Henson, ' "In the Natural Course of Physical Things": Ghosts and Science in Charles Dickens's *All the Year Round*', in *Culture and Science in the Nineteenth-Century Media*, ed. Louise Henson, Geoffrey Cantor, Gowan Dawson *et al.* (Aldershot, 2004), p.116.

[122] During a period of mental distress in which Dickens took many night-walks throughout London, he was drawn to the precincts of the Bethlehem Hospital, where he speculated upon a 'night fancy' that he had: 'Are not the sane and the insane equal at night as the sane lie a dreaming? Are not all of us outside this hospital, who dream, more or less in the condition of those inside it, every night of our lives?' *The Uncommercial Traveller and Reprinted Pieces, etc.* (London and New York, 1964), p.131. It is clear that Dickens was familiar with the case of Nicolai, and with the spectral illusions theory in general. See 'To Be Taken with a Grain of Salt', in Cox and Gilbert, eds, *Victorian Ghost Stories*, pp.55–64. For the relations between mesmerism, the occult and the writings of

Marley was dead, to begin with. There is no doubt whatever about that. The register of his burial was signed by the clergyman, the clerk, the undertaker and the chief mourner. Scrooge signed it. And Scrooge's name was good upon 'Change for anything he chose to put his hand to. Old Marley was as dead as a doornail.[123]

Here it is clear that, as a prelude to the ghost-seeing situation, the fact of Marley's death is forcefully established, with Scrooge himself implicated in the formalities of Marley's passing. Furthermore, Dickens demonstrates that even before Scrooge is visited by the *revenant*, the reader is to understand that Scrooge is a possessed man: he answers equally to both 'Scrooge' and 'Marley' (they had been 'two kindred spirits'), and lives in chambers that once belonged to Marley.[124] Scrooge's supernatural experiences begin innocently enough, with what Esquirol would have termed an 'illusion'. Letting himself in at home at night Scrooge 'saw in the knocker, without its undergoing any intermediate process of change – not a knocker, but Marley's face'.[125] This illusion, a mistaken perception of real objects in the visual field, vanishes rapidly yet forms a psychological gateway to the more serious hallucinations which will afflict Scrooge later on in the story.[126]

Throughout his ghost-seeing experiences Scrooge demonstrates an awareness of the contemporary spectral illusions theory of hallucinations. Using the mantra of 'humbug' he remains steadily incredulous in the face of the sensory data before him:

'You don't believe in me', observed the ghost. 'I don't', said Scrooge. 'What evidence would you have of my reality beyond that of your own senses?' 'I don't know', said Scrooge. 'Why do you doubt your senses?' 'Because', said Scrooge, 'a little thing affects them. A slight disorder of the stomach makes them cheats. You may be an undigested bit of beef, a blot of mustard, a crumb of cheese, a fragment of an underdone potato. There's more of gravy than of grave about you, whatever you are!'[127]

Dickens see Fred Kaplan, *Dickens and Mesmerism: The Hidden Springs of Fiction* (Princeton, 1975). Kaplan points out that on the sale of Dickens's Gad's Hill Library in 1870 the catalogue contained notable works dealing with the supernatural including those of Hibbert, Crowe, Abercrombie, Jung-Stilling, Calmet, von Reichenbach, and Dale Owen. *Ibid.*, p.4.

[123] Charles Dickens, *The Christmas Books* (Ware, 1995), p.7.
[124] *Ibid.*, pp.7, 11, 14.   [125] *Ibid.*, p.14.
[126] As Gurney wrote: 'Illusions, or false perceptions of colour, often precede the appearance of more distinct phantasms. So, in cases of more transient abnormality – such as the well-known *illusions hypnagogiques* – other signs precede the hallucination. The observer, whose eyes are heavy with sleep, begins by seeing luminous points and streaks, which shift and change in remarkable ways; and it is from these as nuclei that the subsequent pictures develop.' Gurney, 'Hallucinations', 181–2.
[127] Dickens, *The Christmas Books*, p.18.

Stating this in spite of the obvious sensual reality of the spectre, Scrooge resembles the heroes of the spectral illusion model, percipients who, like Nicolai, fought against their senses and refused to ascribe reality to objects they were sure had a physiological origin. The remainder of the tale can be read as a spectre-show in which the appearance of so many apparitions bombards and literally frightens Scrooge into a belief in the reality of the spiritual world and a consequent entrance into a community whose members, like Scrooge's nephew, exhibit Christian charity, family love, and compassion in their daily dealings. In this development the space of the bedroom, where falling asleep, dreaming and waking typically take place, is crucial in signifying the potential for the detailed waking dreams. It is here that Scrooge wonders about the reality of his hallucinations and frets over the uncertainty as to whether they belong in the dream-world or the world of reality:

every time he resolved within himself, after mature enquiry, that it was all a dream, his mind flew back again, like a strong spring released, to its first position, and presented the same problem to be worked all through, 'Was it a dream or not?'[128]

While in his bed Scrooge is visited by the ghosts of Christmas past, present and future (indeed the Ghost of Christmas Future becomes a bedpost as he departs) and his inability to distinguish his experiences from waking dreams is complicated by the fact that he is described as being 'much in need of repose', and 'being exhausted, and overcome by an irresistible drowsiness'.[129] Through all of these signifiers the ghost-seeing described in *A Christmas Carol* can be considered as part of the contemporary hallucination discourse which noted the extreme mutability of consciousness and the inability to tell real objects from the externalised representations of the dreaming mind. An unfinished watercolour by Robert W. Buss entitled *Dickens' Dream* demonstrates the Victorian perception of Dickens as a writer who possessed a hallucinatory creativity (see Figure 3).

The notion of waking dreams occurring in the bedroom also dominates Hawthorne's contemporaneous fantasy 'The Haunted Mind':

What a singular moment is the first one when you have hardly begun to recollect yourself after starting from midnight slumber! By unclosing your eyes so suddenly, you seem to have surprised the personages of your dream in full convocation round your bed, and catch one broad glance at them before they can flit into obscurity. Or, to vary the metaphor, you find yourself for a single instant wide awake in that realm of illusions whither sleep has been the passport, and behold its ghostly inhabitants and wondrous scenery, with a perception of their strangeness such as you never attain while the dream is undisturbed.[130]

[128] *Ibid.*, pp.24–5.   [129] *Ibid.*, pp.23, 39.
[130] Nathaniel Hawthorne, *Twice-told Tales* (London and New York, 1932), p.222.

Figure 3 Robert W. Buss, *Dickens' Dream* (1875). Courtesy of the Charles Dickens Museum.

Hawthorne has selected a liminal moment which straddles the phases of sleeping and waking and assumes a revelatory potential in its capacity for veracity.[131] The sleeper, who is 'wide awake in that realm of illusions' has surprised the figments of his dream-world which surround the very corporality of his sleeping body as if (recalling Goya's etching) consciousness itself were a magic-lantern show projecting a spectacle for the delight of the ghost-seer. Yet Hawthorne is conscious of the fact that this metaphor is a self-entertaining narcotic which interrogates the sleeping/waking binary only through the uncertainty of accurately knowing whether the hallucination is a fact or fiction: 'The distant sound of a church clock is borne faintly on the wind. You question with yourself, half seriously, whether it has stolen to your waking ear from some grey tower that stood within the precincts of your dream.'[132]

---

[131] The poetic value of dreams and dreaming would play a strong part in transcendentalism. See Ralph Waldo Emerson, 'Demonology', *North American Review* 124:255 (1877), 180–1. Compare with Thoreau's conviction that dreaming while awake was the most truest and most heroic form of life. See Jeffrey E. Simpson, 'Thoreau "Dreaming Awake and Asleep" ', *Modern Language Studies* 14:3 (1984), 55.

[132] Hawthorne, *Twice-told Tales*, p.222.

Dickens's and Hawthorne's fictions demonstrate that the hallucination, as the most popularly known form of 'cognitive slippage',[133] was being used as a prominent literary trope in the supernatural fiction of the 1840s, and indeed, was forming the very conceptual basis of the uncertain realism evident in the framework of the Victorian ghost story. Julia Briggs wrote:

The philosophical problem of whether apparently supernatural phenomena have any independent existence or are created in the human imagination, with all its implications for a 'living' universe, or a totally subjective human vision are implicit in the question most basic to the ghost story, 'Was it real or imaginary?'[134]

These ghost stories also illustrate that the metaphor of dreaming while awake continued to be used to explain and rationalise reports of ghost-seeing in hallucination debates of the mid-nineteenth century, proving that this expression was neither a survival of romantic poetics nor an isolated psychiatric metaphor.[135] Thus, in his writings on the supernatural and abnormal psychological states, Hawthorne applied the logic of dreaming while awake to literary production, a process that occurred more frighteningly elsewhere during this period. For instance, one commentator wrote of the case of a poet from Edinburgh 'who not unfrequently awakes with the remanent [sic] image of some scene from dreamland in his eye, and it is some time till it evanesces'.[136] Such imaginative poetics were, however, soon to be matched with what appeared to be the objective realisation of the dream-world through the phenomena of spiritualism. Indeed, as a creative writer who had utilised the metaphor of dreaming while awake, Hawthorne himself was convinced that the spiritualistic phenomena reported by mediums were actually projected dreams,

in that the whole material is, from the first, in the dreamer's mind, though concealed at various depths below the surface; the dead appear alive, as they always do in dreams; unexpected combinations occur, as continually in dreams; the mind speaks through the various persons of the drama, and sometimes astonishes itself with its own wit, wisdom, and eloquence, as often in dreams.[137]

---

[133] Theodore R. Sarbin, 'The Concept of Hallucination', *Journal of Personality* 35 (1967), 360.

[134] Julia Briggs, *Night Visitors: The Rise and Fall of the English Ghost Story* (London, 1977), p.22.

[135] Despite this it seems that the first commentator to suggest that Hamlet's experience with the ghost of his father was a hallucination, understood in the modern sense, was Heinrich von Struve in 1876, and there appears to have been no similar argument until W. W. Greg in 1917. See Heinrich von Struve, *Hamlet: Eine Charakterstudie* (Weimar, 1876), p.52; W.W. Greg, 'Hamlet's Hallucination', *Modern Language Review* 12:4 (1917), 401.

[136] Brown, 'Ghosts and Ghost-seers', 401.

[137] Cited in Rita K. Gollin, *Nathaniel Hawthorne and the Truth of Dreams* (Baton Rouge and London, 1979), p.36.

2   Seeing is believing: hallucinations and ghost-seeing

The dreams of the *Geistersehers*: Kant and Schopenhauer on ghost-seeing

The works of Kant and Schopenhauer on ghost-seeing reflected a wide-spread interest in the investigation of occult phenomena within German philosophy which formed an intellectually rich prelude to the eruption of philosophical investigations into modern spiritualism, which began in the United States with the case of the Fox sisters in 1848. Their writings were significant in that they propounded theories of wakeful dreaming from a philosophical basis, analysing the supernatural phenomena considered widespread in Europe before the arrival of modern spiritualism in the 1850s, and thus before the establishment of sceptical and investigative modes of interaction with the ghostly.[1] The occult phenomena being examined by philosophers, physicians and other curious parties in Germany included the phenomena of animal magnetism, second sight, angelic visitations and witchcraft – yet it was the writings of Swedenborg that initiated Kant's personal interest in such marvels. Kant was concerned that the spiritualist speculations of Swedenborg were proving influential within intellectual circles and he resolved to counter this perceived influence with some anti-spiritualist philosophical arguments.[2]

Schopenhauer's essay on ghost-seeing can be seen as a continuation of the Kantian investigation into Swedenborgianism, yet Schopenhauer's own idealist philosophical system proved much more accommodating of the spirit-world than did Kant's early philosophical thought. As such, the essays of Kant and Schopenhauer offer contrary views of ghost-seeing from philosophically idealistic points of view which can be compared and contrasted with the spectral illusions theory of England in the early

---

[1] Although Schopenhauer's essay was published in 1851, the place of ghost-seeing in his philosophy had been established in his main work *The World as Will and Idea* (1818).
[2] For Swedenborg's influence in the nineteenth century see Lynn R. Wilkinson, *The Dream of an Absolute Language: Emanuel Swedenborg and French Literary Culture* (New York, 1996).

nineteenth century and the debates within French psychiatric circles as to whether the hallucination was normal or not. They also demonstrate the uncertainty with which these philosophers encountered the phenomenon of ghost-seeing, and the extent to which they actively integrated – and intellectually responded to – the challenge of contemporary accounts of anomalous phenomena by using the language of the dream-world in general, and the notion of dreaming while awake in particular.

* * *

Kant's *Träume eines Geistersehers, erläutert durch Träume der Metaphysik* (*Dreams of a Spirit-seer Elucidated by Dreams of Metaphysics*), published anonymously in 1766, was presented as a sceptical examination of the mystical theories of Swedenborg, whom Kant considered 'the arch-spirit-seer of all spirit-seers'. Ostensibly the essay was written, we are told, solely to please Kant's friends who urged him to examine the matter, and also to provide some personal justification for going to the trouble and expense of purchasing Swedenborg's main book *Arcana Celestia* (1749–1756), which Kant subsequently judged to be 'stuffed full of nonsense'.[3] However, this tactic of sarcasm and nonchalance merely served to further accentuate the disturbance he felt at the ghostly revelations of 'Schwedenberg' (purposefully spelt wrongly) and indeed the nature and meaning of the hallucination itself.[4] For his contemporaries, Kant's exact purpose in this essay was shrouded in confusion and mystery. Scholars have recently gone some way in explaining the part *Dreams of a Spirit-seer* played in Kant's wider philosophical development. Martin Schönfeld has shown that Kant encountered Swedenborg at a turning point in his precritical project, a philosophical enterprise which had aimed to unify and reconcile Newtonian natural science with metaphysics. In Swedenborg's angelology, Kant saw a nightmarish reflection of his own metaphysical inclinations, a *reductio ad absurdum* of the precritical project as it were.[5] In a brave move, he took a machete to his system and resolved to firmly map out the possibilities of

---

[3] Immanuel Kant, *Theoretical Philosophy, 1755–1770*, trans. David Walford and Rulf Meerbote (Cambridge, 1992), pp.341, 347. Kant's frequent references to the money expended on the book aim to *discredit* the philosophical value of the mystical theology of Swedenborg. *Ibid.*, pp.306, 344, 353. It is said that Kant was among the very few to have bought and read Swedenborg's work during his lifetime. C.D. Broad, *Religion, Philosophy and Psychical Research* (London, 1953), p.126.

[4] Moses Mendelssohn called him 'Mr *Schredenberg*'. Cited in Martin Schönfeld, *The Philosophy of the Young Kant: The Precritical Project* (Oxford, 2000), p.181. In 1918 Ernst Cassirer wrote that Kant's style in this essay 'upset all the traditions of the literature of scientific psychology'. Ernst Cassirer, *Kant's Life and Thought*, trans. James Haden (New Haven, and London, 1981), p.78.

[5] Schönfeld, *The Philosophy of the Young Kant*, p.244.

reasonable philosophy – to ascertain its boundaries, frontiers and limits. This topographical concern dominates the latter part of *Dreams of a Spirit-seer*.

In his descriptions of ghost-seeing, Swedenborg had laid down a challenge to both empiricists and metaphysicians:

> Now on to some evidence. As for angels being human forms, or people, this I have seen thousands of times. I have actually talked with them person to person, sometimes with one, sometimes with several in a group, without seeing anything about their form to distinguish them from man. From time to time I have marvelled at their being the way they are; and to forestall any claim that this is delusion or hallucination, I have been allowed to see them while I was fully awake, that is, while I was aware with all my physical senses and in a state of clear perception.[6]

Here, at the dawn of the hallucination concept, Swedenborg had recognised the risk of pathologisation inherent in his writings, yet ascertaining the state of play he had emphasised his tangible interaction with angels, the fact that he had been fully awake (and not dreaming) when this occurred, and that the situation had surprised him (further distancing the experience from the dream which, typically, did not elicit surprise). Such expressions of the ghost-seeing experience were a challenge for metaphysical philosophers during the Enlightenment, when such writings exposed, to an embarrassing degree, just how occultist most philosophical speculations were. Kant began his critique by locating the self in the world, by 'placing' the human body in the world of experience: 'The body, the alterations of which are *my* alterations – this body is *my* body; and the place of that body is at the same time *my* place.'[7] By locating the body in space, as a place, Kant challenged the idea that a spirit could have a shape or fill any space.[8] Perplexed by the problem of how an immaterial substance could obstruct matter, and how a body could affect a spirit which was neither impenetrable nor offered resistance to the occupation of the space in which it was present, Kant problematised the spiritualistic hypothesis of conscious and empirical spirit-intervention. He did not, however, discount the possibility that the human subject may become aware, from time to time, of the 'influences' of the spirit-world in an indirect or unconscious fashion through awakened representations.[9] This awareness would assume a symbolic character and, by using the apparatus of our consciousness,

---

[6] Emanuel Swedenborg, *Heaven and Hell*, trans. George F. Dole (New York, 1990), p.70.
[7] Kant, *Theoretical Philosophy*, p.312.
[8] *Ibid.*, pp.311–12.   [9] *Ibid.*, p.326.

the sensed presence of a spirit would be clothed in the image of a *human figure*; the order and beauty of the immaterial world would be clothed in the images of our imagination which normally delight our senses in life, and so forth.[10]

Kant thus outlined a naturalistic hypothesis of ghost-seeing which based such a phenomenon firmly within the precincts of the hallucinatory imagination: it is the subject who clothes the ghost, who represents the internal externally. Though naturalistic, Kant maintained that this type of phenomenon could only occur with unusual persons 'endowed with an exceptionally high degree of sensitivity for intensifying the images of the imagination'; that is, recalling the case of Nicolai, people with a predisposition to extreme vivacity or hallucination.[11] In a scenario such as this Kant believed that, because truth and delusion were mixed together to such a degree, where the real spirit-sensation has been transformed into a phantom, it would be hugely difficult to verify the experience, whilst also indicating the pathological and 'visionary' nature of the ghost-seer.[12] Kant's critique did not discount the existence or influence of the ghostly, but nevertheless approached a despairing agnosticism in that it placed true, veridical ghost-seeing beyond the limitations of his community of sensation:

Departed souls and pure spirits can never, it is true, be present to our outer senses, nor can they in any fashion whatever stand in community with matter, though they may indeed act upon the spirit of man, who belongs with them to one great republic.[13]

Kant proposed that such ghost-seers were 'dreaming their dreams' and occupying an imaginary world which was different from the world of common understanding.[14] However, he distinguished the ghost-seers from the waking dreamers: the latter take little notice of the sense-impressions of the external world, while the former 'refer certain objects to external positions among the other things which they really perceive around them'.[15] This distinction, so far as has been ascertained, is unique to Kant's thought and goes a long way to demonstrate the novelty of purpose behind *Dreams of a Spirit-seer*. For Kant, newly awakened from his dogmatic slumbers by David Hume and Jean-Jacques Rousseau, the illusions of metaphysics, of which he was a participant, resembled the dreamlike cogitations of Swedenborg's spiritualism to an almost uncanny degree. Yet Kant notes the differences between the metaphysical dreamer (a dreamer of reason) and the *Geisterseher* (a dreamer of sense)

[10] *Ibid.*, p.327.   [11] *Ibid.*   [12] *Ibid.*, pp.327–8.   [13] *Ibid.*, p.328.
[14] *Ibid.*, p.329.   [15] *Ibid.*, pp.330–1.

are based upon the will-to-deception of the ghost-seer who hallucinates the figments of his imagination through the *focus imaginarius* and projects them into the external world. Such a conjuration or 'deception' he believes is an effect of madness, or an inability of the will to exert its concentrative power:

> Furthermore, it can also be seen from this that, since the malady of the fantastical visionary does not really affect the understanding but rather involves the deception of the senses, the wretched victim cannot banish his illusions by means of subtle reasoning. He cannot do so because, true or illusory, the impression of the sense itself precedes all judgement of the understanding and possesses an immediate certainty, which is far stronger than all other persuasion.[16]

In this situation, Kant concluded that speculations upon the spirit-nature can never be positively thought of due to an acute lack of data, and thus must remain a futile and unnecessary form of investigation.[17] This traumatic episode – described by Susan Meld Shell as a 'metaphys-ical exorcism' – hastened the collapse of Kant's precritical project and heralded his ethical turn to 'a new model of spiritual worldhood that is morally, rather than theoretically, accessible'.[18] Through his examina-tion of the nature of ghost-seeing, as reported by Swedenborg, Kant was convinced that the discipline of metaphysics should be promoted as 'a science of the *limits of human reason*' tied to common-sense and experience, and implicitly aware of the capacity of visionaries to hallu-cinate and dream into the world the content of their imagination.[19] In thus seeking to end the matter, Kant anticipated the evangelical empiricism of the mid-Victorian mental physiologists who, like him, 'wasted their time in order to gain it'.[20] Not for the last time, the ghost-seeing experience had forced the savant into a topographical audit whereby the tactics used to discount the anomalous experience came to reflect and problematise the very intellectual enterprise engaged in.

In 'Über das Geistersehen' ('Essay on Spirit-seeing') of 1851, Schopenhauer took Kant's later concept of the ideality of space and time to launch an idealistic rather than spiritualistic critique of ghost-seeing, seeking to harmonise instances of supernormal phenomena with his own theory of the will – famously identified with Kant's 'unknowable'

---

[16] *Ibid.*, p.335.
[17] *Ibid.*, p.339. On the subtlety of Kant's position vis-à-vis metaphysics see John Hedley Brooke, *Science and Religion: Some Historical Perspectives* (Cambridge, 1991), pp.204–9.
[18] Susan Meld Shell, *The Embodiment of Reason: Kant on Spirit, Generation, and Community* (Chicago and London, 1996), pp.5, 133.
[19] Kant, *Theoretical Philosophy*, p.354.   [20] *Ibid.*

thing-in-itself. In this Schopenhauer essentially turned the precritical Kant on his head. In contrast to Kant in 1766, Schopenhauer was writing during a period when mesmerism and animal magnetism had radically impacted upon intellectual attitudes to the supernormal, especially among the *Naturphilosophen* who were drawn towards the study of the unconscious.[21] 'Whoever at the present time doubts the facts of animal magnetism and its clairvoyance', Schopenhauer declared, 'should not be called a sceptic but an ignoramus.'[22] Presumably believing Kant would have thought differently in the light of such early-nineteenth-century marvels as the Seeress of Prevorst, Schopenhauer also argued that only his theory of the will could unify all such ghostly phenomena in line with the evidence about the natural world. Schopenhauer's theory on ghost-seeing was widely disseminated in Britain and the United States following his posthumous acclaim and his theories formed an influential alternative to the challenge of scientific materialism.[23]

Schopenhauer believed that both metaphysical and empirical arguments against the possible existence of ghosts and apparitions were flawed *a priori*, in that the question of whether or not a spirit could

[21] Matthew Bell, *The German Tradition of Psychology in Literature and Thought, 1700–1840* (Cambridge, 2005), p.208.

[22] Arthur Schopenhauer, *Parerga and Paralipomena: Short Philosophical Essays*: vol. I, trans E.F.J. Payne (Oxford, 1974), p.229. Kant was aware of mesmerism but sounded a sceptical note of caution. See Peter Fenver, *Late Kant: Towards Another Law of the Earth* (New York and London, 2003), p.204. On the influence of animal magnetism in German romanticism see Jürgen Barkhoff, *Magnetische Fiktionen: Literarisierung des Mesmerismus in der Romantik* (Stuttgart, 1995); Bell, *The German Tradition*, pp.167–207.

[23] Corinna Treitel, *A Science of the Soul: Occultism and the Genesis of the German Modern* (Baltimore and London, 2004), pp.36–7. Treitel writes: 'In the 1850s, Schopenhauer's work provided a viable alternative to the materialist cause, and his philosophy became immensely popular among the educated middle classes uncomfortable with the metaphysics of materialism but dedicated to the empirical epistemology of science.' Treitel, *A Science of the Soul*, p.36. It is clear that from the 1870s Schopenhauerian philosophy was central in many debates surrounding the hallucinatory nature of ghost-seeing, not least in Eduard von Hartmann's essay *Der Spiritismus* (1885), which was quickly translated and reprinted in *Light*. Eduard von Hartmann, 'Spiritism', trans. Charles C. Massey, *Light* 5 (22 August 1885), 405–9; (29 August 1885), 417–21; (5 September 1885), 429–32; (12 September 1885), 441–4; (19 September 1885), 453–6; (26 September 1885), 466–9; (3 October 1885), 479–82; (10 October 1885), 491–4. See also Gustavus George Zerffi, *Dreams and Ghosts. A Lecture Delivered before the Sunday Lecture Society, on Sunday Afternoon, 7th February, 1875* (London, 1875); Gustavus George Zerffi, *Spiritualism and Animal Magnetism* (London, 1873); Frederic H. Hedge, 'Ghost-seeing', *North American Review* 133:298 (1881), 286–302; Lazar Hellenbach, 'The Hallucination of the "Unconscious"', trans. 'V', *Light* 5 (17 December 1885), 590–2; 'Alif', 'Religion and Schopenhauer', *Light* 12 (7 May 1892), 221.

actually be present in space was never really the issue at stake. Schopenhauer argued that there was a well-known state of consciousness in which an absent body is perceived as real and present, and yet is not: *the dream*: 'the fact remains that we have a capacity for intuitively representing objects that fill space and for distinguishing and understanding sounds and voices of every kind, both without the external excitation of the sense impressions'.[24] The palpable reality and effects of the dream upon the mind of the sleeper would prove that an intuitive perception of the world is possible without the actual presence of bodies. This proposition consummates, in philosophical form, the ghostly, hallucinatory nature of dreaming which has framed each of the discursive areas that have been examined thus far: however, in contradistinction to the psychological interpretations current in Britain and France, Schopenhauer proposed that the dream came from the faculty of intuitive perception which, like empirical perception, was an organic function of the brain. Schopenhauer then proceeded to examine states of hallucinatory aware-ness in which the dream-world seemed to interpenetrate with the world of external, empirical reality:

Thus there is a state in which we certainly sleep and dream; yet we dream only the reality itself that surrounds us. We then see our bedroom with everything therein; we become aware of people entering the room; and we know that we are in bed and that everything is correct and in order. And yet we are asleep with our eyes shut; we dream; only what we dream is true and real. It is just as if our skull had then become transparent so that the external world now entered the brain directly and immediately instead of by an indirect path and through the narrow portal of the senses.[25]

This 'dreaming of what is true and real' has been called *Schlafwachen* (sleep-waking) Schopenhauer notes, yet he elected to term it *Wahrträumen* (dreaming of reality). Schopenhauer names the active principle in this process the 'dream organ' which is an intuitive sense-apparatus that allows the subject entrance to the noumenal realm of the will, asleep or awake.[26] He regarded this dream organ as the key to explaining veridical

---

[24] Schopenhauer, *Parerga and Paralipomena*, p.238.   [25] *Ibid.*, p.239.
[26] Compare to Johannes Müller's concept of the *Phantastikon*, the imagination or fantasy centre which generates hallucinations and fantasmata in the visual field when stimulated. Berrios, 'On the Fantastic Apparitions', 236. Schopenhauer did not find a sure criterion for distinguishing dream from reality: 'Life and dreams are leaves of the same book. The systematic reading of this book is real life, but when the reading hours (that is, the day) are over, we often continue idly to turn over the leaves, and read a page here and there without method or connection: often one we have read before, sometimes one that is new to us, but always in the same book. Such an isolated page is indeed out of connection with the systematic study of the book, but it does not seem so very different when we remember that the whole continuous perusal begins and ends just as abruptly,

apparitions: significantly, in this regard, he placed the dream organ in contradistinction to the faculty of the imagination. Yet while these apparitions were fundamentally hallucinations in that the proximate cause of the ghost-seeing experience must always come from within the brain, stimulating it to activity, the possibility of a remoter cause for ghost-seeing experiences could also exist. Schopenhauer believed that ghost-seeing could be explained as 'retrospective second sight': ghosts are the vestiges and traces of departed phenomena which become perceivable to the dream organ in rare cases. Ghost-seers merely objectively perceive the world through the dream organ through which they actually dream the real: thus apparitions of the living, the dead, and the dying may be objectively seen in the same way as they are in a fantastical dream. Yet this 'dreaming of the real' is fundamentally a hallucinatory process in that the ghost-seer merely perceives the eidolon of the deceased person, a picture image or representation that originates organically in the dream organ and is initiated by a relic or echo of the deceased.[27]

For Schopenhauer, this theory explains three mysteries about ghost-seeing: why ghosts and phantasms are reported of the recently dead and those who have not been buried, why visions are perceived in darkness, silence and solitude, and, crucially, why the ghost appears in the clothes that the deceased normally wore in life.[28] In each case the dream organ, Schopenhauer argues, is active in producing a hallucination of the senses which relies upon the brain to format the apparition according to immediate data, memory and recollection, and the ingredients of the consciousness regarding the figure perceived.

Accordingly, I suspect that, during such a phenomenon, the consciousness that is certainly awake is veiled, as it were, with an extremely light gauze whereby it acquires a certain yet feeble dreamlike tinge. In the first place, it might be explained from this why those who have actually had such phenomena have never died of fright, whereas false and artificially produced spirit apparitions

and may therefore be regarded as merely a larger single page.' Arthur Schopenhauer, *The World as Will and Idea*: vol. I, trans. R.B. Haldane and J. Kemp (London, 1964), p.22.

[27] In this Schopenhauer echoes ancient Greek myth and ritual where *colossoi* took the place of the dead in society and functioned as a religious sign, a 'double', and an eidolon. See Jean-Pierre Vernant, *Myth and Thought among the Greeks* (London, 1983), pp.305–20.

[28] Schopenhauer, *Parerga and Paralipomena*, p.286. 'Another's lively and anxious thought of us can stimulate in our brain the vision of his form not as a mere phantasm, but as something vividly standing before us and indistinguishable from reality. In particular there are those on the point of dying who display this faculty and therefore at the hour of death appear before their absent friends, even to several in different places at the same time.' *Ibid.*, p.289.

have sometimes had a fatal effect. Indeed actual visions of this kind do not, as a rule, cause any fear at all; but it is only afterwards when we reflect on them that we begin to feel a shudder. This, of course, may be due to the fact that, while they last, they are taken for living persons and only afterwards is it obvious that they could not be.[29]

For Schopenhauer hallucinations and ghost-seeing were neither natural nor supernatural phenomena in the context of a metaphysical system which posited the world-as-will as the inheritor of Kant's thing-in-itself.[30] Thus, while the cause of intuitive perceptions mostly lies within the brain, and these Schopenhauer terms 'hallucinations' proper, there remained the possibility within this philosophical system of clairvoyant visions, mediated by the world-as-will, which transcends all forms of intellect and the *principium individuationis*.

The origin of these *momentous visions* is to be sought in the fact that the mysterious faculty of knowledge which is concealed within us and is not restricted by relations of space and time and is to that extent omniscient and yet never enters ordinary consciousness, but is for us veiled in mystery – yet casting off its veil in magnetic clairvoyance – that the faculty of knowledge has once espied something of great interest to the individual. Now the will, as the kernel of the whole man, would like to acquaint cerebral knowledge with this matter of interest; but then this is possible only by means of the operation in which it rarely succeeds, namely of once allowing the dream-organ to arise in the *state of wakefulness* and so of communicating this its discovery to cerebral consciousness in the forms of intuitive perception either of direct or allegorical significance ... Now all these related to the future; yet even something happening just now can be revealed in this way; however, it naturally cannot concern one's own person, but that of another. For example, the death of my distant friend that takes place at this very moment can become known to me through the sudden appearance of his form, as realistic as that of a living person, without it being necessary for the dying man himself to contribute to this in any way through his vivid thoughts of me.[31]

The agent is unconscious of his ghosting; the origin of such a phenomenon is 'concealed within us'; the crisis-apparition travels via a community of will and is made manifest by the consciousness – Schopenhauer's thoughts on ghost-seeing have strong parallels with the telepathic theory advocated by the SPR towards the end of the century yet are constructed within a referential system that obliged the ghost and the dream to co-habit. Schopenhauer's domestication and naturalisation of ghost-seeing through the medium of the dream organ reflects his idealist systemisation which circumvents the apparent contradiction of 'dreaming of

[29] *Ibid.*, pp.274–5.   [30] *Ibid.*, p.268.   [31] *Ibid.*, p.279.

the real'. His theory, that the ghost-seer is a person who is dreaming while awake, expressed in the sphere of idealist philosophy the acute dissonance with which the concept of hallucination was approached in the nineteenth century. It is also unique in that it offered an ingenious response to how something could be both a dream and a veridical event.

Schopenhauer utilised the notion of dreaming while awake as part of an effort to prove that the activity of the will could negate the very labels 'natural' and 'supernatural', and when causing the percipient to experience an hallucination or see a phantasm, demonstrate the nunciative significance of all that is perceived and represented to the human senses. Schopenhauer did not refer to the spiritualist phenomena in America in his essay but it is curious that he allowed that the question of whether the dead could influence the living remained an open one.[32] Yet despite Schopenhauer's influence, it was Kant's investigations into ghost-seeing that would ultimately prove paradigmatic of an intellectual trend which took off in the mid-nineteenth century following the spread of spiritualism. Kant had challenged the ghost-seeing experiences of a celebrated scientist – considered a genius and a reasonable man by most of his contemporaries – and thus prefigured a genre of criticism that sought to rescue the scientist from spiritualism, to save the (correct) science from the (erroneous) self. The concept of hallucination would form a strategic weapon in the battle to oppose the phenomenological realities of ghost-seeing experience with the intuition and scientific acceptability of common-sense and scepticism.

Hallucinations, spiritualism and pathology

In 1848 the sceptic Charles Ollier expressed the view of many in the mid-nineteenth-century scientific community when he wrote:

> It may be laid down as a general maxim, that anyone who thinks he has seen a ghost, may take the vision as a symptom that his bodily health is deranged. Let him, therefore, seek medical advice, and, ten to one, the spectre will no more haunt him. To see a ghost, is, *ipso facto*, to be a subject for the physician.[33]

The increased medical and psychological knowledge of fallacious perceptions, and the extraordinary public sphere in which they seemed to manifest themselves, soon updated Ollier's *a priori* pathologisation of the ghost-seeing experience. With spiritualism becoming a matter of great

---

[32] *Ibid.*, p.309.
[33] Charles Ollier, *Fallacy of Ghosts, Dreams, and Omens; With Stories of Witchcraft, Life-In-Death, and Monomania* (London, 1848), p.10.

public controversy in the Western world in the 1850s the concept of hallucination became inextricably linked with what was described as the 'epidemic' of spiritualism and 'table-talking'.[34] Following the strong connection made between spiritualism, insanity and hysteria in medical literature, commentators raised severe questions as to the reliability of *any* human testimony that supported the spiritualist claims of material-isations and ghostly intervention, particularly in the years following Crookes' celebrated investigations into Home and Cook.[35] At issue was the extent to which the visual world could be trusted: was the statement 'seeing is believing' a valid one in the context of a rapidly fragmenting epistemological field in which the boundaries between imagination and reality, and sanity and insanity, were becoming ever more fluid and uncertain? The critic George Henry Lewes thought that the statement was a valid one to make but, as he explained, the fallacy lay with confounding vision with inference: 'It is one thing to believe *what* you have seen, and another to believe that you have seen *all* there was to be seen.'[36] In this manner, when a percipient insists that he/she has 'seen a ghost', he/she is making an unwarranted inference which is divorced from the facts presented to the visual sense. Certainly something was seen, Lewes allows, but this prompts a new range of tricky questions such as 'How do you know it was a ghost?', 'Do you

---

[34] See William B. Carpenter, *Mesmerism, Spiritualism, &c., Historically & Scientifically Considered* (London, 1877), p.100.

[35] See Roy Porter and Helen Nicholson, eds, *Women, Madness and Spiritualism*: vol I, *Georgina Weldon and Louisa Lowe* (London and New York, 2003); Bridget Bennett, ed., *Women, Madness and Spiritualism*: vol. II, *Susan Willis Fletcher* (London and New York, 2003). Jung wrote: 'If we plump a good physicist down in the deceptive, magical darkness of a spiritualistic séance, with hysterical mediums plying their trade with all the incredible refinement many of them have at their command, his observation will be no more acute than a layman's.' Jung, *Psychology and the Occult*, p.106. On the belief that spiritualism was a symptom and a cause of insanity see L.S. Forbes Winslow, 'Spiritualistic Madness' (London, 1876); William A. Hammond, *Spiritualism and Allied Causes and Conditions of Nervous Derangement* (London, 1876); Charles Williams, *Spiritualism and Insanity: An Essay Describing the Disastrous Consequences to the Mental Health, Which Are Apt to Result from a Pursuit of the Study of Spiritualism* (London, 1910); Marcel Viollet, *Spiritism and Insanity* (London, 1910). Other commentators countered those who linked spiritualism with insanity. See Eugene Crowell, *Spiritualism and Insanity* (Boston, MA, 1877). From a survey of the asylum population in the USA Crowell, a medical doctor, concluded that out of 23,328 insane persons only 59 were committed for reasons related to spiritualism. *Ibid.*, p.5. See also Susan Elisabeth Gay, *Spiritualistic Sanity: A Reply to Dr. Forbes Winslow's 'Spiritualistic Madness'* (London, 1879); Judith R. Walkowitz, 'Science and the Seance: Transgressions of Gender and Genre in Late Victorian London', *Representations* 22 (1988), 3–29.

[36] George Henry Lewes, 'Seeing Is Believing', *Blackwood's Edinburgh Magazine* 88 (1860), 381.

know what a ghost looks like?', and 'What proof is there that it was not something other than a ghost?'[37]

As noted in the introduction, spiritualism radically interrogated mid-Victorian notions of evidence and evidential proofs. The advice of sceptical commentators such as Lewes was that in the face of the physical phenomena of spiritualism, with its dancing tables and levitations, the observer should maintain a negative agnosticism and not give mediums, considering their propensity to being exposed as fraudulent, the benefit of the doubt. The situation sketched out in the anti-spiritualist discourse was one in which the credulity of the spectators of spiritualistic séances acted against the very notion that they could witness the truth. The late Victorian amateur conjurer Angelo Lewis (whose stage name was 'Professor Hoffmann') held that ordinary observers were 'absolutely untrustworthy as witnesses' because after they experienced magical illusions they described what they *thought* happened, not what actually happened.[38] However, the calibre and respectability of scientific observers such as Alfred Russel Wallace, who was reporting ghost-seeing experiences and had enthusiastically converted to spiritualism, forced mental physiologists to focus upon the hidden workings of the 'normal' mind which seemed to betray the intelligence and common-sense of otherwise normal people.[39] In the critical response to the perceived *trahison des clercs* taking place in the séance rooms of English society there was a continuity of the use of the spectral illusions theory to explain apparitions, yet there was also a return to the Enlightenment tactic of describing such perceptions in pejorative terms. This was contemporaneous with the development of French psychiatry where, as we have already seen, the increased pathologisation of abnormal behaviour secured greater authority for the medical professions and a concomitant enshrining of the notion of subject-specific 'expertise'. Yet, to repeat the point, these psychiatric responses to spiritualism became more problematic as the status of scientific investigators, and the extent of their faith, became clear to the scientific community at large.

With the emergence of new theories of unconscious and contradictory action there was a realisation in medical and psychiatric discourses that subjectivity itself was a haunted entity which, in some cases, was in dire need of reform. One Victorian alienist argued that, just as the human has

---

[37] *Ibid.*, 382.

[38] Cited in 'D.D. Home, His Life and Mission', *JSPR* 4 (1889–1890), 120.

[39] Jon Palfreman, 'Between Scepticism and Credulity: A Study of Victorian Scientific Attitudes to Modern Spiritualism', in *On the Margin of Science: The Social Construction of Rejected Knowledge*, ed. Roy Wallis (Keele, 1979), pp.201–36; Owen, *The Darkened Room*, pp.139–67; Nordau, *Degeneration*, pp.214–18.

two eyes and two ears, so too we have two separate organs of mind, 'two distinct and perfect brains'.[40] According to this view, the fact that Nicolai saw ghosts and yet knew that they were not real was obviously explainable through the theory of a dual-mind structure: 'One brain was, as we so often see, watching the other, and even interested and amused by its vagaries.'[41] For the mental physiologist William B. Carpenter mentation was all a question of the 'Will'. The Will was a faculty concept strongly associated with British psychiatry and open to wildly different interpretations and speculations, but all centred, nonetheless, in a conviction of conscious volitional control.[42] Carpenter demonstrated how supernatural sensations could be automatically produced by mental states characteristic of expectant attention, or acute lack of volition, which allowed beliefs to be experienced as true sensations – phenomenological facts with no actual basis in reality. Following the naturalisation of many facets of the spiritualist repertoire such as mesmerism, table-turning and thought-reading, the seeing and hearing of deceased figures became characterised as a willing hallucination, yet one in which 'unconscious cerebration', or the subliminal mind was active in perverting reality, thus deeply disturbing an empirical epistemology based upon evidence and personal testimony. Carpenter believed that spiritualists could truly *see* the content of their own unconscious and attributed this psychological fact to an unfortunate resignation of their faculty of 'Common Sense'.[43]

Continuing in the tradition of the spectral illusions model, Carpenter radically devalued the evidence of the senses by comparison with the faculty of Common Sense, propounding that these spiritualist sensations could be produced by a variety of mental states: indeed the 'Sensorium'

[40] Arthur L. Wigan, *A New View of Insanity. The Duality of the Mind etc.* (London, 1844), p.35.

[41] *Ibid.*, p.72.

[42] The Metaphysical Society engaged in a debate upon the nature of the will which threw up some interesting, but very different, definitions of the faculty: 'A rational appetite' (Archbishop Manning); 'The desire of an act of our own' (Huxley); 'The power we have of increasing or diminishing the force of our own nature' (R.H. Hutton); 'The *Ego* conscious of itself or acting' (Sidgwick); 'Sense of effort for a purpose' (Stadworth Hodgson); 'Action for a feeling' (G. Croom Robertson); 'Purposive determinative effort' (Carpenter); 'The resultant of motives' (James Knowles); 'Necessity' (James Hinton). Brown, *The Metaphysical Society*, pp.79–80. The strength of the concept of the will in Victorian and Edwardian psychiatry was emphasised by Oppenheim who noted that as late as 1924, and despite a generation of radical neurological findings, the neurologist James Crichton-Browne maintained that the will had a central role in mental states. See Oppenheim, *'Shattered Nerves'*, p.75.

[43] William B. Carpenter, *Principles of Mental Physiology: With Their Applications to the Training and Discipline of the Mind, and the Study of its Morbid Conditions*, 6th edn (London, 1891), p.115.

emerges as a haunted perceptual engine at the mercy of all types of sensation with little distinction between perceptions that are 'real' or 'fictive':

Now when a number of persons who are 'possessed' with the current ideas in regard to Spiritualistic manifestations, sit for some time in a dark room in a state of 'expectant attention', it is comfortable to all scientific probability that they should *see* luminous manifestations, should *smell* flowers, should *feel* the contact of spirit-hands or the voices of departed friends, – just as they are prompted to do by their own course of thought, or by the suggestions of others; the connection of these dreamy imaginings, by bringing common sense and scientific knowledge to bear upon them, being just what the votaries of the doctrine referred-to scornfully repudiate.[44]

Echoing Coleridge's 'willing suspension of disbelief', Carpenter used the symptom of 'suspension of volitional control' to draw attention to the continuity between the variety of phenomena and states of mind which share this major feature. Thus dreaming, delirium, hypnotism, reverie, abstraction, ghost-seeing and indeed insanity were all essentially down to a lack of will-power within the mind of the percipient.[45] A prominent theme underlying this system, it must be noted, was the culture of self-discipline and acute mental observation as propounded by the evangelical religious revival.[46]

In a like manner to Carpenter, the psychiatrist Henry Maudsley accepted that most ghost-seeing cases were in fact instances of hallucination which he defined as

a false perception of one or other of the senses as a person has when he sees hears, or otherwise perceives as real what has no outward existence – that is to say, has no existence outside his own mind, is entirely subjective.[47]

Maudsley classified ghosts, apparitions, witches, visions of Satan and spirits of all kinds under the subjective criteria of a hallucination of the senses. Yet the delusion was not considered to be the cause of mental imbalance but rather 'a condensation from it, and an attempted

---

[44] Carpenter, *Principles of Mental Physiology*, p.165.
[45] *Ibid.*, pp.557, 584. As Oppenheim notes, ' "Failure of the will" was a convenient way to indicate the gravity of the medical problem, without being able to pinpoint its material source.' Oppenheim, *'Shattered Nerves'*, pp.43–4. The spiritualists, with some degree of satisfaction one suspects, drew attention to the spiritualist beliefs of some members of Carpenter's family. See 'F.J.T.', 'Spiritualism in the Carpenter Family', *Light* 1 (27 January 1881), 27.
[46] See 'Mental Epidemics', *Fraser's Magazine for Town & Country* 65 (1862), 490–505; Oppenheim, *'Shattered Nerves'*, p.14. On Unitarianism and mental physiology see Henson, ' "Half Believing, Half Incredulous" ', 255.
[47] Henry Maudsley, 'Hallucinations of the Senses', *Fortnightly Review* 24 (1878), 370.

interpretation of it'.[48] Delusionary phenomena strongly resemble dreams in that they are not the cause of a mental reaction but are, on the contrary, formed by internal and subjective processes: the image generates the feeling. Thus Maudsley was extremely surprised when, on consulting the *Encyclopaedia Britannica*, he found that the issue of whether apparitions existed or not was still considered, in accordance with psychical research, an open one.[49] While agreeing with the medical view that hallucinations were essentially a symptom and a form of morbid phenomena, Maudsley did not doubt that sane people occasionally experienced hallucinations also.[50] He believed that this fact explained the universal belief in ghosts and apparitions which has existed in all communities and in all historical periods. However, he separated his contemporary period, characterised as it was by scientific naturalism, from the past, when superstition was more likely to prevail over knowledge of the workings of the mind. Maudsley wrote that

the reason why no ghosts are seen now, when people pass through churchyards on dark nights, as our forefathers saw them, is that ghosts are not believed in nowadays, while we have gained a knowledge of the nature of hallucinations, and of the frequency of their occurrence, which our forefathers had not.[51]

Despite this assurance of the strength of the hallucination theory of ghost-seeing, Maudsley sounded a note of caution for those who were susceptible to derangement of the senses. He outlined the gradational states between the disorders of healthy and morbid hallucinations, such as giddiness, vertigo, hearing noises and fever, and noted that as in mesmerism, when the suggestion of an idea creates its perception, so

[48] Henry Maudsley, *Body and Mind: An Inquiry into Their Connection and Mutual Influences, Specifically in Reference to Mental Disorders* (New York, 1871), p.84.
[49] Maudsley, 'Hallucinations of the Senses', 373. For Myers the implications of Maudsley's opposition to psychical research smacked of materialism. In a letter to J.A. Symonds of 28 August 1883, Myers wrote: 'But the kind of adversary present to my mind is a man like Dr. Maudsley; – a man for whose private character I can well believe that I should feel much respect, but who represents a school of thought which, if it prevails, will bring the world to the nihilism of brutes of the field. I want to snatch our young Ray-Lankesters as brands from the burning, to save the men whose minds associate religion & the mad house, psychology & the vivisection-table, Love & the Strand.' Cited in Alan Gauld, *The Founders of Psychical Research* (London, 1968), p.142.
[50] However Maudsley explicitly rejected a psychological approach to mental illness in favour of the medical model which was dominant for much of the nineteenth century: 'It is not our business, is not in our power, to explain *psychologically* the origin and nature of any of [the] depraved instants [manifested in typical cases of insanity] ... it is sufficient to establish their existence as facts of observation, and to set forth the pathological conditions under which they are produced; they are facts of pathology, which should be observed and classified like other phenomena of disease.' Cited in Owen, *The Darkened Room*, pp.144–5.
[51] Maudsley, 'Hallucinations of the Senses', 372.

too in the mind of a healthy person a vivid idea can become a visual image. Maudsley cites a case of a man

who had the power of thus placing before his own eyes *himself*, and often laughed heartily at his double, who always seemed to laugh in turn. This was long a subject of amusement and joke; but the ultimate result was lamentable. He became gradually convinced that he was haunted by himself. This other self would argue with him pertinaciously, and, to his great mortification, sometimes refute him, which, as he was very proud of his logical powers, humiliated him exceedingly.[52]

Maudsley warns the reader that the man shot himself at midnight on 31 December of that year. In this account, as in Maudsley's writings in general, hallucinations were strongly linked to morbidity and were considered pathological in nature. However, it should be pointed out that accounts of autoscopy and doubling – sometimes horrific, sometimes comic – popped up throughout the literature on hallucinations. Goethe recorded one such incident when he 'saw, not with the eyes of the body, but with those of the mind, my own figure coming towards me',[53] while one participant at a séance in the 1920s reported that upon speaking to a ghost 'I had the impression that I was talking to myself, but it was some other myself, in a word, that my consciousness was talking to my subconscious.'[54]

To take a French example of the pathological discourse on hallucinations Marcel Viollet, a Parisian physician who worked in a lunatic asylum, believed that the hallucination was essentially a mental automatism wherein an object was interpreted in a special manner so that, where phantasmic apparitions were concerned, 'the imagination is obliged to intervene to be able to suppose these phantoms endowed with such an extension in space as enables them to be perceived otherwise than as described on a vertical plane'.[55] Drawing on his experience as a practising alienist, Viollet pointed to the dangers of spiritualism noting that people with hereditary nervous dispositions have a relentless curiosity with the spirit world, and brought their poor intelligence and weak will-power to the spiritualistic gathering. Regarding spiritualism as a pathological phenomenon, Viollet believed it appealed to weak-minded individuals because it provided a rapid and intense introduction to its faith.

---

[52] *Ibid.*, 377.
[53] Johann Wolfgang von Goethe. *The Autobiography of Goethe: Truth and Poetry: From My Life*, trans. John Oxenford (London, 1848), p.433.
[54] Cited in Zofia Weaver, 'Daniel Dunglas Home Revisited – Evidence Old and New: An Essay Review of *Knock, Knock, Knock! Who's There?*', *JSPR* 72 (2008), 224.
[55] Viollet, *Spiritism and Insanity*, pp.28–9.

Furthermore, spiritualism was to be considered as essentially hallucinatory in its marvels and beliefs:

> Have not the spectators at a spiritistic séance only one ideal: to obtain for themselves the phenomena produced by the medium? And is it not the desire of every believer to enter, no matter by what means, into a *rapport* with spirits, that is to say, to become a typological, auditory, visual, writing, drawing, or speaking medium? And is not everyone going to put forth his utmost efforts towards the arousing of the automatism of his centre, and hence of hallucinatory revelations?[56]

The degenerationist themes lurking within the anti-spiritualist writings of psychologists also began to feature in the new discipline of social anthropology in which the beliefs of modern spiritualism were being reassessed in the light of research into the different stages of development in primitive societies.[57] Edward B. Tylor's writings on the concept of animism,[58] principally his hugely influential *Primitive Culture* (1871), put the analogy between dreams and hallucinations centre-stage as he argued that by taking an 'ethnographic view of the matter', psychology would benefit from the scientific investigation into such an issue.[59] In Tylor's evolutionary scenario primitive man faced two fundamental questions, namely: what is the difference between being alive and being dead, and what status do the human figures that appear in dreams and hallucinations have? Tylor believed that the answer to these questions was that there existed two kinds of existential phenomena: waking life, and a phantom life which is perceived in visionary episodes.[60] With the appearance of the self, and deceased figures, in the dream-world of the primitive man, Tylor argued that this co-existence led to the theory of the ghost-soul conceived as a vapour or shadow, and which has the consciousness and volition of its owner and can appear 'to men waking or asleep as a phantasm separate from the body of which it bears the likeness'.[61] This, Tylor held, was the original source for religious belief.[62] Thus, in Tylor's theory of animism, the sane primitive, in

---

[56] *Ibid.*, p.30.

[57] On the theme of degeneration during this period see Daniel Pick, *Faces of Degeneration: A European Disorder, c.1848-c.1918* (Cambridge, 1989).

[58] For Tylor, 'animism', denoting a belief in the existence of supernatural beings, was a term he preferred to use instead of the more appropriate 'spiritualism' which he rejected on the basis of its contemporary rooting in the world of spiritualistic séances and supernormal phenomena. See George W. Stocking, Jr, 'Animism in Theory and Practice: E.B. Tylor's Unpublished "Notes on 'Spiritualism'" ', *Man* 6:1 (1971), 88.

[59] Edward B. Tylor, *Primitive Culture: Researches into the Development of Mythology, Philosophy, Religion, Art, and Custom*, 2nd edn, vol. I (London, 1873), p.142.

[60] *Ibid.*, p.428.   [61] *Ibid.*, p.429.

[62] Tylor's theory was not entirely original. Thomas Hobbes wrote that it was from this 'ignorance of how to distinguish Dreams, and other strong Fancies, from Vision and Sense, did arise the greatest part of the Religion of the Gentiles in time past, that

waking life, is unable to make a distinction 'between subjective and objective, between imagination and reality, to enforce which is one of the main results of scientific education': in modern terminology this is known as a failure in 'reality discrimination'.[63]

It was from this outline of the individual in thrall to the world of dreams and hallucinations that Tylor propounded a socio-cultural argument that regarded modern spiritualism as a direct revival, or 'survival', of 'savage philosophy and peasant folklore':

It is not a simple question of the existence of certain phenomena of mind and matter. It is that, in connexion with these phenomena, a great philosophic-religious doctrine, flourishing in the lower culture but dwindling in the higher, has re-established itself in full vigour. The world is again swarming with intelligent and powerful disembodied spiritual beings, whose direct action on thought and matter is again confidently asserted, as in those times and countries where physical science had not as yet so far succeeded in extruding these spirits and their influences from the system of nature.[64]

This survival theory of spiritualism sought to explain how ghost-seeing regained its place and meaning in the popular culture of the nineteenth-century individual, and how civilised and elite men could be, on the face of it, as degenerate in their beliefs as the savages analysed by anthropology. Tylor notes, with more than a hint of approval, that only a generation earlier second sight had gone the way of witchcraft in the Scottish

worshipped Satyres, Fawnes, Nymphs, and the like; and now adayes the opinion that rude people have of Fayries, Ghosts, and Goblins; and of the power of Witches'. Thomas Hobbes, *Leviathan*, ed. Richard Tuck (Cambridge, 1991), p.18.

[63] Tylor, *Primitive Culture*, p.445. Nietzsche's theory of dreams was considerably influenced by Tylor. Nietzsche wrote: 'all of us are like the savage when we dream. Faulty recognitions and mistaken equations are the basis of the poor conclusions which we are guilty of making in dreams ... The utter clarity of all dream-ideas, which presupposes an unconditional belief in their reality, reminds us once again of the state of earlier mankind in which hallucinations were extraordinarily frequent, and sometimes seized whole communities, whole nations simultaneously. Thus, in our sleep and our dreams, we go through the work of earlier mankind once more.' Friedrich Nietzsche, *Human, All Too Human*, trans. Marion Faber and Stephen Lehmann (London, 1994), pp.19–20.

[64] Tylor, *Primitive Culture*, pp.142–3. While the doctrine of survivals was most strongly associated with Tylor, it had previously appeared in a more limited form in the writings of J.F. McLennan and Herbert Spencer. See J.W. Burrow, *Evolution and Society: A Study in Victorian Social Theory* (Cambridge, 1966), pp.240–1. On popular religion and debates about the secularising and civilising process see Judith Devlin, *The Superstitious Mind: French Peasants and the Supernatural in the Nineteenth Century* (London, 1987); Thomas Kselman, *Death and the Afterlife in Modern France* (Princeton, 1993); Keith Thomas, *Religion and the Decline of Magic: Studies in Popular Beliefs in Sixteenth and Seventeenth Century England* (London, 1971); Susan K. Morrissey, 'Drinking to Death: Suicide, Vodka and Religious Burial in Russia', *Past and Present* 186 (2005), 117–46.

Highlands as, since it had ceased to be believed, it had therefore ceased to exist among the populace.[65]

Suppose a wild North American Indian looking on at a spirit-séance in London. As to the presence of disembodied spirits, manifesting themselves by raps, noises, voices, and other physical actions, the savage would be perfectly at home in the proceedings, for such things are part and parcel of his recognized system of nature.[66]

Yet Tylor's arguments for the abnormal and savage implications of animism drew strong criticism from A.E. Crawley who argued, conversely, that incidences of hallucinations were probably no more frequent in lower than in higher civilisation, and furthermore, that 'The biological probability is that its frequency, never considerable, decreases the nearer man is to the animals.'[67] Crawley believed that Tylor overestimated the pathological nature of dreams and hallucinations, and suggested that Tylor's theory had been significantly weakened by the findings of experimental psychology, specifically Taine's and Francis Galton's arguments for a continuum of mental states in the human psychology.[68]

As the concept of hallucination developed, the complex nature of human psychology came to the fore in medical and psychiatric discussions about just what constituted the mental processes of the normal, sane mind. With advent of the 'new psychology' in the 1880s, this psychological work increasingly began to take place in the setting of the laboratory.[69] This prioritisation of the experimental framework led to the use of statistical methods to ascertain incidences of psychological phenomena in the general population. It is no surprise, therefore, that the concept of hallucination entered a new phase in its development in which the medical model of the concept came under much pressure

[65] Tylor, *Primitive Culture*, p.143.

[66] *Ibid.*, pp.155–6. Maudsley supported the survival hypothesis. Henry Maudsley, *Natural Causes and Supernatural Seemings* (London, 1886), p.161. Despite this aversion to modern spiritualism, Tylor did attend some séances in London in November 1872. It seems that these experiences, recorded in his diary, left Tylor in a much more uncertain position vis-à-vis mediumship and spiritualistic phenomena than had been the case in the late 1860s. See Stocking, Jr, 'Animism in Theory and Practice', 92–100.

[67] A.E. Crawley, *The Idea of the Soul* (London, 1909), pp.7–8.

[68] The psycho-physical problem, as expounded by Tylor and his successors in social anthropology, occupied a notable role in psychical research, specifically through the writings of William McDougall, who allied belief in animism to post-Myersian investigations into survival. For McDougall, if animism was not accepted by psychical research then any belief in immortality would be put under threat. See William McDougall, *Body and Mind: A History and a Defense of Animism* (London, 1911).

[69] See William L. Courtney, 'The New Psychology', *Fortnightly Review* 26 (1879), 318–28; Rick Rylance, *Victorian Psychology and British Culture, 1850–1880* (Oxford, 2000), p.7.

from the findings of a new generation of experimental psychologists. It was in this context that Galton sought to statistically measure individual differences in mental processes through what was, at the time, the pioneering method of psychometrics.[70]

By asking respondents simple questions relating to the use of mental imagery in their thought-processes Galton amassed some surprising results. He asked scientific friends of his to think of the table they had breakfast on that morning, and consider, in their 'mind's eye', the illumination, definition and colouring of the scene. Galton was 'amazed' by the findings of his survey:

To my astonishment, I found that the great majority of the men of science to whom I first applied protested that mental imagery was unknown to them, and they looked on me as fanciful and fantastic in supposing that the words 'mental imagery' really expressed what I believed everybody supposed them to mean.[71]

Galton proved the facility of using statistical methods into subjective mental processes and concluded that strong visual representation is antagonistic to abstract thought. In general society he found that children and women had a greater capacity for mental imagery than men, perhaps as a result of the 'delight in self-dissection' those sectors of the populace seem to take.[72] Galton then proceeded to conduct a larger survey of 100 individuals, of whom about half were classed as elite male intellectuals. He received replies indicative of a variety of mental visualising states, from perfectly clear and distinct mental imagery to absolutely no visual representative powers. Again, Galton recorded his surprise at the findings of the survey:

In the course of my inquiries into visual memory, I was greatly struck by the frequency of the replies in which my informants described themselves as subject to 'visions'. Those of whom I speak were sane and healthy, but were subject notwithstanding to visual presentations, for which they could not account, and which in a few cases reached the level of hallucinations. This unexpected prevalence of a visionary tendency among persons who form a part of ordinary society seems to me suggestive and well worthy of being put on record.[73]

---

[70] See Francis Galton, 'Statistics of Mental Imagery', *Mind* 5:19 (1880), 301–18.

[71] Francis Galton, *Inquiries into Human Faculty and Its Development* (Bristol and Tokyo, 1998), p.84.

[72] *Ibid.*, p.87. Galton's finding appeared all the more remarkable given that in Western sensory culture women have been traditionally associated with the lower senses of smell and touch rather than that of vision. See Classen, *The Color of Angels*; Vieda Skultans, 'Mediums, Controls and Eminent Men', in *Women's Religious Experience*, ed. Pat Holden (London, 1983), pp.15–26.

[73] Galton, *Inquiries into Human Faculty*, p.155.

His survey of visions, published in *Inquiries into Human Faculty and Its Development* (1883) led Galton to the realisation that there was a definite continuum between all forms of visualisations, from an absence of this faculty to complete hallucinatory experiences. As with Hibbert and Taine, Galton argued that there was a significant prevalence of hallucinations in general society, further deconstructing the absolute demarcations of the psychiatric categories of sanity and insanity.[74] Furthermore Galton de-pathologised incidences of ghost-seeing, writing that seeing 'phantasmagoria' and phantoms was common among many sane and eminent men, including five newspaper editors personally known to him.[75] Galton ascribed to the analogy made between dreams and hallucinations and followed Hibbert in believing that phantasmagoria and visions were made up of recollections of the past and 'blended memories'.[76] Indeed, Galton believed that that the natural hallucinatory world of the individual, as seen in the imagination of the child, was socially repressed and liable to be unearthed only in an epistemic shift that placed a high value was on hallucination cases that demonstrated the 'gift' of the visualising faculty:

Therefore, when popular opinion is of a matter-of-fact kind, the seers of visions keep quiet; they do not like to be thought fanciful or mad, and they hide their experiences, which only come to light through inquiries such as these that I have been making. But let the tide of opinion change and grow favourable to supernaturalism, then the seers of visions come to the front. The faintly-perceived fantasies of ordinary persons become invested by the authority of reverend men with a claim to serious regard; they are consequently attended to and encouraged, and they increase in definition through being habitually dwelt upon. We need not suppose that a faculty previously non-existent has been suddenly evoked but that a faculty long smothered by many in secret has been suddenly allowed freedom to express itself, and to run into extravagance owing to the removal of reasonable safeguards.[77]

---

[74] On this subject see Georges Canguilhem, *The Normal and the Pathological* (New York, 1989).

[75] Galton, *Inquiries into the Human Faculty*, p.166. Galton cites Herschel's recurring visions of phantom faces. See John F.W. Herschel, *Familiar Lectures on Scientific Subjects* (New York and London, 1866), pp.403–4.

[76] Galton, *Inquiries into the Human Faculty*, p.173. See George du Maurier's *Peter Ibbetson* (1891) in which the protagonist is locked in an asylum for the criminally insane and yet can 'dream true' in a kind of 'fourth dimension'. On the role of subjectivity in this novel see Nicholas Daly, *Modernism, Romance, and the 'Fin de Siècle': Popular Fiction and British Culture, 1880–1914* (Cambridge, 1999), pp.158–61.

[77] Galton, *Inquiries into the Human Faculty*, p.177. On the neglect of visualisation and the faculty of the imagination in the Western philosophical tradition see Edward S. Casey, *Imagining: A Phenomenological Study*, 2nd edn (Bloomington 2000), pp.xix–xx.

The views expressed by Galton were about as far away as was possible from those of the mental physiologists of the mid-Victorian period, deeply concerned as they were with the maintenance of common sense and will-power in the mind if it was to have any chance of defeating the encroachments of just such abnormal phenomena as were being canvassed for by Galton. Yet Galton was supported in his methods and findings by the advanced research by the American psychologist Carl E. Seashore. In his landmark paper of 1895, 'Measurements of Illusions and Hallucinations in Normal Life', Seashore demonstrated the sheer scale of perceptual errors which could be detected in the normal, sane individual: experiments which induced hallucinations of warmth, of shapes, and of objects and illusions of weight and touch seemed to radically undermine the medical model of hallucinations. Seashore concluded:

Experiences in all forms of illusion may be realistic. People really see ghosts. If a scientific observer in the bead experiment sees the bead as real although there is no bead, I do not think we can set any limit to what an excited, imaginative person may really see under circumstances favourable for illusion.[78]

The fact is that laboratory-based studies of ghost-seeing in experimental psychology did nothing to contradict the growing consensus that the human mind was an entity with a particular aptitude for 'auto-haunting' and the self-elicitation of visions. The groundbreaking studies of Galton and Seashore, which showed the extent to which the sane could hallucinate, resonated into the early twentieth century in the interviews and tests arranged by Lillien J. Martin which examined in detail the causative factors behind cases of ghost-seeing.[79] One trial was performed with 'Miss T.', a student at Stanford University, who reported biannual visions of a male ghost in her bedroom that had been experienced since childhood. Martin's interview with her subject is of interest to us here:

'Were you afraid of him?' 'No. He fascinates me. I never want him to leave'.
'Why not?' 'I have always felt he would bring me good luck'.
'Why did he come at this time?' 'I do not know. But about five days before, our housemother had remarked that it was about time for my ghost to appear'.
'Did he speak?' 'No'.

[78] Carl E. Seashore, 'Measurements of Illusions and Hallucinations in Normal Life', in *Studies from the Yale Psychological Laboratory*, vol. III, ed. Edward W. Scripture (1895), p.65. For a comprehensive survey of the hallucinations of the sane see Robert Hunter Steen, 'Hallucinations in the Sane', *Journal of Mental Science* 63 (1917), 328–46.
[79] For another example of experimental research into visualisation and imagery see Cheves West Perky, 'An Experimental Study of Imagination', *American Journal of Psychology* 21:3 (1910), 422–52.

'How do you explain this ghost?' 'I have always explained this as an hallucination, yet I have a feeling that it is a spirit and have always felt this. I feel that it comes from another world, of which we know nothing'.

'What do you mean by an hallucination?' 'It is a visual image so firmly fixed in one's mind, that it appears without any conscious effort on the part of the person'.

'Did the ghost bring any message?' 'No'.

'Has it ever brought a message?' 'No'.

Room was darkened. 'Can you see the ghost now?' 'No. But I saw a large rectangle of white'.[80]

On the basis of cases like this, Martin concurred with Galton that the ability to project mental imagery was a major factor in the production of ghosts. Yet, from interviews such as that with Miss T., Martin discovered significant biographical and socio-cultural factors which pointed towards 'a favouring and inhibiting emotional complex' intimately linked to the projection of imagery.[81] This would allow the ghost to be hallucinated in specific circumstances, and repressed or inhibited in other circumstances, depending on the level of psychological or intellectual comfort required. Coming almost a century after Nicolai's narrative, Martin's report advanced the theory that the ghost-seer and his/her socio-cultural construction harboured the true causative factors of the ghost-seeing experience.

This normalisation of the idea of hallucinations in the sane in experimental psychology soon found expression in literary criticism, with George Henry Lewes describing Dickens, shortly after his death, as

a seer of visions; and his visions were of objects at once familiar and potent. Psychologists will understand both the extent and the limitation of the remark, when I say that in no other perfectly sane mind (Blake, I believe, was not perfectly sane) have I observed vividness of imagination approaching so closely to imagination.[82]

A few years later Richard Wagner similarly wrote of Shakespeare as 'one who sees and banns apparitions, one who knows how to take the shapes of men of all times from his own and our eyes so that they shall seem actually alive'.[83] This interest in the hallucinatory abilities of celebrated writers also fed into a new genre of medical history that sought to

---

[80] Lillien J. Martin, 'Ghosts and the Projection of Visual Images', *American Journal of Psychology* 26:3 (1915), 255.

[81] *Ibid.*, 257.

[82] George Henry Lewes, 'Dickens in Relation to Criticism', *Fortnightly Review* 11 (1872), 144. See also Carpenter, *Principles of Mental Physiology*, p.455.

[83] Richard Wagner, *Beethoven*, trans. Edward Dannreuther (London, 1880), pp.84–5.

retrospectively diagnose historical figures judged to have suffered from hallucinatory psychiatric disorders.[84] Pioneering works in this area included L.F. Lélut's studies of Socrates and Pascal, and Maudsley's pathography of Swedenborg.[85] Yet the field was soon dominated by the writings of William W. Ireland – *The Blot upon the Brain* (1885) and its sequel, *Through the Ivory Gate* (1889). Ireland focused on an analysis of controversial figures in religious history such as Muhammad, Joan of Arc, Martin Luther and Swedenborg, all of whom left evidence of extreme psychiatric abnormalities. But, despite his positivistic leanings, Ireland was acutely aware of the damaging secularist implications inherent in a psycho-historical enterprise that threatened to diagnose Martin Luther, for instance, as a lunatic. Instead, following Brierre de Boismont, Ireland approached his subjects with a degree of sympathy and awareness of the historical context where, for instance, Joan of Arc's hallucinations of hearing and sight were deeply connected with the political situation in fifteenth-century France.[86] Through this reluctance to diagnose religious ecstatics as either sane or insane, and use 'hallucination' in a pejorative

---

[84] On the use of the retrospective diagnosis of hysteria in the Salpêtrière school, and its anticlericalist implications, see Jan Goldstein, 'The Hysteria Diagnosis and the Politics of Anticlericalism in Late Nineteenth-century France', *Journal of Modern History* 54:2 (1982), 235–6. The term 'retrospective medicine' was first coined by Émile Littré. See Émile Littré, 'Un fragment de médecine rétrospective', *Philosophie positive* 5 (1869), 103–20. See also Ivan Leudar and Wes Sharrock, 'The Cases of John Bunyan, Part 1. Taine and Royce', *History of Psychiatry* 13:51 (2002), 247–65; Ivan Leudar and Wes Sharrock, 'The Cases of John Bunyan, Part 2. James and Janet', *History of Psychiatry* 13:52 (2002), 401–17.

[85] Louis Francisque Lélut, *Du Démon de Socrate, spécimen d'une application de la science psychologique à celle de l'histoire* (Paris, 1836); Louis Francisque Lélut, *L'Amulette de Pascal, pour servir à l'histoire des hallucinations* (Paris, 1846); Henry Maudsley, 'Emanuel Swedenborg', *Journal of Mental Science* 15 (1869), 169–96. Maudsley's article, which attributed psychotic and epileptic origins to Swedenborg's visions, predictably proved controversial among Swedenborgians, and John Johnson claims that this pressure resulted in its removal from the 1895 edition of Maudsley's *Pathology of Mind*. John Johnson, 'Henry Maudsley on Swedenborg's Messianic Psychosis', *British Journal of Psychiatry* 165:5 (1994), 690–1.

[86] William W. Ireland, *Through the Ivory Gate: Studies in Psychology and History* (Edinburgh, 1890), p.78. Brierre de Boismont held a similar point of view, writing of Ignatius of Loyola: 'These hallucinations, admitting them scientifically to be such, were only the highest expression of his meditations, the result of profound convictions which formed the distinctive trait of the period. The thought which entirely occupied him, took a material and living form, and as Shakespeare beautifully says, he saw it "in his mind's eye", but there was no touch of madness. In this case, the leading idea, instead of being intercerebral, became external; it placed itself before him palpably, and preceded him in all his enterprises. But with him, as with many celebrated personages, hallucination was but the auxiliary of a primary conception.' Brierre de Boismont, *On Hallucinations*, p.380. Eliza Lynn Linton also put forward a contrasting view on the psychological state of religious hallucinators. Linton, 'Our Illusions', 595–6.

sense, Ireland soundly represented the findings of experimental psychology in his chosen sphere of psycho-history:

There is no dividing line between sanity and insanity. As the eye is not perfectly achromatic, the mind is probably never perfectly sane. Some brains work well, at least, on most occasions; many work tolerably; some work ill; a few scarcely work at all. The differences are endless; no two beings are exactly alike.[87]

Following this atomisation of the field of diagnosis, Ireland further complicated the notion of diagnostic categories by outlining a neuropsychology in which the brain featured as the battleground between a healthy and morbid side of the mind which threatened to end in insanity: 'There is a wrestle between reason and unreason; then a rhythmic strophe, and antistrophe, between the sane and the insane hemispheres, as there is an alternation of colours when two hues are presented to each eye.'[88]

The clothes of ghosts

For a philosophy dedicated to propounding all-encompassing doctrines and a single essential metaphysical belief-system concerning this life and the next, it may come as a surprise to learn that spiritualism was a mode of thought very much haunted by the details of its revelation. Issues such as whether a spirit could 'see' in any human understanding of the word, whether spirits could 'see' each other while visiting the terrene world, and whether animals had souls, were just a few of the knotty and sometimes obscurantist debating points that exercised the minds of both spiritualists and anti-spiritualists throughout the nineteenth century.[89] Alongside such 'spiritual' issues as these the spiritualist discourse articulated important concerns with the minutiae and the base *materiality* of its beliefs. One of the most recurring riddles in writings on ghosts and hallucinations within spiritualism and beyond during this period concerned the question of the material apparel of the apparition.

In 1863 the celebrated English illustrator George Cruikshank excitedly announced his 'discovery' concerning ghosts. It does not appear, he wrote,

[87] Ireland, *Through the Ivory Gate*, pp.82–3.
[88] William W. Ireland, *The Blot upon the Brain: Studies in History and Psychology*, 2nd edn (Edinburgh, 1893), p.351.
[89] See, for instance, A. Hulisch, 'Can a Spirit, of Its Own Self, See Another Spirit?', *Light* 8 (17 November 1888), 569–70; Lilian Whiting, 'Do Spirits See Material Objects?', *Light* 17 (31 July 1897), 368–9; Henry Sidgwick, Alice Johnson, Frederic W.H. Myers, Frank Podmore and Eleanor M. Sidgwick, 'Report on the Census of Hallucinations', *PSPR* 10 (1894), 192–3.

THAT ANY ONE HAS EVER THOUGHT OF THE GROSS ABSURDITY,
AND IMPOSSIBILITY, OF THERE BEING SUCH THINGS AS GHOSTS
OF WEARING APPAREL, IRON ARMOUR, WALKING STICKS, AND
SHOVELS! NO, NOT ONE, except myself, and this I claim as my
DISCOVERY CONCERNING GHOSTS, and that therefore it follows, as a
matter of course, that as ghosts *cannot, must not, dare not*, for decency's sake,
appear WITHOUT CLOTHES; and as there can be no such thing AS
GHOSTS OR SPIRITS OF CLOTHES, why, then, it appears that GHOSTS
NEVER DID APPEAR, AND NEVER CAN APPEAR, at any rate not in the
way in which they have hitherto been supposed to *appear*.[90]

If the ghost was an objective reality, why should it be wearing clothes,
and why should it be wearing the very specific clothes that were associated with a deceased person? If the spiritualistic hypothesis was true,
should the soul which has returned to visit the earth not be perfectly
nude, ethereal, or at least clothes-less?[91] This question of spectral
clothing would prove a central point of contention within the popular
literature on ghosts and hallucinations after the spread of spiritualism,
and indeed, in the spiritualist press itself.[92] The contention that 'ghosts
are never without drapery'[93] and the argument that apparitions invariably appeared in dress according to the fashion of the period during
which they lived fed into the general debate as to the reality of the ghostly
world, and went some way to back up the concept that ghost-seeing was
categorically a form of dreaming while awake.

While ghosts had been associated in the popular mind with the
apparel of white linen or deathly shrouds along with accessories such
as clanking chains and preternatural lighting, with the advent of detailed
investigations into the personal testimony of ghost-seers from the
Enlightenment onwards, it soon became clear that the descriptions of
the clothing and appearance of apparitions did not differ from contemporary fashion or seem to surprise the percipient at all. For many
commentators in the nineteenth century this factor was the one
insuperable obstacle to any rational or scientific belief in ghosts.
Ambrose Bierce wrote that to believe in a clothed ghost left one in the

---

[90] George Cruikshank, *Discovery Concerning Ghosts; With a Rap at the 'Spirit Rappers'*
(London, 1863), p.25.
[91] Lang could only account for three or four cases in which a ghost had been reported as
naked. Andrew Lang, *The Book of Dreams and Ghosts* (Hollywood, 1972), p.69.
[92] Crowe, *The Night Side of Nature*, pp.197–8; Swedenborg, *Heaven and Hell*, pp.137–9;
'Leo', 'How Spirits Are Clothed', *Light* 9 (1 June 1889), 268–9; 'M.W.G.', 'Clothes
Spooks', *Light* 10 (29 November 1890), 572. See also Davies, *The Haunted*, pp.33–4.
For a twentieth-century theosophical view on the issue see Robert Crookall, *The Next
World – And the Next: Ghostly Garments* (London, 1966).
[93] John Addington Symonds, *Sleep and Dreams; Two Lectures Delivered at the Bristol Literary
and Philosophical Institution* (London, 1851), p.11.

absurd position of believing that the vital power that made the dead visible also extended to their fabrics:

Supposing the products of the loom to have this ability, what object would they have in exercising it? And why does not the apparition of a suit of clothes walk abroad without a ghost in it? These are riddles of significance. They reach away down and get a convulsive grasp on the very tap-root of this flourishing faith.[94]

The question of the clothes of ghosts left all justifications of ghost-belief open to public ridicule: surely these materialistic facts argued against, or at least drastically complicated, any simple spiritualist belief in ghosts?[95] From this starting point sceptics began to draw attention to all the incongruous accessories of the ghost experience such as spectral stockings, carriages, animals and items such as paper and pens.[96]

One response to this issue was to adopt an idealist position in which the clothes and apparel of the mortal life were somehow connected to the soul of the person on a metaphysical plane of existence. From the argument that clothes were metaphysical ideas, or inextricably linked with the immortal identity of the wearer, it was but a small step to the notion that all ideas, or emblems, may themselves be considered clothes – a position notably discussed at length by Professor Teufelsdröckh in Thomas Carlyle's *Sartor Resartus* (1833–1834).[97] Within Schopenhauer's idealist philosophical system, the clothing of ghosts was proof of his concept that ghost-seers 'dream the real', for the ghost-seer is merely seeing the eidolon (εἴδωλον), Schopenhauer argues, a mental picture of

---

[94] Ambrose Bierce, *The Devil's Dictionary* (London, 2003), pp.103–4.

[95] Herbert Mayo, *On the Truths Contained in Popular Superstitions with an Account of Mesmerism* (Edinburgh and London, 1851), p.61; Camille Flammarion, *Death and Its Mystery: At the Moment of Death*, trans. Latrobe Carroll (London, 1922), p.80; Lionel A. Weatherly and J.N. Maskelyne, *The Supernatural? With Chapter on Oriental Magic, Spiritualism, and Theosophy* (London, 2000), p.103.

[96] Lang, *Dreams and Ghosts*, p.70; G.N.M. Tyrrell, *Apparitions*, rev. edn (London, 1953), p.67. Cruikshank declared that, following the logic of the spiritualist position on the matter, they must be the 'ghosts of stockings'. Cruikshank, *Discovery Concerning Ghosts*, p.26. For a comic take on the clothes-of-ghosts issue see Grant Allen, 'Our Scientific Observations on a Ghost', in *Strange Stories* (London, 1884), pp.321–40.

[97] 'All visible things are Emblems; what thou seest is not there on its own account; strictly taken, is not there at all: Matter exists only spiritually, and to represent some Idea, and *body* it forth. Hence, Clothes, as despicable as we think them, are so unspeakably significant. Clothes, from the King's-mantle downwards, are Emblematic, not of want only, but of a manifold cunning Victory over Want. On the other hand, all Emblematic things are properly Clothes, thought-woven or hand-woven: must not the Imagination weave Garments, visible Bodies, wherein the else invisible creations and inspirations of our Reason are, like Spirits, revealed, and first become all-powerful; – the rather if, as we often see, the Hand too aid her, and (by wool Clothes or otherwise) reveal such even to the outward eye?' Thomas Carlyle, *Sartor Resartus*, ed. Kerry McSweeney and Peter Sabor (Oxford, 1987), p.56.

the deceased person that originated in the dream-organ and was initiated by the trace or relic. Thus the figure of the ghost appears in the clothes that they wore when they alive and known by the percipient.[98] The particular clothing of the ghost was to be explained through the mental associations by which the percipient remembered the agent. It is now a cultural commonplace that clothes and garments represent the living memory of absent people – they function as 'material mnemonics' and prove enormously significant in the process of dealing with the death and absence of a loved one.[99] In the ghost-seeing experiences of percipients in the nineteenth century there exists a tension between the recognition and nomination of the ghost through the materiality of clothes and related accessories, and the doctrinal need to announce the spirituality and immaterial nature of the ghost that was perceived. The French spiritualist Allan Kardec attempted to square this circle by opining that, although spirits are perfect beings, they must present themselves in the gross and earthly manner by which they would be recognised and identified by persons still alive: 'Thus, although as a spirit, he has no corporeal infirmity, he will show himself disabled, lame, humpbacked, wounded, with scars if that is necessary to establish his identity.'[100]

This debate about the clothing of ghosts was extended to examinations of the role of the ghost's armour in *Hamlet* – a prop which encouraged sceptical readers to doubt the reality of the apparition and ascribe a very definite materiality to those who wore it (see Figure 4).[101] In an essay on the ghost-beliefs of Shakespeare, Alfred Roffe responded to such developments by noting that clothes were not merely worn for reasons of warmth or decency, but for aesthetic significance and concern for appearing in noble guise:

Again, no piece of Clothing can be made by hands without being first contrived *in* and *by the Soul*, according to some end. If the Internal World and its inhabitants be *Realities*, the marvel would be the want of Clothing for the latter, and if they had it not, the Skeptics would be the first to see, and justly to ridicule, the incongruity. The question which should be asked, is not, 'where does the Armour, &., come from?' but, 'is there an *Internal Causal World*, in which, as such, there must be all that there is in the *External, Effect World*'.[102]

[98] Schopenhauer, *Parerga and Paralipomena*, p.286.
[99] Ann Rosalind Jones and Peter Stallybrass, *Renaissance Clothing and the Materials of Memory* (Cambridge, 2000), p.32. See also Joan Didion, *The Year of Magical Thinking* (London, 2006), p.37. For a ghost story in which the clothes of the deceased play a major role see James's 'The Romance of Certain Old Clothes', in *Ghost Stories of Henry James*, pp.21–37.
[100] Kardec, *Experimental Spiritism*, pp.137–8.
[101] See Jones and Stallybrass, *Renaissance Clothing*, pp.245–68.
[102] Alfred Roffe, *An Essay upon the Ghost-Belief of Shakespeare* (London, 1851), pp.21–2.

"Alas, poor Ghost!"

Figure 4 George Cruikshank, *Alas, Poor Ghost!* Source: George Raymond, *The Life and Enterprises of Robert William Elliston, Comedian* (London, 1857). In author's collection.

In this scenario clothing assumed a metaphysical origin in which the soul was actively engaged in 'dressing' the personality in a noble fashion. This fashion was designed to be timeless and acted as a sign which could be perceived by the ghost-seer. For Roffe, the presence of the armour of Hamlet's ghost was a logical extension of the fact that it was the ghost of Hamlet's father that was appearing: the idea of the ghost comes with its personal ideas attached.[103] This debate thus raised issues of identity and questions about how the soul was to be accurately discerned by loved ones left behind. The riddle for spiritualists was that if the apparition was in fact an objective reality – a vitally real and supernatural being – then the clothes and accessories of the apparition must also be spiritualised in the same sense as the body of the figure, or the soul of the deceased must be somehow permanently linked to a set of material items. One spiritualist argued that the phenomenon of the dressed ghost was another reason to believe in its reality for it 'would naturally desire to appear in decent attire and also in such a way as to be recognized, and as all spirits are amateur chemists, it could readily improvise a wardrobe from the surrounding elements'.[104] The positivist and spiritualist Adolphe d'Assier admitted to being perturbed by the issue which was 'as inexplicable as the apparition itself'.[105] However, it was symbolic of the uneasiness with which spiritualists faced the question of the materiality of ghosts that Assier rather desperately resorted to citing the philosophy of the ethereal double outlined in *The Seeress of Prevorst*, and then swiftly avoided the issue.[106]

Another way to explain (away) the materiality of ghosts was to use the metaphor of photography. The spiritualist Newton Crosland proposed a 'Spiritual-photographic theory' in which every significant action of life – in the garments people wear, and in the attitudes and gestures of humanity – is vitally photographed or depicted in the spirit-world; and that the angels, under God's direction, have the power of exhibiting, as a living picture, any specific circumstance or features to those who have the gift of spiritual sight, and who are intended to be influenced by the manifestations.[107] Continuing the analogy between the human mind

---

[103] Some spiritualists supported this type of idealist argument. See A.J. Penny, 'Ready-made Clothes', *Light* 7 (3 September 1887), 411–12.

[104] G.G. Hubbell, *Fact and Fancy in Spiritualism, Theosophy and Psychical Research* (Cincinnati, 1901), p.91.

[105] Adolphe d'Assier, *Posthumous Humanity: A Study of Phantoms*, trans. Henry S. Olcott (London, 1887), p.92.

[106] *Ibid.*, p.93.

[107] Newton Crosland, *Apparitions: A New Theory* (London, 1856), p.29.

and the photographic memory, a certain 'Philosophius' in *Ghosts and Their Modern Worshippers* (1892), wrote that:

it would appear that our brain is a kind of photographic plate, which receives the picture of everything we see in miniature, with power to reproduce it both *internally* and *externally*, the external reproduction forming the hallucination. Hence the circumstance, which is a *most important one*, that these hallucinations are the *exact* representations of the originals and that our so-called 'ghosts' appear in those dresses or clothes in which we beheld them during their life-time, even though at the time of their appearance these should no longer be in existence or actually worn by other people.[108]

The issue at stake here was the persistence of memory: were the clothes and the accessories of the ghost-world maintained in some sort of permanent database (under God's direction, or within the unconscious mind), or did the material items themselves contain spiritual matter capable of being perceived under special circumstances?

This latter notion formed the thought behind the pseudo-science of 'psychometry', established when William Denton, an English geologist, published *The Soul of Things: Psychometric Experiments for Re-living History* in 1863 with the aid of some 'sensitive' women, including his wife. In the 1850s, Denton began experimenting with mineral, fossil and archaeological remains and was delighted to find that his sensitive seers could reconstruct the 'history' of each object through the rapid inference of all the light, motion, sound and impressions that have affected the object throughout its presence on earth. In this dizzying situation

the meanest boulder by the roadside would fill more volumes than all our libraries contain. The nail retains the impression made upon it by hammering, the clay by grinding, the brick by burning, the wool of the cloth, every step of the torturing process by which it was transferred from the back of the sheep to the back of the man.[109]

Denton postulated that all humans possess an innate psychometric power, that is, that a percipient can 'time-travel' using the emanations

---

[108] 'Philosophius', *Ghosts and Their Modern Worshippers* (London, 1892), p.12. Kardec wrote: 'Thus the soul really sees but sees only an image daguerreotyped in the brain. In the normal state, these images are fugitive and ephemeral, because all the cerebral parts act freely; but in a state of disease the brain is always more or less enfeebled, the equilibrium no longer exists between all the organs; some alone preserve their activity, while others are in some sort paralyzed; from thence the permanence of certain images, which are not, as in the normal state, effaced by the preoccupations of the exterior life. That is the real hallucination, and the primary cause of fixed ideas.' Kardec, *Experimental Spiritism*, p.149.

[109] William Denton, *The Soul of Things: Psychometric Experiments for Re-living History* (Wellingborough, 1988), p.50.

of an object, and thus 're-live' its history. This interior visuality was held by Denton to radically transform the nature of external knowledge. For if every object, vital or dead, contained all its memories within it, could certain individuals actively hallucinate these impressions via the retina? Denton also used the metaphor of the photographic apparatus to illustrate his belief in the aura, or emanation exuded by bodies onto the external world. He believed that in the world around us radiant forces pass from object to object and

are daguerreotyping the appearances of each upon the other; the images thus made, not merely resting upon the surface, but sinking into the interior of them; there held with astonishing tenacity, and only waiting for a suitable application to reveal themselves to the inquiring gaze.[110]

In this pantheistical belief-system, nature was like a gallery which photographed the passage of time with the foreknowledge that seers would some day 'behold her instructive pictures'.[111] Furthermore, in Denton's opinion, psychometry explained the phenomena of spectral illusions, and answered the problem of the ghost of clothes. Denton believed that in the case of Nicolai, his clothing or the articles on his person contributed to his ghost-seeing. Indeed he hypothesised that Nicolai himself possessed strong psychometric powers:

Nicolai was at this time sensitive enough to see the great picture gallery, or a portion of it at least, where hangs the likeness of all that light ever beheld; and he at length becomes sufficiently sensitive to hear, issuing from the great storehouse of sounds, the condoling words which his friends had uttered, as faithfully registered and repeated to his interior ear.[112]

Denton stressed the practical use that this psychometric faculty would have in disciplines such as history, geology and archaeology, yet he linked this with a forceful argument in favour of the ghost-seeing power of women and believed that by psychometry 'a woman may have in one year a more correct idea of the condition of the earth and its occupants during the geologic periods that any man without it could be in a lifetime'.[113] Thus elective hallucinations were seen as utilitarian and almost messianic in their abilities to transform the state of knowledge, quite literally from the ground up. Denton extended its relevance to solving crimes, fortune-telling and the autoscopic diagnosis of disease.[114]

Despite such spiritualist and pseudo-scientific attempts to explain the clothes of ghosts by analogy with photography and thought-projection, it was the concept of automatic and internal hallucinations that gained the

[110] *Ibid.*, p.31.   [111] *Ibid.*, p.32.   [112] *Ibid.*, p.262.   [113] *Ibid.*, p.287.
[114] *Ibid.*, pp.288, 299, 301.

most credence and support among the scientific community.[115] By proposing that apparitions were in fact hallucinations, the ghost-seeing experience could be deconstructed as a mental creation in which the figures perceived were dressed according to the percipient's memory of that person. Thus the riddle of ghostly accessories was held up as a standard problem in the literature on ghosts which only the concept of hallucination could solve most fully.

The notion that when the percipient was hallucinating she was in fact dreaming while awake was steadily applied to the problem of the clothes of ghosts throughout the nineteenth century. The folklorist and psychical researcher Andrew Lang believed that, with ghosts being hallucinations, and hallucinations being waking dreams, the clothes of the ghost were produced by the percipient in much the same manner as suggestions given under hypnotic trance result in specific details being *seen* by the perceiving mind.[116] The clothes of ghosts were thus the 'stuff that dreams are made of', namely, the mechanisms and constructions of the mind: 'We do not see people naked, as a rule, in our dreams; and hallucinations, being waking dreams, conform to the same rule. If a ghost opens a door or lifts a curtain in our sight, that, too, is only part of the illusion.'[117]

For the SPR, the clothes of ghosts problem became a central reference point in their promotion of a new theory of apparitions based upon the hypothetical veridicality of the hallucinatory experience (not its morbidity, as had been stressed by the medical model). The SPR psychologists Gurney and Myers, with Podmore, used the concept of hallucination as a psychological fact which could be the basis for a utilitarian survey on the incidence of ghost-seeing in the British population, as shall be seen in a later chapter. In this discourse the issue of ghostly garments was raised

---

[115] However, Charles Richet's 'metapsychics' adopted an agnostic attitude to baffling phenomena such as the materialisation of clothes: 'It seems to me much wiser to verify without pretending to understand, and to admit that any explanation we can give can hardly escape being ridiculous. Instead of claiming that unknown powers pertaining to deceased humanity are capable of producing these phenomena, it is better to admit that we are dealing with facts as yet inexplicable, and await further elucidation.' Charles Richet, *Thirty Years of Psychical Research: Being a Treatise in Metapsychics*, trans. Stanley de Brath (London, 1923), p.476.

[116] Lang, *Dreams and Ghosts*, p.70.

[117] *Ibid.*, pp.69–70. Tylor wrote: 'That the apparitional human soul bears the likeness of its fleshy body, is the principle implicitly accepted by all who believe it really and objectively present in dreams and visions. My own view is that nothing but dreams and visions could have ever put into men's minds such an idea as that of souls being ethereal images of bodies. It is thus habitually taken for granted in animistic philosophy, savage or civilized, that souls set free from the earthly body are recognized by a likeness to it which they still retain, whether as ghostly wanderers on earth or inhabitants of the world beyond the grave.' Tylor, *Primitive Culture*, p.450.

as strong evidence for the subjective production of phantasms and not as a representation of the idealist existence of souls with their clothing, as the spiritualists maintained: problematising such beliefs Myers put forward the tricky question, 'how has the meta-organism accreted to itself a meta-coat and meta-trousers?'[118] For Myers, the theory that the percipient was in the position of the clairvoyant when hallucinating a telepathic impression explained the fact that there were no cases of naked ghosts: 'it therefore would be strange if I phantasmally saw the dying man unclothed, – as I have never seen him in life; if he, in his last moments, pictured himself as he has never hitherto pictured himself in colloquy with his friends'.[119] In this sense, the clothing of ghosts, along with their other material accruements, were to be understood as symbolic representations indicative of an effort at recognition or, as Gurney put it, the 'ghosts of *old* clothes'.[120] Yet, for Myers, this situation raised even more questions:

Thus – to come at once to my present purpose – it is usual for a witness to say 'he appeared to me in the dress he habitually wore, and in which I knew him'. In one sense these two clauses mean the same thing. But which of them is the really effective one? If A's phantom wears a black coat, is that because A wore a black coat, or because B was accustomed to see him in one? If A had taken to wearing a brown coat since B saw him in the flesh, would A's phantom wear to B's eyes a black coat or a brown? Or would the dress which A actually wore at the moment of death dominate, as it were, and supplant phantasmally the costumes of his ordinary days?[121]

In her analysis of phantasms of the dead, Eleanor M. Sidgwick made two findings about the clothes of ghosts: in some cases the dress was considered normal daytime wear for the figure by the percipient, yet most narratives mentioned vague costumes 'not specially appropriate to any particular period'. Furthermore she found it remarkable that among cases of 'fixed local ghosts', or haunting ghosts, which could connect a specific costume to the recent dead, there was not a single account worthy of publication.[122] This sceptical attitude was carried on by Podmore who noted that most apparitions were clothed as the percipient was accustomed to see the agent clothed, and not, as we should imagine given the sheer number of crisis-apparitions reported, dressed in bed clothes or night-wear. He therefore believed that the agent did not

---

[118] Edmund Gurney, Frederic W.H. Myers and Frank Podmore, *Phantasms of the Living*: vol. II, p.279.
[119] *Ibid.*, p.294.
[120] Gurney, Myers and Podmore, *Phantasms*, vol. I, p.540.
[121] Gurney, Myers and Podmore, *Phantasms*, vol. II, p.295.
[122] Eleanor M. Sidgwick, 'Notes on the Evidence, Collected by the Society, for Phantasms of the Dead', *PSPR* 3 (1885), 143.

transmit to the percipient any 'superficial content' of his consciousness, but rather 'the underlying massive and permanent elements which represent his personal identity', thus allowing the percipient's imagination to conceive of such an impression through the signifiers of identity, namely clothing and other relics of selfhood. The important point was that it was the percipient that dressed the apparition in its clothes, and not the apparition who 'arrived' already clothed. Indeed, Podmore speculated that for the apparition to rise into the consciousness of the percipient at all, it must be clothed in such a 'remembered' manner.[123] This concept implied that apparitions were made in the mind on the back of an impulse, and did not in fact exist as representations until imagined by the percipient.

This short survey of the problem of the clothes of ghosts in the nineteenth century demonstrates the multifaceted and multi-discursive scope of what, at first glance, seems an obscure and largely irrelevant debating point. On the contrary, throughout the writings of idealists, spiritualists, and psychical researchers the issue of the materiality of the immaterial constantly shadowed attempts to establish a secure epistemology of the ghost-seeing experience and elicited theoretical responses that ranged from the comic to the prescient. That the concept of hallucination gradually became the most legitimate and scientific response to the problem of the clothes of ghosts reinforces the centrality of the concept in framing sceptical arguments in opposition to theories of ghost-seeing that were becoming less believable as the progress of human psychology demonstrated the imaginative mechanisms of the mind. It is a testament to the SPR's dedication to the narrative of scientific naturalism that it took hold of the concept of hallucination and redirected its intellectual outcome away from a scoffing scepticism towards a more nuanced understanding of the psychology of the ghost-seer, a reorientation which reiterated the fact that ideas of a spectral self were becoming more solid and tangible as the nineteenth century developed.

---

[123] Frank Podmore, *The Naturalisation of the Supernatural* (New York and London, 1908), pp.111–12. On this issue Frances Power Cobbe wrote: 'The intersection of the states wherein consciousness yields to unconsciousness, and *vice versa*, is obviously always difficult of sharp appreciation, and leaves wide margin for self-deception; and a ghost is of all creations of fancy the one which bears most unmistakable internal evidence of being *home-made*. The poor unconscious brain goes on upon the track of the lost friend, on which the conscious soul, ere it fell asleep, had started it. But with all its wealth of fancy it never succeeds in picturing a *new* ghost, a fresh idea of the departed, whom yet by every principle of reason we know is *not* (whatever else he or she may have become), a white-faced figure in a coat and trowsers [sic], or in a silk dress and gold ornaments.' Frances Power Cobbe, 'Unconscious Cerebration: A Psychological Study', *Macmillan's Magazine* 133 (1870), 30.

Part II

A science of the soul

Ghost-hunting in the Society for Psychical Research

The Society for Psychical Research

Following the rapid spread of modern spiritualism in Britain in the 1850s and 1860s, rationalist groups and circles of friends with an investigative bent and ambitions to the 'scientific method' had sprung up, chiefly interested in investigating the veracity of the marvellous phenomena emanating from the spiritualist séances. In Britain social clubs and learned groups such as the Ghost Society (founded in Cambridge, 1851–c.1860s), the Phasmatological Society (founded in Oxford, 1879–1885), and the Ghost Club (founded in London, 1882–1936) examined – in varying degrees of formality and application – accounts of ghost-seeing, haunting and spiritualistic phenomena: yet these private groups were strongly elitist and conversational in character, did not operate on a dedicated or widespread basis, and lacked the organisational will to approach the whole area of the supernatural and the 'occult' with an open mind in partnership with the spiritualists, the scientific community, and the wider public.[1] The activities of the Psychological Society of Great Britain (PSGB), which was established by Edward William 'Serjeant' Cox in 1875, represented a major shift in this situation.[2] The PSGB met about twice a month to discuss the scientific investigation of psychology (by which was meant abnormal

---

[1] On the Cambridge Ghost Society see William F. Barrett, 'An Early Psychical Research Society', *JSPR* 21 (1923–1924), 67–71; Oppenheim, *The Other World*, p.123. On the Phasmatological Society see Charles Oman, 'The Old Oxford Phasmatological Society', *JSPR* 33 (1946), 208–17. The Ghost Club only ever had around two dozen active members. Stainton Moses, the Ghost Club's chief personality in its early years, wished it to have a confidential and Masonic atmosphere. See Ghost Club Minutes, vol. VIII, (1918–1925), p.179.

[2] See *Proceedings of the Psychological Society of Great Britain* (1875–1879). On a reappreciation of the PSGB see Graham Richards, 'Edward Cox, the Psychological Society of Great Britain (1875–1879) and the Meanings of an Institutional Failure', in *Psychology in Britain: Historical Essays and Personal Reflections*, ed. G.C. Bunn, A.D. Lovie and G.D. Richards (Leicester, 2001), pp.35–53. See also Luckhurst, *The Invention of Telepathy*, pp.47–51.

psychology and what would be called 'psychical research'), and its
founding membership included important and respectable figures such
as Richard Francis Burton, William Crookes, W. Stainton Moses and
Frederic W.H. Myers. Despite its premature dissolution following
the death of Cox in November 1879, the PSGB represented a new
ghost-seeing-investigative model in late Victorian culture through its
grounding in psychology, its formation of special investigative committees and, perhaps more importantly, its public orientation.[3]

With the establishment of the SPR in London in 1882, investigation
into manifestations of the supernatural entered a new intellectual phase
that was deeply concerned with the psychological and psychical origins
of ghost-seeing. While the original foundation of the SPR was the
consequence of the efforts of a number of spiritualists to place their
beliefs on a sound, unprejudiced and, as befitted the age, scientific footing,
it was a close-knit group of young Cambridge scholars who had
collected ghost stories and investigated spiritualism in the 1870s that
would form the working nucleus of the SPR. It is notable that many of
the early psychical researchers were academics or fellows of the universities of Cambridge and Oxford. Indeed, Alan Gauld notes that
during the period under examination, Trinity College 'was the
undoubted centre of the parapsychological world. Contemporaries
might well have said that psychical research was a form of academic
eccentricity cultivated at Cambridge and spread abroad by persons
educated there.'[4] Through their intellectual quality, diversity and
ambition, as well as their consistent will-to-investigate, these figures
established psychical research as a profoundly influential cultural constant in late Victorian and Edwardian culture. Even a cursory glance
at the membership of the SPR assures one of the calibre and intellectual status of the people who were attracted to psychical research in its
early days as a new discipline that could formulate responses, and
perhaps answers, to the ultimate questions raised by spiritualism.
With members such as William E. Gladstone, Arthur Balfour, Lord
Tennyson, Arthur Conan Doyle, Robert Louis Stevenson, William
James, William McDougall, Henri Bergson, Charles Richet, Sigmund
Freud and Carl Gustav Jung, the SPR resembled a *Who's Who* of the
fin-de-siècle world. What could interest such major personalities from
the worlds of politics, literature and psychology in a London-based

---

[3] On the high proportion of members from the urban professional classes, especially the
legal and judicial professions see Richards, 'Edward Cox'.
[4] Alan Gauld, 'Psychical Research in Cambridge from the Seventeenth Century to the
Present', *JSPR* 49 (1978), 925.

society led by Cambridge University savants and supported by the spiritualist movement?

The will-to-investigate *possibilities* provided the impetus behind the establishment of the SPR: the possibilities of new worlds, new human capacities and new discoveries about the nature of reality and the psyche provided some sense of hope to a generation of thinkers bereft of intellectual assurances and afflicted by religious doubt.[5] It was in this context that psychical research was famously described by Gladstone as 'The most important work, which is being done in the world ... By far the most important.'[6] From the perspective of over a century later, the SPR can be interpreted as a workforce responding to cultural change through its construction of spectro-nunciative discursive fields: Roger Luckhurst has called these 'knowledge networks'.[7] As shall be shown, the SPR connected itself to pioneering trends in the human sciences: from its base in the discipline of experimental psychology the Society reached out to the Nancy school of psychotherapy, adopted a statistical scope which pre-empted that of the mass-observation era, and proposed an advanced theory of hallucination which consummated a century of medical and psychiatric debate. Yet, it is paramount to remember that these epistemic networks, as locations of exchange, were inextricably linked to the haunting spectre of agnosticism (or more accurately, the spectre of spiritual indifference) in Victorian culture, with its injunction to attain positive knowledge in place of the negative.[8] An anecdote illustrative of this meaning is found in the memoirs of Gwen Raverat. Raverat wrote of her uncle Francis ('Frank') Darwin who had participated in the early SPR investigations and subsequently became convinced that spiritualism was fraudulent:

Once Mr. Myers touched Uncle Frank and said: 'Frank, let me *feel* you: a man who really does not WANT immortality'. And Uncle Frank answered: 'Well, Myers, I don't much like myself very much as I am, and I really could not bear the thought of going on for ever'.[9]

---

[5] Edmund Gurney wrote that 'the sense of possibilities that can never be disproved is capable of exercising a pervading effect on the human mind which is absolutely irrelevant to any numerical estimate of odds'. Cited in Gauld, *The Founders*, pp.158–9.

[6] Cited in Frederic W.H. Myers, 'The Right Hon. W.E. Gladstone', *JSPR* 8 (1897–1898), 260.

[7] Luckhurst, *The Invention of Telepathy*. As Robert A. McDermott has noted: 'Psychical research is necessarily a collaborative effort, involving a network of subjects, investigators, editors, publishers, and an enormous amount of financial support.' Introduction to William James, *Essays in Psychical Research* (Cambridge, MA, and London, 1986), p.xv.

[8] See Gauld, *The Founders*, pp.32–65.

[9] Gwen Raverat, *Period Piece: A Cambridge Childhood* (London, 1960), p.189.

Here the uncomprehending Myers significantly placed the non-believer in the position of the ghosts that he sought to investigate, of some supernatural spirit that he had to physically touch, like a modern Doubting Thomas, in order to convince himself of Uncle Frank's reality. To Myers the work of the SPR was, quite literally, a labour of love to rebuild the ruins of religion anew and to confront the modern world with positive and irresistible evidence of survival and a concept of immortality beyond the range of facetious responses, such as Uncle Frank could easily make.

It was through the knowledge networks installed by Myers and the SPR that the ghost-seeing experience was able to escape the factionality trap noted in the introduction. Ghosts, phantasms and hallucinations were from the 1880s simultaneously part of popular, psychical and psychiatric discourses because all were enlisted in the SPR's quest to synthesise and re-conceptualise supernatural experience according to the contemporary grid-system of thought-transference and telepathy. The vastly accommodating mode of the ghost-as-message, or the spectro-nunciative, ultimately contributed to the varied make-up of the cast of the Society with multiple disciplines represented in each issue of its *Proceedings* and personalities outside the SPR inner circle, such as W.T. Stead and Andrew Lang, writing consistently and forcefully on issues of ghost-seeing and thought-transference in the late Victorian periodical press.

The 'Sidgwick Group', as the inner circle in the SPR came to be known, centred on the figure of Henry Sidgwick (1838–1900), a philosopher and professor at Trinity College, Cambridge, who had made his reputation with *The Methods of Ethics* (1874) but who had been engaged in what he described as 'ghostological investigations' from as early as 1858.[10] His standing as a liberal (he was a reformist when it came to women's higher education at Cambridge) and principled figure was immensely extended when he resigned his Fellowship at Trinity in 1869 on coming to the conclusion that he did not support the religious

---

[10] Bart Schultz, *Henry Sidgwick, Eye of the Universe: An Intellectual Biography* (Cambridge, 2004), p.90. One student's observations on the 'Sidgwick Group' are interesting to note: 'Henry Sidgwick was the centre, and with him his two most intimate friends, Frederick Myers and Edmund Gurney. Frederick Myers rang, perhaps, the most sonorously of all, but to me he always rang a little false. Edmund Gurney was, I think, the most loveable and beautiful human being I ever met. This was the Psychical Research circle; their quest, scientific proof of immortality.' Jane Ellen Harrison, *Reminiscences of a Student's Life* (London, 1925), p.55. Gauld estimates that of the chief SPR publications between 1882 and 1900, at least fifty per cent were contributed by the Sidgwick Group and Richard Hodgson. Gauld, *The Founders*, p.313. For Sidgwick's activities in psychical research see Schultz, *Henry Sidgwick*, pp.275–334.

provisos that this post (officially) demanded.[11] As a demonstration of the esteem in which he was held at Cambridge, Sidgwick was almost immediately offered a post as Lecturer in the Moral Sciences, a role that did not require nominal allegiance to the Church of England.[12] Sidgwick, like most of the members of the Group, was the son of an Anglican clergyman, and although he shared the same agnostic malaise of many of the post-Darwinian Victorian intelligentsia, he did not have a closed mind upon religious matters.[13] Indeed he was an enthusiastic member of many intellectual clubs that debated and speculated upon religious and philosophical matters. In his undergraduate days Sidgwick was a member of the famous debating club at Trinity known as 'The Apostles', which was dedicated to the pursuit of Truth and consequently dealt with 'the gravest matters'.[14] He would also later join the renowned Metaphysical Society and the Synthetic Society.[15]

Among the many students Sidgwick attracted to his person in Cambridge, Myers was one of the most promising. A classical scholar and accomplished poet, Myers became a close friend of Sidgwick's from 1869.[16] It was perhaps in this same crucial year of agnostic doubt that the famous foundational walk between the two men took place, an event which Myers recorded in his obituary of Sidgwick in 1900:

In a star-light walk which I shall not forget ... I asked him, almost with trembling, whether he thought that when Tradition, Intuition, Metaphysic, had failed to solve the riddle of the Universe, there was still a chance that from any actual observable phenomena, – ghosts, spirits, whatsoever there might be, – some valid knowledge might be drawn as to a World Unseen. Already, it seemed, he had thought that this was possible; steadily though in no sanguine fashion, he indicated some last grounds of hope; and from that night onwards I resolved to pursue this quest, if it might be, at his side. Even thus a wanderer in the desert, abandoning in despair the fair mirages which he has

---

[11] Sidgwick's wife, Eleanor Balfour, whom he married in 1876, became Principal of Newnham College at Cambridge, an institution Sidgwick helped to found in 1871. He was proud of the fact that Newnham had no chapel for religious services.

[12] Sidgwick would go on to become the Knightsbridge Professor of Philosophy at Trinity.

[13] Gurney, Myers and Podmore were also sons of clergymen. See Gauld, *The Founders*, pp.141–3. For the relationship between clerics-to-be and Cambridge University see Sheldon Rothblatt, *The Revolution of the Dons: Cambridge and Society in Victorian England* (London, 1968), pp.63–5.

[14] Sidgwick and Sidgwick, *Henry Sidgwick*, p.35. Alfred Tennyson, a prominent Apostle, wrote a paper on 'Ghosts' for the group, which was never delivered. Willard Brown observed that Tennyson's 'In Memoriam' owed a lot to the emotional and intellectual environment of the Apostles. Brown, *The Metaphysical Society*, p.6.

[15] Oppenheim, *The Other World*, p.127. R.H. Hutton, ' "The Metaphysical Society": A Reminiscence', *Nineteenth Century* 18 (1885), 177–96. On the Synthetic Society see Brown, *The Metaphysical Society*, pp.252–60.

[16] Sidgwick and Sidgwick, *Henry Sidgwick*, p.196.

followed in vain, might turn and help an older explorer in the poor search for scanty roots and muddy water-holes.[17]

It is interesting to note here both the pioneering tone of these preliminary explorations – the idea that all previous modes of interpretation had failed – and the nomination of ghosts and spirits as primary phenomena of the unseen world, phenomena that Sidgwick and Myers believed deserved to be seriously explained within the positivistic context of the scientific naturalist paradigm.

This discussion of ghostly phenomena may perhaps be explained by the disillusionment and disgust experienced by Sidgwick and Myers with the less 'spiritual' and more grossly 'physical' phenomena of spiritualism such as table-tilting, rapping, slate-writing and materialisation, which were considered base on a spiritualistic level by some, and fraudulent on a physical level by many.[18] In the 1870s Crookes heralded a time when

The increased employment of scientific methods will promote exact observation and greater love of truth among enquirers, and will produce a race of observers who will drive the worthless residuum of spiritualism hence into the unknown limbo of magic and necromancy.[19]

Despite Crookes's hopes, this period was full of cases of blatant fraudulence and trickery, and the public exposures of spiritualist mediums such as Henry Slade, Florence Cook and Mary Showers were part of a more general culture of debunking which claimed many scalps and was perhaps most astutely expressed by Browning's acerbic poem 'Mr Sludge, "The Medium"'. Indeed, the fact that Home, the subject of that notorious satire, was apparently never exposed as a charlatan did not halt the large numbers of declarations from investigators that he must be a fraud nonetheless.[20] Despite the frequent protestations in the spiritualist press that the evidence of conjuration provided by sceptical inquirers was falsified, exaggerated or merely originated in an unconscious automatism of the medium, the whole phenomena of spiritualism, especially its physical phenomena, retained an ambiguous status in the researches of the SPR for some time to come. However, the essential premise of spiritualism – that the dead could communicate with the living – remained an evidential challenge to all curious observers, especially those who practised psychical research.

---

[17] Cited in Gauld, *The Founders*, p.103. On the confusion of actual date of this incident see *ibid.*, p.103.

[18] On the repulsion felt by observers for table-turning and related phenomena see Cottom, *Abyss of Reason*, pp.22–49.

[19] William Crookes, *Researches in the Phenomena of Spiritualism* (London, 1874), p.8.

[20] See Peter Lamont, *The First Psychic: The Peculiar Mystery of a Notorious Victorian Wizard* (London, 2005), pp.149–63.

Sidgwick's eagerness to solve the questions pertaining to the survival of the human personality was painfully contrasted with the many investigative failures he and his acquaintances had already notched up by the 1870s. Yet Sidgwick, like most contemporary commentators, believed that the stakes were too high to risk adopting a frivolous attitude to the matter; either spiritualism was a worldwide fraud which proved once more the capacity for people with the 'will to believe' to be thoroughly deceived, or spiritualism at last provided a sure and empirically valid answer to some of the ultimate questions of human existence. In 1853 the religious thinker Adin Ballou wrote of the aftermath of a world in which spiritualism was proven:

It will convert thousands from gross infidelity. It will cure millions of involuntary semi-scepticism. It will render a future existence *real* to the whole human race. It will reinvigorate every great religious and moral truth, heretofore revealed to mankind. It will intensify all the sublime motives that urge human nature on to a heavenly destiny. It will advance from step to step of demonstration, till death shall be disarmed of its terrors. It will usher in a new era of faith, hope, and charity. It will peaceably revolutionize the religious, moral, and social state of the world.[21]

In the midst of the revolutionary claims of spiritualism's proponents and the bitter denunciations of the scientific establishment, it was felt that some kind of organised scientific society was needed to ascertain the facts of the matter and end the scandal of a situation where, after almost thirty-five years of contentious debate, the reality or unreality of spiritualistic phenomena had not yet been accurately established.

The impetus for the avowed 'scientification' of the nascent psychical research movement came from the controversial experiments of two prominent scientists; William Crookes, the pioneering chemist, and William Barrett, Professor of Experimental Physics at the Royal College of Science for Ireland, Dublin. Sidgwick became enthusiastic about Crookes's hands-on experiments with Cook and Home, which were soon perceived as a crucial public encounter between the scientific establishment and spiritualism.[22] Moreover, Barrett's experiments in 'thought-reading' in Co. Westmeath, Dublin and London in the 1870s and early 1880s fostered an atmosphere of impending scientific evidence for supernormal claims.[23] The theory of thought-reading, that A could

[21] Ballou, *An Exposition of Views*, p.17.
[22] See Trevor H. Hall, *The Spiritualists: The Story of Florence Cook and William Crookes* (London, 1962).
[23] The term 'supernormal' was coined by Myers to describe psychical phenomena. It was intended to be a term expressive of the 'abnormal' rather than the 'supernatural'. See Gurney, Myers and Podmore, *Phantasms*, vol. I, p.xlvi.

consciously know what B was thinking of, opened up for Sidgwick and his fellow investigators new ways of approaching the ultimate questions of psychical research, ways which could be packaged as both experimentally valid and scientifically pioneering. After discussions with Edmund Dawson Rogers, a journalist and spiritualist, Barrett convened a conference on the matter which was held at the headquarters of the British National Alliance of Spiritualists in London on 6 January 1882, and as a result the Society for Psychical Research was formally established on 20 February.[24] The following objects were outlined:

It has been widely felt that the present is an opportune time for making an organised and systematic attempt to investigate that large group of debatable phenomena designated by such terms as mesmeric, psychical, and Spiritualistic.

From the recorded testimony of many competent witnesses, past and present, including observations recently made by scientific men of eminence in various countries, there appears to be, amidst much illusion and deception, an important body of reasonable phenomena, which are *prima facie* inexplicable on any generally recognised hypothesis, and which, if incontestably established, would be of the highest possible value.

The task of examining such residual phenomena has often been undertaken by individual effort, but never hitherto by a scientific society organised on a sufficiently broad basis.[25]

The 'Objects of the Society' demonstrated both the wide berth which the Society gave itself in investigative terms, and the palpable sense of hope that such a scientific society could conclusively explain and synthesise accounts of recent and historic spiritualistic phenomena.

However, despite the ambitious plans of the new Society and the vibrant intellectual atmosphere it initiated, Myers and Edmund Gurney

---

[24] See Edmund Dawson Rogers, 'Origin of the Society for Psychical Research', *Light* 13 (9 September 1893), 429–30. On the founding of the SPR see John Peregrine Williams, 'The Making of Victorian Psychical Research: An Intellectual Elite's Approach to the Spiritual World', PhD thesis, 1984, University of Cambridge, p.162; Brian Inglis, *Natural and Supernatural: A History of the Paranormal from Earliest Times to 1914* (London, 1977), pp.320–1; William F. Barrett, *Death-bed Visions: The Psychical Experiences of the Dying* (Wellingborough, 1986), p.156. The original Council of the SPR consisted of Barrett, Edward T. Bennett, Walter Browne, Alexander Calder, Walter H. Coffin, Desmond G. Fitzgerald, Gurney, Charles C. Massey, W. Stainton Moses, Myers, Francis W. Percival, Podmore, O. Lockhart Robinson, Edmund Dawson Rogers, Balfour Stewart, Morell Theobald, Hensleigh Wedgwood and George Wyld. Barrett was long considered a founding father of the Society even though he grew to dislike the Sidgwicks and frequently disagreed with their findings on controversial matters such as the exposure of the Creery Sisters. See Richard Noakes, 'The "Bridge Which Is between Physical and Psychical Research": William Fletcher Barrett, Sensitive Flames, and Spiritualism', *History of Science* 42 (2004), 438–46.
[25] 'Objects of the Society', *PSPR* 1 (1882–1883), 3.

(1847–1888), another member of Sidgwick's group, only agreed to join the SPR on the condition that Sidgwick would be appointed its first president.[26] This proved to be a wise proviso as Sidgwick, although at first pessimistic about the enterprise, would soon prove to have been the perfect choice for this position; an extremely well connected Cambridge don, he held an open mind on most matters but, unlike many, did not have a habit of pontificating on phenomena he felt were dubious. Thus, with Sidgwick at the head of a group of young friends which included his wife Eleanor M. Sidgwick (née Balfour) (1845–1936), and her brother Arthur Balfour, Myers, and Gurney, the Sidgwick Group formed a stable and driving force within the SPR which would continue until the death of its leader at the end of the century.[27] Never a mass organisation, the SPR consistently punched above its weight; while it obviously led to the creation of the modern discipline of parapsychology, it also fostered pioneering trends in both psychology and philosophy.[28] While it was predominantly bourgeois, the general membership of the SPR was varied in terms of profession, international in scope and welcoming of female participation at the highest level (one historian has estimated that women made up roughly forty per cent of the SPR's membership).[29] Despite its cult of the scientific, the SPR was never able to found a permanent research institute or have dedicated employed investigators, and it remained a privately endowed Society: in fact, most of the successes of the SPR in the 1880s were due to the input and dedication of Gurney, Myers and other members of independent means. In this sense, the worth of psychical research at the time was essentially in its

---

[26] Gauld, *The Founders*, p.138.

[27] Sidgwick was President of the SPR from 1882 to 1884 and again from 1888 to 1892. Alongside Sidgwick's close friendship with Myers, Gurney and Stainton Moses, he had also taught Arthur Balfour and Richard Hodgson at Cambridge. Fraser Nicol notes that the average age on the SPR council was 33. Fraser Nicol, 'The Founders of the S.P.R.', *PSPR* 55 (1966–1972), 347. Frank Podmore (1856–1910), a postal official and co-founder of the Fabian Society, was a peripheral member of the Sidgwick Group but an integral council member of the SPR. On Podmore and the Fabians see Edward R. Pease, *The History of the Fabian Society* (London, 1916).

[28] By the end of 1882 the SPR had about 150 members, rising to 600 in 1886, and close to 1000 by 1900. A common example given of the cutting-edge intellectual outlook of the SPR is the fact that Myers was one of the earliest figures to introduce Sigmund Freud to English audiences with his citation of Freud and Breuer's work on hysteria in 1891. See SPR Archive, MS 74/SPR Cambridge Branch, Minute Book, 1884–1900; Frederic W.H. Myers, 'The Subliminal Consciousness', *PSPR* 9 (1893–1894), 12; Ernest Jones, *Sigmund Freud: Life and Work*: vol. I (London, 1953), p.250.

[29] Mary Walker, 'Between Fiction and Madness: The Relationship of Women to the Supernatural in Late Victorian Britain', in *That Gentle Strength: Historical Perspectives on Women in Christianity*, ed. Lynda L. Coon, Katherine J. Haldane and Elisabeth W. Sommer (Charlottesville, 1990), p.236.

personnel, and thus its limited acceptance in scientific culture depended to a large extent upon the respectability and status of its members and associates. The SPR, largely through the efforts of Barrett, was, however, able to found a sister organisation – the American Society for Psychical Research (ASPR) – in 1885. Despite severe financial difficulties, which led to its amalgamation with the SPR in 1889, the ASPR attracted the participation of influential intellectual figures, especially from the psychological disciplines, such as William James, Josiah Royce and G. Stanley Hall.[30]

After centuries of constant flirtation between occultist explorations and mainstream science, and coming swiftly after the spiritualist craze, the firm public establishment of the SPR expressed both the curiosity and the frustration of its members at the state of affairs regarding the lack of scientific exploration of apparently supernatural matters. However, from the start of the SPR work it was clear that its core philosophical outlook would be sceptical and experimental, an outlook which did not at the time seem to discourage the enthusiastic participation of spiritualists in the SPR.[31] The SPR was not what spiritualists later criticised as a 'Sadducean' organisation with no scope for the integration of spiritual truths – on the contrary at some point almost all the SPR members flitted back and forth from enthusiastic belief in such divers matters as telepathy, the survival of human personality and the authenticity of mediumship, to a die-hard sceptical and fiercely debunking attitude.[32] Despite Tennyson's memorable line, 'For nothing

---

[30] Gauld, *The Founders*, p.148.

[31] Indeed, in 1885 the Oxford Phasmatological Society was of the opinion that 'many of [the SPR's] leading members are persons of avowed spiritualistic leanings, and that their investigations are made to support beliefs already formed, rather than to find out what is to be believed'. SPR Archive, MS 43/Oxford Phasmatological Society Papers; 'The S.P. R. and the C.A.S.', *Light* 3 (3 February 1883), 54. However, there is some evidence that the spiritualists were suspicious of the SPR from the start. Dawson Rogers had some interesting comments to make on how he convinced Stainton Moses (a prominent spiritualist) to become involved in setting up the SPR in early 1882: 'But when I first asked him to attend the [convening] Conference he resolutely refused, because, as he said, he had a shrewd guess that the men who were likely to come to the front in the new Society were not the men to bring impartial minds to the investigation of the phenomena of Spiritualism. This attitude he maintained.' Rogers, 'Origin of the Society for Psychical Research', 430. On the defining role of spiritualists in the setting-up of the SPR see Nicol, 'The Founders of the S.P.R.', 343. Nicol estimates that sixty-eight per cent of the Council, and fifty per cent of the Vice-Presidency, were spiritualists.

[32] 'A Sadducean Bias', *Light* 16 (25 April 1896), 198. Even at this early point a disclaimer was established in the publications of the SPR which in effect advocated primarily a sceptical outlook: '*To prevent misconception, it is here expressly stated that Membership of the Society does not imply the acceptance of any particular explanation of the phenomena investigated, nor any belief as to the operation, in the physical world, of forces other than*

worthy proving can be proven, Nor yet disproven',[33] the SPR were united by optimistic hopes in swiftly placing before the public domain certain incontrovertible facts on spiritualistic matters and thus directing the agenda in what positivism considered the 'scientific' age of society (Auguste Comte's third and final social age after the theological and metaphysical).[34] With the ideal of objective truth and an adherence to the scientific method before them as a means of solving life's greatest mysteries, the researchers expected results one way or the other, results which could serve as an enlightened benchmark for the perennial debates on occult and psychical matters. To this end the SPR was concerned to make a loud impact upon the intellectual community of late Victorian England and this attitude may be seen in the Society's precocious interaction with the media of the time.[35]

The main voice of the Society was the *Proceedings of the Society for Psychical Research*, a high-quality periodical which aimed to combine the findings of on-going experimental research with more abstract and theoretical speculations. From 1884 it also began to publish the *Journal of the Society of Psychical Research* for private, in-house circulation. The *JSPR* was a publication that contained the preliminary research, updates and speculations which formed the basis for the more polished articles that were later published in the *PSPR*, but which for reasons of sketchiness, tact or potential controversy, were not published at once in the *PSPR*. From the beginning it was intended that a SPR library could be established to concentrate in one place the disparate literature on

---

those recognised by Physical Science.' 'Constitution and Rules', *PSPR* 1 (1882–1883), 5. There were quite a few leading figures in the SPR, such as Richard Hodgson and Hereward Carrington, who had made their names as fierce sceptics only to advocate towards the end of their lives some of the spiritualistic beliefs they had previously combated.

[33] Alfred Lord Tennyson, 'The Ancient Sage', in *The Complete Works* (London, 1905), p.548.

[34] Auguste Comte, *System of Positive Polity*: vol. IV (New York, 1969), p.547. In a Comtean manner, the French psychical researcher Charles Richet suggested the existence of four stages of his science of 'metapsychics': the Mythical, the Magnetic, the Spiritist and the Scientific which began with Crookes. Richet, *Thirty Years of Psychical Research*, p.14.

[35] A comment by Gurney, therefore, rings true in this regard. On receiving criticism of the SPR theory of ghost-seeing from Charles S. Peirce, Gurney wrote that it was 'a source of genuine pleasure and profit ... Criticism, as my colleagues and I should allow, and even insist, is what the exponents of every new doctrine must expect; and in the case of a doctrine so new to science as telepathy, the criticism cannot be too searching.' Charles S. Peirce, *Writings of Charles S. Peirce: A Chronological Edition*: vol. VI, *1886–1890*, ed. Nathan Houser and Peirce Edition Project (Bloomington, 2000), p.82. Similarly Myers wrote: 'We must recognise that we have more in common with those who may criticise or attack our work with competent diligence than with those who may acclaim and exaggerate it without adding thereto any careful work of their own.' Frederic W.H. Myers, 'In Memory of Henry Sidgwick', *PSPR* 15 (1900–1901), 459–60.

psychical research and the occult for use by researchers, members and the general public.[36] The SPR was also keen to publicise its work on the subject of ghost-seeing as much as possible in the mainstream press in the 1880s. Thus printed advertisements and letters calling for cases of ghost-seeing, telepathy and haunting became a common feature in newspapers of the period, most notably in *The Times*.[37] Key members of the Society also printed the findings of their own research in periodicals and reviews with a large readership and circulation such as the *Contemporary Review*, the *National Review*, *Nineteenth Century*, and the philosophical-psychological journal *Mind*.[38] Finally the publications of senior members of the SPR such as Gurney, Frank Podmore and Myers's *Phantasms of the Living* (1886); Podmore's *Apparitions and Thought-transference: An Examination of the Evidence for Telepathy* (1894) and *Modern Spiritualism: A History and a Criticism* (1902); and Myers's posthumous *Human Personality and Its Survival of Bodily Death* (1903), received many extended reviews and much attention in the media, not only in the spiritualist and psychical research press, but also in the mainstream high-brow newspapers and journals of the period.

Ghost-hunting in the Society for Psychical Research

The SPR hit the ground running in 1882 with six committees immediately set up, each under the direction of an Honorary Secretary. These were: Thought-reading (Barrett), Mesmerism (George Wyld), Reichenbach Phenomena (Walter H. Coffin), Apparitions and Haunted Houses (Hensleigh Wedgwood), Physical Phenomena (C. Lockhart Robertson) and the Literary Committee (Gurney, Myers).[39] All were based in London except for the Committee on Thought-reading which was directed by Barrett from Dublin. At a glance it appears that each committee was

---

[36] This eventually became the Edmund Gurney Library, founded shortly after Gurney's death.
[37] See Carlos S. Alvarado, 'Psychical Research and Telepathy in Nineteenth-century Issues of *The Times*', *Paranormal Review* 43 (2007), 3–7.
[38] See, for example, William F. Barrett, Edmund Gurney and Frederic W.H. Myers, 'Thought Reading', *Nineteenth Century* 11 (1882), 890–901; Edmund Gurney and Frederic W.H. Myers, 'Visible Apparitions', *Nineteenth Century* 16 (1884), 68–95, 851–2; Frederic W.H. Myers, 'Multiplex Personality', *Nineteenth Century* 20 (1886), 648–66. Most of Gurney's writings on hypnotism were published in *Mind*.
[39] 'Objects of the Society', 3–4. 'Reichenbach phenomena' referred to the alleged luminosity surrounding magnets as observed by Carl von Reichenbach. Reichenbach posited the existence an 'odic force' perceptible by certain sensitives. See F.D. O'Byrne, *Reichenbach's Letters on Od and Magnetism (1852) Published for the First Time in English, with Extracts from His Other Works, so as to Make a Complete Presentation of the Odic Theory* (London, 1926).

pursuing its own distinct path; however, with prominent council members such as Barrett, Myers, Podmore and Gurney heavily involved in more than one committee there was a considerable amount of flexibility and inter-penetration of on-going investigations. Thematically also, with the exception of the Reichenbach Committee, the investigative projects were essentially unified as nunciative phenomena in that they all played host to forms of message-sending which explored the frontiers between the mind, the body and the (contested) spirit world. In this sense, as shall be shown, it becomes apparent that the *total* work of the SPR during this period, illustrated by the subject-matter of the committees, can be placed within the wider context of death rituals and communicatory relations between the living and the dead in late Victorian culture and society.

While mesmerism and hypnotism remained important topics within the SPR (especially for psychologists such as Gurney and Myers), rapid developments in the psychology of hypnotism and the relationship between physical mediumship and abnormal psychology soon took precedence over the more occultist, fluidic speculations of traditional mesmerism. The committee on the so-called 'Reichenbach effects', similarly pseudo-scientific in character, lacked institutional or popular interest and soon faded away.[40] The Committee on Physical Phenomena never produced a report at all in the 1880s for the following reasons: the perceived lack of reputable and respectable mediums, the death of the Committee's main backer Balfour Stewart in 1887, the controversial break with the spiritualist supporters of the SPR following the debunking of the Theosophical Society in 1885 by Richard Hodgson (a prominent psychical researcher originally from Australia), and the general investigative turn against well known physical mediums such as William Eglinton.

In contrast to the subjects of mesmerism, Reichenbach phenomena and the physical phenomena of spiritualism, experiments in thought-reading (the name was soon changed to 'thought-transference' to distinguish the phenomena from the widespread popular entertainments of muscle-reading, code-reading and the popular Victorian 'willing game') began to occupy the time of most of the senior SPR figures. Finally it

---

[40] After a preliminary report which merely mentioned a delay in research, the Reichenbach Committee issued its first and only report in April 1883. The percipient in these experiments was the mesmerist George A. Smith (see below) and its main intellectual force was Barrett. Podmore did not ascribe much significance to the phenomena: 'On the whole, the results of the Committee's researches indicate that the phenomena described by Reichenbach were purely subjective; that they were in fact faint hallucinations, due in most cases, it is probable, to direct verbal suggestion.' Frank Podmore, *Studies in Psychical Research* (London, 1897), p.92.

seemed as if the remarkable evidence collected proved the existence of supernormal faculties, namely 'a belief that a vivid impression or a distinct idea in one mind can be communicated to another mind without the intervening help of the recognised organs of sensation'.[41] This assertion was largely based upon two sets of experiments undertaken by the SPR in 1882 and 1883. The first involved the Creery Sisters, three teenage daughters of a Derbyshire clergyman, whose remarkable successes during their willing game led to participation in card-guessing tests for the SPR.[42] In these tests, which greatly impressed Barrett, Myers and Gurney, the sisters seemed to score 'hits' far above chance even with variables such as involuntary actions, collusion and conscious or unconscious deception taken into account.[43]

Through the Creery tests the SPR sought to earn their experimental spurs, so to speak, and emphasised that through their 'perpetual vigilant watch' they had never detected any fraud or dishonesty in the proceedings.[44] Crucial also in laying the foundations for the SPR's belief in telepathy were the thought-transference tests involving two young men based in Brighton who ran a 'second-sight' performance there: George A. Smith and Douglas Blackburn. These tests typically involved Blackburn's apparent thought-transmission of random names, images and colours to the blindfolded Smith, who sat behind him in the same room. Smith's successful 'hits' went beyond the possibility of chance-coincidence and seemed to occur despite the precautions of the SPR members present. Gurney personally attested to Smith's character and employed him as his private secretary from 1883 to 1888: he was 'excellent at tracing impostures', Gurney wrote in a letter to William James.[45] Following the Creery and Smith/Blackburn experiments, thought-transference became one of the abiding themes of the SPR in the 1880s and 1890s and the hypothesis of supernormal communication was rapidly expanded into the subject-matter of most of the other committees, featuring prominently in speculations regarding mesmeric rapport, somnambulism and the physical phenomena on display during séances.

Yet the thought-transference hypothesis was most fully and fruitfully integrated into theories regarding hallucinations, apparitions, phantasms and the alleged appearances of the dead – subject areas which soon

---

[41] William F. Barrett, Edmund Gurney and Frederic W.H. Myers, 'First Report of the Committee on Thought-reading', *PSPR* 1 (1882–1883), 13.
[42] See Trevor H. Hall, *The Strange Case of Edmund Gurney* (London, 1964), pp.55–63.
[43] Barrett, Gurney and Myers, 'First Report on Thought-reading', 24.
[44] *Ibid.*, 27.   [45] Cited in Gauld, *The Founders*, p.181.

became the remit of the Literary Committee. In the reports of the Literary Committee the role of thought-transference was seen as central in determining the difference between delusive and veridical hallucinations, and this differentiation opened up the genre of supernatural hallucinations to scientific explanation and exposition. The increased speculations about thought-transference, and its wider implications for theories of hallucinations and apparitions led to its second name-change in the space of a year with Myers famously coining the word 'telepathy' from the Greek 'tele' (distant) and 'patheia' (feeling).[46] The term 'thought-transference', limited in its scope to the transference of thoughts or specific psychic ideas, could not, the SPR felt, accommodate the more sophisticated mental action needed express the externalisation of such complex phenomena as hallucinations of the living and lengthy auditory and vocal hallucinations.[47]

Under the committee system of collective authorship the investigations of apparitions immediately featured prominently in the *PSPR*, with both the Committee on Haunted Houses and Apparitions and the Literary Committee issuing reports in 1882 on cases of ghost-seeing and the investigative methods they would be pursuing in such cases.[48] Recognising the huge popular interest in this particular genre of psychical research, the SPR made it clear that the evidential value it required for validation disqualified the majority of cases that would be submitted. The testimony of a single witness with the backing of hearsay would *not* constitute sufficient grounds for claiming the objective reality of an apparition of a dying or dead person; rather multiple witnesses of credible standing would be required to contribute to a cumulative body of data which could be analysed with a view to developing a statistically grounded theory of ghosts.[49] However, as the vast majority of cases involved a single witness, and thus could not be verified on a collective scale, apparitions and hallucinations were dealt with according to their veridical nature, i.e. their external agreement with recorded reality, such as dated letters, the detailed knowledge of clothing, or the coincidence with the death of the apparition. As Sidgwick remarked in forceful terms in his opening address to the SPR in July 1882: 'Scientific incredulity

---

[46] William F. Barrett, C.C. Massey, W. Stainton Moses *et al.*, 'First Report of the Literary Committee', *PSPR* 1 (1882–1883), 147.

[47] Williams, 'The Making of Victorian Psychical Research', p.204.

[48] It would appear that early in the apportioning of work the original Committee on Apparitions and Haunted Houses relinquished the area of ghosts and apparitions to the Literary Committee.

[49] William F. Barrett, A.P. Perceval Keep, C.C. Massey *et al.*, 'First Report of the Committee on Haunted Houses', *PSPR* 1 (1882–1883), 105.

has been so long in growing, and has so many and so strong roots, that we shall only kill it, if we are able to kill it at all as regards any of those questions, by burying it alive under a heap of facts.'[50] More so than with the phenomena of thought-transference, the investigations into apparitions depended upon the *suffocating* nature of the body of evidence, a corpus which would kill off and 'bury alive' the inevitable challenges from mainstream science to a new psychical theory of ghosts and ghost-seeing.

Despite the seeming prevalence of ghosts, wraiths and spirits in every-day life, the Committee on Haunted Houses and Apparitions seemed to encounter some reluctance on the part of their prey. The Committee wrote about how it had been asked why it did not simply gather a dozen disbelievers in a haunted house and leave them there overnight in order to settle the question once and for all. But, as the Committee humo-rously remarked, ghosts 'like aerolites, seem to be no respecters of persons; and no amount of scientific watchfulness will make them come to order'.[51] However, this reluctance on the part of the ghost was not to blame for the results of most cases, as the SPR paid equal attention to the psychical state of the ghost-seer. The first case investigated by the Society set a benchmark for future standards in the nature of the tale and the investigative response to it. It concerned an apparition that had appeared over a hundred times to an artist, 'Mr. P.', at his studio in Chelsea. The apparition usually appeared in broad daylight and was so lifelike that the artist managed to produce a portrait of his constant visitor who was 'a young man of about twenty-five, with the right arm torn away from the shoulder, and a strangely mournful, pleading expres-sion in the eyes'.[52] The two SPR investigators (unnamed) involved in the case proceeded to interview and interrogate the owners of the house, who did not report any supernatural occurrences. They did, however, relate the story of a distressing suicide which occurred there, but the investigators did not find secure grounds to connect it with the artist's apparition. Thus, in the absence of corroborative testimony, or evidence that the apparition was of a veridical nature, the investigators labelled it a morbid hallucination brought on by sudden physiological movements:

With one exception, it invariably appeared to Mr. P. floating in air behind the rails of the staircase, when he was washing his brushes at the end of his day's work. The sudden quickening of the circulation, caused by the change of

[50] Henry Sidgwick, 'President's Address', *PSPR* 1 (1882–1883), 12.
[51] Barrett, Keep, Massey *et al.*, 'First Report of the Committee on Haunted Houses', 114–15.
[52] *Ibid.*, 102.

position and rapid movement after a period of some hours passed in a sedentary or stationary posture, would be precisely one of the conditions we should look for as calculated to develop any latent predisposition to spectral illusions. There is, however, one circumstance which makes us waver in our diagnosis of this case. On the occasion above referred to as exceptional, Mr. P. saw the figure in his studio. He was sitting before his easel with his back to the door one winter's morning, when, as he assured us, he felt that someone was in the room, and, turning round, he saw the apparition a few feet from him. This intrusion appears to have annoyed him, and he uttered an impatient exclamation, upon which the figure slowly vanished. If Mr. P.'s remembrance of this incident is completely accurate, there would certainly seem to be some degree of justification for his own firm belief in the objective nature of the phantom; since hallucination which affects sensation in two modes – what we may call hallucination of two dimensions – is at all events uncommon. However, in the absence of more conclusive evidence, we must be content to regard the presumption in favour of the objective nature of this apparition as, at least, too weak to afford us ground for action.[53]

The recourse to the physiological theory of apparitions as spectral illusions emphasised the SPR's epistemic continuity with the extensive quasi-scientific literature on the nature of ghosts and hallucinations that existed since the Enlightenment. Furthermore, the picturesque and representational quality of the ghost, alongside the seeming lack of veridicality, and the artistic vocation of the percipient led to a natural degree of scepticism on the part of the investigators. This, the first report of an apparition case recorded in the *PSPR*, can thus be seen as a deft move designed to portray the cool and sceptical credentials of the SPR from the beginning, a diagnosis-cum-interpretation favoured by the diplomatic and almost apologetic final sentence recorded above.[54]

It was undoubtedly the lack of sensational eyewitness experience on the part of SPR investigators in matters spectral which led them toward the more pedestrian methods of collecting and collating masses of material, and issuing circular requests for data to friends of the Society and the major newspapers and journals with a view to future developments. It was soon evident that ghost-hunting had begun to dominate the labours of the Literary Committee, which had been set up as a processing department for Myers, and especially Gurney, to wade

---

[53] *Ibid.*, 103.

[54] This choice of case proved a rather fortunate one for the SPR as the next case examined, the alleged ghost-seeing of 'Mr. X.Z.', was soon revealed to be a hoax. See Barrett, Keep, Massey *et al.*, 'First Report of the Committee on Haunted Houses', 106–7; Hall, *The Strange Case of Edmund Gurney*, pp.68–70. Indeed, the 'Mr. X.Z.' case bears more than a passing resemblance to Walter Scott's much-anthologised ghost story 'The Tapestried Chamber'.

through biographies, documentation and correspondence for cases of a spectral or telepathic nature with evidential or theoretical value: it became the engine room of the SPR in its early years, knocking out four substantial reports in the *PSPR* from 1882 to 1884. In its first report the Committee outlined its methodology for verifying and classifying testimony regarding ghost-seeing. It preferred a personal interview with the percipient (the person who had experienced the supernormal occurrence), and expressed the wish to 'hear his story told in a manner which pledges his honour to its truth'.[55] Here the cultural notions of *tellability* and its hierarchical requirements, which would play a key role in the SPR discourse on ghosts and ghost-seeing, are first encountered in a bald manner. This is further demonstrated by a footnote to the quote above which notes that if the case concerns the testimony of an illiterate person the narrative may be accepted as authentic on the authority of the local clergyman. Clearly then, the SPR developed an *a priori* notion of an accredited ghost story which relied upon the non-sensational account of a literate and respectable member of the public willing to communicate with the SPR.[56] If the desired requirement of personal acquaintance with the person who experienced the occurrence was not possible, then cross-examination by letter would be a necessary procedure, an avenue which proved to be the primary method of verification for the SPR in the 1880s; some 10,000 letters were sent to correspondents by the Literary Committee in 1883 alone.[57]

Luckhurst has suggested that the tales sent in to the SPR operated like rumours through their citational character and the possibility of their further transmission.[58] Following this train of thought, the SPR's sociological work concerning ghosts, phantasms and hallucinations may be viewed as a kind of 'open secret' – a public-private site of exchange, comparison and statistical calculation in which the SPR personnel were operators in a knowledge-grid, working for the public weal. Indeed, the

---

[55] Barrett, Massey, Moses *et al.*, 'First Report of the Literary Committee', 117.

[56] In 1887 Gurney complained that a critic of the SPR had 'taken a rather unfair advantage of the fact that, though much time has been spent in forming a judgement as to witnesses' characters by personal interviews, and often by prolonged correspondence, I have expressly avoided giving the results in the shape of definite testimonials'. Peirce, *Writings*, p.91.

[57] William F. Barrett, C.C. Massey, W. Stainton Moses *et al.*, 'Second Report of Literary Committee', *PSPR* 2 (1884), 45.

[58] Luckhurst, *The Invention of Telepathy*, p.151. Tyndall wrote: 'Scientific theories sometimes float like rumours in the air before they receive complete expression. The doom of a doctrine is often practically sealed, and the truth of one is often practically accepted, long prior to the demonstration of either the error or the truth.' John Tyndall, *Fragments of Science*: vol. II, 6th edn (New York, 1905), p.356.

Literary Committee themselves envisaged psychical researchers 'Working unseen among multitudes who belong to no learned bodies and have no scientific pretensions.'[59] Thus it is possible to regard the Sidgwick Group as an elite, or secret society within the SPR from its very beginning, committed to promoting a scientific naturalist theory of ghosts through the participation of selected witnesses. It should be recalled that the *JSPR*, which published deeply sceptical articles on issues such as theosophy and physical phenomena, contributed to the alienation of spiritualist members of the SPR who regarded it as a divisive and exclusive forum.[60] By stretching this theme of secrecy from the internal activities and politics of the SPR and applying it to the form and content of the ghost-seeing cases it collected we may begin to fully appreciate the project of psychical research in this area.

The presentation of accounts of ghost-seeing by accredited corres-pondents, and annotated by the SPR, represented a development from an earlier stage in the spiritualist press, where cases were loudly presented, towards a more mature intervention released at an ambient volume, at once hidden and affective. Georg Simmel wrote that the secret

produces an enlargement of life: numerous contexts of life cannot even emerge in the presence of full publicity. The secret offers, so to speak, the possibility of a second world alongside the manifest world; and the latter is decisively influenced by the former.[61]

By utilising the liminal space between sociation and secrecy, the 'second world' of ghosts and ghost-seeing could be investigated by the SPR with a generally liberated sensibility attuned to both the popular concept of the ghost and the new psychical concepts surrounded by the emerging idea of telepathy. In this sense Luckhurst's point that the fact that the SPR conducted their investigations privately demonstrated its class-based make-up may be countered with the argument that it was the subject-matter of psychical research, and in particular the SPR's interest in ghost-seeing, which led to the SPR being, necessarily, a society that welcomed spontaneous public avowals of ghost-seeing, while remaining an exclusive bourgeois (epistolary) society that showcased the high standards of its evidence and cautious approach to testimony.[62] Thus the two-guinea fee

---

[59] William F. Barrett, C.C. Massey, W. Stainton Moses *et al.*, 'Third Report of the Literary Committee: A Theory of Apparitions. Part I', *PSPR* 2 (1884), 110.

[60] For a sustained attack on the work of the early SPR with regard to the early deaths of Gurney and Podmore see Hall, *The Strange Case of Edmund Gurney*.

[61] Georg Simmel, *The Sociology of Georg Simmel*, ed. Kurt H. Wolff (New York and London, 1950), p.330.

[62] Luckhurst, *The Invention of Telepathy*, p.56. Some of Habermas's comments about the bourgeois public sphere are pertinent to this issue: 'Reason, which through public use of

for annual membership in the SPR can be compared with the tariff of 100 louis charged by Anton Mesmer for entry into his 100-member 'Society of Harmony' in the second, and more secretive, phase of his Parisian residency, as part of his aim of making mesmerism an inductable and exclusive power, while also maintaining a concern for its public status and humanitarian interventions.[63] I would suggest that, like mesmerism, the SPR's ghost-hunting activities emerged on the one hand, as a secretive, or exclusive, performance, expressed in the *preference* for upper-class ghost-seers, membership fees, and a two-tier publication policy, while on the other hand the SPR stood for a public-private partnership as part of its aim to foster paradigmatic intellectual shifts among the populace. It was this double-naturedness – a result of the SPR's commitment to investigating (and editing) a previously repressed 'second world' under the scientific naturalist paradigm – that gave the SPR the institutional capital to propose a theory of ghosts, but it was this same characteristic which ultimately resulted in the failure of the theory to gain scientific acceptance. Indeed, writing in *Nature*, H.G. Wells attacked the SPR's easy acceptance of testimony from all quarters and particularly criticised the fact that much of its evidence for telepathy derived from 'persons usually youthful and coming from a social level below that of the investigators'.[64]

In their presentation of case narratives, the SPR were concerned to offer up prototypes of a modern and scientifically empirical ghost story. The SPR seemed to make a virtue of the fact that their ghost stories were quite banal and nothing like the popular conception of the haunting ghost, dragging chains through an old mansion or lamenting a

the rational faculty was to be realized in the rational communication of a public consisting of cultivated human beings, itself needed to be protected from becoming public because it was a threat to any and all relations of domination. As long as publicity had its seat in the secret chanceries of the prince, reason could not reveal itself directly. Its sphere of publicity had still to rely on secrecy; its public, even as a public, remained internal. The light of reason, thus veiled for self-protection, was revealed in stages. This recalls Lessing's famous statement about Freemasonry, which at that time was a broader European phenomenon: it was just as old as bourgeois society – "if indeed bourgeois society is not merely the offspring of Freemasonry".' Jürgen Habermas, *The Structural Transformation of the Public Sphere: An Inquiry into a Category of Bourgeois Society*, trans. Thomas Burger and Frederick Lawrence (Cambridge, 1989), p.35. This public sphere, Habermas notes, was to a large extent structured by the intimacy of the letter. *Ibid.*, pp.48–9.

[63] See Alan Gauld, *A History of Hypnotism* (Cambridge, 1992), pp.8–10. Gauld also mentions the reported generosity of Mesmer when faced with a provincial physician who could not afford entry into the Society of Harmony: 'Mesmer surreptitiously slipped him the requisite amount, thus, as it were, paying his left hand with his right hand.' *Ibid.*, p.22.

[64] H.G. Wells, 'Peculiarities of Psychical Research', *Nature* (6 December 1894), 121.

tragedy. As early as the first issue of the *PSPR* the Committee on Haunted Houses and Apparitions wrote:

Further, we must warn future readers that the details of the evidence are in many cases not only dull, but of a trivial and even ludicrous kind; and they will be presented for the most part in the narrator's simplest phraseology, quite unspiced for the literary palette. Our tales will resemble neither the *Mysteries of the Udolpho* nor the dignified reports of a learned society.[65]

This positioning of the ghost narratives collected by the SPR, as distinct from popular and clichéd gothic tales, points to the recognised liminal status of the empirical ghost story that emerges neither as an experimentally valid piece of fieldwork nor even as an interesting or readable ghost story. Thus many critics of the SPR's theory of ghosts had what amounted to aesthetic objections to the type of ghosts described in their reports. Chief among them was the American philosopher Charles S. Peirce who noted the 'stupidity' of these ghosts:

They seem like the lower animals. If I believed in them, I should conclude that, while the soul was not always at once extinguished on the death of the body, yet it was reduced to a pitiable shade, a ghost, as we say, of its former self.[66]

Yet the researchers capitalised on this situation, and the similarity and greyness of accounts was believed to contribute to the evidential value of testimony, which in its matter-of-fact tone and protestations of corroboration aimed to use a journalistic tone of presented fact: Gurney wrote that such tales 'ought to absolutely *reek* of candour'.[67] Exaggeration and embellishment of stories were to be mistrusted, and the Society was proud of the fact that the ghost stories reported were 'far more likely to provoke sleep in the course of perusal than to banish it afterwards'.[68] Here, as elsewhere, we can learn much about the ghost-seer from the type of ghost being described. By the 1880s the typical fantastic or haunting ghost of English oral and popular culture was

---

[65] Barrett, Keep, Massey *et al.*, 'First Report of the Committee on Haunted Houses', 118.
[66] Peirce, *Writings*, p.62.
[67] Gurney cited in Deborah Blum, *Ghost Hunters: William James and the Search for Scientific Proof of Life after Death* (London, 2007), p.94. See also Gurney, Myers and Podmore, *Phantasms*, vol. II, p.272.
[68] Barrett, Keep, Massey *et al.*, 'First Report of the Committee on Haunted Houses', 117–18. By the end of the century Arthur Machen had declared that the SPR 'has dealt a fatal blow at the ghost of literature'. Arthur Machen, 'Ghosts and Dreams', *Literature* 5 (1899), 168. In a similar vein August Strindberg wrote in *Inferno* (1897): 'Spirits have become positivists, in harmony with the times, and are therefore no longer content to manifest themselves only in visions.' August Strindberg, *Inferno; and from an Occult Diary*, trans. Mary Sandbach (Harmondsworth, 1979), pp.145–6.

simply not *fashionable* any more, at least within psychical research.[69] Ghosts, spirits and spectres, as phenomena embedded within popular literary-oral and spiritualist culture were to be either pushed aside as unsubstantiated superstitions or else examined through the medium of the scientific and experimental standards which the SPR championed, standards which held an increasingly ambiguous status in the main-stream spiritualist movement. Rather, it was the sober, mute and, need-less to say, unprepossessing ghost which tended to predominate in the narratives published by the SPR as part of its commitment to accumu-lating generically typical ghost stories. This quantitative, rather than qualitative methodology of reducing ghosts to statistics, as opposed to sensational experiences, was certainly a novel approach to the area, an approach that was in tune with the new sociological trends of the period and which aimed to develop a critical mass of evidence from witnesses whom they considered to be of a high character. In short, the SPR developed a montage-approach to ghost-hunting with a view to synthe-sising recurring themes within an experimentally valid framework. The SPR mindset is reminiscent of Kant's cryptic remark on ghost stories: 'I am sceptical about each one of them individually, but I ascribe some credence to all of them taken together.'[70]

From the beginning the SPR was concerned to arrange the miscellan-eous cases of ghost-seeing into a workable whole through the subdivision of categories and the establishment of a scientifically orientated language of dealing with apparitions. Thus, in apparition cases the scenario described always involved an 'agent', the originator of the hallucination, and a 'percipient', the perceiver of this hallucination. While this termin-ology sought to link apparition-cases with the quasi-scientific language

[69] Andrew Lang wrote of the type of ghost stories which involve the spirits of the dead being active in animals: 'This kind of ghost story one seldom or never hears in drawing-rooms, but it is the prevalent and fashionable kind among the peasantry, for example, in Shropshire.' Andrew Lang, 'The Comparative Study of Ghost Stories', *Nineteenth Century* 17 (1885), 624. Lang was possibly thinking of the kind of ghost stories recorded in Charlotte Sophia Burne's *Shropshire Folk-lore: A Sheaf of Gleanings* (1883). Henry James, familiar with the SPR publications, drew attention to the scientific character of their ghost stories: 'The new type [of ghost story] indeed, the mere modern "psychical case", washed clean of all queerness as by exposure to a flowing laboratory tap, and equipped with credentials vouching for this – the new type clearly promised little, for the more it was respectably certified the less it seemed of a nature to rouse the dear old sacred terror.' Henry James, *Literary Criticism: French Writers, Other European Writers, the Prefaces to the New York Edition*, ed. Leon Edel and Mark Wilson (New York, 1984), p.1182.
[70] Kant, *Theoretical Philosophy*, p.338. This quote can be compared to the SPR's speculations on the evidence of ghost-seers: 'It is only when the various bits of testimony are put side by side that their real significance can be appreciated.' Barrett, Keep, Massey et al., 'First Report on Haunted Houses', 114.

and themes of telepathic communications, it did not merely imply that the 'sender' was an active object and the 'receiver' a passive object. In some cases the situation became a confused state of affairs with the percipient being the active party (whether conscious or unconscious), while in other cases the agent seemed to demonstrate peculiarities consistent with those of a percipient. However at this point the original scheme of classification proposed was: agent and percipient both in normal condition, percipient in abnormal condition, agent in abnormal condition, and agent and percipient both in abnormal condition.[71]

Cases given precedence under this classification were 'causal apparitions' or appearances that were veridical, which could be strongly connected to real documented events. J.G. Keulemans contributed an account of an apparition to the SPR in 1882 which may be taken as typical for cases of its kind:

In December, 1880, he was living with his family in Paris. The outbreak of an epidemic of small-pox caused him to remove three of his children, including a favourite little boy of five, to London, whence he received, in the course of the ensuing month, several letters giving an excellent account of their health. 'On the 24th of January, 1881, at half-past seven in the morning, I was suddenly awoke by hearing his voice, as I fancied, very near me. I saw a bright, opaque, white mass before my eyes, and in the centre of this light I saw the face of my little darling, his eyes bright, his mouth smiling. The apparition, accompanied by the sound of his voice, was too short and too-sudden to be called a dream: it was too clear, too decided, to be called an effect of imagination. So distinctly did I hear his voice that I looked round the room to see whether he was actually there. The sound I heard was that of extreme delight, such as only a happy child can utter. I thought it was the moment he woke up in London, happy and thinking of me. I said to myself, "Thank God, little Isidore is happy as always." ' Mr. Keulemans describes the ensuing day as one of peculiar brightness and cheerfulness. He took a long walk with a friend, with whom he dined; and was afterwards playing a game at billiards, when he again saw the apparition of his child. This made him seriously uneasy, and in spite of having received within three days the assurance of the child's perfect health, he expressed to his wife a conviction that he was dead. Next day a letter arrived saying that the child was ill; but the father was convinced that this was only an attempt to break the news; and, in fact, the child had died, after a few hours' illness, at the exact time of the first apparition.[72]

However, alongside cases of this type, which quite literally related to life and death, the SPR received many accounts of ghost-seeing which, while veridical, did not seem to fit any spiritual, or even broadly utilitarian

---

[71] Barrett, Massey, Moses et al., 'First Report of the Literary Committee', 118–44.
[72] Ibid., 126–7.

context. The following is another example of the purposeless and sometimes bizarre nature of some of these cases of causal apparitions:

It was a very wet Sunday afternoon in 1835 or '36, Mrs. Clay being at home
and Mr. Clay at service in the gaol where he was chaplain. Rather before his
usual time Mrs. Clay heard her husband return, enter the house by the back
door under the window of the room she was in, hang up his coat and hat, saw
him enter the room, and, standing at the door, heard him remark what a wet
day it was, and then, after her reply, he went upstairs. As he did not return,
Mrs. Clay ran upstairs to seek him, and concluded he had gone out again as she
could not find him. A little later the whole occurrence was *re-enacted*, and on
her asking her husband why he had gone out again, he assured her he had not
done so, but had then only just come back from service. This time it was the
real Mr. Clay.[73]

With all the enthusiasm of a new and eager society the SPR had, on the
basis of the positive results of the Committee on Thought-transference
(which published three detailed reports in 1882 and 1883), and the sheer
quantity of ghost cases submitted and researched that pointed to the
activity of supersensuous contact of one mind upon another, made the
link between telepathy and ghost-seeing a thematic constant in investigations into both phenomena throughout the 1880s. Going beyond this
they had pushed theories of ghosts forward into a new and fascinating
quasi-scientific context with the assumption that telepathy was a reality,
the reality and primary phenomenon of psychical research thus far.[74]
The innate optimism contained in this psychical approach to the supernatural, which avoided spiritualistic concepts in favour of a modern sense,
indeed cult, of scientific discovery, yet promised answers to some of the
most intractable questions of human existence, can be seen in the lyrical
language which the researchers sometimes allowed themselves to slip into.
For instance, the Literary Committee passionately declared:

There is the *maximum* of stimulus which the sense of a rising cause, of an on
flowing tide, can give; there are the alluring gleams of a dawning order; there is
the excitement of a time when individual efforts, however humble, may contribute
in a sensible measure towards the establishment of an important truth.[75]

[73] Barrett, Massey, Moses *et al.*, 'First Report of the Literary Committee', 146.
[74] As Luckhurst put it: 'Telepathy was coined as a strategy to protect a terrain of scientific
legitimacy.' Luckhurst, *The Invention of Telepathy*, p.148. However, Sidgwick voiced a
typical tone of doubt. While he was personally convinced of the reality of the
phenomena he could understand why others were not as yet. In 1884 he wrote that
the case of thought-transference 'is one in which no one can say exactly how much
evidence is wanted; we have to balance conflicting improbabilities; and the
improbabilities are of a kind that we have no scales to weigh exactly'. Sidgwick,
'President's Address', 153.
[75] Barrett, Massey, Moses *et al.*, 'First Report of the Literary Committee', 155.

The sociology of the psychical ghost story

On reading the SPR's literature on apparitions, phantasms and haunting ghosts it quickly becomes clear that the *mode* and *form* of interaction in reported ghost stories was just as important as the *content* of interaction – however fantastic the narrative related may be. For of great interest to the SPR was the fact that the steady trickle of cases sent in to its rooms at 14 Dean's Yard and investigated by researchers pointed, through their banality, the respectability of their senders and their common themes, to the existence of a substructure of supernormal activity all over the Empire. Through its evocation of this 'second world' in late Victorian society – a world buzzing with the ghostly transmissions and receptions of 'agents' and 'percipients', 'senders and receivers' – the SPR sought to acclimatise the reading public to truths they believed waited just around the corner. They fully believed that the question of apparitions, a question that was possibly of most latent concern to the public, was entering a new interpretive phase: 'It is coming at the same time to seem more *important*, and to seem more *soluble*.'[76] This momentum found voice with the 'Theory of Apparitions' expounded in the *PSPR* in two parts in 1884 by the Literary Committee. Here the SPR located a new typology of spontaneous telepathic ghost stories that may previously have been put down to anxiety, hypochondria, hysteria, imagination or occurrence of spectral illusions by percipients. The Committee laid out the status of such cases:

For the main difficulty in collecting cases of this sort is that, even if they do occur, they are not likely to be observed or remembered. Their theoretical importance is (very naturally) not discerned; they are thought trivial and purposeless – merely incredible, without either pathos or dignity. In reality, no narratives are more significant, or cast a more searching ray on the obscure pervasive co-sentiency of man and man.[77]

Thus from the outset the success or failure of the SPR theory of apparitions depended to a significant extent upon public participation in the investigative enterprise, a large-scale participation that had not been necessary in the experimental thought-transference tests but was crucial if the ghost-seeing was to be scientifically proved to occur in society. Gurney left his readers in no doubt that their place in the enterprise reflected the democratic intentions of the SPR:

But though 'psychical research' is certain in time to surmount ridicule and prejudice, and to clear for itself a firm path between easy credulity on the one

---

[76] Barrett, Massey, Moses *et al.*, 'Third Report of the Literary Committee', 109.
[77] *Ibid.*, 129.

side and easy incredulity on the other, the rate of its advance must depend on the amount of sympathy and support that it can command from the general mass of educated men and women. In no department should the democratic spirit of modern science find so free a scope: it is for the public here to be, not – as in anthropological researches – the passive material of investigation, but the active participators in it.[78]

This openness was also a natural result of the SPR's adherence to contemporary philosophical empiricism and especially what J.P. Williams has called the Society's 'liberal epistemology', an operating mode which laid emphasis upon freedom of discussion, inquiry and participation, and the free availability of information relating to specific supernormal cases.[79]

The SPR was active in a phase of the history of science in which the scientific naturalism of the 1840s–1870s, propelled by the strength of the scientific societies and the momentum of the Darwinist controversy, gave way to the *fin-de-siècle* establishment of what Frank Miller Turner termed 'public science' – a discourse aimed at persuading institutional powers on contested topics and challenging popular conceptions of subjects which it was believed should best be dealt with by the 'professionals'.[80] In this intellectual context psychical research appealed to the educated classes in order to develop the sense of professionalism which could facilitate their drive towards the popularisation of the scientific instinct. Myers described psychical research as 'the left wing of Experimental Psychology' and he and Gurney compared the trials of psychical research with the opposition of the establishment to the new disciplines of anthropology and eugenics – other proto-/pseudo-sciences battling for scientific recognition and widespread application towards the end of the nineteenth century.[81] As psychical research sought to carve out a space for itself among the experimental sciences in the public sphere, Myers wrote that the SPR had had to 'create a public' of its own, a constituency neither sceptical nor superstitious.[82] It is therefore significant that, as the SPR developed and members of all points of view became active in the direction of psychical research, adjustments in the arrangements for collective and corporate responsibility were deemed necessary. In 1884 Sidgwick

---

[78] Gurney, Myers and Podmore, *Phantasms*, vol. II, pp.273–4.

[79] Williams, 'The Making of Victorian Psychical Research', p.64. In his study Logie Barrow explored what he termed the 'democratic epistemology' of plebeian spiritualism. Barrow, *Independent Spirits*, pp.146–212.

[80] See Frank Miller Turner, 'Public Science in Britain, 1880–1919', *Isis* 71:4 (1980), 589–608.

[81] Frederic W.H. Myers, 'The Drift of Psychical Research', *National Review* 24 (1894), 191; Edmund Gurney and Frederic W.H. Myers, 'Apparitions', *Nineteenth Century* 15 (1884), 791–2.

[82] Myers, 'The Drift of Psychical Research', 190.

announced a clarification in the rules of the Society: responsibility for views now lay primarily with individual authors and not with the Council or Society as a whole. This was ostensibly done to encourage more participation from scientific observers and reassure prospective members of the SPR. However, the disclaimer also demonstrated the increasingly contentious nature of articles written under the banner of specific committees, and acted as a support for members who had individual viewpoints or minority reports to contribute.

While it counted many established scientists among its members and workers, it was rare that an SPR pronouncement was able to achieve acceptance among the scientific periodical press: psychical research then, as now, was most frequently lambasted by mainstream science for its lack of replicable experiments under test conditions. The possibility of fraud (unconscious or otherwise) and incompetence on the part of the investigator were also common criticisms of psychical research from the psychological community, yet the argument that all human testimony was potentially erroneous, while being perhaps the most favoured 'common-sensical' response of scientific critics, was an argument which also featured strongly in the SPR's own literature, in its meta-critical moments, we might say.[83] Shadowing these internal debates on the use of testimony as evidence was David Hume's short essay 'On Miracles'

---

[83] Significant in this regard are C.C. Massey, 'The Possibilities of Mal-observation in Relation to Evidence for the Phenomena of Spiritualism', *PSPR* 4 (1886–1887), 75–99; Henry Sidgwick, 'Note on Mr. Massey's Paper', *PSPR* 4 (1886–1887), 99–110; Richard Hodgson and S.J. Davey, 'The Possibilities of Mal-observation and Lapse of Memory from a Practical Point of View', *PSPR* 4 (1886–1887), 381–495; Frederic W.H. Myers, 'Resolute Credulity', *PSPR* 10 (1895), 213–43. In a dialectical relationship with sceptical arguments against the credulous was the argument that a refusal to believe in the testimony and evidence for the supernatural was itself a form of mental illness. One mid-Victorian mesmerist wrote: 'The curious spectacle which is exhibited at the present day, of a large number of individuals not only obstinately refusing to believe facts supported by a body of evidence amply sufficient for their establishment, but actually priding themselves upon their own obtuseness, and designating their more gifted and less prejudiced contemporaries as credulous dupes or unprincipled impostors, is a phenomenon fraught with so much interest to the cerebral physiologist ... Amongst other "extraordinary popular delusions", let us examine that strange hallucination which leads its victims to mistake the narrowness of their own mental vision for superior clearsightedness, and deceives them into attributing to greater penetration what proceeds in reality from inferior sagacity.' 'X.P.', 'Believers and Disbelievers; or, Who are the Fools?', *Zoist* 4 (1846–1847), 435. See also Alfred Russel Wallace, 'The Psychological Curiosities of Scepticism. A Reply to Dr. Carpenter', *Fraser's Magazine for Town & Country* 16 (1877), 694–706. For an interesting exploration of the attempts to pathologise belief in the testimony for spiritualism and the counter-attacks which pathologised a *refusal* to believe in the testimony of spiritualism see Heather Wolffram, 'Parapsychology on the Couch: The Psychology of Occult Belief in Germany, c.1870–1939', *Journal of the History of the Behavioral Sciences* 42:3 (2006), 237–60.

from his *An Enquiry Concerning Human Understanding* (1748). Here Hume famously defined a miracle as

a violation of the laws of nature; and as a firm and unalterable experience has established these laws, the proof against a miracle, from the very nature of the fact, is as entire as any argument from experience can possibly be imagined.[84]

Although Hume was examining religious-orientated phenomena such as miracle-working, his arguments were frequently applied by sceptics to supernatural events in general. Hume further outlined a principle of superior evidence and expressed doubt as to whether a miracle has ever or could ever take place:

Upon the whole, then, it appears, that no testimony for any kind of miracle has ever amounted to a probability, much less to a proof . . . no human testimony can have such force as to prove a miracle, and make it a just foundation for any such system of religion.[85]

Here Hume placed limits upon the validity and verifiability of all human testimony, and thus provided the basis of a sceptical language, which would attack the philosophical foundations of Christianity through the Enlightenment, and into the nineteenth century his debunking of miracles would become a rationalist manifesto.[86] Despite many members of the SPR coming from the same rationalist-empirical tradition as Hume and his sceptical supporters, human testimony would ultimately prove the primary mode of evidence for the Society in its verification of phantasms of the living and of the dead.[87] While at times the SPR investigators could resemble incredulous governmental officials, a harsh line towards witnesses was considered justified in cases of testimony so remarkable.[88]

---

[84] David Hume, *An Enquiry Concerning Human Understanding and Concerning the Principles of Morals*, ed. L.A. Selby-Bigge, 3rd edn (Oxford, 1975), p.114.
[85] *Ibid.*, p.127.   [86] Inglis, *Natural and Supernatural*, pp.138–9.
[87] Countering the Humean position Sidgwick wrote: 'The greater the marvel, the better must be the testimony; of that common-sense has no doubt; but it is impossible to say precisely what accumulation of testimony is required to balance a given magnitude of marvel.' Henry Sidgwick, 'The Canons of Evidence in Psychical Research', *PSPR* 6 (1889–1890), 4. See also Wallace's arguments against Hume, in Alfred Russel Wallace, *On Miracles and Modern Spiritualism* (London, 2000), pp.1–28. See the criticisms of Hume's argument in Andrew Lang, *The Early Sociology of Religion*: vol. IV, *The Making of Religion*, ed. Bryan S. Turner (London, 1997), p.17; Edmund Gurney, *Tertium Quid: Chapters on Various Disputed Questions*: vol. I (London, 1887), pp.227–73.
[88] Williams has contrasted Sidgwick's activity in promoting the rigorous investigation of applicants to the 'Society for Organising Charitable Relief', with his principles of thorough investigation of the percipients who made a claim to the SPR. Williams, 'The Making of Victorian Psychical Research', pp.111–13. See also Myers, 'Resolute Credulity', 213.

The SPR did not generally utilise Humean scepticism – leaving that to their critics – and instead attempted to support testimony with secondary modes of verification. In expressing the truth of supernormal experiences, legal depositions were considered out of the question early on so direct interviews were deemed crucial in decision-making about cases: in that way the SPR could vet people they considered 'hysterical' or 'imaginative'.[89] Even so, despite this vetting and the high proportion of attestations from upper-class and respectable figures who claimed they had seen apparitions, it was still felt within the SPR that the absolute conviction of percipients and was not enough. Gurney further stressed the value of personal interviews in the cause and his frustration at the inability to translate this form of proof to the page.[90] It was argued that a characteristic of the modern empirical ghost story was that it emphasised the value of the *evidence* (literally 'clear to the vision') *of presence*, of both the percipient and the investigator interviewing the percipient on site. Yet ultimately Gurney was extremely reluctant to rely upon this type of private, oral testimony, and this reluctance proved frustrating for him. Indeed, in his correspondence and case notes on the matter, it is significant that Gurney employed the same kind of phenomenologically charged language that ghost-seers were using in their narratives. For instance, in a letter to Eleanor M. Sidgwick he explained:

> It is a bore not to be able to communicate, even to you, the total effect of them [interviews with ghost-seers] on my mind. In almost all instances the case, as I now read it on paper, seems to give a comparatively feeble impression of its remarkableness & genuineness. There has not been much chance of *formally* improving the Evidence; but one gets such a strong impression of the way the percipient's experiences *stood out* ... I don't think this *added* impression, on seeing & cross-examining the witness, could occur so often in a set of exaggerated & trumped up reports. It is very fortifying, but, as I say, it can't be communicated.[91]

In a similar letter to William James in 1887 Gurney mentioned his 'real feeling of irritation & discontent at having been the only outsider who was present, & the only one who had had a chance of getting the impression which *deserved* to be got', and despaired at adequately transferring *his* impression of the witness to the sceptical reader.[92] In the absence of presenting the percipient to the reader in all his/her

---

[89] Barrett, Massey, Moses *et al.*, 'Second Report of the Literary Committee', 48.

[90] See for instance 'We do not expect the results to be as crucial for persons who were not present.' Gurney, Myers and Podmore, *Phantasms*, vol. I, p.29.

[91] Gurney to Eleanor M. Sidgwick, 21 August 1884, SPR Archive, MS 49/Eleanor Sidgwick Correspondence.

[92] Cited in Gauld, *The Founders*, p.106.

authenticity, Gurney sought to tie up other testimonial loopholes that would inevitably be brought against such extraordinary claims. As part of the cumulative strategy he attempted to spread 'responsibility' for a narrative among as many respectable persons as possible, and urged all his correspondents to allow their names to be published, a move which was, by and large, successful, although in cases where this was not permitted the impression was given that the percipient was well known and respected by the SPR and that this should prove authentication enough for sceptical critics.

Building on this reliance for face-to-face communication and the veracity of human testimony, it comes as no surprise that psychical researchers were deeply involved in statistical theory such as pioneering the design of experiments through advanced randomisation techniques. Indeed, they optimistically proclaimed that the ultimate questions of existence 'may hereafter be solved in the market-place, by the Method of Averages and by tables of statistics'.[93] Gurney was alerted to the possibilities in applying advanced experimental methodology to the subject of telepathy by a paper on *suggestion mentale* by Charles Richet that was published in 1884.[94] In their investigations into telepathic phenomena – investigations which in their nature necessitated safeguards and a thorough objectivity if results over and above chance were ever to be distilled and popularised – the SPR constructed a knowledge network, sophisticated for its time, based upon the statistical innovations which would lead to the cherished *accumulation* of the isolated facts mentioned above. Indeed, it was the notion of a distillation of results – the belief that the revolutionary results of psychical research would emerge almost as tiny leftovers from massive trials, rather than as highlighted results – which points to the SPR's engagement with Victorian theories of scientific logic. In this regard Williams has noted how the SPR relied heavily upon John Stuart Mill's 'method of residues' as outlined in his *A System of Logic* (1843).[95] Mill believed that the method of residues was

[93] Barrett, Massey, Moses *et al.*, 'Third Report of the Literary Committee', 113.
[94] On the application of statistics to psychical research see F.Y. Edgeworth, 'The Calculus of Probabilities Applied to Psychical Research I', *PSPR* 3 (1885), 190–9; F.Y. Edgeworth, 'The Calculus of Probabilities Applied to Psychical Research II', *PSPR* 4 (1886–1887), 189–208; John Venn, *The Logic of Chance: An Essay on the Foundations and Province of the Theory of Probability, with Especial Reference to Its Logical Bearings and Its Application to Moral and Social Science, and to Statistics*, 3rd edn (London and New York, 1888), pp.236, 256–7; Ian Hacking, 'Telepathy: Origins of Randomization in Experimental Design', *Isis* 79:3 (1988), 427–51.
[95] Williams, 'The Making of Victorian Psychical Research', p.15.

one of the most important among our instruments of discovery. Of all the methods of investigating laws of nature, this is the most fertile in unexpected results: often informing us of sequences in which neither the cause nor the effect were sufficiently conspicuous to attract of themselves the attention of observers.[96]

In a similar fashion, the SPR's attempt to promote a scientifically valid theory of the ghost relied almost exclusively upon the epistolary input of the ghost-seeing public which, by its sewing-together, could enshrine the *remains* of investigation as causative.

This hope – that the smoking gun of 'evidential residue' was a logical possibility – found its physical expression in the materiality of the ghost-seeing narratives received by the SPR. Oliver Lodge recorded an anec-dote, worthy of quoting in full, which demonstrates the hands-on nature of Gurney's techno-textual practice during this period:

All the furniture in this study, including the floor, was littered over with an orderly collection of extracts, some of them done up into packets, the nucleus of a book which he was preparing, and which ultimately appeared under the title *Phantasms of the Living*, by Edmund Gurney and others. The book struck me as a meaningless collection of ghost-stories which he was classifying and arranging ... Attention to such [gruesome] tales seemed to me a futile occupation for a cultivated man, but Gurney evidently regarded seriously the narratives he had been collecting, and thought he had a clue whereby some of these stray legends or asserted experiences could be rationalised and brought under a coherent scheme.[97]

Here it must be remembered that the form of the ghost story, its physicality and mode of public presentation, were as important as the content in the SPR enterprise. Lodge's comments thus draw attention to the very real connection between the organised chaos collected by the SPR and the 'rationalised' theory of ghosts that would emerge from this structural system. Sidgwick had himself, anonymously at first, defrayed the costs of a new system of reference whereby the hundreds of cases of ghost-seeing were type-printed on slips of paper or cyclostyled for open viewing and critique at the SPR headquarters. This techno-textual process can be compared to Emily Dickinson's practice of sewing her poems together into packets, a practice which one critic has cited as an example of nineteenth-century 'domestic technologies of publication'.[98]

---

[96] John Stuart Mill, *Collected Works of John Stuart Mill*: vol. VII, ed. J.M. Robson (London, 1973–1974), p.398.

[97] Cited in Gordon Epperson, *The Mind of Edmund Gurney* (London, 1997), p.81.

[98] Jeanne Holland, 'Scraps, Stamps, and Cutouts: Emily Dickinson's Domestic Technologies of Publication', in *Cultural Artifacts and the Production of Meaning: The Page, the Image, and the Body*, ed. Margaret J.M. Ezell and Katherine O'Brien O'Keeffe (Ann Arbor, 1994), pp.139–81.

While it was stressed that 'the fact of printing or exhibiting these slips does not imply that any conclusion has been arrived at by the Committee as to the precise value of any one of them', this in itself recognises the authority that the printed word possessed in this context.[99] Thus, in a similar manner to Dickinson, who also denigrated the aura of the published, the SPR's arrangement, cataloguing and editing of their raw material signifies their intentions of engaging with the epistemological marketplace. With the textual technology of referencing established, the spirit of collecting and hoarding could be consciously accepted by the SPR as being an integral part of the ghost-hunting enterprise:

We hope that something of the *collector's* spirit may be aroused in many minds for the service of the inquiry ... We would ask that some of this energy may be transferred to a field where there is still a harvest more ample than the labourers can gather in; namely, the collection of definite psychological facts.[100]

The SPR needed to 'harvest' a culturally contested form of evidence – the 'psychological facts' and statistics of apparitions – and promoted itself as a secure repository for ghost stories, an institute of cultural disembarrassment, it might be said. This was reinforced by the cataloguing system itself whereby specific classes of apparitions were placed together: for example, the 'G' series collected narratives relating to the idea of the 'ghost', that is, phantasms of the dead.[101] A point repeated at length by the SPR was that they could never have enough narratives relating to ghosts, apparitions and veridical hallucinations in particular, further stressing their role as legitimate management for ghost-seeing narratives.

In what way could these managers of the culture of the ghost in late-nineteenth-century Britain 'create a public' in Myers's sense? In what form was this public conceived and understood? As has been noted above, the SPR's intellectual orientation harboured anxieties about the scientific value of oral testimony and valued the technology of the textual

---

[99] Barrett, Massey, Moses *et al.*, 'Second Report of the Literary Committee', 45. After *Phantasms of the Living* was published the cases were no longer printed on slips but instead featured in the *JSPR*. See also Podmore's remarks on the issue. 'The evidential standard to which a narrative must attain before being printed even for consideration by the Literary Committee has never, of course, been rigidly defined. It has naturally risen since the Committee began its work, but even now it should be borne in mind by Members reading the Journal that the Committee do not pledge themselves individually or collectively to any estimate of the value of a story as evidence for supernormal phenomena by printing it for consideration in the Journal.' Frank Podmore, 'Phantasms of the Dead from Another Point of View', *PSPR* 6 (1889–1890), 230.

[100] Barrett, Massey, Moses *et al.*, 'Second Report of the Literary Committee', 51.

[101] Podmore, 'Phantasms of the Dead', 230.

communication. It would be too simplistic to argue that the SPR's archiving of ghost-seeing narratives was an all-out assault upon an oral tradition that was based on informal transmission, indirect occurrence and memorial residue. I would suggest that an illustrative concept is needed to understand the SPR's conflicting and uneasy attitude toward both types of testimony. The sociological aspects of the SPR ghost story we have noted in this section – the 'second world' beneath the manifest, the liberal epistemology and epistolary nature of the ghost-hunting enterprise, the textual technology – are all aspects of a greater format and may be subsumed under a meta-theme which articulates the sense of shared feeling, of a sender/receiver relationship, that comes across in SPR discourse: *community of sensation* will express this psycho-sociological network. This happy phrase was widely used in the SPR literature on mesmerism, hypnotism and telepathy to express the intimate relationship between the operator/agent and the subject/percipient, and is here taken to represent the SPR's *sympathetic* relationship to ghost-seers in the general public.[102]

The expressive relationship behind this notion of a community of sensation, on both a telepathic-scientific and cultural-sociological level, was crucial in the attempted legitimisation of the modern psychical ghost story of the 1880s. For it must be remembered that the empirical ghost story was not an immaterial construct silently experienced in isolation and registered by a single percipient. Rather it was something that was made, pieced together, passed around, told and thought about, forgotten and remembered, and written and received. The SPR could not reject their rapport with a popular culture which held the evidence it needed; it is recalled that Gurney contrasted psychical research from anthropology because his ghost-seers were not passive, but active participants in the research undertaken. In this context it becomes significant that Dickens's self-declared 'communion' with his readership was largely predicated on his oral delivery of narrative.[103] Malcolm Andrews has demonstrated how Dickens's public readings fostered a reciprocal relationship between reader and listener that allowed 'the transmission of feelings, unrefined, spontaneous' to be legitimately passed from receiver to sender and vice versa.[104] Alison Winter has also shown how during

---

[102] See, for instance, William F. Barrett, Edmund Gurney, Frederic W.H. Myers *et al.*, 'First Report of the Committee on Mesmerism', *PSPR* 1 (1882–1883), 224; Podmore, *Modern Spiritualism*, vol. I, pp.132–40.

[103] See Malcolm Andrews, *Charles Dickens and His Performing Selves: Dickens and the Public Readings* (Oxford, 2006).

[104] *Ibid.*, p.18. Dickens once described an idea for a story: 'Open a story by bringing two strongly contrasted places and strongly contrasted sets of people, into the connexion necessary for the story, by means of an electric message. Describe the message – *be the*

the same era mesmeric experiments provided remarkable evidence for the idea of a fluid psyche:

They portrayed thought as the exercise of separate mental faculties. There was a mutual relation between mental and physical powers, and mind and brain were likened to an electric machine. Mesmerism also suggested connections between people that ran contrary to the stereotyped images we have of Victorian bodies as self-contained, discrete in their own skulls and skins. People's identities extended beyond the visible border of the body, flowing into one another.[105]

Feeding into these ideational realities, the SPR's community of sensation would be held together by reciprocally dealing with visible, auditory and tactile apparitions as impressions that were transferred to it, and as such, as phenomena feasible in scientific naturalism. Furthermore, fears of being accused of hysteria, psychological lassitude or even madness were allayed by the SPR which made clear that the type of ghost-seeing it privileged had an external and verifiable origin:

In virtue of their having their real cause *outside* the percipient, and so in a way conveying true information, we may describe death-wraiths and the like as *veridical* hallucinations; but as projections of the percipient's own mind, by which his senses are deluded, we hold them to be altogether on a par with morbid hallucinations.[106]

In this community of sensation, it was made clear, experiences that were typically pathologised by medical and psychiatric critics would not be so summarily diagnosed by the SPR: rather the Society was the natural home for the rational ghost-seer and their ghosts, where empiricism and science were twin gods and trust was codified through their resolutely naturalist theories of ghost-seeing and frequent appeals for more public input.[107]

That it was the ghost story which was the lynchpin of this community of sensation should not be surprising; structurally the ghost story lies betwixt and between oral and literary traditions, traditions that, in this context, need not necessarily be thought of as conflictive.[108] As a genre,

message – flashing along through space – over the earth, and under the sea.' Cited *ibid.*, p.261.
[105] Winter, *Mesmerized*, p.117.
[106] William F. Barrett, C.C. Massey, W. Stainton Moses *et al.*, 'Fourth Report of the Literary Committee: A Theory of Apparitions. Part II', *PSPR* 2 (1884), 168.
[107] See, for instance, Sidgwick, 'Notes on the Evidence', *PSPR* 3 (1885), 149.
[108] See David Vincent, 'The Decline of the Oral Tradition in Popular Culture', in *Popular Culture and Custom in Nineteenth-century England*, ed. Robert D. Storch (London and New York, 1982), pp.20–47.

the ghost story could be equally read silently to oneself and delivered verbally to an audience, given that both activities were performative and, to reiterate a point made above, spectro-nunciative in nature. Indeed both activities are synthesised in Henry James's *The Turn of the Screw* (1898) when the narrator reads to a gathering at Christmas-time a ghost story he once received from a governess. Henry James, of course, dictated *The Turn of the Screw* to his typewriting secretary William MacAlpine: in 1901 his brother William James sat with a blank sheet of paper waiting for the just-deceased Myers to communicate with him from the other world: the sheet remained empty, we are told.[109] The intimate performances of Henry and William James demonstrate how the psychical ghost story, publicly mediated through the SPR, formatted the sociological structure of a community of sensation through an occult epistolary discourse. As Friedrich Nietzsche wrote during this era, 'Our writing tools are also working on our thoughts.'[110]

This structural sensibility should be kept in mind as we turn to examine the most common apparition being described in the *PSPR* – the 'crisis-apparition'. This was manifested in cases where the agent entered an abnormal or traumatic state, that is to say, a mortally danger- ous or dying situation, and unconsciously appeared to the percipient in the form of a hallucination of the senses – possibly due to a pre-existing personal rapport with the percipient or a strong psychical connection with the locality of the occurrence. This type of ghostly occurrence was usually a family affair with, for example, dying sons appearing to their shocked mothers, or else involved the loss of a close friend or acquaint- ance and could thus be verified in death records as to the factual reality of the event of the death. To prove the fact of the ghost-seeing episode was another matter entirely, yet it was the subject of the crisis-apparition that allowed the SPR to make its most sustained, publicised and

---

[109] James complained of MacAlpine's response, or lack thereof, to his tale: ' "Do you know", he said to a friend some years later, "I wrote that story with the intention of terrifying every reader, and in the course of its composition, I thought it would be a total failure. I dictated every word of it to a Scot [MacAlpine], who never from the first to the last betrayed the slightest emotion, nor did he ever make any comment. I might have been dictating statistics. I would dictate some phrase that I thought was blood- curdling; he would quietly take this down, look up at me and in a dry voice say 'What next?' " '. Cited in H. Montgomery Hyde, *Henry James at Home* (London, 1969), p.147. See Thurschwell, *Literature, Technology, and Magical Thinking*, pp.86–114. On William James and Myers see Axel Munthe, *The Story of San Michele* (London, 1991), p.257. On the links between the SPR and *The Turn of the Screw* see E.A. Sheppard, *Henry James and 'The Turn of the Screw'* (Auckland and London, 1974), pp.116–211; Mark Seltzer, 'The Postal Unconscious', *The Henry James Review* 21 (2000), 197–206.

[110] Cited in Friedrich A. Kittler, *Gramophone, Film, Typewriter*, trans. Geoffrey Winthrop- Young and Michael Wutz (Stanford, 1999), p.200.

controversial claim. With the network of a community of sensation established after a few years of research, the SPR could translate late Victorian attitudes on death and dying through the medium of the scientific ghost and could link its interest in thought-transference, telepathy and supernormal communication with the more precarious theories clustered around the moment of death and the possibility of survival. Thus, the SPR forcefully began to advance the rather surprising theory that it was 'phantasms of the living' and not the ghosts of the dead which held the most evidential, experimental and speculative value. The classic representation of this exploration remains *Phantasms of the Living* (1886).[111]

[111] Gauld writes of *Phantasms*: 'Since Gurney's time every serious discussion of crisis-apparitions has taken its start from his classification and arrangement of them. To pass from even the ablest of previous works to *Phantasms of the Living* is like passing from a mediaeval bestiary or herbal to Linnaeus' *Systema Naturae*.' Gauld, *The Founders*, p.164.

Phantasms of the living

A book on apparitions from the perspective of psychical research had been promised from the SPR as early as 1882, and in August 1883 a meeting was held by the Council to discuss what to do with the some 400 cases involving apparitions already collected. A resolution was subsequently passed which authorised Gurney and Myers to compose a book on apparitions which would be published with the support of the SPR.[1] Gurney and Myers were joined in this enterprise by their fellow council member Frank Podmore. The resulting work, *Phantasms of the Living*, was a two-volume collection of 701 cases dating mostly from the later part of the nineteenth century, indicative of the reality of ghost-seeing, mostly visual, and coincidental with the death of persons; at around 1400 pages *Phantasms* is thus a veritable blue book on ghosts and ghost-seeing in late Victorian society. This would be the Society's first major intervention in contemporary print culture, a supernatural compendium in the guise of a collection of cases which were 'spontaneous' – that is cases taken from the field that were non-induced, uninvited and quite unlike the experimental research which had taken place at Dean's Yard, in Brighton, and at Barrett's rooms in Dublin.

Phantasms eschewed the supernatural in favour of the scientific-naturalist. The use of the word 'phantasm' served two functions. Firstly, it could refer to a much wider variety of apparitions that were not necessarily centred on the visual sense such as auditory, tactile or olfactory hallucinations. Phantasm was a word suggestive of a wider field of interest and could be seen as a phenomenological construct designed to integrate the disparate nature of experiential apprehension and expression into one endorsed word. Secondly, the authors emphasised from the beginning that they were concentrating on phantasms of the dying and

---

[1] Barrett, Massey, Moses *et al.*, 'First Report of the Literary Committee', 118; Barrett, Massey, Moses *et al.*, 'Second Report of the Literary Committee', 44.

the just-dead, i.e. phantasms of the living. By calling crisis-apparitions phantasms – that is by connecting them to the hallucination discourse – by dealing with the living, and by linking the topic to what they believed was scientifically proven, both by the quantity and quality of results obtained, the SPR sought to modernise the ghost story within the precepts of scientific naturalism.[2] As Gurney wrote:

> The appearance of an absent person's figure to several spectators at once has had in it something specially startling; and when associated with the idea of death, it has almost inevitably suggested a material or 'ethereal' spirit – an independent travelling ghost. But as soon as the experience is analysed, it is found to involve nothing new or antagonistic to scientific conceptions.[3]

The SPR's impassioned rejection of the use of popular phrases such as 'ghosts', 'supernatural' and 'occult' in their literature fitted in with their agenda of classifying apparitions, which though subjective, as primarily mental phenomena, thus dragging them away from popular spiritualist beliefs and into the realms of scientific possibility.[4]

There was some tension in the SPR Council over the portioning of work on the project: it appears that Myers was disappointed that he was not appointed the main author of the work.[5] Then, as now, it was clear that Gurney was the obvious choice to direct such an enterprise: a fluent writer, he had a cool mind prone to neither the baffled incredulity of Sidgwick nor the poetical and sometimes over-the-top romanticism of Myers.[6] Gurney was a handsome and talented psychical researcher who was acquainted with many important figures in Victorian society, including Samuel Butler and George Eliot.[7] From his earliest years Gurney had strong ambitions as a musician and musical theorist, and a

---

[2] See Ralph Noyes, 'The Other Side of Plato's Wall', in *Ghosts: Deconstruction, Psychoanalysis, History*, ed. Buse and Stott, p.253. For the psychoanalytical use of 'phantasm' to signify the unconscious see Louis Althusser, *Writings on Psychoanalysis: Freud and Lacan*, trans. Jeffrey Mehlman (New York, 1996), pp.103–4.

[3] Gurney, Myers and Podmore, *Phantasms*, vol. II, p.225.

[4] See William F. Barrett, *On the Threshold of the Unseen: An Examination of the Phenomena of Spiritualism and of the Evidence for Survival after Death* (London, 1917), p.152. For an example of spiritualist opposition to the SPR's theory of ghosts see 'X', 'The Telepathic Theory', *Light* 5 (14 March 1885), 121–2; Ghost Club Minutes 4 (1899–1903), 136.

[5] See Gauld, *The Founders*, p.161.

[6] Myers wrote of Gurney, 'while his instincts were mainly aesthetic, his powers were mainly analytic'. Frederic W.H. Myers, 'The Work of Edmund Gurney in Experimental Psychology', *PSPR* 5 (1888–1889), 360. For the differences between Myers and Gurney see John Beer, *Post-Romantic Consciousness: Dickens to Plath* (Basingstoke, 2003), pp.44–76.

[7] It is commonly reported that Eliot was so enchanted by Gurney that she used him as the model for Daniel Deronda. Hall, *The Strange Case of Edmund Gurney*, p.2.

treatise – *The Power of Sound* (1880) – has been lauded as one of the most important contributions to musical aesthetics ever written.[8] However, lack of success in this field prompted career changes to law and medicine, and then psychical research, to which he moved full-time in 1882.[9] As an independently wealthy and respectable figure who was prepared to settle down and make psychical research the focus of his career (a status that was unique in the SPR at the time), Gurney naturally took the lead in most of the SPR projects. Between 1882 and his death in 1888, Gurney managed to serve on multiple committees, to extensively experiment on thought-transference in Brighton, to act as Honorary Secretary of the SPR from 1883, and to edit the *PSPR*. Furthermore, alongside *Phantasms*, he wrote *Tertium Quid* (1887), a two-volume collection of essays on a variety of topics such as pain and the ethics of vivisection, and half a dozen essays on hypnotism contained in the *PSPR* and *Mind*. It is therefore no surprise that William James described Gurney as the '*worker*' of the SPR, who 'exhibited a colossal power of dispatching business and getting through drudgery of the most repulsive kind'.[10] Fraser Nicol carried out a valuable informal survey on who actually performed the interviews contained in *Phantasms* and found that of the 185 occasions where the interviewer was named, Gurney held 105 interviews, Podmore 30, Sidgwick 14, and Myers 5 – a finding which attests to the remarkable investment which Gurney personally placed in the *Phantasms* project.[11] A manic-depressive throughout his life, Gurney frequently became sombre in the midst of this huge SPR workload and told friend and fellow-sufferer William James that 'the mystery of the Universe and the indefensibility of human suffering' were always on his mind – a theme that is frequently encountered in *Tertium Quid*.[12]

Phantasms was originally intended for publication in 1884, however the sheer scope of the project proved too much and the labours continued until 1886. The work is a huge compendium of tales, mostly from Britain, of many different hues with speculative comments interspersed by Gurney and book-ended by a long introduction and conclusion from Myers. The SPR set huge store by the evidential quality of the material collected through laborious correspondence, the double checking of newspapers and death registers, and witness-hunting all over Britain and the Empire. Indeed, the SPR Archive in the University Library,

[8] Rollo Myers, 'Edmund Gurney's "The Power of Sound"', *Music and Letters* 53 (1972), 36.
[9] Epperson, *The Mind of Edmund Gurney*, p.53.
[10] James, *Essays in Psychical Research*, p.92.
[11] Nicol, 'The Founders of the S.P.R.', 354.   [12] Cited in Gauld, *The Founders*, p.156.

Cambridge, contains a large Bradshaw's railway map of the British Isles with some seventy towns and cities, from Inverness to St Ives, marked in red ink as having been visited by investigators seeking to authenticate ghost-seeing narratives. This feeling of professional rigour and evidential legitimacy was maintained by the high degree of self-awareness of the problems of testimony among the researchers in *Phantasms*: indeed, chapter 4 of *Phantasms* was devoted to a meta-criticism of the evidence for spontaneous telepathy, including a tour-de-force history of the witchcraft craze and the fallacies of testimony it illustrated. Such was the anticipation regarding the book that Sidgwick, as President of the SPR, considered the publication of *Phantasms* the 'real crisis in the history of the Society'.[13] Similarly aware of the critical and landmark nature of the work, Myers introduced the book by urging a kind of great rebellion among percipients in society, calling on people to resist the taboo that existed on not investigating ghostly phenomena. He also proposed psychical research as a domain in between science and theology where the distorted optics of both would be corrected:

It should surely be needless in the present day to point out that no attempt to discourage inquiry into any given subject which strongly interests mankind, will in reality divert attention from the topic thus tabooed. The *savant* or the preacher may influence the readers of scientific hand-books, or the members of church congregations, but outside that circle the subject will be pursued with the more excited eagerness because regulating knowledge and experienced guidance are withdrawn.

And thus it has been with our supernormal phenomena. The men who claim to have experienced them have not been content to dismiss them as unseasonable or unimportant. They have not relegated them into the background of their lives as readily as the physiologist has relegated them into a few paragraphs at the end of a chapter. On the contrary, they have brooded over them, distorted them, misinterpreted them. Where *savants* have minimised, *they* have magnified, and the perplexing modes of marvel which the textbooks ignore, have become, as it were, the ganglia from which all kinds of strange opinions ramify and spread.[14]

Again, the SPR was represented as a secure and legitimate bureau for the supernormal experiences of the general public: its liminal status – between religion and science – offered the kind of 'regulating knowledge and experienced guidance' which other epistemic structures could not. In this context Luckhurst has written that the narratives contained in *Phantasms* constitute 'a set of *doxai*, a shadow-record of beliefs and semi-legitimate knowledges that dealt with material that failed to find sanction

[13] Sidgwick and Sidgwick, *Henry Sidgwick: A Memoir*, p.406.
[14] Gurney, Myers and Podmore, *Phantasms*, vol. I, p.lviii.

in orthodox channels of information'.[15] Freed from scientific superstition, psychical research could emerge as a kind of heterodox science of the educated classes and could provide the possibility of a factual basis for beliefs formerly confined to religious or occult discourses or the cultural sphere of oral storytelling. Yet, as shall be demonstrated, this liminal status of psychical research implied a very different relationship with revealed religion than scientific naturalism, especially as expressed in the disciplines of geology and biology, had so far cultivated.[16]

Before examining the subject of crisis-apparitions, *Phantasms* surveyed examples of a specific genre of ghost-seeing that seemed to overlap somewhat with the evidence collected in the study of thought-transference and telepathy. These cases, located somewhere between the spontaneous and the experimental, involved an agent consciously willing the transference of an image or idea to the percipient, who was in a normal state and at a distance. An account given by Stainton Moses provides an fascinating description of how one might make oneself into an apparition:

One evening early last year, I resolved to try to appear to Z, at some miles distance. I did not inform him beforehand of the intended experiment; but retired to rest shortly before midnight with thoughts intently fixed on Z, with whose room and surroundings, however, I was quite unacquainted. I soon fell asleep, and awoke next morning unconscious of anything having taken place. On seeing Z a few days afterwards, I inquired, 'Did anything happen at your rooms on Saturday night?' 'Yes', replied he, 'a great deal happened. I had been sitting over the fire with M, smoking and chatting. About 12.30 he rose to leave, and I let him out myself. I returned to the fire to finish my pipe, when I saw you sitting in the chair just vacated by him. I looked intently at you, and then took up a newspaper to assure myself I was not dreaming, but on laying it down I saw you still there. While I gazed without speaking, you faded away. Though I imagined you must be fast asleep in bed at that hour, yet you appeared dressed in your ordinary garments, such as you usually wear every day.' 'Then my experiment seems to have succeeded', said I. 'The next time I come, ask me what I want, as I had fixed on my mind certain questions I intended to ask you, but I was probably waiting for an invitation to speak'.

A few weeks later the experiment was repeated with equal success, I as before, not informing Z when it was made. On this occasion he not only questioned me on the subject which was at that time under very warm discussion between us, but detained me by the exercise of his will some time after I had intimated a desire to leave. This fact, when it came to be communicated to me, seemed to account for the violent and somewhat peculiar headache which marked the morning following the experiment; at least I remarked at the time there was no apparent cause for the unusual headache; and, as on

---

[15] Luckhurst, *The Invention of Telepathy*, p.151.
[16] Gurney, Myers and Podmore, *Phantasms*, vol. I, p.lii.

the former occasion, no recollection remained of the event, or seeming event, of the preceding night.[17]

It is notable here that the concept of 'will' informs both the actions of both agent and percipient: Moses 'willed' that he would appear, while 'Z' managed to use the powers of *his* will to detain the apparition against its own will. A similar case, cited in *Phantasms*, involved the spontaneous appearance of 'Mr. S.H.B.' to some acquaintances.

On a certain Sunday evening in November, 1881, having been reading of the great power which the human will is capable of exercising, I determined with the whole force of my being that I would be present in spirit in the front bedroom on the second floor of a house situated at 22, Hogarth Road, Kensington, in which room slept two ladies of my acquaintance, viz., Miss L.S.V. and Miss E.C.V., aged respectively 25 and 11 years.[18]

In this instance it is clear that the phantasmisation of the self took on the trappings of a parlour game, with the ladies reportedly terrified to see the apparition of Mr. S.H.B. indiscreetly standing by their bedside. Indeed the testimony of Mr. S.H.B. tends to suggest that he had acquired a distinct advantage in his social relations with the opposite sex:

Besides exercising my power of volition very strongly, I put forth an effort which I cannot find words to describe. I was conscious of a mysterious influence of some sort permeating in my body, and had a distinct impression that I was exercising some force with which I had hitherto been unacquainted, but which I can now at certain times set in motion at will.[19]

Mr. S.H.B. seems to have haunted the ladies in question, who signed their surname 'Verity' in the testimonials: he reported that in 1882 he fell into a mesmeric sleep with the image of a bedroom at a house in Clarence Road in his mind where Miss Verity and her two sisters resided, intending to appear in the bedroom at 12 p.m. and remain there 'until I had made my spiritual presence perceptible to the inmates of that room'. Subsequently the married sister of Miss V., Mrs. L., reported to Mr. S.H.B. that she had encountered his apparition at 12 p.m.:

when she was wide awake, she had seen me enter the bedroom and walk round to where she was sleeping, and take her hair (which is very long) into my hand. She also told me that the apparition took hold of her hand and gazed intently into it.[20]

---

[17] *Ibid.*, pp.103–4.   [18] *Ibid.*, p.104.   [19] *Ibid.*, p.105.
[20] *Ibid.*, pp.106–7. This case was used by the *Saturday Review* as an example of the impropriety of thought-transference: 'There is a certain person, it seems, who is able, by going thoughtfully to sleep, to make his spook appear to certain young ladies of his acquaintance after they have retired to rest. Not only so, but it has been known, on more

Of course, these cases of self-phantasmisation raised curious questions about the nature of the self and its relationship with the conscious mind. If Stainton Moses could appear at a distance as himself, with prepared questions, did this not suggest the existence of a soul or spirit capable of leaving the earthly body, whilst also retaining the essence of its personality? If Mr. S.H.B. could project his phantasm, seemingly at will, to ladies he was connected with did this not suggest the discovery of a new culture of sympathy between individuals which could transcend the limitations of space, and very possibly the ultimate limitation of death? What these instances demonstrate is that the community of sensation was much more than a spontaneous phenomenon which, it was believed, could only occur in critical situations; rather, as these cases illustrate, such a rapport was considered part of an experimental projection of the human personality within the realms of everyday life, radically investing sociability with new public meanings and, in the case of Mr. S.H.B., new threats to privacy and distinct selfhood.

Phantasms included many such stories that resembled cases of experimental thought-transference in the banality of the impression received. Cases of non-lethal telepathic hallucinations included one contributed by John Ruskin of a woman who reported being struck on the lip at the same time as her absent husband, the case of a clergyman who 'knew' when his daughter arrived safely in India, and the case of a father who had a feeling that his child had fallen out of the bed many miles away.[21] It should be noted from the examples of anxiety displayed in these cases that received feelings of pain and apprehension were more readily reported to the SPR than feelings of pleasure and enjoyment.[22] Myers related that while collecting such cases of apparitions, the authors were struck by the number of veridical, as opposed to morbid or merely casual, hallucinations or alleged apparitions that occurred near the moment of a death. Following this they made the link between these crisis-apparitions and the on-going experiments in thought-transference. The following may be taken as a typical case collected in *Phantasms* and presented as part of a cumulative argument in favour of the scientific ghost:

On Thursday, the 16th day of December, 1875, I had been for some little time on a visit at my brother-in-law's and sister's house near London. I was in good

occasions than one, to go to the length of pulling their hair. But if any spook can be so indiscreet as this, it seems to follow that experimental telepathy might produce compromising results.' 'Spookical Research', *Saturday Review of Politics, Literature, Science, and Art* 62 (1886), 650. For a similar 'compromising' episode involving telepathy see W.B. Yeats's account in Ghost Club Minutes 7 (1910–1917), 126–8.

[21] Gurney, Myers and Podmore, *Phantasms*, vol. I, pp.188, 192, 196–7.
[22] *Ibid.*, pp.242–3.

health, but from the morning and throughout the day I felt unaccountably depressed and out of spirits, which I attributed to the gloominess of the weather. A short time after lunch, about 2 o'clock, I thought I would go up to the nursery to amuse myself with the children, and try to recover my spirits. The attempt failed, and I returned to the dining-room, where I sat by myself, my sister being engaged elsewhere. The thought of Mr.——— came into my mind, and suddenly, with my eyes open, as I believe, for I was not feeling sleepy, I seemed to be in a room in which a man was lying dead in a small bed. I recognised the face at once as that of Mr.———, and felt no doubt that he was dead, and not asleep only. The room appeared to be bare and without carpet or furniture. I cannot say how long the appearance lasted. I did not mention the appearance to my sister or brother-in-law at the time. I tried to argue with myself that there could be nothing in what I had seen, chiefly on the ground that from what I knew of Mr.———'s circumstances it was most improbable that, if dead, he would be in a room in so bare and unfurnished a state. Two days afterwards, on December 18th, I left my sister's house for home. About a week after my arrival, another of my sisters read out of the daily papers the announcement of Mr.———'s death, which had taken place abroad, and on December 16th, the day on which I had seen the appearance.

I have since been informed that Mr.——— had died in a small village hospital in a warm foreign climate, having been suddenly attacked with an illness whilst on his travels.[23]

This case contains all the hallmarks of the psychical ghost story; depression of percipient – spontaneous hallucination – assurance of wakefulness – lack of documentation or witness verification – textual announcement of death – death of agent suddenly and at a distance from the percipient. It was made quite clear that while Myers and Gurney already believed telepathy proved on the basis of the 1882–1883 tests and subsequent researches, *Phantasms* would aim to prove it all the more in a sphere, which although nunciative, had not been previously connected in any scientific fashion with notions of thought-transference. It was through the evidence of cases such as this that it was hoped the scientific community would be persuaded that ghost-seeing was a natural and verifiable occurrence in the physical world.

This collection of cases of apparitions and analysis of ghost-seeing would be a sociological test case of the telepathic hypothesis in a format that was spontaneous or unconscious, rather than induced or experimental. It was assumed that in most cases of crisis-apparitions the agent was unconscious of the ghostly connection with the percipient, although in some, like the experimental cases mentioned above, the percipient was on the agent's mind. The connection between the telepathic theory and unconscious, or automatic actions was championed by Myers who

---

[23] *Ibid.*, pp.265–6.

placed the scope and significance of the telepathic discovery alongside the discovery of the unconscious: 'In a certain sense it may be said that this hidden action of one mind on another comes next in order of psychical discovery to the hidden action of the mind within itself.'[24] Yet as *Phantasms* shows, the unconscious discovered by the SPR was decidedly thanatropic in tone, for the book is drenched in death and dying: over half the cases included dealt with an attested occasion when a percipient's ghost-seeing experience either coincided with or shortly followed the death of an agent.[25]

Thus among the 668 cases of spontaneous telepathy in this book, 399 … are death-cases, in the sense that the percipient's experience either coincided with or very shortly followed the agent's death; while in 25 more cases the agent's condition, at the time of the percipient's experience, was one of serious illness which in a few hours or a few days terminated in death. Nor, in this connection, can I avoid once more referring to the large number of cases in which the event that befell the agent has been death (or a very near approach to it) by *drowning or suffocation.*[26]

As this quote demonstrates, *Phantasms* is a primary source for late Victorian attitudes to death and dying, and it is the purpose of the remainder of this section to follow the SPR in its attempt to map out this ghost-seeing unconscious within the remit of scientific naturalism.

With such a community of sensation operating in Britain it is no surprise to see the theme of international telepathic communication coming out strongly, especially bearing in mind the huge numbers of British citizens who emigrated to the Empire in this period.[27] Recent research has shown how the content of psychopathological delusions can change through time and can respond to shifts in social, scientific and political contexts.[28] The fact that late Victorian Britain imagined itself at the core of an imperial community found expression in the content of a large number of the psychical ghost stories of the period. *Phantasms* quite literally had to map out certain cases of ghost-seeing with many narratives involving the death

---

[24] *Ibid.*, p.lxii.
[25] 'Impressions of death, illness, or accident are the almost unbroken rule.' *Ibid.*, pp.242–3.
[26] Gurney, Myers and Podmore, *Phantasms*, vol. II, p.26.
[27] Between 1815 and 1914 around 16 million people emigrated from Britain to the Empire. See Stephen Constantine, 'Introduction: Empire Migration and Imperial Harmony', in *Emigrants and Empire: British Settlement in the Dominions between the Wars*, ed. Stephen Constantine (Manchester and New York, 1990), p.1. See also Noyes, 'The Other Side of Plato's Wall', p.252.
[28] B. Škodlar, M.Z. Dernovsek and M. Kocmur, 'Psychopathology of Schizophrenia in Ljubljana (Slovenia) from 1881 to 2000: Changes in the Content of Delusions in Schizophrenic Patients Related to Various Sociopolitical, Technical and Scientific Changes', *International Journal of Social Psychiatry* 54:2 (2008), 101–11.

of an agent far from Britain, proving even more strongly to psychical researchers the power of telepathic rapport to traverse huge amounts of space in order to reach its target. This vast geographic diaspora of potentially dying British persons comes out in the cosmopolitanism of *Phantasms* with ghost-seeing cases involving the apparitions of agents from Australia, South Africa, Burma and India, all *ipso facto* informing the percipient of their demise days before they could otherwise have known.[29] In long distance cases such as these, death compacts, the practice of making a promise to notify or appear to a loved one at the moment of death, proved a common occurrence among friends, lovers and relatives, further enhancing rituals of personal death-arrangements that were not mediated through traditional religious practices or expressions.[30]

While the metaphor of telegraphy had been present in the spiritualist discourse from its inception, the telegram as a nunciative object became a central constituent of the psychical ghost story as part of a general uploading of the dying body into a wider international tele-technological network attuned to the demands of instant knowledge and notification of crisis.[31] Here the body as an intuitive telephonic system in itself replaced a religious faith-system limited to a locality. In a recent study Molly McGarry has argued for the importance of epistolary exchange in American spiritualist circles as a means of consolation and connection.[32] In an era of emergent individualism and social atomisation, distance from the other has increased the subject's pain of loss and necessitated new methods of cultivating a reassuring intimacy. Sending and receiving letters had, even before the development of modern spiritualism, served

---

[29] See, for instance, Gurney, Myers and Podmore, *Phantasms*, vol. I, pp.324–5, 336, 375–6, 378–9, 551–2.

[30] See *ibid.*, pp.527, 531–2. Handley argues that colonial ghost-seeing in the eighteenth century 'functioned as emotional manifestations of anxiety and absence following enforced separation from well-loved friends and family, or following death'. Handley, *Visions of an Unseen World*, p.191.

[31] On this theme see Luckhurst, *The Invention of Telepathy*, pp.148–80; Warner, *Phantasmagoria*, p.248; Mark Seltzer, *Bodies and Machines* (New York and London, 1992); Laura Otis, 'The Metaphoric Circuit: Organic and Technological Communication in the Nineteenth Century', *Journal of the History of Ideas*, 63:1 (2002), 105–28; Mark Twain, 'Mental Telegraphy', in *Literature and Science in the Nineteenth Century: An Anthology*, ed. Laura Otis (Oxford, 2002), pp.99–103; Stefan Andriopoulos, 'Psychic Television', *Critical Inquiry* 31:3 (2005), 618–37; Jeremy Stolow, 'Techno-religious Imaginaries: On the Spiritual Telegraph and the Circum-Atlantic World of the Nineteenth Century', in *Institute on Globalization and the Human Condition Working Paper Series*, ed. William Coleman (Hamilton, ON, 2006). Myers was especially interested in wireless telegraphy and even 'stimulated' Oliver Lodge to some of his discoveries in the area. Gauld, *The Founders*, p.276.

[32] Molly McGarry, *Ghosts of Futures Past: Spiritualism and the Cultural Politics of Nineteenth-century America* (Berkeley and London, 2008), p.25.

this inter-subjective purpose, a situation that was most lyrically described by Nathaniel Hawthorne in a letter of 1839 to his fiancée Sophia Peabody:

I feel as if my letters were sacred, because they are written from my spirit to your spirit. I wish it were possible to convey them to you by other than earthly messengers – to convey them directly into your heart, with the warmth of mine still lingering in them. When we shall be endowed with our spiritual bodies, I think they will be so constituted, that we may send thoughts and feelings any distance, in no time at all, and transfuse them warm and fresh into the consciousness of those whom we love. Oh what a bliss it would be, at this moment; if I could be conscious of some purer feeling, some more delicate sentiment, some lovelier fantasy, than could possibly have had its birth in my own nature, and therefore be aware that my Dove was thinking through my mind and feeling through my heart! Try – some evening when you are alone and happy, and when you are most conscious of loving me and being loved by me – and see if I do not possess this power already. But, after all, perhaps it is not wise to intermix fantastic ideas with the reality of our affection. Let us content ourselves to be earthly creatures, and hold communion of spirit in such modes as are ordained to us – by letters (dipping our pens as deep as may be into our hearts); by heartfelt words, when they can be audible; by glances – through which medium spirits do really seem to talk in their own language – and by holy kisses, which I do think have something supernatural in them.[33]

Hawthorne's dream of an instant, intimate communion of one self with another, invisible self, demonstrates how Victorian culture already possessed the substructure or grid-system from which later notions of actual thought-transference could emerge. *Phantasms* used this framework established by the postal service, and in the age of telegraphy illustrated how the intuitive body could compete with contemporary technology in the speed of the message-delivering service, functioning as a regulator of melancholy, anxiety and grief. One case demonstrates this upgrading of the percipient's encounter with loved ones in the world:

During the whole afternoon I remained in this state of dismal wretchedness. All at once a telegram arrived from home, informing me that my grandmother was taken very ill, and that she was earnestly longing for me. There I had the solution of the riddle. Nevertheless from that hour my melancholy gradually decreased, and in spite of the telegram it completely disappeared in the course of the afternoon. In the evening I received a second message, to the effect that the danger was over. In this way the second phenomenon, the rapid decrease of my wretchedness – a circumstance which in itself was surprising, inasmuch as the melancholy should naturally rather have *increased* after the receipt of the first

[33] Nathaniel Hawthorne, *The Letters, 1813–1843*, ed. Thomas Woodson, L. Neal Smith and Norman Holmes Pearson (Columbus, 1984), pp.294–5. See also David M. Henkin, *The Postal Age: The Emergence of Modern Communications in Nineteenth-century America* (Chicago and London, 2006).

news – received its explanation. For the afternoon was just the time when the change in the patient's condition for the better took place; and the danger to her life once over, her yearning for my presence had decreased; while simultaneously my anxiety was dispelled.[34]

Of note here is the percipient's rhetoric of an emotional equilibrium, a bodily economics which can be affected by the crisis far away as it ebbs and flows: the percipient's melancholy 'gradually decreased' and 'completely disappeared' when it should have '*increased*'. Just as Hawthorne speculated on the bliss of being 'thought through' an intimate, in this case the community of sensation between the agent and the percipient has been envisaged through the rhetoric of regulation and the 'riddle' of emotional dis-equilibrium elevated to an input–output issue.

While crisis-apparitions defied the limits of geography and distance to make themselves known to percipients, the SPR also received some contrasting cases of intimacy at very close proximity. An example of one such case would be the following of a married couple that recounted how they dreamt the same dream whilst in bed together:

The dream you ask me to narrate took place in 1856, at Neuilly, near Paris. I had a vivid impression that I was dying, and awoke with a start to hear my husband sobbing so painfully that I aroused him to ask what was the matter, upon which he said that he had dreamt that I was just on the point of dying. These two dreams must have occurred to both of us simultaneously, and seem to me to be a curious instance of thought-transference. I may add that there was such great sympathy between my husband and myself that, one day not long before his death, I well remember his saying that we should soon not need the communication of *speech*.[35]

Here, again, we find evidence that the sympathetic community between two people is understood to such a degree that the limitations of the human senses are transcended: lovers have become members of one another. In cases of distance, as in cases of close proximity, what remains the same is the community of sensation that is held to exist between friends and family. Such interventions of the supernatural within loving relationships continued to appear in *Phantasms* with the almost playful organisation of death compacts between people who wished to appear to a loved one as they died, a genre of ghost-seeing which recalls the self-phantasmisation of the living mentioned above. The SPR recorded a few cases of this sort in *Phantasms* and indeed many of the leading members

---

[34] Gurney, Myers and Podmore, *Phantasms*, vol. I, p.274.
[35] *Ibid.*, p.316. For a later example of the same situation see Bernard J. Duffy, *Food for Thought: A Treatise on Memory, Dreams and Hallucinations* (London and Dublin, 1944), p.116.

of the Society made promises of this kind, pledging to colleagues that they would attempt to return from the other-side to provide proof of existence after death if proof was to be had. It becomes clear through reading *Phantasms* that the figure of the ghost presumed the existence of new methods of proving and perceiving intimate relations. The telepathic theory of ghost-seeing, particular to the SPR, not only suggested the apprehension of a loved one passing away, but also the targeting of the percipient as a person with whom the agent had a special rapport, sympathy and affection. It was in this context of transgressing the boundaries between self and non-self, and between life and death, that Barrett suggested that telepathy could serve a revolutionary part in fundamentally altering the way that people interact and communicate with each other, as if the world were governed by a politics of intimacy, or as I have suggested, a community of sensation:

If we were involuntarily sharers in one another's pleasures and pains, the brotherhood of the race would not be a pious aspiration or a strenuous effort, but the reality of all others most vividly before us; *the* factor in our lives which would dominate all our conduct. What would be the use of a luxurious mansion at the West End and Parisian cooks if all the time the misery and starvation of our fellow creatures at the East End were telepathically part and parcel of our daily lives? On the other hand what bright visions and joyous emotions would enter into many dreary and loveless lives if this state of human responsiveness were granted to the race![36]

Thinking about telepathy provided psychical researchers with the framework for revolutionising the concept of community, for by mapping out the range and depth of psychological action at a distance they hypothesised the existence of a spectral self capable of confirming intimacy across space and time. As the physicist and psychical researcher E.E. Fournier d'Albe wrote:

the 'self' of the socially normal man is not limited to his own body or wealth. It is a varying entity, extending over other persons 'near and dear' to him, acquiring perhaps a wider range, possibly co-extensive with his race or state or nation.[37]

The fact that we can never experience death, but are forced to deal with the loss of the other, is one of the main origins of community, of social and spiritual cohesion in the face of traumatic atomisation. The philosopher Jean-Luc Nancy has argued that capitalist modernity leaves the individual exposed in relation to the death of the other but also offers a new revelation. Community

---

[36] Barrett, *On the Threshold of the Unseen*, pp.294–5.
[37] E.E. Fournier d'Albe, *New Light on Immortality* (London, 1908), pp.41–2.

is the presentation of the finitude and the irredeemable excess that make up finite being: its death, but also its birth, and only the community can present me my birth, and along with it the impossibility of my reliving it, as well as the impossibility of my crossing over into death.[38]

From the themes that have been dealt with so far it should be clear that, as a shared discourse, a supernormal community of sensation based upon an investigative framework, the SPR's establishment of the psychical ghost story was a sociological enterprise designed to locate and map out the possibilities of 'community spirit' in the renovated world of spectral modernity. Indeed Gurney extended the concept of rapport from one signifying a pre-existing channel of transference between kin or loved ones to a concept of sensual community, 'consisting not in old-established sympathy, but in similarity of immediate mental occupation' – a concept more amenable to interpretations of collective ghost-seeing. Barrett's utopian representation reminds one that the boundary between science and science-fiction was an inherently fluid one in the *fin-de-siècle* period, particularly within the SPR which was associated with many pioneering physicists and experimental scientists.[39] Telepathy was being conceptualised in an era when science-fiction was becoming scientific-fact at breakneck speed and the technological revolution of telephones, telegraphs, phonographs, photographs, x-rays and spectroscopes posited the real magic of communication, the capture of reality and visions of the invisible. It is therefore no surprise to learn that telepathic and ghost-seeing speculations frequently took place through the metaphors of telecommunications. For instance, Barrett compared the scientific hostility to the telepathic hypothesis with the discovery of the telephone: 'Thus for anyone to deny the possibility of the electronic telephone, as some scientific sceptics did in my hearing in 1877, it is of no importance compared with competent witnesses who have seen and heard the telephone.'[40] In a context such as this the idea of 'phantasms of the living' did not seem such a bizarre notion, at least to the young, ambitious and intellectually radical SPR leadership eager to make an impact in mainstream science. The sensuous/spiritual community mapped out by the SPR emerged in tandem with spectral technology, but was fundamentally a response to the threat of individual isolation in

[38] Jean-Luc Nancy, *The Inoperative Community*, trans. Peter Connor, Lisa Garbus, Michael Holland and Simona Sawhney (Minneapolis and London, 1990), p.15.

[39] Erwin N. Hiebert, 'The Transformation of Physics', in *Fin de Siècle and Its Legacy*, ed. Mikuláš Teich and Roy Porter (Cambridge, 1990), pp.235–53; Richard Panek, *The Invisible Century: Einstein, Freud, and the Search for Hidden Universes* (London, 2004); Noakes, 'The "Bridge" ', 446–55.

[40] Barrett, *On the Threshold of the Unseen*, p.23.

a world of death, a world where community was based upon regular, face-to-face communication with the living.

However, in order to promote a naturalistic interpretation of ghost-seeing Gurney was forced to compartmentalise death and the moment of death:

We are, of course, accustomed to regard death as a completely unique and incomparably important event; and it might thus seem, on a superficial glance, that if spontaneous telepathy is possible, and the conditions and occasions of its occurrence are in question, no more likely occasion than death could be suggested. But on closer consideration, we are reminded that the actual psychical condition that immediately precedes death often does not seem to be specially or at all remarkable, still less unique; and that it is this actual psychical condition – while it lasts, and not after it has ceased – that really concerns us here. Our subject is phantasms *of the living*: we seek the conditions of the telepathic impulse on the hither side of the dividing line, in the closing passage of life; not in that huge negative fact – the apparent cessation or absence of life – on which the common idea of death and of its momentous importance is based.[41]

The problem that the SPR faced was how to distinguish between the dead and the quasi-dead – how to distinguish between the cessation of life and of the cessation of its psychical, unconscious effects on the living. As a result, Gurney implemented a temporal range of twelve hours from the moment of death in which the phantasm would remain within the remit of naturalism and remain a phantasm of the *living*. The promotion of this time-range was due, firstly, to uncertainty about the exact time of the 'crisis' experience, and the fact that the different time-zones in the Empire often confused matters further. Gurney's theory presumed that the telepathic impression could remain latent for hours or days within the unconscious mind before making itself known – materialising, as it were – through the mechanism of subjective hallucination. This was given experimental support by Gurney's thought-transference tests in the early 1880s in which the agent would, for example, taste some salt, only to find that the percipient's consciousness of the taste sensation sometimes became latent or deferred.[42] It was believed that the emergence of the latent hallucination to the conscious mind could be triggered by a variety of situations such as the quiet, darkness and psychological interiority which characterised the state of sleep, or the impression of a locality, or house, associated with the agent. Secondly, by allotting a time-frame to the moment of death and the moment of

[41] Gurney, Myers and Podmore, *Phantasms*, vol. I, p.230.   [42] *Ibid.*, p.56.

ghost-seeing, Gurney sought to break up the supernaturalism of the ghost story and place it as a phenomenological event within a rationalised temporal culture. While this echoed Arthur Schopenhauer's theory of latency, Gurney's theory must be understood in terms of the unconscious anxieties of late Victorian culture where death was no longer a simple event, but rather a moment in time that became steadily broken up, fractured and resisted as the century progressed, and thus invested with new conflicting sensibilities.[43] Even the fact of a person's death in the nineteenth century was something which was never absolutely certain. The London Society for the Prevention of Premature Burial was founded in 1896 at the end of a century which witnessed the development of a whole range of bizarre tests and the widespread manufacture of in-grave gadgets and security coffins designed to prevent the horror of being buried alive.[44] As I shall now suggest, this fracturing of the fact of death was analogous to the fracturing and atomisation of the dying individual.

Phantasms argued that contrary to popular conceptions apparitions were not typically seen after a murder or other crimes – there was little evidence for 'haunting' or vengeful ghosts in the book. Rather the most common type of ghost-seeing experience involved the simple death of a loved one recorded in a basic epistolary transcript with no overt references to religion, occultism or spiritualism. In the absence of such reference points it becomes clear that apparitions were assuming a leading role as unconscious compensations in the face of the more traditional death rituals of the mid-nineteenth century. As one historian has put it: 'Knowing the dead could not return to haunt the living, the Victorian middle classes began to haunt the dead, visiting them in cemeteries and communicating with them through spiritualist mediums.'[45] While this may appear a simple argument at first glance – that the ghost was the figuration of death-denial – one should not ignore the SPR's argument that these cases of ghost-seeing were not coincidental but actually *caused*, in a telepathic manner, by the dying person. For this assertion to attain any cultural acceptance changes in attitudes

---

[43] Schopenhauer, *Parerga and Paralipomena*, vol. I, p.235. On the shifting attitude to death see Ivan Illich, *Limits to Medicine: Medical Nemesis: The Expropriation of Health* (London, 1976), pp.189–94.

[44] See Jan Bondeson, *Buried Alive: The Terrifying History of Our Most Primal Fear* (New York and London, 2001). It is significant that Joseph Taylor, the author of a book which ridiculed the fear of ghosts as childish and superstitious soon after wrote *The Danger of Premature Interment* (1816).

[45] John R. Gillis, *A World of Their Own Making: Myth, Ritual, and the Quest for Family Values* (New York, 1996), p.210.

towards the dead were needed. Philippe Ariès provides evidence of just such a change in attitudes: he argues that in order for belief in the communication with spirits to spread in society the traditional idea of the *homo totus* – or man as one unit, body and soul – had to be challenged by the counter-idea of the soul as being independent of the body: 'The soul then became the essential principle of the individual, his immortal part.'[46] This was, of course, something which was a basic tenet in the various forms of spiritualism and occultism in late Victorian England, especially among theosophists who focused much of their teachings on the activities of the soul on the so-called 'astral plane'.[47] Alongside this shift in focus, Ariès proposes that during the nineteenth century a 'revolution in feeling' occurred in which new relations of affectivity between loved ones meant that the 'death of the other' was no longer tolerated. Indeed, it caused a 'crisis' in the self, 'made the separation of death more painful and invited the bereaved person to compensate for his loss through memory or some more or less precise form of survival'.[48]

If the argument of Ariès is followed and a 'crisis' situation is ascribed to the bereaved subject, then the psychical ghost story, as expressed through cases of crisis apparition, begins to emerge as a distinctly socio-historical construction based upon modern expressions of psychological loss.[49] In this way crisis-apparitions reflect the 'dying to know' attitude consistent with the scientific epistemology of the period.[50] By adhering to a naturalistic orientation, demonstrated in the pseudo-scientific theory of latency, *Phantasms* charted a complex terrain in which the unconscious desires and fears of ghost-seers suggest that the community of sensation, as a new type of public-private intimate relationship, offered an outlet for expressing the fractured and conflicting emotions mentioned by Ariès within the framework of a progressive knowledge network: philosophy and 'learning to die' were once again synonymous with each other. While *Phantasms* was loath to state it as such, the underlying message of ghost-seers who experienced crisis-apparitions was one which sought a science of the soul, or at least a naturalistic system that allowed for the nunciative influence of

---

[46] Philippe Ariès, *The Hour of Our Death*, trans. Helen Weaver (London, 1983), p.456. See also Swedenborg, *Heaven and Hell*, pp.337–43.

[47] See for instance Charles W. Leadbeater, *The Astral Plane: Its Scenery, Inhabitants and Phenomena* (London, 1895).

[48] Ariès, *The Hour of Our Death*, p.471.

[49] Ariès believed that due to the absence of the idea of purgatory, the dead were more likely to be seen as 'pseudoliving' in Protestant rather than Catholic environments. *Ibid.*, pp.462–3.

[50] George Levine, *Dying to Know: Scientific Epistemology and Narrative in Victorian England* (Chicago and London, 2002).

disembodied persons, even if the message given was merely the self-reflexive visual statement: 'I am dead.' Here the medium, popularly transmitted, advertises itself.

Yet to what extent did Protestantism provide fertile ground for a type of ghost-seeing experience that implied a naturalistic or psychical explanation, that is, what the percipient would consider a non-superstitious interpretation of the crisis-apparition? Although from the late seventeenth century there had been a considerable dissipation in hostility towards the idea of non-demonic ghosts and prayers for the departed, Protestant churches, from Anglicanism to Nonconformism, continued to lay down strictures upon how the living could be intimate with the dead. The issue of theodicy, especially following the mass death of World War I, caused many church-goers to question the suitability of Protestant orthodoxy as a framework for solace and intellectual certainty.[51] Fundamentally, for a culture denied the doctrine of purgatory as a mediating concept, ghost-seeing expressed a type of humanism that neither religion in its orthodox or spiritualistic varieties, nor materialistic science could offer.[52]

'The "modern man in search of a soul" ', Jung wrote, 'abhors dogmatic postulates taken on faith and the religions based on them. He holds them valid only in so far as their knowledge-content seems to accord with his own experience of the deeps of psychic life. He wants to know – to experience for himself.'[53] Jung believed that most of the occultist and psychical movements of the period that considered themselves 'scientific' were actually religious in character, yet in the 1880s the SPR actively repressed the religious implications of the telepathic theory of ghost-seeing, judging it better to keep on the right side of scientific thinking. However, as shall be examined, these latent religious speculations would come to the fore towards the end of the century as the SPR sought to prove the existence of the soul and more than ever began to constitute a 'surrogate faith' for percipients caught between religion and science.[54] One of the reasons for the success of the SPR-structured community of sensation as a ghost-seeing network was that it offered Christians and agnostics a feasible riposte to the back-draught from the 'crisis of faith', that is, an epistemological framework attuned to the intellectual atmosphere of the age.

---

[51] John Harvey, 'Revival, Revisions, Visions and Visitations: The Resurgence and Imaging of Supernatural Religion, 1850–1940', *Welsh History Review* 23:2 (2006), 80.
[52] See Greenblatt, *Hamlet in Purgatory*, pp.102–50. Turner, *Between Science and Religion*, p.107.
[53] Carl Gustav Jung, *Modern Man in Search of a Soul*, trans. W.S. Dell and Cary F. Baynes (London, 1984), p.239.
[54] Oppenheim, *The Other World*, p.152.

Rene Kollar has examined how in England the Anglican Church sought to combat the spread of spiritualism by appealing to traditional rituals and doctrines that had previously been downplayed in its public ceremony.[55] Chief in this strategy was the promotion of the doctrine of the communion of saints (*communio sanctorum*), the notion that the living and the dead were equally part of the spiritual body of Jesus Christ under a congregation that transcends the limits of time and space. By the mid-nineteenth century the doctrine had become a feature which Catholics were marketing as a significant contrast to the perceived alienation of Protestants from the dead:

> Protestantism breaks up the consoling union of the children of God, removes the Saints from us to an unapproachable region, and leaves no trace of a living, active Communion between the Church on earth and the Church in heaven. Death, if we would believe Protestantism, ends all Communion between brethren. The dead are dead, is the climax of the icy, deathlike, and deadening doctrines of Protestant theology.[56]

While the doctrine of the communion of saints was put forward as an alternative to spiritualist beliefs, in practice the doctrine tended to confuse most Anglicans who were attracted to the more simple spiritualist framework that allowed for a direct link with the souls of the departed.[57] Although Kollar focuses on the first three decades of the twentieth century, it can safely be argued that Anglicans in the late nineteenth century faced the similar awareness that a gap existed between their own attitudes towards death (as expressed in the phenomenon of the crisis-apparition) and the anti-spiritualist strictures of the established Church.[58] In the 1880s it was the SPR's community of sensation with its implications

---

[55] Rene Kollar, *Searching for Raymond: Anglicanism, Spiritualism, and Bereavement Between the Two World Wars* (Lanham, 2000).

[56] Francis Xavier Weninger, *Protestantism and Infidelity: An Appeal to Candid Americans*, 10th edn (New York, 1865), p.79.

[57] For instance, in 1933 Reverend Charles Tweedale wrote: 'the Communion of the Saints must consist largely of communion with the "dead". Communion means fellowship, mutual intercourse. There can be no effective fellowship and mutual intercourse without communication. Psychic phenomena constitute the only effective and recognizable means of this communion with the dead and with the Spirit-world.' Cited in Kollar, *Searching for Raymond*, p.23. See also Alan Wilkinson, *The Church of England and the First World War* (London, 1978), pp.174–7.

[58] Myers wrote: 'The Cosmic Order is not an order of isolation, but of interpenetration of kindred souls. We recognize that the Universe is good from the fact that its constituent consciousnesses are organized into unity by the very instinct which makes their highest joy. *Therefore* it was that Love was dear to us, because Love was the fulfilling of the Law. Telepathy was but the outer, the objective aspect of that inward and ancient flame; of that passion whose community is now imperfect, and its duration transitory, and its intensest rapture akin to pain; but which shall yet achieve a pervading intimacy, and

of scientific acceptability which attracted a congregation willing to believe in and express its rhetoric which, while it did not explicitly state it as such, heralded the survival of the human soul. As Roland Barthes notes of this period, 'the cry from the heart of that positivist age runs thus: if only one could believe scientifically in immortality!'[59]

While such higher theological speculations represented a significant factor of the Protestant and spiritualist discourses, on the ground the psychical ghost story inculcated itself firmly within the normality of everyday life. The manifestation situation of the ghost-seeing experience generally seemed to reflect a passive state of mind on the part of the percipient – about as far away from the agent's traumatic crisis as was possible. Indeed most ghosts, like accidents, tended to happen within the security of the home, and many of the cases recorded in *Phantasms* were reported to have taken place in the bedroom where an encounter with the uncanny resonates most fully (as has been shown in the Neuilly case above).[60] When the narrative relied upon visual sightings, as was typically the case, the apparition was usually distinctly recognised and most commonly described as being pale, melancholy and misty; it was noted that the apparition figure rarely induced horror in the percipient. These observations illustrate the generic *normality* of the psychical ghost-seeing experience and further amplify the naturalistic foreground of the SPR ghost, a foreground in which the fantastic could be tamed and the uncanny could be domesticated.

Yet it was through this very normality that themes of dread and feelings of impending calamity could come to dominate *Phantasms*: while premonitions, presentiments and physical reactions to forebodings were a common trope of popular ghost stories, the fact that the psychical ghost-seeing experience integrated everyday life within its remit allowed it to express the emotional states which seemed to lurk beneath the levels of conscious awareness. Gurney's suspicion that percipients may have had other ghostly trials, or other buried moments when they believed they had occult evidence that someone was dead, and that they remembered only the 'hits' and forgot the 'misses', is a plausible one, and suggests a general culture of anxiety over the death of

enter upon an endless continuance, and become capable of a flawless joy. The Communion of Saints will be the very substance of the life everlasting.' Myers, 'The Drift of Psychical Research', 207. In 1906 Oliver Lodge delivered an address to the SPR entitled 'The Communion of Saints'. See Oliver Lodge, 'Memorial to Mr. Myers at Cheltenham', *JSPR* 13 (1907–1908), 148–52.
[59] Roland Barthes, 'Textual Analysis: Poe's "Valdemar"', in *Modern Criticism and Theory: A Reader*, ed. David Lodge, 2nd edn (Harlow, 2000), p.156.
[60] For some examples of bedroom hauntings see Davies, *The Haunted*, p.48.

the other with a concomitant prediction, or presentiment, complex. Some examples will illustrate these types of seemingly inexplicable emotional states:

All at once a dreadful feeling of illness and faintness came over me, and I felt that I was dying. I had no power to get up to ring the bell for assistance, but sat with my head in my hands utterly helpless.

I was overwhelmed with a most unusual sense of depression and melancholy. I shunned my friends and got 'chaffed' for my most unusual dullness and sulkiness. I felt utterly miserable, and even to this day I have a most vivid recollection of my misery that afternoon.

I experienced a *strange sadness* and depression … I wrote off to my brother, closed my desk, and felt compelled to exclaim quite aloud, 'My brother or I will break down'. This I afterwards found was the first day of his fatal illness.[61]

These examples show that the moments preceding the ghost-seeing experience were not, as was typically the case in the ghost stories of popular culture, filled with a sense of fear or horror or comedy, but rather with feelings indicative of dread, anxiety and a sense of angst, responses which have a distinctly modern resonance. Nicolas Abraham has theorised the phantom as representing a gap within the mind of the percipient, a kind of secret buried in a crypt.[62] In the cases collected in *Phantasms* the ghost of the dying person can be interpreted as using the emotions of the percipient to express itself and to fill the gap, in Abraham's sense, that was left by the loss of a loved one: what comes across most strongly is that ghost-seeing, for many people in Victorian society, was a form of auto-haunting. It is the peculiarity of these modern presentiments and foreboding messages that the moment of death is not exclusively the phenomenon expressed, for feelings of mortal danger, trauma and personal crisis seem to cause the same level of alarm as death-portents:

About 3 months ago as I was sitting, quietly thinking, between 5 and 7 p.m., I experienced a very curious sensation. I can only describe it as like a cloud of calamity gradually wrapping me round. It was *almost* a physical feeling, so strong was it; and I seemed to be certain, in some inexplicable way, of disaster to some of my relations or friends, though I could not in the least fix upon anybody in particular, and there was no one about whom I was anxious at the time.[63]

---

[61] Gurney, Myers and Podmore, *Phantasms*, vol. I, pp.273, 278, 281.
[62] Nicolas Abraham, 'Notes on the Phantom: A Complement to Freud's Metapsychology', trans. Nicholas Rand, *Critical Inquiry* 13:2 (1987), 287–92.
[63] Gurney, Myers and Podmore, *Phantasms*, vol. I, p.271.

Passages such as this, which are scattered throughout *Phantasms*, suggest through their use of specific phenomenological language that it is the percipient who is the person in mortal danger, not the agent: it is almost as if death is being simulated and expressed through the intuition of dread. Henri Bergson, in *L'Évolution créatrice* (1907), suggested that if sympathy, or intuition, could reflect upon itself 'it would give us the key to vital operations', just as in the opposite manner intelligence developed leads one to scientific discoveries about inert matter.[64] Of course, the idea that one can sympathetically feel oneself in the position of the dead other was not new in the late nineteenth century. In *The Theory of Moral Sentiments* (1759) Adam Smith sketched out a kind of memorial economic system whereby the dead are compensated for *their* loss:

> The tribute of our fellow-feeling seems doubly due to them now, when they are in danger of being forgot by every body; and, by the vain honours which we pay to their memory, we endeavour, *for our own misery*, artificially to keep alive our melancholy remembrance of their misfortune.[65]

Smith suggested that our sympathy with the 'dreary and endless melan-choly' of death comes not from any religious or metaphysical belief in the afterlife but 'from our putting ourselves in their situation, and from our lodging ... our own living souls in their inanimated bodies, and thence conceiving what would be our emotions in this case'.[66] While for Smith the dead are owed their due for being located outside the living market-place, the accounts contained in *Phantasms* show that the SPR's community of sensation facilitated the coincidence of feeling which allowed percipients to take on physical and emotional sympathy with the dead who still existed. Therefore, in *Phantasms* one can trace the transformation of the traditional trope of the supernatural prophecy into a modern psychological self-fulfilling prophecy, an auto-prophesying or prediction complex, attuned to the desire for sympathy with the disap-peared loved one. As Bergson put it, 'intuition may enable us to grasp what it is that intelligence fails to give us, and indicate the means of supplementing it'.[67]

Central to what was described in Part I was the notion, whether implied or denied, that one could 'dream reality' or 'dream the dead alive'. In this regard Hendrika Vande Kemp's observations on dreaming

---

[64] Henri Bergson, *Creative Evolution*, trans. Arthur Mitchell (Lanham, 1984), p.176.
[65] Adam Smith, *The Theory of Moral Sentiments*, ed. D.D. Raphael and A.L. Macfie (Oxford, 1976), p.13. Italics are mine.
[66] *Ibid.*, p.12. For eighteenth-century constructions of the affectual realm see Chris B. Jones, *Radical Sensibility: Literature and Ideas in the 1790s* (London, 1993).
[67] Bergson, *Creative Evolution*, p.177.

in the nineteenth century prove useful to the development of this chapter's investigation. Vande Kemp noted:

Just as it was commonly accepted that the dead were seldom dreamed of as dead, it was also believed that dreams of one's own death never went beyond the funeral. The mind was said to be not only reluctant to conceive death, but also *unable*, for death does not lie within personal experience. The dreaming mind could no more picture death than the waking one. This phenomenon reinforced the nineteenth century notion of the closed mind: dreams must reconstitute the dreamer's own experiences.[68]

As we have seen, the analogy between dreaming and ghost-seeing was firmly established in multiple discourses by the latter part of the nineteenth century. Such a cultural-referential constant raises interesting questions about whether death could be *represented* in an obvious manner at all, if it was simply *simulated* in a naturalistic fashion in accordance with the remits of psychical research, or if, following Abraham, the fact of death (or death-desire) was *entombed* or buried alive. In any case it was clear that the intra-psychic mentation of the dreamer/ghost-seer and not the meaningful content of the dream/ghost was the direction in which psychological research was heading by the turn of the twentieth century.[69] Such a thematic orientation was not ignored by psychical research. When examining the class of coincidental dreams, Gurney was struck by the number of dreams that involved the death of someone known to the dreamer. This finding was supported by an SPR mini-census on death dreams examined in *Phantasms*. Gurney asked,

Millions of people are dreaming every night; and in dreams, if anywhere, the range of possibilities seems infinite; can any positive conclusion be drawn from such a chaos of meaningless and fragmentary impressions? Must not we admire the force of the obvious *a priori* argument, that among the countless multitude of dreams, one here and there is likely to correspond in time with an actual occurrence resembling the one dreamed of, and that when a dream thus 'comes true', unscientific minds are sure to note and store up the fact as something extraordinary, without taking the trouble to reflect whether such incidents occur oftener than pure chance would allow?[70]

Gurney sought to localise a specific and unique event in the dream-world of public society in order to ascertain whether the hypothesis of chance

[68] Hendrika Vande Kemp, 'Psycho-spiritual Dreams in the Nineteenth Century, Part I: Dreams of Death', *Journal of Psychology and Theology* 22:2 (1994), 104.
[69] See Havelock Ellis, 'On Dreaming of the Dead', *Psychological Review* 2:5 (1895), 458–61. See also Peirce's critique below. On death dreams in Freud see *The Interpretation of Dreams*, pp.347–70, 558.
[70] Gurney, Myers and Podmore, *Phantasms*, vol. I, p.299.

or coincidence could be weakened, and by extension, the telepathic theory of ghost-seeing strengthened: Gurney therefore chose the event of death. He asked if, between 1874 and 1885, the percipient had vividly dreamt of the death of a person known to them. He received 5360 answers, 166 of which indicated that they had in fact dreamt of the death of someone known to them. From this Gurney tentatively concluded that 1 in 26 people out of the general population recalled a death dream during this period.[71] Although such a survey did not prove crisis-apparitions as a scientific fact, it demonstrated to the SPR that by applying their legitimising statistical methodology to dream narratives, the scientific hypothesis of crisis-apparitions could be brought closer within the realms of possibility, further distancing the subject from sceptics who claimed that the chances of the death dream coinciding with an actual death were remote to say the least. The general public of Britain in the 1880s, *Phantasms* suggests, had death on the brain.

Criticisms of *Phantasms of the Living*

Phantasms of the Living was the SPR's dramatic entrance into late Victorian print culture, and this in itself, apart from its radical findings, merited a spirited response in the print media. The first major reaction came when *The Times* devoted a leader to *Phantasms* on 31 October 1886 entitled 'How Many Senses Have You?' Here the reviewer readily recognised the remarkable nature of the volumes and their importance for the scientific world and outlined for the reader the main theses of *Phantasms*:

1. Experimental evidence proves the existence of telepathy.
2. Testimony proves the existence of phantasms of the living.
3. Phantasms of the living are instances of telepathic action.

Of these three suggestions, the critic was not convinced that the third had been sufficiently proved beyond doubt. While admitting that the book had not been examined in detail for the review, the critic believed that what was now called telepathy had appeared down the ages under many different forms and went on to note: 'We have no right to assume that we know all that can be known of the phenomena of the human consciousness, or that the unknown will not reveal itself if interrogated in the proper way.' However, the critic believed that the issue of apparitions was fundamentally different from that of telepathy, arguing that experimentation in cases of ghost-seeing fails altogether, while observation can only ever be indirect. It was argued that the ghost-seer as a unit

---

[71] *Ibid.*, p.305.

of evidence was not scientifically valid and such a person could never actually relate what they saw, but only what they *think* they saw: 'To explain them [apparition cases] by telepathy is surely, in the present condition of our knowledge, to beg the whole question.'[72]

According to *The Times* 'in order to establish the objective reality of the apparitions we should have to examine minutely the mental history and condition' of all percipients who claim to have seen phantasms. With this, and many other questions regarding the validity of its cherished evidence, the SPR was keen to counter allegations that their cases were merely the hysterical reports of the hallucinations of women and clergymen, categories of people supposedly naturally inclined towards the marvellous.[73] In *Phantasms* Gurney had estimated that out of 527 percipients concerned in the hallucinations of sight and hearing which were included as evidence of the telepathic hypothesis of apparitions, 241, or more than 46 per cent, were males; 286, or less than 54 per cent, were women; 28, or between 5 and 6 per cent, were clergymen or ministers of religion. As an explanation for this, Gurney offered a characteristically bourgeois-epistolary response: 'The slight preponderance of female informants may probably be due to their having, as a rule, more leisure than men for writing on matters unconnected with business.'[74] Yet judging by the review in *The Times* it was clear that the SPR's reliance on human testimony to prove the reality of ghost-seeing would be the main criticism to be directed at *Phantasms*.

In his criticism A. Taylor Innes, a Scottish lawyer writing in *Nineteenth Century*, asked a very specific question of the authors: 'Where Are the Letters?' He praised *Phantasms* as a promising enterprise, but as it was a piece of work predicated on the testimony of percipients who claimed not to know of the agent's death before seeing the phantasm, Innes requested that the authors publish the letters which have 'crossed', i.e. the percipient's letter home, or to a third party, describing the ghost-seeing incident and their fears for the loved one, post-marked and dated, and thus indicative of a genuinely supernatural event. While the authors made clear in *Phantasms* that the evidential basis of the claims being made were dependent upon extremely accurate documentation, they had not actually published any of these crucial letters.[75] Innes

---

[72] 'How Many Senses Have You?', *The Times* (30 October 1886), 9.

[73] For instance, rejecting the London Dialectical Society's invitation to participate in its investigations into spiritualism, Thomas Huxley responded that he had better things to do than to '[listen] to the chatter of old women and curates in the nearest cathedral town'. *Report on Spiritualism*, p.229.

[74] Gurney, Myers and Podmore, *Phantasms*, vol. II, p.3.

[75] A. Taylor Innes, 'Where Are the Letters?', *Nineteenth Century* 22 (1887), 178.

complained that in cases such as that of the clergyman who claimed to have phantasmically hugged his fiancée, the letters and memoranda describing the incident were burned; others were lost, missing, of suspicious value, or simply had not been conducive to offering absolute proof. Innes's criticism demonstrated the fact that for the SPR the status of the letter was both proof and its opposite; Gurney's chaotic production of *Phantasms*, as witnessed by Lodge, while aiming to be cumulative had failed to find The Letter that could offer positive proof of the ghost: 'If such a letter exists', wrote Innes, 'it is worth a thousand guineas in the market, and its destination is a guarded glass case in the British Museum.'[76]

Gurney took up the gauntlet and in his reply repressed the epistolary fetishism of the SPR, arguing that verbal communication to another person present was more common in the ghost-seeing scenario than an immediately written letter, especially in a proximate family situation. Furthermore in cases where documentation was mentioned, Gurney stressed that he himself possessed many of the diaries in question. Even though many of the letters had been lost or thrown away, Gurney argued that this was a common occurrence among the general public which, unfortunately, did not realise the cumulative importance of their letters to the psychical research project: 'Their interest is wholly in their own isolated case, as a mere event, not as material for scientific deductions.'[77] Gurney maintained that there was a substantial body of evidence for spontaneous telepathy, and while there were no 'crossed' letters there were many other forms of evidence such as corroborative testimony from honest, respectable people, and the only reason for not accepting this evidence 'would be the hypothesis of a wilful forgery, committed long ago in anticipation of a coming race of psychical researchers'.[78] In other words, Gurney requested that critics take the Kantian approach to the matter, and judge the phenomena on the basis of montage and common sense. Yet Innes was not convinced, and as a lawyer observed how the SPR had discredited the theosophical movement by a close analysis of the 'Mahatmas' letters, supposedly supernaturally sent to Madame Blavatsky:

And yet – the question must be put whether the Society, in issuing its most important publication in 1886, and since that date in dealing with the problem as to testimony which was then raised, has not been in ever increasing danger of a lapse in the very direction which it has condemned.[79]

[76] *Ibid.*, 182.
[77] Edmund Gurney, 'Letters on Phantasms: A Reply', *Nineteenth Century* 22 (1887), 525.
[78] *Ibid.*, 531.
[79] A. Taylor Innes, 'The Psychical Society's Ghosts: A Challenge Renewed', *Nineteenth Century* 30 (1891), 766.

In another challenge for Gurney the *Saturday Review* lampooned the SPR in three articles in late 1886 on the backdrop of the publicity surrounding *Phantasms*, referring to them as the 'Society for Spookical Research' and their studies as 'spookology'. Gurney's writing style was attacked as cumbersome and circular, and the review asserted that 'the great majority of those who accept his arguments will do so, not because they have been convinced by them, but because they agreed with him beforehand'.[80] It was argued that with a subject-matter as controversial as this no one person's testimony was to be accepted considering the human tendency to tell lies, to hoax and to misremember. With many cases dismissed as too reliant upon memory and hearsay, and in the absence of contemporary documentation, the cases of ghost-seeing reproduced in *Phantasms* were judged as not having gone beyond the possibility of hoax or chance-coincidence.[81] As with Innes, the *Saturday Review* critic connected the SPR with the Theosophical Society, writing gleefully about the 'feuds between the rival admirers and exponents of spooks',[82] and proposing that regardless of whether a spook is theosophical and occult, or psychical and telepathed, they were both spooks of the same category and 'but for practical purposes there is no difference between them':[83]

It is a great pity that the Society for Spookical Research should go for Mme. Blavatsky, and that Mme. Blavatsky should be down on the Society for Spookical Research like a thousand bricks. It makes so little difference whether spooks are telepathed about, generally accidentally, by promiscuous person, or whether the Thibetan Adepts go spooking astrally through the world on the strength of being fifth or sixth rounders. If they would but recognize it, spookologists and theosophists are all in the same boat, and ought to be each other's dearest friends. It is true that Mme. Blavatsky uses the word spook in some highly technical sense of her own, but the practical distinction between a British spook cropping up at that very moment and an astral presence bringing a message about nothing in particular is really far too fine for the general public.[84]

It was ironic that in the criticisms of Innes and the *Saturday Review* the SPR were consistently linked with its *bête noire*, the Theosophical Society, and had its telepathic theory of ghost-seeing attacked as occultist and theosophical in nature. That the SPR, which had itself 'debunked' the Theosophical Society in 1885 as an unscientific and fraudulent movement, was associated

---

[80] 'Spookical Research', 649.   [81] *Ibid.*, 649.

[82] 'Spooks and Their Friends', *Saturday Review of Politics, Literature, Science, and Art* 62 (1886), 750.

[83] 'What Is a Spook?', *Saturday Review of Politics, Literature, Science, and Art* 62 (1886), 773.

[84] 'Spooks and Their Friends', 751.

with such occultist teachings must have been galling to its leadership. Yet it was doubly ironic that in the case of *Phantasms* the authority of letters was *again* the issue at the heart of the controversy: the presence of the Mahatmas letters, the critic noted, had 'continually undermined Blavatsky's authority as well as their own' and resulted in Hodgson's findings against the Theosophical Society: the absence of documented and dated letters indicative of telepathic ghost-seeing similarly undermined the SPR's attempt to prove the ghost, at least in the periodical press.

A different type of criticism was to come from America, where Charles S. Peirce had read *Phantasms* with much interest and was moved to publish a stinging article on the book in late 1887 which initiated a sustained controversy with Gurney.[85] In this article, published in the *Proceedings of the American Society for Psychical Research*, Peirce put forward eighteen different conditions which he argued rendered many of the strongest crisis-apparition cases in *Phantasms* invalid: these ranged from suspicions about anxiety, intoxication, unreliability and delirium, to more general arguments about the validity of the statistical methodology and data used and the reliability of the three authors as investigators.[86] To his credit Gurney responded with vigour to the attack and exposed Peirce's mistaken readings of many of the cases he cited, scoring hits in the process. At this point contrasting interpretations of what it was that 'anxiety' connoted became important in the debate. Countering Peirce's argument that anxiety about the state of health of the agent precluded the inclusion of such a case as evidence conducive to the reality of crisis-apparitions, Gurney wrote:

Anxiety is clearly a condition which admits of all degrees, while at the same time it cannot be accurately measured, but all that logic demands is that coincidental cases should be excluded when the anxiety was acute enough to be regarded with any probability as the sufficient cause of the hallucination. A person who has been for some time ill, but whose condition has not been seriously dwelt on, is in fact not a bit more likely to be represented in a friend's hallucination than the friend's most robust acquaintance.[87]

Peirce, on the contrary, believed in the existence of a subconscious current of anxiety towards people with whom the percipient was in deep sympathy: this not only radically challenged the speculations in

---

[85] This article was probably written in response to a positive review of *Phantasms* by Peirce's friend and colleague William James, published in *Science* on 7 January 1887. See James, *Essays in Psychical Research*, pp.24–8. See also Charles S. Peirce, 'Telepathy and Perception', in *Collected Papers of Charles Sanders Peirce*, vol. VII, *Science and Philosophy*, vol. VIII, *Reviews, Correspondence, and Bibliography*, ed. Arthur W. Burks (Cambridge, MA, 1966), pp.359–97.
[86] Peirce, *Writings*, pp.74–81.   [87] *Ibid.*, p.86.

Phantasms but also exposed the ghost-seeing consciousness as inherently haunted by an unrecognised stream of anxiety towards loved ones. For if anxious thoughts about people are constantly in our mind, subconscious or not, then consciously known details such as their age and state of health could prove crucial in the probability of a crisis-apparition occurring 'naturally', that is, when the sympathetic percipient enters a mental state conducive to such a hallucination emerging: and as both Peirce and Gurney stressed, this discourse was predicated on probabilities. Peirce was willing to allow that this mental state could

produce a wonderful exaltation of sensibility. In such a condition perceptions of the truth may be reached which are founded on differences of sensation so slight that even an attentive scrutiny of the field of consciousness may not be able to detect them, and which may be almost magical in their effects.[88]

However, the existence of such a faculty drastically increased the chances of the crisis-apparition being a coincidental hallucination and not, as *Phantasms* maintained, part of the growing probability that ghost-seeing was a scientific fact. Innes had criticised the epistolary fallacies of the SPR's work; Peirce had focused his attack on the false and emotionally charged messages inherent in the community of sensation.

In his criticisms of *Phantasms*, published in *Mind*, the idealist philosopher, and ASPR member, Josiah Royce followed Peirce's train of thought by focusing on the role of memory disorders in the ghost-seeing experience. Royce was certain that the majority of the percipients described in *Phantasms* were 'haters of all superstitions, whose own personal honesty is undoubted, and whose memory is generally good'.[89] He was therefore puzzled by why such rational, sane and trustworthy people claimed to have experienced death-warnings at the moment of the agent's death:

Why should such tales be told at once, or very soon after the accident, and before the *ordinary* errors of imaginative memory could have time to distort the facts? Why should the experiences be sporadic for such people, so as to be almost wholly isolated in their lives, and so as not especially to affect their beliefs thenceforth?[90]

Royce's own hypothesis was that *Phantasms* illustrated cases of a not yet recognised type of '*instantaneous hallucination of memory, consisting in the fancy, at the very moment of some exciting experience, that one has*

---

[88] *Ibid.*, p.118.
[89] Josiah Royce, 'Hallucination of Memory and "Telepathy" ', *Mind* 13:50 (1888), 245.
[90] *Ibid.*

EXPECTED *it before its coming'*.[91] What this hypothesis suggested was that ghost-seers were actually remembering the future: on hearing of a loved one's death the percipient suddenly declares that he/she saw an apparition or had a death-warning at the moment of the other's death. The mechanics of such a hallucination were unknown to Royce, but he speculated that they would occur rarely among the sane and could possibly pass from one percipient to another, especially if they were members of the same family. Royce explicitly linked this type of hallucination of the memory, or 'double memory', with the notion of déjà-vu, yet the idea of telepathic ghost-seeing, for Royce, resembled a more morbid version of déjà-vu in that it was not immediately corrected by the self and could persist on in life as a conviction. Royce proposed, therefore, that *Phantasms* had revealed a hitherto unproven hallucination of the human memory, and not as the authors claimed, the reality of telepathy. In this, rather ironically, the scientific merit of the project had been justified: 'If it is the truth as such that we want to "bag", it is not ours to decide whether the truth shall turn out to be a wild goose or some other fowl.'[92] Royce's counter-argument of double memory highlighted the increased strength of dynamic psychiatry in its interpretations of the psychology of the sane, and also pointed towards the focus on double, or split, personalities as a concept which could explain contradictory behaviour in psychiatric patients.[93] Thus criticisms of the SPR's theory of ghost-seeing proved useful in combating the 'veridical' in life: psychologists were exposing the fact that the mind could not be trusted – for every conviction that an event occurred, or something was seen, even on a collective scale, the psychologist could respond with empirical and experimental evidence of everyday delusions and disorders.

The strong critical reaction to *Phantasms* from American commentators continued with the publication of a review by G. Stanley Hall in the first issue of the *American Journal of Psychology*. Hall used this entrance as an opportunity to challenge the SPR's claims to membership in the discipline of experimental psychology.[94] Hall, who had been a sceptical

---

[91] *Ibid.*

[92] *Ibid.*, 248. For a history of memory disorders during the period, see German E. Berrios and M. Gil, 'Will and Its Disorders: A Conceptual History', *History of Psychiatry* 6:21 (1995), 87–104.

[93] On this topic see Ian Hacking, *Rewriting the Soul: Multiple Personality and the Sciences of Memory* (Princeton, 1995). The concept of paramnesia would be used in a psychoanalytical context elsewhere to explain the SPR's crisis-apparitions. See Leonard T. Troland, 'The Freudian Psychology and Psychical Research', *Journal of Abnormal Psychology* 8:6 (1914), 405–28.

[94] It is interesting to note the circumstances behind the establishment of the *American Journal of Psychology*: 'Hall was given his opportunity when R. Pearsall Smith, a

voice on the Council of the ASPR, argued that the authors of *Phantasms* were biased in favour of the telepathic hypothesis, and by going back to the Creery and Smith/Blackburn tests, he criticised the poor and unscientific test-conditions which informed the belief that telepathy was proven. Hall was especially suspicious of the 'decline effect' in the Creery case; this highlighted the finding that as the test conditions became more stringent and the girls were isolated from their father, the remarkable successes of the early tests began to decline: 'it is strange that this decline should coincide step by step with closer study of them, and still more so that all the girls should lose this marvelous power *simultaneously!*'[95] Yet perhaps Hall's most damning criticism of the telepathic theory of ghost-seeing was his argument that the SPR's conception of cumulative or quantitative proof was biased in favour of their own hypotheses:

The cumulative method has the advantage of encouraging the bias above referred to both by mutual countenance and evidential appearances, but in science it is the competent minority that is usually right and the majority that is usually wrong. One man who would exhaust all the resources of modern science in precautions in this field, would be more authoritative than all the parlor sceances [sic] together. What is to be chiefly desiderated is not the multiplication of instances, but more systematic and prolonged study of such cases as have been already found, the use of more cautions against error, the probability of which would be shown so incalculably great could the calculus be intelligently applied to their estimation.[96]

Hall intervened in the debate as an influential representative of experimental psychology, asserting his community's disenchanted and elite expertise, and repudiated psychical research as a scientific method, at least in its positive-investigative mode. Hall's insistence that the SPR would be put to better use by a negativist study of the sheer ingenuity of fraud and error, conscious and unconscious, seriously undermined the research into crisis-apparitions presented in *Phantasms*. While Peirce reacted to Gurney's use of probability theory to prove the prevalence of ghost-seeing, Hall was concerned that psychical research would

spiritualist member of the American Society for Psychical Research, offered him $500 to start a journal. Smith assumed that the *Journal* would be favourable to psychical research; to what extent Hall tacitly encouraged that assumption is unknown.' Dorothy Ross, *G. Stanley Hall: The Psychologist as Prophet* (Chicago and London, 1972), p.170. Ross goes on to note that Hall envisaged his journal to have a thoroughly scientific character with no room for speculative pieces: 'Hall also excluded psychical research.' *Ibid.*, p.171. On James's negative reaction to the *Journal* see *ibid.*, pp.176–8. In its review of the first issue of the *Journal*, *Mind* pointed out Hall's 'searching' review of *Phantasms*. 'Notes', *Mind* 13:49 (1888), 149.

[95]   G. Stanley Hall, 'Psychological Literature', *American Journal of Psychology* 1:1 (1887), 134.
[96]   *Ibid.*, 144.

disturb the project for the institutionalisation of psychology, would queer its pitch so to speak, when the discipline needed to be 'kept, in the severest sense, experimental and scientific'.[97] In this scenario telepathy was denounced as a popular superstition and ghost-seers a top-down and Anglocentric construction: 'If good hypnotic subjects are more numerous in France than in England, it would seem that ghost seers are most common among cultivated classes in England.'[98]

Phantasms had received criticisms which, while strongly repulsed, nevertheless stung Gurney and the SPR who, while accepting significant methodological attacks and, to a certain extent, the satirical sniping, had also depended upon the strength of the experimental telepathic evidence to push through their hypothesis on apparitions. *The Times* had not accepted the telepathic hypothesis of ghost-seeing; Innes and the *Saturday Review* mercilessly took the SPR to task for its lack of documentation to prove its theory; Peirce and Hall offered more searching criticisms based upon the fundamental fallacies of such testimony, and opposed the SPR's use of the 'scientific' label to frame its researches into ghost-seeing. While sympathetic to the ambitions of *Phantasms*, Royce had nevertheless undermined its findings by highlighting the risk of unconscious deception. Thomas Kuhn has argued that for radical new theories to stand a chance of success in a scientific field, then that field must be in a state of crisis.[99] Yet there was no general crisis threatening the materialistic framework of scientific naturalism. On the contrary, it was the SPR which was in a state of crisis: the crisis which Sidgwick described had arrived, the SPR had sought out a positive critical response, but *Phantasms*, despite commendations of the authors' diligence and ambition, had hardly dented the scientific-naturalist consensus that the psychical ghost was unproven and fundamentally *unscientific*. Scientific naturalism, represented mostly by experimental psychologists, had built upon the mid-century reaction of mental physiology to spiritualism and rejected the SPR's suit. Even worse, the criticism from America, coming from figures connected with the ASPR, attested to the harsh reaction against spiritualism and psychical research that was spreading from the ASPR itself through the east-coast academies, especially following the publication of the Seybert Commission Report into spiritualism in 1887 which detailed numerous incidences of fraud among mediums.[100]

[97] *Ibid.*, 146.   [98] *Ibid.*
[99] Thomas Kuhn, *The Structure of Scientific Revolutions*, 3rd edn (Chicago and London, 1996), pp.66–76.
[100] *Preliminary Report of the Commission Appointed by the University of Pennsylvania to Investigate Modern Spiritualism* (Philadelphia, 1887). See also Blum, *Ghost Hunters*, pp.117–18, 132–3.

The increased sense of alienation from both theology and mainstream science in psychical research circles contributed to Sidgwick's own personal state of crisis in 1888.[101] This same critical language appears in Sidgwick's Presidential Address of that year:

> To me it appears that we have reached a crisis in our history – not perhaps a very critical crisis, rather one likely to be prolonged and mild – but yet a crisis of which it is important that we should thoroughly understand the nature, in order that we may guard against the dangers it involves.[102]

After noting the 'calamity' of Gurney's death in 1888, Sidgwick went on to express his general disenchantment with the closed mindset of scientific naturalism. Putting his faith in 'the younger and more open-minded part of the scientific world' Sidgwick repeated the injunction to collect fresh and well-attested cases indicative of telepathy and pointed the Society in the direction of a widespread census which would attempt, yet again, to prove the prevalence of ghost-seeing in everyday life.[103]

If there were any doubts that this period was a critical one for the status of the SPR's theory then further events removed them. As noted above, one of the major criticisms of *Phantasms* was the unscientific nature of the Creery tests and the Society's reliance upon them as part of their evidence for telepathy. It was thus unfortunate that *Phantasms* declared 'it is to those trials that we owe our conviction of the possibility of genuine thought-transference between persons in a normal state',[104] for one of the last contributions from Gurney before his death was a note later published in the *PSPR* in 1888 which announced that two of the Creery Sisters had been detected in late 1887 using a code of signals to each other to obtain 'hits' in the card-guessing game, and a third sister admitted to using a signalling system in the early experiments.[105] The SPR was therefore obliged to judge all the previous experiments with the Creery girls invalid by default, much to the dismay of Barrett.[106]

---

[101] See Sidgwick and Sidgwick, *Henry Sidgwick: A Memoir*, pp.484–5. It is notable that around 1890 Sidgwick changed his 'keynote' text – a kind of recurrent mental mantra/expression – from 'But this one thing I do, forgetting those things that are behind, and stretching forth unto those that are before, I press towards the mark', to the more negative 'Gather up the fragments that are left, that nothing be lost.' *Ibid.*, p.125.

[102] Henry Sidgwick, 'President's Address', *PSPR* 5 (1888–1889), 271.

[103] *Ibid.*, 272.   [104] Gurney, Myers and Podmore, *Phantasms*, vol. I, p.29.

[105] Edmund Gurney, 'Note Relating to Some of the Published Experiments in Thought-transference', *PSPR* 5 (1888–1889), 269.

[106] Barrett steadily refused to discard the results of these thought-transference experiments following the exposure, regarding them as 'unimpeachable'. Oppenheim writes that this episode represented Barrett's 'first deviation from the attitude of impartial

The various code-systems used – coughing, sneezing, yawning, movements of the eyes, scraping of the feet – were so physically obvious that the episode proved highly embarrassing for the SPR, and was a further example to sceptics of psychical research that the spectre of childish trickery and fraud relentlessly haunts those who seek physical proof of the unseen.[107] From this point onwards it is discernible that, within the SPR, the writings of Podmore and Myers began to represent diametrically opposing trends. Podmore's *Apparitions and Thought-transference* (1894) was billed as a more accessible and readable update of *Phantasms*. Podmore seemed to accept some of the criticisms that had been levelled at *Phantasms*, particularly, following the Creery revelations, with regard to evidence supplied by respectable percipients that later turned out to be false, bogus or exaggerated.[108] On the other hand, Myers stayed stubbornly loyal to his and Gurney's belief in the cumulative power of evidence for telepathy, evidence that could survive the rare occasions when fraud, dishonesty or unconscious error was detected. But, in contradistinction to Gurney, Myers began to further develop the quasi-spiritualist theories which had begun to emerge in his conclusion to *Phantasms* and he increasingly bemoaned the reductionist cosmological scenario of the scientific naturalist model where the world 'is made of ether and atoms, and there is no room for ghosts'.[109]

Phantasms of the dead

In the first circular released to SPR members and associates in July 1883 the following notice appeared:

The Committee on Haunted Houses invite information on any unusual occurrences seemingly confined to particular localities, such as bell-ringing, unseen footsteps,

---

scientific inquiry that characterized his earlier ventures into psychical research'. Oppenheim, *The Other World*, p.360. See also Gauld, *The Founders*, p.148.

[107] For the wider spiritualist movement, 1888 proved an *annus horribilis* as Margaret and Kate Fox confessed that their mediumistic powers were fraudulent. See Reuben Briggs Davenport, *The Death-blow to Spiritualism: Being the True Story of the Fox Sisters, as Revealed by Authority of Margaret Fox Kane and Catherine Fox Jencken* (New York, 1888).

[108] 'It may be added that some of the criticisms called forth by *Phantasms of the Living*, and our further researches, have led us to modify our estimate of the evidence in some directions, and to strengthen generally the precautions taken against the unconscious warping of testimony.' Frank Podmore, *Apparitions and Thought-transference: An Examination of the Evidence for Telepathy* (New York, 1915), p.xvii.

[109] Cited in Turner, *Between Science and Religion*, p.31. 'Had Gurney lived, he rather than Myers would have written a large-scale résumé of the S.P.R.'s work, and the public image of psychical research would have been more acceptable to psychologists.' Gauld, *The Founders*, p.339.

&c.; but, especially, apparitions of any kind. It should be specially noted whether these phenomena were observed at fixed periods or on certain days of the year. There are houses bearing on this kind of reputation in most localities; and it would be of real service if any member would take pains to sift the rumours current about such houses in his own neighbourhood, and, if possible, track them to their source. It may probably be often found that the reputation of being 'haunted' is due to easily explicable sources of noise or disturbances, and it is eminently desirable that all such cases should be distinctly cleared up.

We shall gladly avail ourselves of any opportunity which our members may be able to procure for us of personally investigating occurrences of this nature. As the pecuniary value of a house is sometimes thought to be endangered by a reputation for being haunted, we may here repeat the statement which refers equally to communications received by all the Committees – viz., that all information will be regarded as confidential, when it is so desired.[110]

Despite this positive (and positivistic) start, the Committee on Haunted Houses immediately ran into difficulties in this most 'supernatural' of the many classes of ghost-seeing. A major problem in the cases of haunting and *revenants* collected was the perceived devaluation in the property concerned. This fear on the part of the ghost-seer or home-owner, it was argued, severely limited the amount of cases the Committee could investigate; indeed it delivered only two reports, in 1882 and 1884. In its second report the Committee argued for the reality of haunted houses yet raised the issue of the problematic behaviour of such 'haunting ghosts' which did not appear regularly or according to any specific time, date or anniversary, and which tended to glide like magic-lantern figures when moving, and perhaps most perplexing of all, which appeared to be without any object in their return: 'A figure is seen, and that is all.'[111]

Yet perhaps the most problematic factor which the SPR faced in its investigation of haunted houses was their association with the ghosts of the dead, a situation which would lead the Society toward the more contentious issues surrounding the notion of phantoms and their 'spirit' or soul-essence, and why it was that such a spirit remained in a certain location. This meant that the Society would be drawn into dealing with decidedly supernatural themes redolent of popular culture, such as the ghost of a murdered person returning to demand justice, or apparitions which tended to inspire terror in their observers, a situation which the SPR did not especially relish. An interesting example of the type of cases the SPR received about haunted houses was the ghost-seeing experience

---

[110] 'Circular No. 1', *PSPR* 1 (1882–1883), 301.
[111] W.D. Bushell, F.S. Hughes, A.P. Perceval Keep *et al.*, 'Second Report of the Committee on Haunted Houses', *PSPR* 2 (1884), 139–40.

sent in by a clergyman which occurred in 'one July morning in the year 1873'. The incident happened in the percipient's bedroom in an old house where he was living with his brother and a servant woman, having moved in about four months previously. One night, after locking the bedroom door and putting out the light he fell into 'a sound dreamless sleep' only to be awakened at around 3 a.m.:

Opening my eyes now I saw right before me the figure of a woman, stooping down and apparently looking at me. Her head and shoulders were wrapped in a common grey woollen shawl. Her arms were folded, and they were also wrapped as if for warmth, in the shawl. I looked at her in my horror, and dared not cry out lest I move the awful thing to speech or action. I lay and looked and felt as if I should lose my reason.[112]

After an undetermined space of time the apparition went backwards towards the window and gradually disappeared through growing more transparent by degrees. Concerned by the effect this experience could have upon the value of his household, financial and otherwise, and his personal reputation as a known ghost-seer, the clergyman did not report the nightly visitation. However, it appears that this ghost did not discriminate in who it was that she appeared to. Two weeks later at breakfast his brother reported seeing the same 'villainous looking hag' which had quite upset him. In addition, four years later the clergyman's young nephew reported seeing the apparition of an old woman going upstairs, which inspired terror in the boy. Soon the clergyman heard rumours that the house was indeed haunted by the ghost of an old woman:

A gentleman with whom we became acquainted in the neighbourhood, started when we first told him of what we had seen, and asked how we never heard that a woman had been killed in that house many years previously, and that it was said to be haunted. He is a sober-minded, religious man, an Englishman of middle age, the most unimaginative man I ever met, but he says he firmly believes we actually saw what he described.[113]

The unimpeachable details of the third-party gentleman would be just what the SPR required as basic facts to footnote such a case of ghost-seeing. Yet despite such assertions of testimonial validity, the SPR in the 1880s did not devote nearly as much attention to phantasms of the dead as they did to phantasms of the living due in part to the uneasy connection between actual ghosts and the spiritualist movement, but also because at this stage Gurney, Myers and Podmore were united in their sceptical attitude towards the clichéd notions of terrifying ghosts, especially considering the rapid developments they had made with the telepathic theory

---

[112] *Ibid.*, 141.   [113] *Ibid.*, 142.

of apparitions which depended upon a scientific, and relentlessly positivistic, language of psychology and psychical states in order to make an intellectual impact. Fundamentally, therefore, the leaders of the SPR felt uneasy dealing with phenomena that implied the existence of a metaphysical realm without sufficient evidence to back it up. There would be no room for the complications surrounding the concept of the 'restless spirit' or haunting ghost in a Society already lampooned at length for its interest in ghost-seeing and linked to such occultist groups as the Theosophical Society. This awareness of ridicule informed Gurney's objections to rival notions of the 'ethereal' or 'gaseous' ghost.[114]

Eleanor M. Sidgwick was a psychical researcher known as an extremely cool observer and a person whose mathematical training informed her sceptical and logical frame of mind when it came to the issue of ghost-seeing. While her 1885 paper 'Note on the Evidence, Collected by the Society, for Phantasms of the Dead' did not come to a firm conclusion either way on the matter, Sidgwick laid out the attested facts and so-called evidence in a manner which revealed her deep scepticism. As she wrote:

The existence, therefore, of phantoms of the dead can only be established, if at all, by the accumulation of improbabilities in which we become involved by rejecting a large mass of apparently strong testimony to facts which, as recounted, would seem to admit of no other satisfactory explanation: and in testing the value of this testimony we are bound, I think, to strain to the utmost all possible suppositions of recognised causes, before we can regard the narrative in question as even tending to prove the operation of this novel agency.[115]

Sidgwick found no foundation at all for the popular conception that the ghost only haunted old houses, and no significant evidence linking ghost-seeing to a particular crime or tragedy. For Sidgwick (who, incidentally, believed in the evidence for telepathy as collected by the SPR and published in *Phantasms*), the notion that phantasms of the dead could exist contradicted the twelve-hour theory of latency propounded by Gurney, and dragged the SPR's theory of apparitions far beyond such positivistic limitations into a religious and spiritualistic sphere more reminiscent of traditional ghost-folklore than of modern psychological case studies. Sidgwick surveyed four theories of phantasms of the dead:

1. the popular view of the actual existence in space of the apparition;
2. that the apparition has no actual existence in space but is a telepathic hallucination;

---

[114] Gurney, Myers and Podmore, *Phantasms*, vol. II, p.169.
[115] Eleanor M. Sidgwick, 'Note on the Evidence', 70.

3. that the first appearance of the apparition is a subjective hallucination and it is spread like a telepathic infection to other percipients;
4. that there are subtle psychical influences in 'haunted houses' which produce a hallucination in the percipient.[116]

Yet none of these theories struck her as particularly plausible and Sidgwick ended her study with a plea for percipients not to view hallucinations as a pathological sign. She wrote:

it is to be hoped that all who take an intelligent interest in the subject, and have the good fortune to live in haunted houses themselves, and to see ghosts, will help in the search for the truth, by finding out all they can, both about their own experiences and those of others, and about the history of the houses they live in.[117]

While Myers and Gurney were reluctant to deal with the topic of phantasms of the dead in *Phantasms*, both wrote articles, published in the *PSPR* in 1889, that raised the question of the possible existence of such phenomena.[118]

Psychical researchers such as Lord Rayleigh (John William Strutt) and Myers found no contradiction in the notion that the dead could exert a telepathic influence on the living, arguing that it was merely a matter of stretching the qualifying criteria for the impact of the psychical energy of the agent past the twelve-hour limit imposed by Gurney in *Phantasms*.[119] Ghost-seeing cases where collective percipience was indicated were, for the SPR, the trickiest to deal with for they seemed to point towards the simplest explanation – a spiritualist one; that is, that the apparition was objective. To explain collective cases of ghost-seeing Gurney had proposed an amalgamation of two theories, that of a joint affection (or community of sensation) between B and C, caused by the agent A, and a direct transference of the hallucination between B and C:

Where A, the distant agent, is in *rapport* both with B and C, it is possible to suppose that B and C are jointly and independently impressed by A, though the particular form – the hallucination – in which they simultaneously embody their impression is still an effect of B's mind on C's, or of C's on B's. The joint impression from A may be conceived as having in itself a tendency to facilitate this farther effect – that is to say, psychical communication between B and C may find a readier and wider channel at the exceptional moments when they are

[116] *Ibid.*, 146–8.   [117] *Ibid.*, 149.
[118] Gurney, Myers and Podmore, *Phantasms*, vol. II, p.284.
[119] Lord Rayleigh wrote: 'To my mind telepathy with the dead would present comparatively little difficulty when it was admitted as regards the living.' Cited in Renée Haynes, *The Society for Psychical Research 1882–1982: A History* (London, 1982), p.9.

attuned by a common telepathic influence than, *e.g.*, when one of them is staring at a card and the other is endeavouring to guess it.[120]

Myers challenged this rather complicated theory in his conclusion to *Phantasms*. Here, he raised significant doubts about the validity of the telepathic hypothesis of ghost-seeing in explaining the occurrence of cases where multiple people witnessed the same crisis-apparition. Part of these doubts regarded to agency: exactly *who* initiated the ghost-seeing experience, the agent or the percipient? And are crisis-apparitions in any way reciprocal? Myers suspected that clairvoyance was the central faculty in the ghost-seeing experience, but in this, as he realised, he was going beyond the evidence so far collected by the Society. He simply could not conceive of the percipient as being a passive figure in the ghost-seeing scenario and hypothesised a '*clairvoyant invader*' who is the agent-as-percipient. This invader, Myers argued, could discern a distant scene in which he could generate a hallucinatory vision, although this so-called 'invasion' may be subliminal or confused by the death-crisis.[121] Thus, in this situation, the percipient becomes an active agent,

so that A dies and A's phantom appears to B, and A is set down simply as an agent, and B is set down as the only percipient concerned. But in such cases I hold that A is quite as truly a percipient as B is but that the shifting of the threshold of consciousness which accompanied his perception, – whether that shift were from waking to sleep-waking or from life to death, – prevents him, even if his consciousness is shifted back again, from recalling or recording that perception as a link in his chain of normal memories.[122]

The site of the ghost-seeing experience becomes a '*phantasmogenetic centre*' wherein a space is spiritually or psychically invaded and A becomes a symbolic vision liable to perception by anyone in the locality.[123] Yet these theories were, it seemed, undermined *a priori* by the existence of unconscious latency:

the recollection of an act of clairvoyance is itself an occurrence as rare as is the perception of an apparition; it involves the same difficult translation of a quasi-percept from the supernormal to the normal consciousness. The very act of clairvoyance presupposes a psychical condition as far removed as may be from the stream of every-day sensation.[124]

While, compared to Gurney's theory, this was a simpler way of explaining how ghost-seeing could be collective, it still faced the problem of

[120] Gurney, Myers and Podmore, *Phantasms*, vol. II, p.267.
[121] *Ibid.*, p.311.   [122] *Ibid.*
[123] Frederic W.H. Myers, *Human Personality and Its Survival of Bodily Death* (New York, 1909), p.177.
[124] Gurney, Myers and Podmore, *Phantasms*, vol. II, p.303.

latency and deferment, and crucially it had no cumulative evidence to back it up, given that the agent was by definition soon dead, and therefore in no position to attest to reciprocity. What is discernible in this debate is that Myers was perceptibly moving towards a synthetic outlook which relied more upon speculative concepts of the human personality (or soul) and its vital message-sending characteristics than it did upon the quantity of evidence available. The community of sensation, originally established to provide the sociological framework through which a naturalistic theory of ghost-seeing could be built, was gradually being extended to account for post-mortem apparitions; for the SPR this was, as Myers himself put it, a 'momentous step'.[125]

Indeed Gurney in 'On Apparitions Occurring Soon after Death', read posthumously to the Society by Myers in 1889, provided cases in which his theory of latency was not applicable and the agency of a 'decedent' must be supposed. He reminded his readers that *Phantasms* had dealt with post-mortem cases, but had nevertheless included them under the twelve-hour rule: 'We had to suppose that the telepathic transfer took place just before, or exactly at, the moment of death; but that the impression remained latent in the percipient's mind, and only after an interval emerged into his consciousness.'[126] While Gurney still maintained that the evidence for phantasms of the dead was not as strong as that for phantasms of the living, he believed that the theory of latency was now open to revision due to the pressure of so many cases apparently involving the phantasms of the deceased where a psychical or physical condition on the agent's side 'comes into existence at a distinct interval after death', i.e., that the dead may appear to the living.[127] Gurney published a case submitted to the SPR by Kate M. Clerke in 1884 that fits in with this theme. In 1872 while staying in a hotel in Sorrento with her two daughters she saw the figure of an old woman in a shawl in her bedroom:

She stood motionless, silent, immovable, framed by the doorway, with an expression of despairing sadness, such as I had never seen before. I don't know why I was frightened, but some idea of its being an imbecile or mad woman flashed through my mind, and in an unreasoning panic I turned from the drawing-room door, with its melancholy figure, and fled through the bedrooms to the terrace. My daughter, on hearing of my fright returned to the rooms, but all was in its wonted stillness; nothing was to be seen.[128]

---

[125] Frederic W.H. Myers, 'On Recognised Apparitions Occurring More Than a Year after Death', *PSPR* 6 (1889–1890), 13.
[126] Edmund Gurney and Frederic W.H. Myers, 'On Apparitions Occurring Soon after Death', *PSPR* 5 (1888–1889), 406.
[127] *Ibid.*, 407.   [128] *Ibid.*, 466–7.

Clerke subsequently received a visit from the local padre who, on hearing her tale, declared that she had seen the old mistress of the hotel who had died, six months before, in the room over hers. Yet Gurney was still loath to attach any of the popular notions of ghosts to such cases arguing that they were 'transitional ghosts' occupying a midway position between the phantasms which appeared at the moment of death and the traditional 'haunting' ghost: naturalistic terminology and respectability was paramount here, as always.[129]

In a contradistinctive move, Myers attempted a radical redefinition of what it was that was termed the 'ghost'. To be sure, Myers disputed the popular notion of the ghost as a deceased person permitted to return by Providence in order to communicate with the living. Myers pointed out that: there was no evidence for this 'permission' given by an unseen force; as examples of self-projected phantasms proved, it was not certain that the ghost was, in fact, the *real* personality of the deceased; there was little evidence for any specific motivation to communicate on the part of ghosts.[130] Instead, Myers proposed to define the ghost as 'a manifestation of persistent personal energy, – or as an indication that some kind of force is being exercised after death which is in some way connected with a person previously known on earth'.[131] Using the analogy of post-hypnotic suggestibility, where the percipient may suddenly act upon, or react to, suggestions made by the hypnotiser in the past, Myers presented an idea of the ghost as an automatic phenomenon, devoid of the usual behaviour and motivation of normal 'waking' life:

It may be entirely absorbed in the fulfilment of an idea implanted in the decedent's mind in his earthly days, or impressed upon him at the moment of death. Thus we may conceive a murdered man, for instance, as feeling persistently that he ought not to have been murdered, – that his existence should still be continuing in his earthly home. And if his apparition is seen in that house, we need not say that he is 'condemned to walk there', but rather that his memory or his dream goes back irresistibly to the scene which in a sense he feels that he still belongs.[132]

Myers's notion of the ghost as an automatic phenomenon implied a radically phantasmagorical and haunted world, a site of previous events, memories and dreams that never disappear from the visual world, but can be relayed through hallucinatory vision. Thus the dreams of the dead become a real phenomenon capable of being externalised, and passed on, in the real world of the living. It was by using the analogy with dreams that Myers could posit the real world as merely one stratum

---

[129] *Ibid.*, 476.   [130] Myers, 'On Recognised Apparitions', 14–15.   [131] *Ibid.*, 15.
[132] *Ibid.*, 34.

of many states of existence that sometimes interpenetrate with varying levels of consciousness, from intelligent communication, to subliminal messages, to the dreamlike or nonsensical action of reported ghosts. In this system a communication from the departed remained a veritable communication, yet one that must be examined through the two laws governing post-mortem manifestations: firstly, the idea of telepathy, already fully rehearsed within the SPR and the keystone for psychical interpretations of the ghostly world, and secondly, what Myers called the 'multiplex personality', the idea that the human mind possesses many strata of consciousness and memories and may play host to the 'uprushes' of the subliminal consciousness.[133]

With Gurney and Myers's shift to investigation of phantasms of the dead, the SPR was exploring treacherous terrain, for the notions of such phenomena as phantoms and haunting ghosts veered close to the popular conceptions of the ghostly world as publicly expressed by the, frequently plebeian, spiritualists that the Cambridge-educated savants distrusted as credulous and unscientific. Yet Myers held that his psychical theory of phantasms of the dead was a likely one precisely *because* of its foreignness to imaginative concepts of ghosts in popular culture and literary ghost stories:

> And thus, absurdly enough, we sometimes hear men ridicule the phenomena which actually do happen, simply because those phenomena do not suit their preconceived notions of what ghostly phenomena ought to be; – not perceiving that this very divergence, this very unexpectedness, is in itself no slight indication of an origin outside the minds which obviously were so far from anticipating anything of the kind.[134]

Yet in response to this Podmore published an article in the *PSPR* which poured cold water on Myers's speculations and laid out the strict evidential standards which, he believed, any case alleging the activity of phantasms of the dead must pass. The case, Podmore argued, should prove veridicality either by being a collective vision, by the percipient(s) receiving information that was not known at the time, by the recognition of the phantasm in question, by the discovery of human remains at the haunted site, or by the presentation of evidence as to a 'tragic event' having occurred at the haunted site. Analysing the cases which Myers had put forward in his article, Podmore remained unconvinced that the manifestations of the departed had been so proved: in his opinion there was very little separating the characteristics of the ghost, with its lack of veridical messages, from the subjective hallucination.[135] Furthermore, if

---

[133] *Ibid.*, 47.   [134] *Ibid.*, 16.   [135] Podmore, 'Phantasms of the Dead', 237.

it were true that hallucinations are in any way hereditary, contagious or capable of being telepathically communicated to another person in the same locality, then arguments in favour of a subjective agency to explain cases of haunting ghosts would be strengthened immeasurably.[136]

Podmore's writings after the publication of *Phantasms* show that naturalistic telepathy was as far as he was willing to go to explain the ghost-seeing experience, and he persistently stuck to the hallucination theory so current in the nineteenth century. While Podmore concentrated on the perceptual errors of ghost-seers, arguing (especially when it came to phantasms of the dead) that 'a strong mythopoeic tendency' was at work, Myers began to investigate the higher questions which such subjects inspired. For Myers the question posed had changed from 'Do phantasms of the dead exist?' to 'Does man survive?'[137] Thus the SPR researches and investigations into ghost-seeing came to assume cosmic significance for Myers. As he wrote in 1890, 'it is the most important problem in the whole range of the universe which can ever become susceptible of any kind of scientific proof'.[138] The same questions and sense of yearning that Myers and Sidgwick expressed during their 'star-light walk' in 1869 remained unresolved as the century reached a close. Podmore (who, unlike Myers had actually been a card-carrying spiritualist in the 1870s) did not, at this stage, have the same sense of existential crisis that constantly affected Sidgwick, Gurney and Myers: the former memorably noted the 'alternatives of the Great Either-Or seem to be Pessimism or Faith'.[139] Escape from the spectre of agnosticism could come from acceptable proof of ghosts which would lead man towards a true understanding of the universe and a perfect knowledge of the true nature of life. In this situation Myers placed an enormous obligation upon percipients to send in cases urgently to the SPR which would answer the doubts as to the reality of disembodied agencies, and which would prove sceptics such as Podmore wrong. This was a scenario in which, as Myers put it, 'Human testimony is on trial':

It remains, that is to say, to be seen whether Science can accord to honest testimony (of a kind which can rarely be confirmed by direct experiment)

---

[136] *Ibid.*, 243.   [137] *Ibid.*, 231.

[138] Frederic W.H. Myers, 'A Defence of Phantasms of the Dead', *PSPR* 6 (1889–1890), 315.

[139] Sidgwick and Sidgwick, *Henry Sidgwick: A Memoir*, p.340. Gurney's writing sometimes displayed a note of nihilism: 'If for the worst and most permanent suffering there were no possibility of arrangement of hope, if I found in myself and all around me an absolute conviction that the individual existence ceased with the death of the body, and that the present iniquitous distribution of good and evil was therefore final, I should in consistency desire the immediate extinction of the race.' Cited in Epperson, *The Mind of Edmund Gurney*, p.79.

a confidence sufficient to bear the strain put upon it by the marvellous matters for which that testimony vouches. I believe that the veracity, the accuracy of our informants, taken *en masse* will ultimately support that strain, and that the world will be convinced of veridical apparitions as the world has been convinced of meteorites.[140]

Both Podmore and Myers believed telepathy to be sufficiently proved; yet Myers insisted that the proof of this phenomena was but a hint of further and greater revelations to come in the area of the human personality and believed that telepathy destroyed the 'purely physiological synthesis of man, and opens a doorway out of materialism which can never be shut'.[141] Myers was now announcing his movement towards a speculative grand synthesis which would unite the multifarious, and sometimes contradictory, phenomena which the SPR had been investigating since 1882. Myers's grouping together of ghost-seeing, sensory automatism, telepathy, mesmerism/hypnotism and mediumship was directed toward the aim of achieving a scientific demonstration of the existence of the human soul: such a demonstration was no longer absolutely necessary it seems. Thus, by 1891 at least, Myers was a spiritualist in all but name: for psychical research this represented a return of the repressed, the repackaging of basic spiritualist philosophy through the superstructure of abnormal psychology.[142] *Human Personality and Its Survival of Bodily Death* suggests that the soul became the greatest ghost of all, and one which, unlike the more empirical variety reported and collected in the field, Myers could actually experience for himself.

A science of the soul?

In his essay of 1901, 'Frederic Myers's Service to Psychology', William James placed Myers's thought within a romantic type of psychological investigation, as distinguished from the classic-academic type.[143] The epitome of this romantic, and deeply poetic, approach to psychical research was Myers's magnum opus *Human Personality and Its Survival*

---

[140] Myers, 'A Defence of Phantasms of the Dead', 316.   [141] *Ibid.*, 318.
[142] See Frederic W.H. Myers, 'Science and a Future Life', *Nineteenth Century* 29 (1891), 628–47. Sidgwick noted in his diary for 20 July 1884: 'F.W.M. getting steadily more theosophical in his own theory.' Cited in C.D. Broad, 'The Life, Work, and Death of Edmund Gurney', C.D. Broad Papers. Gauld argues: 'It was in part Myers' studies of phantasms of the dead that led him to conviction [of survival]; but what clinched matters was a message from Edmund Gurney which he received through Mrs. Piper in 1890.' Gauld, *The Founders*, p.322. Myers's increasing orientation towards spiritualism apparently led to a rapprochement between the spiritualist movement and the SPR. See 'After Twelve Years', *Light* 14 (27 January 1894), 42.
[143] James, *Essays in Psychical Research*, pp.193–4.

of Bodily Death, like *Phantasms* a two-volume work, which was posthumously published in 1903. As a collection of the psychical research that Myers was engaged in from the mid-1880s to his death in 1901, it propounded an intellectual synthesis of the varied supernormal phenomena which had been studied by the SPR in its first two decades, including such phenomena as hypnotism, hysteria, genius, phantasms of the dead and sensory and motor automatisms in a grand system based in equal measure upon a psychology of the unconscious and an intellectual yearning for certainty in the realm of the cosmic. It is the double nature of Myers's thought – the fact that this yearning, always present within the Sidgwick Group, was here no longer repressed – which will conclude this chapter. For it was with the publication of Myers's *Human Personality* – which has not unjustly been described as a 'religio-scientific gospel' and 'the Bible of British psychical researchers' – that the search for tangible evidence of post-mortem existence was psychologised, legitimised *and* re-spiritualised, thereby profoundly influencing a new generation of spiritualists and psychical researchers and largely superseding the quest to naturalistically prove the telepathic theory of ghost-seeing.[144]

What were the characteristics of this 'romantic psychology', and how did it affect the SPR's interpretation of ghost-seeing? Myers had demonstrated a distinct intellectual trajectory from his belief in the telepathic hypothesis of ghost-seeing, to a postulation of a clairvoyant invasion in his afterword to *Phantasms*, to an independent view of the concept of phantasms of the dead based upon the 'psychorrhagic' mechanism of the agent who, by an in-built, and unconscious, ability, had been able to 'break the soul free' and appear to a percipient or collective percipients as a hallucination. So, with his articles on the subliminal consciousness coming to the forefront of his activities in the SPR, Myers began to propagate the notion of the soul as a valid unit of analysis in psychical research, thereby leapfrogging the Sidgwick Group's unfinished quest to prove phantasms of the living. The shift behind Myers's development can be traced to his researches during the 1890s in the concept of the 'subliminal self' – a faculty that he believed was present in all subjects, not only hysterics or the hypnotised. By 1894 he had decided that he was on the left wing of psychical research and began a personal project to establish scientific proof of survival, or at least, an empirically valid

[144] W.H. Mallock cited in Turner, *Between Science and Religion*, p.129; René Sudre cited in Carlos S. Alvarado, 'On the Centenary of Frederic W.H. Myers's *Human Personality and Its Survival of Bodily Death*', *Journal of Parapsychology* 68 (2004), 18. *Human Personality* continues to exert a significant influence in psychology, parapsychology and psychical research. See especially Edward F. Kelly, Emily Williams Kelly, Adam Crabtree *et al.*, eds, *Irreducible Mind: Toward a Psychology for the 21st Century* (Lanham 2006).

'science of the soul'.[145] For this, Myers needed to conceptualise a mind-structure that would involve a multiplex concept of the mind with many streams and strata of consciousness co-existing with each other and problematising the notion of unitary and stable selfhood:

> I suggest ... that the stream of consciousness in which we habitually live is not the only consciousness which exists in connection with our organism. Our habitual or empirical consciousness may consist of a mere selection from a multitude of thoughts and sensations, of which some at least are equally conscious with those that we empirically know. I accord no primacy to my ordinary waking self, except that among my potential selves this one has shown itself the fittest to meet the needs of common life. I hold that it has established no further claim, and that it is perfectly possible that other thoughts, feelings, and memories, either isolated or in continuous connection, may now be actively conscious, as we say, 'within me', – in some kind of co-ordination with my organism, and forming some part of my total individuality. I conceive it possible that at some future time, and under changed conditions, I may recollect all; I may assume these various personalities under one single consciousness, in which ultimate and complete consciousness, the empirical consciousness which at this moment directs my hand, may be only one element of many.[146]

The mystical inclinations in this mind-structure are evident in Myers's belief that man lives in two interpenetrative worlds, the material and the 'methetherial', or spiritual, which is where the soul finds its natural environment. These two planes of existence – the earthly and the cosmic – correspond to Myers's division of the supraliminal and subliminal selves and he was convinced that humans possessed a soul, a spirit or a transcendent self the properties and powers of which could be glimpsed in the occurrence of supernormal phenomena.[147] Owing to this atomistic mind-structure, the theories of Myers departed distinctly from those propounded by spiritualists who retained a belief in the unitary human personality and individual soul that visited loved ones for the purposes of communication.[148] However, it is clear that for Myers, psychology and spiritualism were interlinked disciplines, allowing him to justify an intense focus beyond telepathy into the precarious realms of metaphysical speculation. This could be regarded as an answer to Tyndall's famous call in 1874 for science to 'wrest from theology, the entire domain of cosmological

---

[145] Myers, 'The Drift of Psychical Research', 191.
[146] Cited in Turner, *Between Science and Religion*, pp.123–4.
[147] John J. Cerullo, *The Secularization of the Soul: Psychical Research in Modern Britain* (Philadelphia, 1982), pp.102–3.
[148] On the confusion surrounding Myers's definition of the soul see Gauld, *The Founders*, pp.300–12.

theory',[149] but, ironically, actually led to a cultural re-orientation which solidified psychical research's twentieth-century status as a deviant, or border science.[150] This categorisation was made a lot easier given the non-objective and, as Podmore would have put it, the 'mythopoeic' character of Myers's thought: like Gurney he simply *needed* to find the Universe friendly.[151] In this way, *Human Personality* was in accord with the Europe-wide 'revolt against positivism' that prefigured the emergence of various intuitionist philosophies in the 1890s.[152] Indeed, Myers's romanticist psychology may be regarded as the foreground for a desperately lyrical, emotional and frequently confusing quest to re-establish the place of religion at the heart of the human sciences, to the extent that by the turn of the century the activities of the SPR represented, in the words of Oppenheim, a 'surrogate faith'.[153] Critics thereby judged the SPR to be a quasi-scientific organisation with well-meaning but unprofessional members committed to proving the spiritual nature of man. Expressing the thoughts of many in the twentieth century, L.S. Hearnshaw wrote:

The truth perhaps rather is that both in Myers and the other early psychical researchers, scientific method was never pushed to its final limits. Their theories were ultimately shaped by the wishes and yearnings which decided them to undertake the task.[154]

This return to religion (understood as non-specific and eclectic) was explicitly laid out by Myers in his Presidential Address to the Society in

---

[149] Tyndall, *Fragments of Science*, vol. II, p.210.

[150] Seymour H. Mauskopf notes that psychical research/parapsychology 'is paradigmatic of marginal science in that it has always attracted the mantle of scientific method and objectivity and attracted outstanding intellectuals and scientists to its support, particularly in the late nineteenth century'. Seymour H. Mauskopf, 'Marginal Science', in *Companion to the History of Modern Science*, ed. R.C. Olby, G.N. Cantor, J.R.R. Christie and M.J.S. Hodge (London, 1990), p.876. On the question of whether psychical research is a pseudo-science or not see Thomas Hardy Leahey and Grace Evans Leahey, *Psychology's Occult Doubles: Psychology and the Problem of Pseudoscience* (Chicago, 1983); Seymour H. Mauskopf and Michael R. McVaugh, *The Elusive Science: Origins of Experimental Psychical Research* (Baltimore and London, 1980); R.G.A. Dolby, 'Reflections on Deviant Science', in *On the Margins of Science: The Social Construction of Rejected Knowledge*, ed. Roy Wallis (Keele, 1979), pp.9–47; H.M. Collins and T.J. Pinch, 'The Construction of the Paranormal: Nothing Unscientific Is Happening', in *On the Margins of Science*, ed. Wallis, pp.237–70.

[151] Gauld, *The Founders*, p.149.

[152] H. Stuart Hughes, *Consciousness and Society: The Reorientation of European Social Thought, 1890–1930* (London, 1959), pp.33–66.

[153] Oppenheim, *The Other World*, p.152.

[154] L.S. Hearnshaw, *A Short History of British Psychology 1840–1940* (London, 1964), p.160.

1900 where he spoke of 'the sheer moral need of discovering a future life, if the cruel injustices of this life are to be conceived as compatible with a First Cause worthy of love or worship'.[155] Furthermore he stated that the task that the SPR set itself was to prove the *'preamble of all religions'*.[156] The members of the Sidgwick Group all experienced the same fear of the abyss in an agnostic world; however, unlike Gurney, who died an early death, and Sidgwick, who was neither a psychologist nor a poet, it was left to Myers to attempt to articulate a science of the soul on behalf of the SPR. In this sense, Myers's thought could hardly be accepted as legitimately 'scientific', no matter how far contemporaries' understanding of the term could be stretched.[157] With Myers, Oliver Lodge remarked in 1901, 'the word science meant something much larger, much more comprehensive: it meant a science and a philosophy and a religion combined. It meant, as it meant to Newton, an attempt at a true cosmic scheme.'[158] Through the theories and case studies presented in *Human Personality* Myers believed he had provided empirical evidence for the existence of the soul. He especially focused on motor automatisms such as automatic writing and drawing, telekinesis, and possession to the detriment of sensory automatisms, of which ghost-seeing was the most prominent. This movement 'from terrene to transcendental things' neglected the Society's traditional utilisation of statistical method and all but burnt its bridges with scientific naturalism.[159] It was the shift toward metaphysical system-making which made investigations into different classes of ghost-seeing largely superfluous. As Renée Haynes notes, in the first decades of the twentieth century the SPR's investigations into ghost-seeing were scaled back as interest into the phenomenon of mediumship and automatisms came to the fore.[160]

---

[155] Frederic W.H. Myers, 'Presidential Address', *PSPR* 15 (1900–1901), 110.
[156] *Ibid.*, 117.
[157] Although *Human Personality* was swiftly included as part of the course for the examination for the Fellowship of Philosophy at Trinity College, Dublin. See 'Lecture by Professor Barrett', *Freeman's Journal* (26 March 1909).
[158] Oliver Lodge, 'In Memory of F.W.H. Myers', *PSPR* 16 (1901–1903), 7. Myers himself wrote: 'by the word "scientific" I signify an authority to which I submit myself – not a standard which I claim to attain. Any science of which I can here speak as possible must be a *nascent* science – not such as one of those vast systems of connected knowledge which thousands of experts now steadily push forward in laboratories in every land – but such as each one of those great sciences was in its dim and poor beginning, when a few monks groped among the properties of "the noble metals", or a few Chaldean shepherds outwatched the setting stars.' Myers, *Human Personality*, p.2.
[159] Gurney, Myers and Podmore, *Phantasms*, vol. II, p.316.
[160] Haynes, *The Society for Psychical Research*, p.44. This interest in the mental and physical phenomena of spiritualism was, of course, always present in the SPR. Of special note were the Society's investigations of Eusapia Palladino and Leonora Piper which

Indeed, following the publication of papers on phantasms of the dead during 1889–1890 by Gurney, Myers and Podmore, there was no significant SPR work carried out on ghost-seeing until Eleanor M. Sidgwick's 'sequel' to *Phantasms* – a renewed study of phantasms of the living – was published in the *PSPR* in 1923.[161] This shift in concern was aided by the development of abnormal psychology (especially the concept of multiple personality disorder), and the publications of classic works on mediumship and religious experiences sympathetic to psychical research such as Théodore Flournoy's *From India to the Planet Mars* (1900) and *Spiritism and Psychology* (1911), and William James's *The Varieties of Religious Experience* (1902).

This gradual disappearance of interpretations of non-spiritualistic, or scientifically orientated, ghost-seeing can be manifestly explained by the intellectual shifts in the SPR caused by the deaths of most of its major figures. By the turn of the century the Sidgwick Group had all but disappeared (Hodgson died in 1905 and Podmore in 1910) and the momentum and sense of optimism that had infused the early period of the SPR's activities all but dissipated. Spiritualism had survived the *fin-de-siècle* and despite its becoming more controversial than ever, with fraud becoming more elaborate – and in the case of spirit photography more technological – the movement was to witness its second great flowering following World War I under the inspiration of Arthur Conan Doyle's proselytising and Lodge's influential work *Raymond: or, Life and Death* (1916). Marching forward with similar pace were intellectual movements aligned with the new techno-scientific age that, as was demonstrated above, either repelled the scientific claims of the SPR or disregarded it as a relic of Victorian neo-spiritualism. From a historical perspective, the failure of the Society to break through into mainstream science by the turn of the century appears to have resulted in a paring-down of the movement to its default position and basic core emotion: hope. Even at the moment of the dissolution of the Sidgwick Group, Podmore, a peripheral member (and one of its most sceptical), could write in his farewell letter to the dying Sidgwick:

I am not sure now that I very much care whether or not there is a personal, individual immortality. But I have at bottom some kind of inarticulate assurance that there is a unity and a purpose in the Cosmos: that our own lives, our own

involved the Sidgwick Group, Hodgson and William James. See Gauld, *The Founders*, pp.221–74.
[161] Eleanor M. Sidgwick, 'Phantasms of the Living: An Examination and Analysis of Cases of Telepathy between Living Persons Printed in the "Journal" of the Society for Psychical Research Since the Publication of the Book "Phantasms of the Living", By Gurney, Myers, and Podmore, in 1886', *PSPR* 33 (1923), 23–429.

conscious soul, have some permanent value – and persist in some form after death. And if you will let me say it – you and some others, just by being what you are, constantly revive and strengthen that assurance for me. I feel that there is a meaning in things![162]

While Podmore was hardly accepting the Myersian assertion of the survival of the soul, the movement of prominent members of the SPR towards a belief in spiritualism was undeniable. This trend was nowhere more prominently seen than in the conversion of such a forceful and sceptical figure as Richard Hodgson, the psychical researcher who, it is recalled, had exposed the theosophical movement as fraudulent in 1884 and was generally the scourge of mediums worldwide.[163]

Thus by the end of the 'heroic' period of psychical research, it was clear that spiritualism had made its spectral return. While scientific naturalists sympathetic to psychical research would be forgiven for thinking that the SPR 'had a great future behind it', the classic thought-transference tests of the early 1880s still undermined the legitimacy of the Society which, it must be remembered, assumed that telepathy was a given. The unlikely reappearance of George A. Smith who, after Gurney's death, had gradually dropped out of SPR activities in the 1890s, further tarnished the Society's reputation. After leaving the SPR, Smith had turned to the new wonders of cinematography and began making ghostly films in Brighton from 1897, leading Michael Balcon to call him 'the father of the British Film Industry'.[164] The type of films he made during this period attest to the interest which the spectro-nunciative still held for Smith, and also shows the extent to which such subject-matter could be at home both in the SPR scientific experiments on telepathy and the new mass entertainment of ghostly films.[165] While pointing to a cultural current able to broadcast itself

---

[162] Frank Podmore to Henry Sidgwick, 27 August 1900. Henry Sidgwick Papers.
[163] After his death Hodgson was reported to have returned in spirit form. See James, *Essays in Psychical Research*, pp.253–360. It was not until 1932 that Eleanor Sidgwick declared that she was 'a firm believer both in survival and in the reality of communication between the living and the dead'. Cited in Helen de G. Salter, 'Impressions of Some Early Workers in the S.P.R.', *Journal of Parapsychology* 14:1 (1950), 33.
[164] Cited in Frank Gray, ed., *Hove Pioneers and the Arrival of Cinema* (Brighton, 1996), p.30.
[165] Gray writes about Smith's interest in uncanny themes: 'A number of "lost" films from 1898 best illustrate this interest: *The Corsican Brothers* ("One of the twin brothers returns home from shooting in the Corsican Mountains, and is visited by the ghost of the twin. By extremely careful photography the ghost appears quite transparent."), *Photographing a Ghost* ("A Photographer's Studio. Two men enter with a large box labelled 'ghost'. The photographer scarcely relishes the order, but eventually opens the box, when a striking ghost a swell steps out. The ghost is perfectly transparent, so that the furniture, etc., can be seen through his 'body'."), *Faust and Mephistopheles* ("Faust discovered in his study.

equally in the sphere of science and spectacle, such a postscript, given the performance background of Smith, seriously dents the validity of Gurney's experimental trials in the 1880s and reinforces the 'double nature' which has been identified as being an integral part of the SPR. Furthermore, in a damaging episode for the SPR reminiscent of the Creery case, Smith's partner in the SPR tests, Blackburn, confessed in 1908 that they were in fact fraudulent.[166] It is thus largely unsurprising that in his study of the early SPR Alan Gauld has pointed out that, to the best of his knowledge, 'the nearest any member of the Society got to encountering a ghost was to hear odd raps and other minor noises in the Brighton house occupied on behalf of the S.P.R. in 1888–1889 by Mr. G.A. Smith'.[167] That Smith, and not any member of the Sidgwick Group, had the closest thing to an actual ghost-seeing experience recorded by a Society member is surely an unfortunate conclusion and one that throws a revealing light on all that has been discussed above.

★ ★ ★

'Crisis' has been a word much used in this chapter to describe the activities and subject-matter of the SPR, and, indeed, the personal feelings of some of its members: however, perhaps the word 'prolepsis' would more adequately describe the essence of the SPR project on ghost-seeing. Luckhurst has noted how for the SPR, legitimacy always had 'a proleptic structure' – acceptance was always just around the corner, it was believed: soon the savants could no longer deny the deluge of good evidence. Telepathy went from being a parlour game, to a working hypothesis, to a solid belief in a matter of years: at no point, however, did it become a fact accepted by the scientific community.[168] Yet the SPR did have the community of sensation which provided it with a framework, a symbolic language, and a huge repository of ghost stories on which the Society could build a telepathic theory of ghost-seeing. Unfortunately, even this community seemed to abandon the SPR as the expected influx of well-attested case narratives post-*Phantasms* never

---

Mephistopheles appears in a cloud of smoke (fine effect), offers Faust renewal of youth if he will sign bond"), *The Mesmerist, or Body and Soul* ("Professor Fluence is in his study visited by an old lady who wishes to see some 'Mesmerism'. Professor mesmerises little girl and proceeds to draw her 'spirit' from her body. Little girl's spirit leaves her body and walks over the furniture. 'Spirit', which is quite transparent, is finally conducted back to the body, and mesmerist awakens his subject, much to the relief of the old lady")'. Gray, *Hove Pioneers*, p.30.

[166] See Hall, *The Strange Case of Edmund Gurney*, pp.125–49. The Smith–Blackburn episode has been used by Hall to suggest that Gurney committed suicide in 1888. For a counter-argument see Gauld, *The Founders*, pp.179–82.

[167] Gauld, *The Founders*, p.196. See Podmore, 'Phantasms of the Dead', 309–13.

[168] Luckhurst, *The Invention of Telepathy*, p.73.

materialised. In 1886 William James had ominously announced, 'Either a flood of confirmatory phenomena, caught in the act, will pour in ... or it will *not* pour in – and then we shall legitimately enough explain the stories here preserved as mixtures of odd coincidence with fiction.'[169] In the next chapter the renewed SPR attempt to prove the ghost through the use of the concept of hallucinations of the sane is traced, but for now it is sufficient to note that the greatly anticipated deluge of well-attested and documented ghost-seeing cases in the 1890s never occurred. As R.G.A. Dolby notes,

> widespread popular interest in a deviant science is difficult to maintain. Once the issue is no longer novel it loses newsworthiness unless it can continue to produce new and varied achievements. Thus, it is common for popular deviant sciences to die away rapidly as fashionable discussion turns to other things.[170]

In the end, as expressed by James, the SPR project to prove the validity of ghost-seeing was essentially epistolaric in praxis. The fact that James (and later Bergson) understood this, and yet still believed in the SPR theory of ghost-seeing, attests to the strength of the community of sensation and the success of the 'quest' in proving the ghost as a form of *natural history*, as they put it.[171] In his review of *Human Personality* James regretted that Myers 'was cut off by death before he could write his direct discussion of the evidence for spirit-return'.[172] In a sense James's statement was soon contradicted: the true sequel to this epistolary enterprise, and one which lies outside the boundaries of this study, may be found in the episode of the 'cross correspondences' – a complex attempt to prove post-mortem existence in which different mediums in different parts of the world received communications from the 'spirits', which primarily included Myers, Sidgwick and Hodgson, that were then compared and combined to form 'veridical' messages.[173]

This chapter has worked through a relatively narrow frame of reference. The SPR's promotion of the telepathic theory of ghost-seeing was the first and most remarkable attempt to scientifically prove the ghost. However, the SPR's second great attempt to prove the ghost in late

---

[169] James, *Essays in Psychical Research*, p.27.
[170] Dolby, 'Reflections on Deviant Science', p.20.
[171] James, *Essays in Psychical Research*, p.211; Henri Bergson, *Mind-Energy: Lectures and Essays*, trans. H. Wildon Carr (London, 1921), p.65. Myers also used the analogy between psychical research and natural history. 'Correspondence', *JSPR* 4 (1889–1890), 149. On the natural-historical approach to psychical research see Mauskopf and McVaugh, *The Elusive Science*, pp.6–7.
[172] James, *Essays in Psychical Research*, p.212.
[173] See Oppenheim, *The Other World*, p.132; Luckhurst, *The Invention of Telepathy*, pp.253–6.

Victorian Britain deserves to be placed within its own context, that is, within the inter-disciplinary hallucination discourses of the nineteenth century. Through this examination the place of the SPR ghost emerges within a much more holistic and contestative environment than was possible to map out within this chapter, and the reasons for the great 'institutional failure' of the SPR ghost-seeing project, touched upon above, are dealt with at more length. The next chapter also serves to introduce some of the metaphorical aspects of the ghost-seeing experience, as the oneiric dimension of the hallucinatory experience became the most consistent expression to describe how sane people saw ghosts.

5   The concept of hallucination in late Victorian psychology

The concept of hallucination in the Society for Psychical Research

The general approach of the scientific and medical establishment to the activities of psychical research was epitomised by a note in *Lancet* that announced the formation of the SPR and referred to its series of

what must surely be serio-comic interrogatories to the public in relation to 'hallucinations' and 'dreams'. An invitation is thrown out to all the weak-minded people who think they have seen 'ghosts' or 'spectres', or been 'touched' by mysterious shades, and to all the dreamers who dream dreams of the nature of 'coincidences', to state their experiences.[1]

Here it is clear that the subject-matter of the SPR had been grouped under the signifier of the 'weak-will' familiar to the anti-spiritualist discourse in abnormal psychology which pathologised both the phenomena themselves, *and* the urge to seriously investigate such issues. *Lancet* wondered if any philosophical society of presumably sane men had the moral right to invite the supernatural accounts of 'the mad folk outside Bedlam', the 'crazy public'. The author of the note warned that such investigations could have disastrous consequences for people with 'weak brains' given that all spiritualistic phenomena must be considered morbid.[2] While the manner in which the medical model viewed psychical research was extreme, it is significant vis-à-vis the topic of this chapter that the canvassing methodology behind the SPR was represented as heterodoxical and a dangerous threat to the mental health of the population.

This situation confirms that the SPR concept of hallucination represented a rupture in the standard descriptive psychopathology of the nineteenth century which had followed the later thought of Kant in specifically keeping the form of a psychological disorder apart from its

---

[1] 'Psychical Research', *Lancet* (22 December 1883), 1104.   [2] *Ibid.*

particular content.[3] While the *fact* of the hallucination would be fully examined by Gurney, it was the *content* of the hallucination which really became the major debating point in psychical research in the 1890s, thus creating the possibility for a more psychological and socio-cultural model of hallucination to emerge in opposition to prevailing interpretive trends which medicalised and pathologised hallucinatory experience.[4] This was never going to be easy: by the last two decades of the nineteenth century the medical model of hallucination had become based on the concept of dissociation, increasing the sophistication and experimental support of pathological arguments. In the first movements towards a rival model for psychical research, Gurney closely examined the mechanism of hallucination in an essay of 1885.[5] Gurney began by citing Taine's view that all instinctive judgements of visual, auditory and tactile percepts could be considered hallucinations, yet noted that to adopt such a view would lead one to describe ghost-seers such as Nicolai as *less* hallucinated than a healthy person, in that Nicolai specifically investigated his phantoms on the assumption that they originated in his mind.[6] To define Nicolai's ghost-seeing as a case of hallucinatory experience proper, Gurney included an important criterion of memory-investigation: thus a sensory hallucination would be '*a percept which lacks, but which can only by distinct reflection be recognised as lacking, the objective basis which it suggests*'.[7] This use of the reflective faculty distinguished hallucinations from the imagery of day-dreams and night-dreams, for in both cases there is no need for 'distinct reflection' to distinguish what are self-evidently the internal products of the mind from an objective reality.[8]

By the late Victorian period it had become evident to psychologists that the issue of whether the object of sensation existed in reality was actually irrelevant to the hallucination debates. Instead the mechanisms and significance of the hallucinatory process itself came under attention. The spectral illusion theorists had stressed the peripheral and retinal origin of hallucinations; in contrast to this Esquirol had outlined the argument that hallucinations had a central origin in the brain. Taking elements of both viewpoints, Gurney proposed that the hallucination had its origin in the brain as an organ of the mind, but also that the senses participated in its

---

[3] See German E. Berrios, 'Historical Background to Abnormal Psychology', in *Adult Abnormal Psychology*, ed. Edgar Miller and Peter J. Cooper (Edinburgh, 1988), p.32; Karl Jaspers, *General Psychopathology*, trans. J. Hoenig and Marian W. Hamilton (Manchester, 1963), pp.58–9.
[4] On the content of hallucinations see Parish, *Hallucinations and Illusions*, pp.185–220.
[5] See also Barrett, Massey, Moses *et al.*, 'Third Report of the Literary Committee', 167–70.
[6] Gurney, 'Hallucinations', 163.   [7] *Ibid.*   [8] *Ibid.*, 164.

mechanism.[9] In this psychical theory of hallucinations the ideas of the French psychologists Jules Baillarger and Alfred Binet proved important to Gurney. In his defence of the central-origin theory, Baillarger had put forward three major arguments: significant peripheral stimulation fails to develop the hallucination; the frequent correspondence between visual, tactile and olfactory hallucinations argues against sensual abnormalities as the source of the hallucination; and hallucinations often refer to dominant thoughts and ideas in the imagination of the percipient.[10] Yet for Gurney, Baillarger ignored the existence of external excitants which initiated the central creation and projection of the hallucination. For evidence of this Gurney examined the experimental hypnosis undertaken by Binet at the Salpêtrière clinic. In his treatment of five hysterical girls Binet verbally induced visual hallucinations in them while they were in the somnambulist stage of hypnotism. Binet went on to publish impressive findings which suggested that the hallucination could be suppressed by a screen, that the hallucination took the bilateral form as in external vision, that mechanical pressure on the eye doubled the hallucination, and that a mirror could reflect the hallucination experienced.[11] Binet's conclusion that the visual hallucinations examined by him seemed to exist in a point in space outside the percipient's mind moving as the eye moves – the *point de repère* – and were subject to normal optical illusions allowed Gurney to speculate that it was this point in space that provided the entry point of external excitation into the brain, where the central origin of the hallucination could be created. Yet, beyond Binet, Gurney concluded that hallucinations must first take shape as ideas before they are converted into sensory projections. Thus the creative force for the hallucination is ideational but it sets in motion the sensory machinery which executes the idea: hallucinations have a centrifugal origin.[12] Such a development proved the breakthrough that the SPR needed to propound a new model of hallucination.

The 'Report on the Census of Hallucinations'

While Gurney stayed well inside the precincts of mainstream psychological discourse in his essay on hallucinations (which was published in both the *PSPR* and *Mind*), this outline would provide the SPR with

[9] See Gurney, Myers and Podmore, *Phantasms*, vol. I, pp.464–95.
[10] Gurney, 'Hallucinations', 168–9.
[11] Alfred Binet, 'Visual Hallucinations in Hypnotism', *Mind* 9:35 (1884), 413–14.
[12] Gurney, 'Hallucinations', 192, 195, 198. For other centrifugal theories, such as those offered by the German psychiatrists Wilhelm Griesinger, Richard von Krafft-Ebing and Emil Kraepelin see Parish, *Hallucinations and Illusions*, pp.113–21. See also Sidgwick, Johnson, Myers, Podmore and Sidgwick, 'Report', 137.

a basis on which to construct a scientifically valid concept of hallucination to run in tandem with, and psychologically explain, the telepathic theory of ghost-seeing which had been expounded in *Phantasms of the Living*. Yet there remained the problem of large-scale evidence: where was the statistical verification that could translate 'coincidental hallucinations' into actual cases of ghost-seeing? In a remarkably prescient article of 1848 the Scottish chemist Samuel Brown had summarised the essential problem of ghost-seeing in the age of modern investigation:

> The synchronism of the apparition with the hour of death is the important point here, and it is the only one. Yet no man is in a condition to settle it scientifically: and it will never be settled until all the apparitions of absent friends, occurring during a given time throughout a given population, shall be collected, and until the number of these which were coincident with deaths be thereafter eliminated. The proportion of the coincidences to the negations will show whether the former can be comprehended under the doctrine of chances. Until this vast and difficult collection and comparison of instances be undertaken and completed, no scientific judgement can be pronounced.[13]

A census of 5705 people on the question of hallucinations and their possible veridicality was conducted by Gurney and published in *Phantasms*. This small survey had found, Gurney argued, that chance-coincidence could not explain many incidences of veridical hallucinations, and therefore the issue merited a more extensive census in the future. The fallout from the publication of *Phantasms*, both the sustained criticism it had received and the sense of anti-climax among SPR members, prompted the Society to push ahead with plans for a much larger survey on incidences of spontaneous hallucinations and ghost-seeing experiences than had been conducted in *Phantasms*. It was hoped that such a survey would supply the SPR with the proofs it needed to demonstrate to the scientific establishment that crisis-apparitions and related phenomena existed and were capable of statistical quantification. The momentum behind this project was rendered all the more necessary following the sudden and tragic death of Gurney: what would become the Census of Hallucinations developed into a memorial for – and attempted intellectual legitimisation of – the SPR's most important early member. While this was planned internally in the SPR from as early as 1884, the co-operation of the larger scientific and psychological community was deemed necessary to throw the net of quantitative impact as wide as possible.[14]

---

[13] Brown, 'Ghosts and Ghost-seers', 404.
[14] See Barrett, Massey, Moses *et al.*, 'Second Report of Literary Committee', 48.

The interests of the SPR occupied a major role in the proceedings of the International Congress of Experimental Psychology, which took place in Paris in August 1889.[15] Sidgwick, Eleanor M. Sidgwick, Myers and his brother, the physician A.T. Myers, represented the SPR, while William James attended in his capacity as a founding member of the ASPR. It is a significant fact that, apart from the four psychical researchers, Francis Galton was apparently the only other English psychologist in attendance at the Congress. The Congress, which was co-ordinated, in the noted absence of Jean-Martin Charcot, by Germain-Théodore Ribot and Charles Richet, outlined three main areas for collective investigation; namely, a statistical inquiry into the hallucinations of the sane, the validity of the heredity approach to psychology, and the problem of hypnotism.

Surprisingly, the issue of the census of hallucinations was dealt with rapidly and with little or no dissension (although Pierre Janet unsuccessfully argued that cases of hallucinations of the insane and hysterical be studied alongside those of the sane and normal).[16] The Congress

[15] Originally called 'The Congress of Physiological Psychology', the attendees changed the name of the gathering to 'The International Congress of Experimental Psychology' during the course of the debates.

[16] The Congress was largely dominated by the sessions on the nature of hypnotism and related phenomena with Richet and Delbœuf strongly arguing, against Janet, that normal, non-hysterical patients could be hypnotised. At stake here was the outcome of the long-running dispute between the Nancy and Salpêtrière schools of psychiatry. See Robert G. Hillman, 'A Scientific Study of Mystery: The Role of the Medical and Popular Press in the Nancy–Salpêtrière Controversy on Hypnotism', *Bulletin of the History of Medicine* 39:2 (1965), 163–82; Ruth Harris, *Murders and Madness: Medicine, Law and Society in the 'Fin de Siècle'* (Oxford, 1989), pp.171–85; André Robert LeBlanc, 'On Hypnosis, Simulation, and Faith in the Problem of Post-Hypnotic Suggestion in France, 1884–1896', PhD thesis, 2000, University of Toronto, pp.12–14; Bertrand Méheust, *Somnambulisme et médiumnité*: vol. I, *Le Défi du magnétisme* (Paris, 1999), pp.471–597. In 1889 the Salpêtrière perspective on hypnosis achieved its apotheosis with the publication of Janet's dissertation *L'Automatisme psychologique*. From the SPR's point of view it was clear that Nancy was emerging as the victor of the dispute, with Bernheim's work on suggestion in particular demonstrating how the induction of hypnosis was prevalent in all psychological types and could not be considered a morbid symptom in itself, but rather a useful method of psychotherapy. In his critique of Janet's work, Myers wrote: 'Hypnotisability indicates neither health nor disease; but merely a facility of communication or alteration between different strata of the personality. The facility of such interchange (like other capacities of strong organic reaction to given stimuli) may be harmful or helpful according to the circumstances of each case. It is probable that those who are morbidly unstable to begin with will be hypnotisable also. And thus it is found on the whole (though with considerable divergence between observers) that hypnotised subjects are specially hypnotisable. But this fact constitutes no presumption whatever that all hypnotisable subjects will be morbid. As well might one say that because drunken men fall very sound asleep, therefore everyone who falls asleep must be more or less drunk.' Frederic W.H. Myers, 'Professor Pierre Janet's "Automatisme psychologique"', *PSPR* 6 (1889–1890), 193.

authorised the screening question put forward by the SPR, and proposed 1892 as the date for the presentation of its report which would be under the management of Sidgwick, but mostly compiled by Eleanor M. Sidgwick. While it was suggested that the management of the Census be in the hands of 'experts', it was soon realised that the envisaged level of statistical gathering demanded a more bottom-up approach if a large figure was to be raised. At this stage Sidgwick believed that at least 50,000 answers to the Census question would be needed for a strong report one way or the other.[17] As part of this development William James believed that collectors hostile or indifferent to the theory of telepathy as outlined by psychical research were more than welcome to participate.[18]

In the event, the 'Report on the Census of Hallucinations' was delivered in preliminary format at the next International Congress of Experimental Psychology, which was held in London in 1892, and was fully published by the SPR in 1894, taking up most of the *PSPR* published that year. Collecting began in April 1889 and was halted in May 1892 when the figure of 17,000 was reached, a figure significantly lower than Sidgwick's envisaged total.[19] Despite appeals for input placed in periodicals such as *Mind, Nineteenth Century, New Review, The Review of Reviews* and not least the *PSPR*, the SPR had found it difficult to sustain a high level of collecting.[20] The collectors were 410 in number; 223 women and 187 men, of whom about half were either members of the SPR or friends of members, and it was claimed that the majority, 'about nine-tenths', were 'educated' and up to the standard of the professional class.[21]

The Census sought to ascertain what proportion of people in the general population had experienced a sensory hallucination while in a wakeful state. The screening question put to percipients was:

---

[17] Arthur T. Myers, 'International Congress of Experimental Psychology', *PSPR* 6 (1889–1890), 185.

[18] William James, 'The Congress of Physiological Psychology at Paris', *Mind* 14:56 (1889), 616.

[19] About 16,000 of the answers came from Britain or other English-speaking countries with the remaining 1000 made up of contributions from Brazil, Russia and mainland Europe. See Sidgwick, Johnson, Myers, Podmore and Sidgwick, 'Report', 159.

[20] See Henry Sidgwick, 'Address by the President on the Census of Hallucinations', *PSPR* 6 (1889–1890), 7–12; W.T. Stead, 'Wanted, a Census of Ghosts!', *The Review of Reviews* 4 (1891), 257–8. Sidgwick noted that, if each of the roughly 700 members and associates of the SPR collected 25 cases, they would soon have 35,000 to work with. Henry Sidgwick, 'Address by the President. Second Address on the Census of Hallucinations', *PSPR* 6 (1889–1890), 407–28.

[21] Sidgwick, Johnson, Myers, Podmore and Sidgwick, 'Report', 34–5.

Have you ever, when believing yourself to be completely awake, had a vivid impression of seeing or being touched by a living being or inanimate object, or of hearing a voice; which impression, so far as you could discover, was not due to any external physical cause?[22]

This question, which was delivered 'impartially and unselectively' to men and women over the age of 21,[23] was ambiguously worded, as noted by the authors themselves, in that the proviso – *'when believing yourself to be completely awake'* – was a subjective judgement and not proof of actually being objectively and verifiably in a wakeful state.[24] Of the 17,000 answers, 2272 were in the affirmative, but after close analysis and adjustments, many of these were deemed invalid due to a misunderstanding of the question, an unreliable answer or an answer which indicated an organic, delusive or dreaming origin of the hallucination. The Report thus found that 1684 people who had answered Yes to the screening question were valid percipients: that is, 9.9% of respondents claimed to have experienced a hallucination at some point in their lives, and that this was a generally a unique experience.

Of the total number of hallucinations, 1112 were primarily visual in sense, 494 were auditory, and just 179 were tactile.[25] The Report's finding that 7.8% of men and 12% of women respondents had experienced a hallucination, a ratio of three female percipients to every two males, corresponded with Gurney's earlier statistics on the relation between hallucinatory experience and gender,[26] and also supported Galton's claims in his *Inquiries* that women have a markedly stronger visualising capacity than men.[27] The Report also found that hallucinations were most frequent

---

[22] *Ibid.*, 33.   [23] *Ibid.*, 34. On the class make-up of the census see *ibid.*, 35.
[24] 'Strictly interpreted, for instance, it may be held to include impressions occurring during sleep, if the percipient while asleep, believed himself to be awake; and a few of those who answered understood the phrase in this sense.' *Ibid.*, 34.
[25] *Ibid.*, 44–7. Out of the visual hallucinations, about 95, or 9% of the total, were collective hallucinations. *Ibid.*, 303. The predominantly visual quality of hallucinations may be compared with the findings of some dream surveys conducted in the 1890s in which vision was at the head of the hierarchy of sense modalities, followed by audition, tactility and the sense of smell. See Mary W. Calkins, 'Statistics of Dreams', *American Journal of Psychology* 5:3 (1893), 311–43; Sarah C. Weed, Florence M. Hallam and Emma D. Phinney, 'A Study of the Dream-consciousness', *American Journal of Psychology* 7:3 (1896), 405–11. See also Robert Armstrong-Jones, 'Dreams and Their Interpretation, with Special Application to *Freudism*', *Journal of Mental Science* 63 (1917), 210. Writing in 1975, Celia Green and Charles McCreery found that in cases of apparitions 84% related to the sense of sight, 37% involved the sense of hearing and 15% the sense of touch. Celia Green and Charles McCreery, *Apparitions* (London, 1975), p.80.
[26] Gurney, Myers and Podmore, *Phantasms*, vol. II, p.3.
[27] Sidgwick, Johnson, Myers, Podmore and Sidgwick, 'Report', 152–4.

among 20–29-year-olds.[28] On the issue of the mechanism of hallucination, the Report was supportive of Gurney's centrifugal theory of origin, arguing that in cases of ghost-seeing the sensory organs were involved only secondarily in the process, with the cerebral activity of the brain being excited by visual, auditory or tactile impulses similar to or indistinguishable from those presented by the peripheral organs.[29] The authors of the Report were keenly aware of the inevitable criticisms that would be directed at their evidential methodology, and so included a chapter devoted to an examination of the trustworthiness of the results obtained. Here they largely ruled out issues such as the possibility of deception, the danger of positive selection of percipients, and temporary or permanent forgetfulness as negligible, improbable and guarded against.[30]

Being an SPR enterprise, the Report indicated its special interest in solving the question of 'coincidental' or 'veridical' hallucinations through a comparison between these cases with non-coincidental cases. From there it was hoped that a possible physical basis for telepathy would be discovered. It also dealt with the issue of phantasms of the dead, holding that the establishment of such a possibility would offer proof of a continued existence after death and lead to the conclusion that telepathy is a spiritual faculty allowing for communication between different spheres of existence.[31] However, this quasi-spiritualist hypothesis was largely held at bay in the Report, and the fact that such cases were rare and difficult to prove impelled the authors to remain, for the moment, in the safer territory of the faculty of telepathy between living people.[32] Similarly, phenomena such as collective hallucinations, premonitions and local cases of haunting were all held to be evidentially weaker than the crisis-apparition class of phenomena, but ultimately explainable on the basis of the telepathic hypothesis. Supporting the speculations contained in the *PSPR* and *Phantasms*, the Report noted the tendency of visual hallucinations to assume the familiar form of the figure the percipient was accustomed to see, and a significant lack of any cases of ghost-seeing which resembled the romantic or gothic ghost of popular culture. Through the gradual honing of valid testimonies, the Report

---

[28] With reference to the Report, Slade and Bentall note that this age group is at maximum risk for developing schizophrenia. Peter D. Slade and Richard P. Bentall, *Sensory Deception: A Scientific Analysis of Hallucination* (London and Sydney, 1988), p.69.

[29] Sidgwick, Johnson, Myers, Podmore and Sidgwick, 'Report', 148.

[30] *Ibid.*, 56–69.   [31] *Ibid.*, 365.

[32] This was widely regretted by the spiritualists who, however, did nonetheless praise the standard of report produced. The editor of *Light* wrote, 'There is no Parliamentary Blue-book of the year which will much surpass this in the matter of well-sifted evidence.' 'The Census of Hallucinations', *Light* 14 (29 September 1894), 462.

published a close analysis of strong cases of hallucinations coinciding with the death of the person seen, heard or felt, and thus indicative of a telepathic transmission.

The calculations of chance-coincidence in the Report were as follows: the average annual death-rate for England and Wales between 1881 and 1890 being about 1 in 19,000, out of a sample of 19,000 cases of ghost-seeing, 1 would necessarily be a death-coincidence according to the general probability of a person dying on any given day in 365 days. However, by taking 30 strong cases of death-coincidence out of the number of 1300 recognised hallucinations, a 1 in 43 chance of seeing a crisis-apparition was reached, 440 times the normal chance. By contrast, according to the average death-rate, 570,000 (30 times 19,000) apparitions would be expected to be perceived in order to produce the 30 death-coincidences selected by the authors. On the basis of these figures, the authors believed themselves entitled to view the connection between the death of a person, and the appearance of the apparition of that person in hallucinatory form, as a proven fact beyond the realm of chance and therefore indicative of the existence of telepathy.[33]

The Report published sixty-two cases that they believed were among the strongest veridical hallucinatory incidents beyond the realm of chance or coincidence. However, they quickly faced a familiar problem in the SPR's culture of ghost-hunting: the crucial lack of verifiable documentation. In the sixty-two cases, twenty-four percipients had been interviewed as part of the Report, yet only six had written notes at the time of the hallucination which could be checked against the time of death of the agent. But, 'In only one of them has the note been preserved, and then only in ambiguous form, but in three others ... there is evidence, independently of the percipient's memory, that the note was made at the time.'[34] The SPR explanation for this gaping lack of evidence this time was a cultural one: quite a small amount of the general population keep diaries; the percipient would not naturally write of the ghost-seeing experience in a letter, especially if her close friends and family were within oral contact; percipients afraid of being designated superstitious would be reluctant to immediately note the event, and would probably not actually do so until the death event had confirmed the hallucination.[35]

The following case may be taken as typical of the manner in which cases designated as strong examples of death-coincidences were presented in the Report (note the internal inconsistency as to whether the experience was designated a dream or not):

[33] Sidgwick, Johnson, Myers, Podmore and Sidgwick, 'Report', 246.
[34] Ibid., 211.   [35] Ibid., 221–2.

From Mrs. J. P. Smith.

Amble, Northumberland, January 17th, 1891.

'In June, 1879, I was a teacher in Macclesfield. A friend, Mrs. ——, was near her confinement. She told me she was afraid she would die. I went into the county of Durham for a holiday. While there I was roused from sleep by Mrs. —— as I supposed. She was shaking me, and saying, "I have passed away, but the baby will live." Then the figure left the room by the door. I got out of bed and went to my sister and related the incident. We agreed to make a note of it. Next day I received a letter from a friend in Macclesfield saying that Mrs. —— was dead but the baby was alive.

[I was] in the best of health and about 29 years of age.

No other persons were present.'
  Mrs. Smith, who is the mistress of the Infants' School at Amble, informs us that this is the only experience of the kind she has ever had, and that to the best of her recollection the apparition was seen about an hour or two after the death.
  Unfortunately, neither the note made at the time nor the letter announcing the death has been preserved, but we have received the following letter of corroboration from Mrs. Smith's sister:—

203, Elswick-street, Leichhardt, Sydney, Australia, *November 2nd,* 1891.

'I distinctly remember my sister coming into my room and waking me up to tell me of her dream, which was as follows:—
  That she had dreamt that a lady friend of hers some miles away had appeared to her and said she was dead; but that her baby would live. The dream had evidently impressed my sister very much, as she seemed quite agitated, and we said we would note it down, and to our utter astonishment the next morning my sister received a letter to say that her friend had passed away that same night. ANNIE BROWN.'
  It will be observed that Mrs. Smith's experience is here referred to as a dream. That this is not her own view of it appears from the following account given by Professor and Mrs. Sidgwick of an interview which they had with her on September 16th, 1891. The account was written within two hours of their seeing Mrs. Smith, from notes made at the time.
  'The figure appeared twice on the same night. The first time was in the breaking dawn of a June morning, before there was any sun. It woke her, and she heard the words she mentions, but she did not get out of bed, and was probably only half awake. The second time the same thing happened, but she is quite sure she was awake. It appeared at the left hand side of her bed, and, after speaking, it moved very quickly round the bed and apparently through the door, which was at the right hand side of the bed parallel to the head and hidden by the curtains, so that she did not see it go out. The figure went as if in a great hurry. It seemed to be dressed in drab; the face was seen – it seemed exactly as in life. She felt no fear, nor sense of the supernatural – only anxiety to question further – and regarded it as real until, running after the figure downstairs, she became convinced that it was a vision. She felt as she ran as

though she would have caught it up, had she not had to open the door. It was about 5 o'clock when she went to her sister, which she did at once after the second vision. Mrs. —— had told her she thought she should not live, but Mrs. Smith had thought little of this, and it had quite passed out of her mind. She was in no anxiety. Mrs. —— was no special friend of hers. Her children came to Mrs. Smith's school, and she was interested in them. She did not know why Mrs. —— should have told her of her expectation of dying; but she said at the same time, 'If I go, you will be very kind to my children.' The friend who wrote telling her of the death mentioned it casually – especially as sad because of the young children. She mentioned the time as in the early hours of the morning, and it struck Mrs. Smith when she got the letter that the vision had been coincident with the death, but she did not verify this by ascertaining the exact time of the death.

Mrs. Smith told us that when she communicated what she had seen to her sister, the latter said it must have been just a very vivid dream, to which she replied, "Well, it was a very vivid one, then", or words to that effect.'

This case was not known to the collector beforehand.

This is another case where there is more than a mere coincidence, since information as to the death was given and also as to the survival of the baby. It perhaps adds to the force of the evidence for telepathy here, that the dying mother is likely, from the circumstances of the case, to have had Mrs. Smith specially in her mind at the time of the death.[36]

In this manner, the Report offered the well-organised empirical data which Gurney had craved, and continued the great thesis underlying *Phantasms*: the moment of death was not a single occurring event, but an atomised experience which represents a fulcrum for supernormal activity that may be scientifically verifiable. The Report made the claim that sensory hallucinations tend to increase as the death of the agent approached, strongly clustered around the moment of death, and continued for a short time following death before gradually receding as time passes. To the SPR, the conclusion was unavoidable 'that there is no discontinuity at the moment of death, – no sudden transition from a state in which communication with the living is possible to a state to which it is not'.[37]

Dreaming while awake

One of the most surprising findings of the Report were the statistics which showed the prevalence of sensory hallucinations experienced when the percipient was in bed or had just been sleeping: in thirty-eight per cent of visual cases, thirty-four per cent of auditory cases and forty-four per cent of tactile cases the hallucination had taken place in this manner. Considering what a small amount of time the average person spent in

[36] *Ibid.*, 214–16.   [37] *Ibid.*, 376.

their bed, the authors observed, these figures were striking.[38] The SPR's answer to this finding was that a state of repose or abstraction was either necessary, or more likely, proved beneficial to the telepathic impression being manifested as a hallucination. This was the interpretation put forward by Gurney as part of his theory of latency. However, the authors of the Report were aware of the critical implications such blatant statistics suggested: surely the percipients were experiencing a hypnagogic illusion, or a sensory deception in the dark and quiet of the night, or more obviously still, were not in fact awake, but in the borderland between wake and sleep, and therefore still dreaming? Pre-empting such sceptical speculations, the authors outlined a standard sleep-waking paradigm which, while it allowed for the definition of the dream as a pure hallucination, postulated that in each person's dream-scenario there was an 'unmistakable chasm, which he crosses in the conscious transition from sleep to waking'.[39]

Yet it was precisely the promotion of this paradigm that was attacked in the only major critique of the Report from the psychiatric or psychological disciplines, Edmund Parish's *Hallucinations and Illusions: A Study of the Fallacies of Perception* (1897).[40] Here, the German psychologist argued that experimental psychology had proved that the average person was capable of gross errors in the judgement of their subjective states and the status of their consciousness. Parish made the now familiar point that the content and mechanisms of dreams and hallucinations were remarkably similar, and, citing the findings of Maury, demonstrated how visual, auditory and tactile phenomena experienced during sleep could greatly influence the dream narrative, an area not sufficiently explored by the Report.[41] Another way that it was extremely difficult to distinguish dreams from hallucinations, Parish stressed, was the fact that both types of phenomena maintained the same status when lodged in the memory and recovered at a later stage: after the death of the agent.

---

[38] *Ibid.*, 171.

[39] *Ibid.*, 71. The Report did note a small number of exceptional cases in which the dream blended into a hallucination. See, for instance, *ibid.*, 71–2.

[40] This was a translation and expansion of Parish's earlier work *Über die Trugwahrnehmung* (1894). Rather bizarrely, Gauld judged that Parish's criticisms were 'not worth summarising'. Gauld, *The Founders*, p.184. William James considered Parish's main argument 'by far the strongest objection yet made' to the Report. James, *Essays in Psychical Research*, p.77.

[41] See, for instance, Wilhelm Wundt, *Lectures on Human and Animal Psychology*, trans. J.E. Creighton and E.B. Titchener (London, 1901), p.321. For a contemporary study which proposed an essential psychological unity between sleeping and waking life see Weed, Hallam and Phinney, 'A Study of the Dream-consciousness', 405–11. See also Parish, *Hallucinations and Illusions*, pp.96–7.

Parish supported the arguments that Royce put forward in his criticism of *Phantasms* that cases of veridical hallucinations were in fact hallucinations of memory, or *hallucinations rétroactives*:[42]

> The frequent recital of an interesting occurrence tends to imprint a distinct picture of it on the mind, and the vividness of the mental image serves further to confirm the percipient's conviction of having been fully awake at the time – a delusion common with persons in a drowsy, half-asleep condition. It is not, then, much to be wondered at if gradually all subsidiary detail fades away, until finally there remains in the memory only two points of cardinal importance – the hallucination itself, and the conviction of having been fully awake.[43]

Writing in 1897, Havelock Ellis, who was editor of the Contemporary Science Series which published *Hallucinations and Illusions*, seemed to agree with Parish's belief that cases of dreaming while awake were dissociative. Ellis believed that the phenomenon of 'hypnagogic paramnesia', or mistaking what has happened in a dream for what has taken place in real life, was in fact an internal hallucination and could explain the determining influence of dreams in human culture as 'a means whereby waking life and dream life are brought to an apparently common level'.[44]

The typical uncritical attitude and lack of surprise exhibited in many of the hallucination narratives further suggested a mental attitude consistent with a dreamy state of dissociation.[45] Indeed it was Parish's comparison between the psychological state of mind in crystal-vision

---

[42] Parish, *Hallucinations and Illusions*, pp.277–86. For Beaunis's notion of 'waking somnambulism' see LeBlanc, 'On Hypnosis, Simulation, and Faith', p.37.

[43] Parish, *Hallucinations and Illusions*, p.106. The paradox of attempting to answer the question, 'Am I asleep?', existed in ancient philosophical debates and haunted Cartesian rationalism: it was noted above that Schopenhauer found it difficult to ascertain legitimate criterion for differentiation between dream and reality. Plato has Socrates present Theaetetus with the familiar riddle: ' "The question is asked, what proof you could give if anyone should ask us now, at the present moment, whether we are asleep and our thoughts are a dream, or whether we are awake and talking with each other in a waking condition." ' Needless to say, Theaetetus cannot conceive of any such proof, given that the two states of being have exact correspondences and that the imagination may imagine one is dreaming while awake, and while awake we may believe that we are in a dream state. Plato, *Theaetetus; Sophist*, trans. Harold North Fowler (London, 1921), p.63.

[44] Havelock Ellis, 'A Note on Hypnagogic Paramnesia', *Mind* 6:22 (1897), 284.

[45] On the passivity of the percipient: 'Hallucinators usually just stand and marvel. Typically, they feel no desire to probe, challenge, or query, and take no steps to interact with the apparitions. It is likely . . . that this passivity is not an inessential feature of hallucination but a necessary precondition for any moderately detailed and sustained hallucination to occur.' Daniel C. Dennett, *Consciousness Explained* (London, 1991), p.9. On the concept of dissociation as it related to psychical research see Carlos S. Alvarado, 'Dissociation in Britain during the Late Nineteenth Century: The Society for Psychical Research, 1882–1900', *Journal of Trauma & Dissociation* 3:2 (2002), 9–33.

and the narratives of ghost-seeing published in the Report that led him to his thesis that a dissociative consciousness was common to both. Parish's evidence for this conclusion was largely textual, and indeed he paid tribute to the honesty of the percipients and the care of the collectors for publishing such narratives in full and in their original language.[46] In Parish's reading, case narratives of veridical hallucinations were full of hints and betrayals indicative of the dreaming-while-awake state of mind:

In December 1886 I was awakened one night by my children ... I attended to them, and lay down again. Suddenly there was a nun standing before my bed.

Early in the morning, while still in bed, I suddenly saw (I believe I was fully awake) the figure of my mother, who had died two years before. (She often appears to me in dreams and when half asleep, but never so distinctly as on this occasion.)

At the time referred to (according to my recollection between 1 and 2 A.M., towards the end of November 1879) I felt as though a hand touched me on the right shoulder, and turning round I seemed to see the form of my friend, Lieutenant Chr—— ... I could in nowise explain the occurrence as I believed myself to be fully awake. According to my usual habit I was studying, and absorbed in the book I was reading, but was nevertheless, as I certainly believe, fully awake.[47]

Here it is manifestly apparent that Parish designated as 'dream' what the SPR called subjective hallucinations.[48] But this designation relied upon an instinctive psychological judgement on the basis of certain 'textual markers' that predominate in the psychical ghost story, markers such as 'I had gone to bed', 'I was awoken suddenly in the middle of the night', and, indeed, the post-hallucination belief in its veridicality or death-coincidental status.[49] William B. Carpenter had written about

---

[46] Parish, *Hallucinations and Illusions*, pp.292–3.
[47] *Ibid.*, pp.343, 345, 96–7. Eleanor Sidgwick responded: 'Now all that we are concerned with from the statistical point of view is the percipient's classification of his experience. He must, after it is over, and when he is in a completely wakeful and normal state, attribute to it the waking quality, – recollect and class it as a waking hallucination. It was in order to avoid any begging of the very question Herr Parish raises, that, in collecting the statistics, we inquired – not as to the fact of the percipient's being awake when the hallucination occurred – but as to his belief about it.' Eleanor M. Sidgwick, '*Zur Kritik des Telepathischen Beweis Materiels*. By Edmund Parish. Leipzig. 1897', *PSPR* 13 (1897–1898), 595. See also Sidgwick's response to Parish's designation of death-coincidental cases as waking dreams. *Ibid.*, 596–7.
[48] However, the co-identity of dreams and hallucinations had been noted by Gurney in *Phantasms*. Gurney, Myers and Podmore, *Phantasms*, vol. I, p.484. See Peirce's criticisms that some of the cases in *Phantasms* were not sufficiently separated from dreams. Peirce, *Writings*, pp.123–4.
[49] Hans-Jürgen Bachorski outlines what marks a text as a dream: 'When a sequence within a text begins with a phrase such as "she dreamt the following" or "she had a heavy dream", a shift in the type of text follows. Just as literary texts, for example, may involve a "fictionality

the extreme difficulty in ascertaining the difference between dreaming and reality, 'the past *mental* experience having been as complete in the one as in the other'.[50] For Parish, any connection with the world of sleep or dream became modifying clauses in the hallucination account, even if, as shown above, the percipient repeatedly stressed the belief that they were awake. Parish thus radically altered the whole topography of the SPR enterprise by moving the psychological goal posts behind the percipient on the basis of a dissociative *point de départ* which highlighted the *a priori* fallacy of the reports of ghost-seeing. The conscious mind was something that could not be trusted when it came to ghost stories; indeed it was the mind itself that was steadily revealing itself to be haunted by the uncertainty of knowing what was dream and what was not, of knowing what was a ghost and what was a hallucination.

Parish's criticisms of the Report, based upon the fundamental difficulty of distinguishing when the subject was awake, asleep, or dreaming, certainly proved the resilience of the notion of dreaming while awake and its new application in the context of the concept of dissociation at the turn of the century. In this regard it is notable that despite its interventions and pioneering studies in abnormal psychology, the SPR concept of dissociation eschewed any emphasis of pathology or trauma in its construction of the ghost-seer.[51] On the contrary, the SPR use of the notion of dreaming while awake, as seen in the writings of Podmore and Lang in the 1890s, remained consistently embedded in a post-spiritualist discursive framework which, while emphasising the endless possibilities of deception – given that the hallucination was identified with the dream – also stressed the advent of the telepathic hypothesis as the most scientifically grounded theory of ghost-seeing that could explain the small number of veridical hallucinations that were outside the bounds of chance.[52]

---

pact", which calls upon the reader to regard certain events and narrative strategies as possible, but by no means everything in the account as true, other signals serve to establish the horizon of a specific genre. The expression "once upon a time" at the beginning of a story, for example, not only promises that what follows will be a fairy-tale, but also functions as an abbreviated installation of a system of rules which determines what can happen or be said in the text – and what must not occur or be said. Such "textual type markers" can take the most various forms.' Hans-Jürgen Bacorski, 'Dreams That Have Never Been Dreamt at All: Interpreting Dreams in Medieval Literature', trans. Pamela E. Selwyn, *History Workshop Journal* 49 (2000), 98–9.

[50] Carpenter, *Principles of Mental Physiology*, pp.455–6.
[51] Alvarado, 'Dissociation in Britain', 10–11.
[52] While not a senior member of the SPR, Lang was an associate of the Society and a frequent contributor to the *PSPR* and psychical research debates in general. See Rev. M.A. Bayfield, 'Andrew Lang and Psychical Research', *PSPR* 26 (1912–1913), 419–30.

By the end of the nineteenth century Podmore had emerged as one of the most articulate sceptics in psychical research and the chief supporter of the SPR concept of hallucination. Podmore believed that hallucination was the most plausible explanation for the reported experiences perceived in spiritualistic séances, and those of Home in particular.[53] As a prominent member of the SPR, Podmore was more than familiar with contemporary experiments in hypnosis where sane, normal and intelligent people were easily induced into experiencing the most bizarre hallucinations. This experimental evidence of the fallibility of human perception, allied to the historical evidence of hallucinatory epidemics and hysteria encouraged sceptics to actively minimise, in order to solidify, the scope of scientifically provable supernormal phenomena. Thus, much like Sidgwick, in his investigations into ghost-seeing phenomena Podmore was extremely loath to go beyond the framework of what he believed to be all but certainly proved, namely, the telepathic theory of ghost-seeing.[54]

In this way Podmore sought to explain the marvels witnessed by spiritualists as hallucinations due to the strong presence of 'emotional excitement and the strained expectation which are characteristic of the religious epidemic'.[55] It will be seen that this language is reminiscent of Carpenter's notion of 'expectant attention', and indeed, in his writings *contra* the mediumship of Home, Podmore approached the common-sense scepticism of that great anti-spiritualist. Furthermore, Podmore was more suspicious of the narratives of non-elite ghost-seers than most of his colleagues. In reply to W.B. Yeats, who suggested that investigators should perhaps show more humility towards the popular view of ghosts, Podmore stated that 'he preferred the evidence of educated to that of uneducated: and he would not, as a rule, choose to base a scientific theory of ghosts on folk-lore and the fairy tales current among peasantry'.[56] Yet in his theory of hallucination Podmore did not neglect the fact that the unique atmosphere of the spiritualistic séance – the darkness, anticipation and ruses of the participants – could contribute to unconscious mal-observation and sensory hallucinations among elite

---

[53] Podmore, *Studies in Psychical Research*, p.121. Podmore was the *bête noire* of spiritualists. See Oppenheim, *The Other World*, p.34. The minutes of the Ghost Club show that members were complaining that Podmore, in the research for his *History of Spiritualism*, was determined to prove Stainton Moses a fraud. Ghost Club Minutes 4, 151. See Lang's oppositions to Podmore's theory. Andrew Lang, 'Mr F. Podmore's "Studies in Psychical Research" ', *PSPR* 13 (1897–1898), 606–7.
[54] See Frank Podmore, *Apparitions and Thought-transference: An Examination of the Evidence for Telepathy* (New York, 1915).
[55] Podmore, *Studies in Psychical Research*, p.122.
[56] Cited in 'General Meeting', *JSPR* 4 (1889–1890), 174.

scientific observers. As an example of how this atmosphere dominated the experience of the séance Podmore pointed to the witness testimonies contained in the *Report on Spiritualism* of the London Dialectical Society. For instance, the account of Mrs Honywood's experience at a séance with Home in 1869:

> The room was lighted by a dull fire, and a lamp in the back room. The window was open, and some showy lamps outside, gave it all the appearance of moonlight streaming in at the window. The table rose to a height of two feet, and waved gently in the air; Mr. Home soon passed into a trance, and requested Capt. S– to extinguish the lamp; the back room was only lighted by the light from the lamps outside, and the front room by the fire which had burned low, and only flickered up from time to time. Mr. Home walked over to the open window and stood there, his figure clearly defined by the light outside; between him and the outer a shadow seemed to fall like a veil, and gradually it assumed the form of a head and shoulders advancing and retreating, the left arm outstretched. To me it appeared like gauze, now transparent, and again opaque, but never distinct, or material.[57]

In such physical conditions as these, Podmore felt it was inevitable that participants would be at risk of hallucinating such marvels as the spirit hands and levitations characteristic of Home's repertoire. Yet, in his analysis of the crisis apparitions as reported to the SPR, Podmore did not use the term 'hallucination' in the pejorative sense of a fallacious perception, but took it as a legitimate psychical and mechanistic concept which was a channel for the telepathic impulse. Maintaining that such a veridical hallucination was still a subjective dream, Podmore approached Schopenhauer's theory that one could 'dream the real':

> we find no justification for regarding the vision as other than purely subjective. It is just a dream, the product of the seer's own phantasy. That in some cases it coincides with the death of the person whose image is seen does not make the image more real. That remains a dream image – but a dream initiated by an impulse received from the brain of the dying man.[58]

In *The Book of Dreams and Ghosts* (1897), Lang noted that the theory that ghosts were merely dreams that occurred when the subject believed himself to be awake was the educated opinion during the eighteenth century: by contrast the definition of a ghost as a hallucination constituted

---

[57] Cited in *Report on Spiritualism*, pp.366–7.
[58] Podmore, *Studies in Psychical Research*, p.247. Later Podmore speculated that mediums such as Home and Blavatsky may have had some sort of psychological ability to cause people to see certain visions and dream dreams. Podmore, *Modern Spiritualism*: vol. II (London, 1902), p.268.

the 'modern doctrine of ghosts'.[59] As with most of the psychological and psychiatric community of the nineteenth century, Lang advocated a synthesis of these two positions: that ghost-seeing was dreaming while awake:

Now, the ghostly is nothing but the experience, when men are awake, or *apparently* awake, of the every-night phenomena of dreaming. The vision of the absent seen by a waking, or apparently waking, man is called 'a wraith'; the waking, or apparently waking, vision of the dead is called 'a ghost'.[60]

Thus collective hallucinations have their parallel in the phenomena of 'collective dreaming while awake'.[61] Lang echoed Parish in his conviction that percipients may sleep, or exist in a semi-somnolent state without being at all aware of it.[62] But along with Podmore, Lang used this theory of dreaming while awake to promote the possibility that some of these hallucinatory dreams were more than coincidental, indeed suggestive of 'mental telegraphy', or telepathy, a theory which he believed had the 'advantage of reducing the marvellous to the minimum'.[63] At issue here was the chance-coincidence that a dream of someone dying coincided in time with their actual death. Lang believed, as did Podmore, that it was all a question of evidence. Furthermore, he speculated upon what was needed to attain an answer to the question one way or another, that is, the 'perfect apparition'.[64] This thought-experiment was a ghost which could affect the subject on a multi-sensual level, but also, crucially, affect the physical world around it in a location outside that of the séance-room and SPR narratives, in the visible, public and legal world of assurance and veracity. Such a ghost, Lang concluded, could not be considered a hallucination, telepathic or otherwise.[65]

---

[59] Lang, *The Book of Dreams and Ghosts*, p.vi.   [60] *Ibid.*, p.3.

[61] *Ibid.*, pp.4–5.

[62] However, see Lang's substantial criticisms of Parish. Lang, *The Early Sociology of Religion*: vol. IV, *The Making of Religion*, pp.337–51.

[63] Andrew Lang, *Cock Lane and Common-sense* (London, 1894), p.28.

[64] See also Tyrrell, *Apparitions*, pp.77–80. Dennett, however, believed that a so-called 'strong hallucination' was impossible: 'By a strong hallucination I mean a hallucination of an apparently concrete and persisting three-dimensional object in the real world – as contrasted to flashes, geometric distortions, auras, afterimages, fleeting phantom-limb experiences, and other anomalous sensations. A strong hallucination would be, say, a ghost that talked back, that permitted you to touch it, that resisted with a sense of solidity, that cast a shadow, that was visible from any angle so that you might walk around it and see what its back looked like.' Dennett, *Consciousness Explained*, p.7.

[65] Lang, *Cock Lane and Common-sense*, pp.204–6.

Some conclusions

The SPR had organised the Census of Hallucinations in order to empirically verify the experimental evidence for telepathy. They had received the
co-operation and institutional backing of the discipline of experimental
psychology (as represented by the Congresses of 1889 and 1892) in this
enterprise and justifiably expected it to make a serious impact in the debate
on the concept of hallucination and its possible veridicality. Judged on this
basis, the SPR failed to dislodge the medical model of hallucinations which
had proved so resilient throughout the nineteenth century: the 'perfect
apparition', capable of objective verification once and for all, had never
materialised. Disappointingly for the SPR's attempts to secure intellectual
backing for its concept, the only major criticism of the Report was
the intervention of Parish who significantly pointed in the direction of the
concept of dissociation and subliminal consciousness as the next destination for the hallucination concept. Parish had utilised the dreaming-while-
awake metaphor that was common to most commentators but, more so
than anyone yet, had stressed the actual subjective inability to know when
one was dreaming, and by extension, to know when one was being deceived
by an apparently veridical hallucination. A conclusion such as this radically
undermined the SPR's attempt to base a theory of ghost-seeing on the post-
hallucinatory testimony and documentation of respected percipients.

Manifest criticisms of the Report centred on the fact that a significant
proportion of the collectors were attached, directly or indirectly, to the
SPR, and that the statistical methodology used was far from ideal.
The latter criticism challenged the calculation of the statistical chances of
such a death-coincidence which failed to show the chances of the average
individual of dying.[66] The SPR had banked on utilising the path-breaking
mass-observation model of psychological profiling, and lost. Despite these
manifest criticisms, it is certain that, on a latent level, the Report suffered
the same fate as *Phantasms* in that the scientific community at large could
not accept that the telepathic theory of ghost-seeing was a scientific possibility, instead regarding it as either a fallacy, a delusion or an example of
the mythopoetic impulse behind the quest for new paradigms. The fact
that the Report – the second great crisis of the Society – did not contribute
to the establishment of psychical research as a legitimate scientific
approach by 1900 led to the gradual decline of the SPR as a central unit
of the 'new psychology', and, in the absence of Myers and Sidgwick, the
end of its 'heroic phase'.

---

[66] See Tyrrell, *Apparitions*, p.20.

If the last two decades of the nineteenth century did not bring the hoped-for establishment of psychical research as a legitimate science, the future heralded bleaker prospects. The rise of behaviourism, especially in the United States from the 1910s, discredited subjectivism as a psychological criterion and introspection as an experimental method.[67] As outlined in John B. Watson's landmark *Behavior: An Introduction to Comparative Psychology* (1914), human behaviour was to be examined on the same plane as that of animal behaviour and grounded in the experimental laboratories of the new academic psychology faculties. With its emphasis on rigid control and the use of test-instruments, and an intellectual orientation towards what Bruno Latour has termed 'technoscience',[68] behaviourism did not tolerate the studies of consciousness and the mind–body problem which had dominated the discipline of psychology in the nineteenth century.[69] It is thus significant that it was the prominent psychical researcher William James who bucked the behaviourist trend in the United States by resisting the spread of standardised laboratory tests and a rigid definition of 'science'.[70] This profound shift in the discipline of psychology made the investigations and speculations characteristic of psychical research seem Victorian and outdated, dangerously subjective in character, and ultimately useless in any attempt to understand human psychology. Investigations into the possible veridicality of hallucinations and the quest for objective proof of survival were simply not offered a place within the new academic atmosphere of the early twentieth century where metaphysical speculation, however empirical in methodology, was not welcome.

Writing in 1912, the experimental psychologist Raymond Dodge noted:

I suppose that no reputable scientist would venture to publish any ... alleged discovery in the physical sciences without a careful investigation of his instruments under the precise conditions under which they were used. His statement of instrumental variability, latency, and constant errors would

---

[67] This trend displayed the influence of phrenological doctrines. See John M. O'Donnell, *The Origins of Behaviorism: American Psychology, 1870–1920* (New York and London, 1985), p.73.

[68] Bruno Latour, *Science in Action: How to Follow Scientists and Engineers through Society* (Cambridge, MA, 1987), p.174. See also Deborah J. Coon, 'Standardizing the Subject: Experimental Psychologists, Introspection, and the Quest for a Technoscientific Ideal', *Technology and Culture* 34:4 (1993), 757–83; Robert Boakes, *From Darwin to Behaviourism: Psychology and the Minds of Animals* (Cambridge, 1984), p.139. In 1894, Edward Scripture, at the Yale Laboratory, wrote 'we can do as much for education and mental life in general as physics does for railroads, bridges, and electrical engineering'. Cited in O'Donnell, *The Origins of Behaviorism*, p.139.

[69] Boakes, *From Darwin to Behaviourism*, p.136.

[70] Coon, 'Standardizing the Subject', 778.

212 A science of the soul

constitute data for a scientific evaluation both of his technique and of his experimental results.[71]

Despite the best efforts of the SPR, the ghost-seeing percipient could be neither standardised nor conceived as an experimental instrument due to the community of sensation framework which underwrote the rise of psychical research in Britain: this was based not upon prevailing mechanical or techno-scientific metaphors, but upon deeply emotional and affective states which were in themselves unreliable in an experimentalist context. Furthermore as an emerging science itself, experimental psychology was threatened by the SPR, especially considering the latter's undoubted impact on the discipline in the late Victorian period. The SPR's use of pioneering statistical methods and the 'liberal epistemology' it espoused were denigrated through suspicions of an underlying spiritualist or metaphysical agenda. In contrast to the amateurish, voluntarist and elitist character of the SPR, the focus in academic psychology was now upon creating a new breed of professional experts.[72] The rise of behaviourism in Britain and the United States and the consolidation of experimental psychology worked against the SPR, as indeed it also did against psychical research elsewhere.

Fundamentally though, telepathy and the telepathic theory of ghost-seeing had neither contributed to a paradigm shift in psychology nor been codified into a single, dynamic and empirically rooted concept. The Census of Hallucinations had not resulted in the expected breakthrough of psychical research into the hard sciences, and the borders of the mind were once again heavily policed after the *fin-de-siècle* flirtation and interlinking between the 'new psychology' and psychical research.[73] It is from this point that the beginnings of the discipline of parapsychology may be located, which, with its cult of the laboratory, and its emphasis on the scientifically and statistically verifiable, was from the start orientated towards studies of extra-sensory perception (ESP) and psychokinesis (PK), rather than on the concept of hallucination, or the subject of crisis-apparitions in particular. In the context

---

[71] Cited in *ibid.*, 766.

[72] Scripture did not include contemporary psychical research within the remit of the 'new psychology': 'The objections to psychical research lie in its unscientific methods of experimentation and in the air of occultism in while the whole is enveloped. If the investigators were trained in the psychological laboratory, we might expect interesting discoveries in regard to mind, while at the same time the repellent mysticism would disappear along with odic force, animal magnetism, thought-transference, and other ghosts.' Cited in Harlow Gale, 'Psychical Research in American Universities', *PSPR* 16 (1897–1898), 584.

[73] Deborah J. Coon, 'Testing the Limits of Sense and Science: American Experimental Psychologists Combat Spiritualism, 1880–1920', *American Psychologist* 42:7 (1992), 143–51; Rhodri Hayward, 'Demonology, Neurology, and Medicine in Edwardian Britain', *Bulletin of the History of Medicine* 78 (2004), 37–58.

of the 'discovery of the unconscious', the dominance of behaviourism, and the cultural trend towards a techno-scientific ideal of research and experimentation, using chosen individuals who were witnesses to ghost-seeing as part of scientific methodology, and using spontaneous phenomena in general, became profoundly distrusted as the irrational nature of the mind was further elucidated.[74]

While the emerging philosophies of the unconscious played a mediating role between psychology and the supernatural in the first two decades of the twentieth century[75] – particularly in the work of Théodore Flournoy – debates in psychical research related to the concept of hallucinations, and by extension the telepathic theory of ghost-seeing, never again assumed such intellectual status and comparative innovation as did the debates which took place in the 1880s and 1890s. Despite the pioneering role the SPR played in outlining theories and concepts of unconscious and subliminal mentation linked to supernormal (non-pathological) faculties, the contesting work of Pierre Janet, in particular, became more widespread and the concept of dissociation, with all its implications of morbidity, influenced the writings of a new generation of psychotherapists on the concept of hallucination, among whom psychoanalytic thinkers were prominent. John Cerullo has argued that what he terms the Myersian model of the 'secular soul' was eclipsed at the beginning of the twentieth century by Freudian models of the self 'that could serve the exigencies of modern social organization better than those of psychical research'.[76] Although in 1911 Flournoy could write: 'It will be a great day when the subliminal psychology of Myers and his followers and the abnormal psychology of Freud and his school succeed in meeting, and will supplement and complete each other', such an envisaged rapprochement never took place.[77] On the contrary, the

[74] Judith Devlin writes: 'By the end of the nineteenth century ... the Enlightenment's confidence in the essential rationality and natural virtue of man had been shaken, and psychiatry was ready to present man to the world, with great success, as an irrational creature who could only with difficulty know himself. Psychology revealed man not so much as the conqueror of nature but as being beset by anxiety and uncertainty, sometimes overwhelmed by the strangeness of the world. Seconded by art and literature, it proposed a picture of man different from that espoused by the Enlightenment.' Devlin, *The Superstitious Mind*, p.230.

[75] Flint, *The Victorians and the Visual Imagination*, p.284.

[76] Cerullo, *The Secularization of the Soul*, p.xiii. See also Graham Richards, 'Britain on the Couch: The Popularization of Psychoanalysis in Britain 1918–1940', *Science in Context* 13:2 (2000), 183–230.

[77] Théodore Flournoy, *Spiritism and Psychology*, trans. Hereward Carrington (London, 1911), p.vii. Flournoy also neatly appends the traditional triad of cultural revolutions with Myers in mind: 'We cannot foretell, at the present time, what the future has reserved for the spiritist doctrine of Myers. If future discoveries confirm his thesis of the intervention of the discarnate, in the web and the woof of our mental and physical worlds, then his name will be inscribed in the golden book of the initiated, and, joined to

highly symbolic meeting between William James and Freud at Clark University – via Stanley Hall – demonstrated the extent to which psychoanalysis gazumped many elements of psychical research in the end. Despite an aversion to Freud's dream theory (not coincidentally he suspected Freud of 'being a regular hallucine' in this regard), James was reported to have said to Freud 'The future of psychology belongs to your work.'[78]

Throughout their respective careers, Freud and Jung displayed ambivalent attitudes towards psychical research, and this tension towards the scientific study of the supernatural was evident in their concepts of hallucination.[79] Freud followed the close regressivist analogy between modern children and primitive adults that had been prevalent since Tylor, ascribing hallucinations to a lack of complex experiences.[80] In Freud, that which is wished for 'was simply presented in a hallucinatory manner, just as still happens to-day with our dream-thoughts every night'.[81] When satisfaction was denied the hallucination was abandoned and the reality-principle was established. Hallucinations, therefore, were not separated from fantasies and day-dreams, given that all phenomena were placed under the pleasure principle.[82] Jung addressed the issue of ghost-seeing more directly than Freud, yet he saw hallucinations primarily in terms of the creative unconscious with all its symbolism and archetypal imagery, and not, as the SPR urged, in terms of positivistic scientific naturalism.[83] For instance, Jung wrote of auditory hallucinations:

those of Copernicus and Darwin, he will complete the triad of geniuses who have most profoundly revolutionized scientific thought, in the order, Cosmological, Biological, Psychological.' Flournoy, *Spiritism and Psychology*, pp.66–7. See also Troland, 'The Freudian Psychology and Psychical Research', 405–28; Wilfrid Lay, *Man's Unconscious Spirit: The Psychoanalysis of Spiritism* (New York, 1921).

[78] Cited in Robert I. Simon, 'Great Paths Cross: Freud and James at Clark University, 1909', *American Journal of Psychiatry* 124:6 (1967), 832.

[79] For Freud's relationship with psychical research see Thurschwell, *Literature, Technology, and Magical Thinking*, pp.115–50; Luckhurst, *The Invention of Telepathy*, pp.269–76. This chapter has not dealt with the sexual causes and content of hallucinations. On this see Troland, 'The Freudian Psychology and Psychical Research', 428. It is interesting that Freud conceived of his sexual theory as the only alternative to the 'black tide' of occultism, a subject he feared Jung was all too easily drawn towards. See Carl Gustav Jung, *Memories, Dreams, Reflections*, trans. Richard Winston and Clara Winston (London, 1963), pp.147–8.

[80] Freud, *The Interpretation of Dreams*, p.720; Michael Cole, *Cultural Psychology: A Once and Future Discipline* (Cambridge, MA, and London, 1996), p.15.

[81] Sigmund Freud, *The Standard Edition of the Complete Psychological Works of Sigmund Freud*: vol. XII, *1911–1913: The Case of Schreber, Papers on Technique and Other Works*, ed. James Strachey with Anna Freud (London, 1958), p.219.

[82] See Robert Caper, *Immaterial Facts: Freud's Discovery of Psychic Reality and Klein's Development of His Work* (London and New York, 2000).

[83] See Jung's foreword to Aniela Jaffé, *An Archetypal Approach to Death Dreams and Ghosts* (Einsiedeln, 1999).

Hallucinations of this kind usually derive from the still subliminal, maturer personality which is not yet capable of direct consciousness, as observations of somnambulists show. In the case of primitive medicine-men they come from a subliminal thinking or intuiting which at that level is not yet capable of becoming conscious.[84]

The failure of the SPR concept of hallucination to establish itself was part of a wider intellectual defeat of the psychological model of hallucinations in which the discontinuity model of psychological normality held sway in psychiatric practices. This led to a marked abandonment of widespread studies into the hallucinations of the sane which continued long into the twentieth century.[85] On the other hand, in our contemporary psychiatric context the concept of hallucination is unhesitatingly used in the symp-tomatology of schizophrenia,[86] leading to the popular belief that visual hallucinations are uncommon in the general population and are probably prominent symptoms of major mental disorder.[87] Perhaps one way of

---

[84] Carl Gustav Jung, *The Symbolic Life: Miscellaneous Writings*, trans. R.F.C. Hull (London, 1977), p.461.

[85] An important exception was the SPR's mass-observation survey of 1947 in which 1519 people replied, with 217 in the affirmative, thus echoing the results of the Census published in 1894. D.J. West, 'A Mass-Observation Questionnaire on Hallucinations', *JSPR* 34 (1948), 187–95.

[86] Visual hallucinations occur in about twenty-four per cent of schizophrenic patients, forty to seventy per cent of delirious patients, and up to seventy per cent of manic-depressive patients. See D.W. Goodson, P. Alderson and R. Rosenthal, 'Clinical Significance of Hallucinations in Psychiatric Disorders: A Study of 116 Hallucinatory Patients', *Archives of General Psychiatry* 24 (1971), 76–80; R.H. Mott, I.F. Small and J. Anderson, 'Comparative Study of Hallucinations', *Archives of General Psychiatry* 12 (1965), 595–601. The latest edition of the *Diagnostic and Statistical Manual of Mental Disorders* includes hallucination as a characteristic symptom of schizophrenia. American Psychiatric Association, *Diagnostic and Statistical Manual of Mental Disorders*, 4th edn, *DSM-IV-TR* (Washington, DC, 2000), pp.299–300.

[87] See, for instance, G.W.C. Hanks and N. Cherny, 'Opiod Analgesic Therapy', in *Oxford Textbook of Palliative Medicine*, ed. D. Doyle, G.W.C. Hanks and N. MacDonald, 2nd edn (Oxford, 1998), pp.331–55. On the assumption that hallucinations are pathognomonic, see Mark W. Mahowald, Sharon R. Woods and Carlos H. Schenck, 'Sleeping Dreams, Waking Hallucinations, and the Central Nervous System', *Dreaming* 8:2 (1998), 93. Yet in a recent study about half of patients in a hospice reported recently experiencing visual hallucinations. These were usually of a hypnagogic or hypnapompic nature, and were usually figures of relatives or loved ones. They were not frightening and patients had been afraid of being thought 'mad' if they reported the hallucinations. Averil Fountain, 'Visual Hallucinations: A Prevalence Study among Hospice Patients', *Palliative Medicine* 15:1 (2001), 19–25. For discrepancies in the *DSM-IV* categorisation of hallucination see Mitchell B. Liester, 'Toward a New Definition of Hallucination', *American Journal of Orthopsychiatry* 68:2 (1998), 305–12. For a survey see R.P. Bentall, 'The Illusion of Reality: A Review and Integration of Psychological Research on Hallucinations', *Psychological Bulletin* 107:1 (1990), 82–95. For a speculative view see Julian Jaynes, *The Origins of Consciousness in the Breakdown of the Bicameral Mind* (London, 1993).

re-interpreting the concept of hallucination is through a comparison between contemporary psychological and psychiatric theories of hallucination with nineteenth-century theories that were grounded in the dreaming-while-awake assumption. It is hoped that this chapter contributes to further research in this area. In a similar revisionist vein Sophie Schwartz has suggested the existence of a 'historical loop' between the dream research of the nineteenth century, and that of the late twentieth century, which, following the cognitive revolution, and research on REM sleep, returned to the phenomenological perspective of Maury and Hervey de Saint-Denys, and moved away from the behaviourist and psychoanalytical denigration of given (manifest) mental facts.[88] The existence of just such a loop was made clear in R.R. Llinás and D. Paré's landmark article of 1991, 'Of Dreaming and Wakefulness', which argued for the co-identity of REM sleep and the state of wakefulness: 'Let us formally propose then *that wakefulness is nothing other than a dreamlike state modulated by the constraints produced by specific sensory inputs.*'[89] At the dawn of the millennium the metaphor of dreaming while awake has proven to be remarkably resilient as a kind of psychological poetic in both description and implication.

★ ★ ★

This part concludes by noting the existence of a general intellectual shift following the Enlightenment towards the conceptualisation of the ghost as a fallacy or error, a negative unit of experience behind which lurked a mental disorder of some sort. This was in contrast to what had gone before where the ghost was considered a positive unit, an intruding presence that, some argued, had to be proved *not* to be real rather than the opposite. For intellectuals arguing against the existence of ghosts, the description 'dreaming while awake' was a resilient, easily applicable and culturally redolent diagnostic for a person in a state of hallucination. For intellectuals arguing for the existence of ghosts, and the existence of a ghost-seeing faculty, incorporating a scientific concept of hallucination became a logistical necessity, especially in a post-spiritualist context. Through their contemporary hallucination discourse the SPR attempted to prove, once again, the telepathic theory of ghost-seeing. Yet despite their attempts to strictly define and police the boundary between sleeping and waking, critics of the 'veridical hallucination' proposition applied, in the Kantian manner, the familiar dreaming-while-awake

---

[88] Schwartz, 'A Historical Loop'.
[89] R.R. Llinás and D. Paré, 'Of Dreaming and Wakefulness', *Neuroscience* 44:3 (1991), 525. See also Mahowald, Woods and Schenck, 'Sleeping Dreams'.

rejoinder in a pejorative and dissociative sense hostile to any attempt to 'naturalise the supernatural', thus solidifying a metaphor which exhibited structural resilience and multifaceted utilisation, and finally came to resemble something like a standard sceptical and quasi-sceptical response to ghost-seeing experience.[90]

[90] See, for instance, Oliver St John Gogarty: 'I believe in ghosts: that is, I know that there are times, given the place which is capable of suggesting a phantasy, when those who are sufficiently impressionable may perceive a dream projected as if external to the dreamy mind: a waking dream due both to the dreamer and the spot.' Oliver St John Gogarty, *As I Was Going down Sackville Street* (Dublin, 1994), p.193; Claire Russell, 'The Environment of Ghosts', in *The Folklore of Ghosts*, ed. Hilda R. Ellis Davidson and W.M.S. Russell (Bury St Edmunds, 1981), p.128.

Epilogue: towards 1920

In this study I have brought the figure of the ghost closer to that of the ghost-seer. In doing so I have shown how thinking about ghosts came to express the spectralisation of the self in the modern world. From the phantasmagoric dislocation, through the notion of dreaming while awake, to the attempt to prove the telepathic theory of ghost-seeing, it became clear that the figure of the ghost radically altered the course of psychological thought, forcing sceptics and believers alike to confront the essential psycho-tropism of the individual towards the ghost. I have outlined some of the cultures of belief and debunking, networks of cross-pollination and formations of the orthodox and heterodox which were central to the construction of meaning between the Enlightenment and the twentieth century, as if ghosts were themselves the Rorschach tests of modernity. Recent scholarship has challenged Max Weber's famous thesis of the disenchantment of the world, and instead argued that wherever religion or superstition have been defeated or superseded new secular forms of magic have swiftly taken their place.[1] Thinking about ghosts and ghost-seeing in the modern age shows how such strategies of re-enchantment were applied to the supernatural in a period which saw the rise of secularism, the triumph of science and the consolidation of society as a spectacle. Whether spectral illusionists, scientific spiritualists, sceptical scientists or spiritual scientists, investigators into ghost-seeing made space for the emergence of a spectral self, a third way in a psychological modernity that embraced seeming contraries with aplomb.

Such a project could go on into paratactic infinity: Kant's ghost-busting project echoed Baruch Spinoza's ironic analysis of ghost-seeing in the 1670s and prefigured Marx and Engels's spectro-centric attack on

---

[1] See Cook, *The Arts of Deception*; During, *Modern Enchantments*; Joshua Landy and Michael Sale, eds, *The Re-enchantment of the World: Secular Magic in a Rational Age* (Stanford, 2009).

Max Stirner in 1846;[2] William Howitt argued that 'the American spiritualism is but the last new blossom of a very ancient tree'[3]; André Breton's surrealism was haunted by the ghostly nineteenth-century Paris of Charles Baudelaire, the Comte de Lautréamont and Arthur Rimbaud;[4] the smoke-and-mirror tricks which featured so strongly in Schiller's *Der Geisterseher* reappeared in the emotional machinations of spirit photography in the later nineteenth century. Giacomo Leopardi wrote of an amusing incident in Florence in 1831 in which the citizens gathered outside a house on successive nights to see a phantom which mysteriously threw its arms about but was otherwise quite still. After the police intervened the phantom was discovered to have been a distaff which, when blown by the wind, took on a spectral appearance.[5] This incident found its uncanny echo in a Dublin case of 1884 when crowds of people gathered each night outside an establishment on Westmoreland Street to see an apparition, clothed in white, appear at the window. Driven to their wits' end, the police decided to solve the mystery and sent up an officer who explained to the disappointed crowd that there was no ghost after all, and that any sudden appearance and disappearance of light on the window had probably been occasioned by 'the accidental opening and shutting' of a back door.[6]

The ghost is that which is always at our backs, over our shoulder: it can manifest itself as the past, the double, the other self. Centuries after Leonardo da Vinci advised his students to hallucinate their creations by staring onto a blank wall, Edward Coit Rogers, a critic of spiritualism, sketched out a process of auto-haunting that demonstrates how this innate capacity to envision had become updated by the Victorian period to echo the existence of an other ghostly self, hemispheric, insecure, atomised. 'If you wish to see the spectre of a particular person as an outstanding reality,' Rogers wrote,

let your mind impress this upon the brain by a clear and definite conception, at the same time burn a certain combination of narcotics in the room where you are, and, while the smoke of the narcotics is curling up from the

---

[2] See Baruch Spinoza, *The Ethics and Selected Letters*, trans. Samuel Shirley (Indianapolis, 1982), pp.248–9; Karl Marx and Friedrich Engels, *The German Ideology. Part One, with Selections from Parts Two and Three, Together with Marx's 'Introduction to a Critique of Political Economy'*, ed. C.J. Arthur (London, 1970).

[3] William Howitt, *The History of the Supernatural in All Ages and Nations and in All Churches Christian and Pagan: Demonstrating a Universal Faith*: vol. I (London, 1863), p.18.

[4] See Shane McCorristine, 'Last Nights in Paris: Exploring Lautréamont's Surreal City', *The History Review* 15 (2005), 115–35.

[5] Giacomo Leopardi, *Thoughts; and, The Broom*, trans J.G. Nichols (London, 2002), pp.8–9.

[6] 'Ghost Hunting', *Irish Times* (31 May 1884). On similar cases in nineteenth-century England see Davies, *The Haunted*, pp.90–4.

chafing-dish, fix your gaze upon it, and the precise spectre shall make its appearance as if taking its form out of the smoke. It shall appear as an outstanding reality, – a living person, ghostly, indeed, but with whom you may hold converse, – give and receive both questions and answers ... on approaching the spectre, *there is a sensation as if one were going against a strong wind, and were being driven back.*[7]

Henrik Ibsen in *Ghosts* (1881) and James Joyce in 'The Dead' (1914) both used ghosts in this capacity as the representations of that which must be faced and struggled against, just like the wind. It was the nightmare of early modern Christians such as John Glanvill that a general decline in ghost-belief would result in the triumph of atheism: that the baby would be thrown out with the bathwater. What Glanvill did not envisage was that disenchantment would result in a radical *re-enchantment* of the world, but this time in a manner more psychologically haunting than ever before: whenever a ghost was chased away or explained away it came back, took root and possessed the mind in a different manner.

For Ibsen, we are all ghosts who are smothered by throbbing forces which 'cling to us all the same, and we cannot shake them off',[8] while Joyce's Gabriel Conroy memorably imagines a spectral presence, brought to life through a melody, as if 'some impalpable and vindictive being was coming against him, gathering forces against him in its vague world'.[9] Just as Schiller's Prince was turned into a ghost-seer precisely at the moment when his ghost-seeing was revealed to be false, Gabriel's epiphany in 'The Dead' is that the disenchantment of the world only cleared the air for the realisation that he also 'ghosts' the world through the reverberations of his own consciousness:

The air of the room chilled his shoulders. He stretched himself cautiously along under the sheets and lay down beside his wife. One by one, they were all becoming shades ... Other forms were near. His soul had approached that region where dwell the vast hosts of the dead. He was conscious of, but could not apprehend, their wayward and flickering existence. His own identity was fading out into a grey impalpable world: the solid world itself, which these dead had one time reared and lived in, was dissolving and dwindling.[10]

---

[7] Edward Coit Rogers, *Philosophy of Mysterious Agents, Human and Mundane, etc.* (Boston, MA, 1856), p.240. Italics are mine.

[8] Henrik Ibsen, *A Doll's House; Ghosts*, trans. William Archer (New York, 1911), p.280. For a contemporary view on Ibsen as a ghost-seer see Benjamin de Casseres, 'Ghosts and Their Makers', *New York Times* (10 June 1910).

[9] James Joyce, 'The Dead', in *The Oxford Book of Irish Short Stories*, ed. William Trevor (Oxford, 2001), p.264.

[10] *Ibid.*, p.266.

With this oracular position of the modernist ghost in mind, this study sought to limit and organise how thinking about ghosts and ghost-seeing developed. Ghost-seeing experience has been examined through the debates, problems, dreams and representations that emerged in multiple locations which were all equally embedded in their times and therefore amenable to contextual and theoretical interpretations. Yet like the ghost, this conclusion is left in the curious position of mirroring the implications of its subject matter: what I hope to have shown through this study is that the ghost haunts us with possibilities, not certainties; ambivalence, not assurance; horizons, not destinations.

Therefore, I want to end with questions rather than answers. Jean-Michel Rabaté poses the question that lies at the heart of modernity: 'Can we speak of "ghosts" without transforming the whole world and ourselves, too, into phantoms?'[11] In like mode Elaine Scarry asks, given the innate hallucinatory capabilities of humans, why it is that we do not *always* see ghosts.[12] The instinctive response that these two questions provoke is the realisation that the ghost has become no dead 'survival' of past superstition, but is rather alive and well in the psyche and that ghost-seeing experience is fundamentally an attempt to authenticate the mind itself, an attempt that is doomed to mere glimpses of veracity as if reality, truth, actuality and all the other haunted Words of human cultural systems, exist at some vanishing point and cannot be simply re-translated into a new ideology (one thinks of the innumerable regenerations of Kant's 'unknowable' thing-in-itself).[13]

Throughout the nineteenth century we come across innumerable examples of thinking about the mind as a haunted entity. As Max Stirner declared as part of the prelude to his exorcism of bourgeois ideology in *The Ego and Its Own* (1845):

Man, your head is haunted; you have wheels in your head! You imagine great things, and depict to yourself a whole world of gods that has an existence for you, a spirit-realm to which you suppose yourself to be called, an ideal that beckons to you. You have a fixed idea![14]

Echoing Stirner, the American psychiatrist George M. Beard wrote in 1879 that it was 'not our houses but our brains that are haunted'.[15]

---

[11] Jean-Michel Rabaté, *The Ghosts of Modernity* (Gainesville, 1996), p.xxi.
[12] Elaine Scarry, 'On Vivacity: The Difference between Daydreaming and Imagining-under-Authorial-Institution', *Representations* 52 (1995), 13.
[13] Thomas Laqueur, 'Why the Margins Matter: Occultism and the Making of Modernity', *Modern Intellectual History* 3:1 (2006), 119.
[14] Max Stirner, *The Ego and Its Own*, trans. Steven Byington (London, 1982), p.43.
[15] George M. Beard, 'The Psychology of Spiritism', *North American Review* 129 (1879), 67.

Responding to the establishment of the SPR in 1882, the *Pall Mall Gazette* proposed that the idea of the ghost was innate in the evolutionary sense and that 'a sort of blank form answering to the concept of a ghost must most probably be potentially present in almost every human brain'.[16] However, it seems that we have gone from believing we are innately haunted to facing up to the disquieting revelation that we are innately ghostly agents. In a lecture of 1914 W.B. Yeats, who was deeply interested in incidents that could be termed 'dream leakage', spoke of the case of a lady

who, engaged in house-hunting, came across a house in the country which she recognized as a house familiar to her in her dreams. On applying to the house-agent concerning it, he said that it had the reputation of being haunted, 'but', he added, 'you need have no fear of the ghost – *you are the ghost!*' He had recognized her resemblance to the phantom which 'haunted' the house.[17]

Walter de la Mare's weird ghost fiction from the 1920s onwards also exemplifies this trend. His short story 'The Looking Glass' (1923) is the tale of an imaginative little girl interested in the haunted garden next door who comes to the sudden realisation: ' "The Spirit is *me*: *I* haunt this place!" '[18]

* * *

Although there is a certain danger in using 1914 as a convenient bench-mark in thinking about cultural change, we cannot ignore the sense that a general re-enchantment took place in England regarding the place of

[16] 'Psychical Research', in *The Fin de Siècle: A Reader in Cultural History, c.1880–1900*, ed. Sally Ledger and Roger Luckhurst (Oxford, 2000), p.279.

[17] Cited in Peter Kuch, ' "Laying the Ghosts"? – W.B. Yeats's Lecture on Ghosts and Dreams', in *Yeats Annual No.5*, ed. Warwick Gould (London, 1987), pp.127–8. It is possible that this narrative assumed the status of an archetype during this period. Another commentator who presented a version of the tale (entitled 'The Dream House') wrote 'There is a certain strange story which I have come across, in various forms, over and over again. I have never read it in any book, paper or magazine, though, for aught I know, it may have been told in print as often as it has been related by word of mouth by persons interested in such matters … The true explanation must be, I think, that the experience is a common one with psychic people.' Jessie Adelaide Middleton, *Another Grey Ghost Book: With a Chapter on Prophetic Dreams and a Note on Vampires* (London, 1915), p.207. Yeats related another example of such dream leakage to the Ghost Club: 'Brother Yeats spoke of his having been lately in Sussex engaged in writing a play and one of the imaginary characters in this play appeared on several occasions to a girl living in the neighbourhood and, while she was dreaming. The dreams were recurrent and of a terrifying kind.' Ghost Club Minutes 7 (1910–1917), 234.

[18] Walter de la Mare, *Short Stories, 1895–1926*, ed. Giles de la Mare (London, 1996), p.38. Given the uncanny shudder that these two examples provoke, it is no coincidence that two of the most successful supernatural films of the past few decades, *The Sixth Sense* (1999) and *The Others* (2001), use the trope of the protagonists finding out they are in fact the ghosts in the ghost story.

the dead in society following the outbreak of World War I. In 1899 an article appeared in the *Fortnightly Review* entitled 'The Dying of Death'; in 1908 the Dublin-based physicist E.E. Fournier d'Albe complained that 'Death is all but dead.'[19] Yet as Freud predicted in 1915, the mass slaughter would lead to new attitudes towards death and the dead. Almost immediately spiritualists, psychical researchers and Christians sought a higher meaning in what was taking place and soon found evidence that the efforts of a whole generation of young men had immense spiritual relevance. Winifred Kirkland in *The New Death* (1918) crystallised this point of view:

With an intensity that only a world-ruin could have wrought, plain people everywhere are making trial of immortality as the sole speculation to nerve our action instantly needed, and to safeguard the future that it is our duty instantly to reconstruct.[20]

Following Arthur Machen's factional lead in his supernatural short story 'The Bowmen', books such as *War and the Weird* (1916) by Forbes Phillips and R. Thurston Hopkins, Rosa Stuart's *Dreams and Visions of the War* (1917), and Hereward Carrington's *Psychical Phenomena and the War* (1918) portrayed the soldier's life in spiritual terms, with ghosts, angels and spectral armies interceding to aid soldiers in what was explicitly described as spiritual warfare against a German enemy imagined as mechanistic, materialistic and demonically militaristic.[21] Amid the grief on the home front there was an outpouring of spiritual belief as new generations of bereaved turned to spiritualism to contact their dead.[22] The enthusiasm of Oliver Lodge and Arthur Conan Doyle, who had both lost sons in the war, in lecturing and writing on spiritualism in the post-war period, offered to a collective audience the solace that they had privately experienced. In this sense the wonder was not, as Margaret Oliphant once pointed out in a ghost story, that the dead returned, but

[19] J. Jacobs, 'The Dying of Death', *Fortnightly Review* 72 (1899), 264–9; Fournier d'Albe, *New Light on Immortality*, p.1.

[20] Winifred Kirkland, *The New Death* (Boston, MA, and New York, 1918), p.41.

[21] Hereward Carrington, *Psychical Phenomena and the War*, new edn (New York, 1920), p.8. Some spiritualists looked on the spread of the German Reformation ('dull German Protestantism') to England in the sixteenth century as the first act in a spiritual war that had resulted in the dis-communion of the English from heaven and a victory for 'gross materialism'. Forbes Phillips and R. Thurston Hopkins, *War and the Weird* (London, 1916), p.36.

[22] See Jenny Hazelgrove, *Spiritualism and British Society between the Wars* (Manchester, 2000); Jay Winter, *Sites of Memory, Sites of Mourning: The Great War in European Cultural History* (Cambridge, 1995); Paul Fussell, *The Great War and Modern Memory* (New York and London, 1975).

that the dead did not *necessarily* return to communicate with the living. In a valuable study Julie-Marie Strange has recently argued that we should not think in terms of an absence or presence of grief during this period, but in terms of a management process of the bereavement experience.[23] All over Britain, parents turned to mediums, psychics and spiritualist organisations as tangible options, among many, to manage their loss. One undoubtedly sensational method of fostering a sense of connection with the dead was through the phenomenon of spirit photography, which had been invented at the outset of the American Civil War in 1861. Although there were as many types of spirit photographs as there were spirit photographers, they generally involved the photographing of a living person (frequently in mourning) with deceased loved ones appearing alongside or wraithlike in the background (see Figure 5 and Figure 6). Alongside the spread of new spiritualistic media such as ouija boards and automatic writing, spirit photography experienced a great flowering in England in the first two decades of the twentieth century as the bereaved sought visual evidence of their dead, a situation which led to the founding of the Society for the Study of Supernormal Pictures in 1918 to investigate the matter.[24] Even though by 1920 the phenomena of materialisation had become more sophisticated, with 'apports' and ectoplasm added to the spiritualist repertoire, there was also a return to belief in the face of fraud and whimsy.[25] The case of Conan Doyle and the Cottingley Fairies in the early 1920s demonstrates how proofs of the other world were becoming, at the same time, as tangible as they were fantastic and as understandable as they were ridiculous.

Coming at the end of over a century of investigations into the ghost as a subjective experience, the remarkable drama directed by the SPR did not have its sequel. Its position as a kind of supra-ghost-seer in late Victorian culture soon became eroded as the energy behind the epistolary and mass-statistical foundations of the great public investigations into ghost-seeing and hallucinations was redirected towards other disciplines, movements and belief systems. In the decade or so before the

---

[23] Julie-Marie Strange, *Death, Grief and Poverty in Britain, 1870–1914* (Cambridge, 2005), pp.194–229.
[24] See Andreas Fischer, ' "The Most Disreputable Camera in the World": Spirit Photography in the United Kingdom in the Early Twentieth Century', in *The Perfect Medium: Photography and the Occult*, ed. Clément Chéroux, Andreas Fischer, Denis Canguilhem and Sophie Schmit (New Haven and London, 2005), pp.72–91; Martyn Jolly, *Faces of the Living Dead: The Belief in Spirit Photography* (London, 2006).
[25] See Corinne Montenon, 'Materialisation Phenomena in British and French Spiritualism and Psychical Research, c.1870–1920', PhD thesis, 2004, University of Birmingham.

Figure 5 Spirit photographs of deceased family members alongside Georgiana Houghton. Source: Miss [Georgiana] Houghton, *Chronicles of the Photographs of Spiritual Beings and Phenomena Invisible to the Material Eye: Interblended with Personal Narrative* (London, 1882). Courtesy of the University Library, Cambridge.

Figure 6 *Mrs Shaw and Mrs Coates' Daughter, Agnes Tweedale Simpson.*
Source: James Coates, *Photographing the Invisible: Practical Studies in
Spirit Photography, Spirit Portraiture, and Other Rare but Allied
Phenomena* (London and Chicago, 1911). © the British Library
Board. Shelfmark 08637.i.38.

discipline of parapsychology began to emerge with J.B. Rhine and others at Duke University, a number of other psychical research organisations were founded which challenged the dominance of the SPR: the Paris-based Institut métapsychique international (1919); the British College of Psychic Science (1920); Hereward Carrington's American Psychical Institute and Laboratory (1920); Harry Price's National Laboratory of Psychical Research (1925). From 1929 Price's sensational investigations into Borley Rectory (labelled by him 'The Most Haunted House in England' in a book of the same name) signalled the arrival of a new type of ghost-hunter who, though media-savvy and weighed-down with equipment and investigative gadgets, redirected thinking about ghosts towards the traditional idea of the ghost as a malevolent force or a restless spirit – a feature of popular culture that survives to this day.[26]

Perhaps the realisation that the ghost is a soporific psychic reality can be brought out further through the posing of another question – a question perhaps ultimately central to the investigation of modernity itself: for which of the James brothers was ghost-seeing a more 'real' phenomena? One might speculate that the answer to such a question would go some way to unravelling the riddle of consciousness, if such an answer were ever obtainable. However, a suggestion may be made which, while not answering the question, can frame a response. Just as play and seriousness are not necessarily antithetical categories, so ghost-seeing 'fact' and ghost-seeing 'fiction' need not exist in conflict with each other but are rather dynamically inter-related and cross-pollinating.[27] Crisis-apparition narratives, séance-room perceptions and oral ghost stories could all equally be framed as 'fact' or 'fiction' according to the shifting factors of belief, context or technique. Similarly, the idea of ghosts as spectres of the self, as the projections of the subjective mind, allows sceptics, believers and those in between to label ghost-seeing as equally a real, truthful and authentic experience. Such an open-ended situation radically disturbs all attempts at ghost-seeing investigation in the modern age, a situation that was astutely discerned by the philosopher and SPR member F.C.S. Schiller:

Ghost stories are what, on the whole, we desire them to be: they fulfil their function best by remaining as they are. They were never intended to be verified or investigated, and if they could be made scientifically valuable they would cease

[26] Jacqueline Simpson, 'Ghosts', in *Encyclopedia of Death and Dying*, ed. Glennys Howarth and Oliver Leaman (London and New York, 2001), p.208.
[27] For an interesting account linked to this thought see Peter Lamont, 'Magician as Conjurer: A Frame Analysis of Victorian Mediums', *Early Popular Visual Culture* 4:1 (2006), 21–33.

to be so emotionally, and would no longer serve to surround terrestrial existence with the foil which entrances its brilliancy.[28]

To be or not to be? This is the great ontological/hauntological question of *Hamlet* and all subsequent re-stagings of the ghost. *Spectres of the Self* has shown that ghost-seeing will be real or it will not be at all. Like the orgasmic dream that simultaneously declares its truth and its falsehood, the ghost-seeing experience poses questions that are central to how the mind works in any given cultural context.

Survivals have a knack of surviving.

---

[28] F.C.S. Schiller, *Humanism: Philosophical Essays* (New York, 1969), pp.246–7.

Appendix

'A Memoir on the Appearance of Spectres or Phantoms occasioned by Disease, with Psychological Remarks. Read by *Nicolai* to the Royal Society of Berlin, on the 28th of February, 1799.' Source: *Journal of Natural Philosophy, Chemistry and the Arts* 6 (1803), 161–79.

Philosophers divide the human being into body and mind, because the numerous and distinct observations we make on ourselves oblige us to consider man particularly, as well in respect to his corporeal as his mental functions. Other philosophers have supposed that this subject might be treated with greater perspicuity by considering man as composed of body, soul, and mind. There can be no doubt but that these, and even more divisions might be invented. Such philosophers, however, have by no means considered that arbitrary systematic divisions, do not constitute an investigation of nature, and that philosophy often becomes more uncertain the more precisely we endeavour to distinguish and separate what nature has closely united. Sub-divisions in speculation seem as necessary as fences in fields, both are in themselves unproductive, and the more they are multiplied and extended the greater is the diminution of the fertility.

For my part, I will confess, that I do not know where the corporeal essence in man ceases, or where the mental begins; though I admit of the distinction, because the extreme differences can be clearly perceived. If we divide man into three parts, we shall be far from removing the difficulties, as we should be were we even to follow those modern philosophers who regard the thinking subject alone as the real Being (*Ego*), and consider all external appearances as confined to the ideas of conscious beings. The greatest and most peculiar difficulties in the philosophic knowledge of the human subject consists in this, that we have never yet been able clearly and distinctly to ascertain the internal association of those striking differences which we observe in our being. Neither the most subtle physiology nor the finest speculative philosophy, has yet been able to explain the union of thought and physical

229

operations. We may indeed doubt whether the labours of our German philosophers, though founded jointly upon modern speculation and modern chemistry, will be attended with any greater success. Extreme caution is most undoubtedly requisite to prevent our becoming too intimately and habitually acquainted with certain hypothetical notions respecting things really unknown, so as to mistake them for truths and deduce erroneous conclusions.

It is much to be feared that the hypotheses and postulates of speculation will be of little value in this case; though to us they may seem very consistent and clear, while we regard them only in a certain point of view. An attention to experimental proof may bring us nearer to our aim, though its perfect accomplishment will perhaps never be within the reach of human investigation. Experiments or facts may show the corporeal as well as the mental functions in several lights, and in such as we never can perceive by mere speculation.

Though it is truly said that the first principles of nature are placed beyond our reach, yet an endeavour to penetrate into the interior of nature will always prove beneficial to the human mind; as long as we do not presume to have completely investigated the subject; but continue our exertions by uniting the observations of facts with deliberate reasoning.

Since men have forgotten that what philosophy has separated is not on that account separated in nature, and since from the earliest ages, the mind and body of man have been considered as if distinct from each other, numberless questions have arisen which have given room for much controversy, without having met with any satisfactory answer. For example: Whether after the dissolution of the body, the spirit (or mind) continues to exist without the body? Whether the spirit can act without the body, and in what manner? And lastly, it is also a question, Whether, as we consider a disembodied spirit not only in a state of separate continual existence, but also in a state of continual existence and continual action *amongst us*, a mere spirit and its actions cannot become perceptible to our senses? – Whether the figure of a spirit (and in particular that of a deceased person) may not be seen? and, Whether a sound proceeding from it may not affect the ear of the living? All the knowledge usually considered as possible to be had of a departed spirit is confined to seeing and hearing; for as far as my information extends, the devil is the only spirit that enjoys the privilege of affecting the sense of smell at his departure.

We have less motive for disputing about the absolute possibility of seeing a spirit, because the idea of a spirit is so indistinct and vague, and because the words spirit and body in considering man, do in reality indicate mere relative notions. It is inconsistent with every known law of nature to suppose that those terms of relation adopted by us solely for the purpose of investigating the nature of man do themselves possess any separate and independent existence. This argument causes a suspicion of deceit or imposition always to attach to narratives of the apparitions of disembodied spirits. But those who are inclined to see and hear spirits, are not satisfied with this summary solution; they appeal to experience, against which no maxim *a priori* can hold. This is only required, that the experience must be true and well attested.

Individuals who pretend to have seen and heard spirits are not to be persuaded that their apparitions were simply the creatures of their senses. You may tell them of the impositions that are frequently practised, and the fallacy which may lead us to take a spirit of our imagination by moon-light for a corpse. We are generally advised to seize the ghosts, in which case it is often found that they are of a very corporeal nature. An appeal is also made to self-deception, because many persons believe they actually see and hear where nothing is either to be seen or heard. No reasonable man, I think, will ever deny the possibility of our being sometimes deceived in this manner by our fancy, if he is in any degree acquainted with the nature of its operations. Nevertheless, the lovers of the marvellous will give no credit to these objections, whenever they are disposed to consider the phantoms of imagination as realities. We cannot therefore sufficiently collect and authenticate such proofs as show how easily we are misled; and with what delusive facility the imagination can exhibit, not only to deranged persons, but also to those who are in the perfect use of their senses, such forms as are scarcely to be distinguished from real objects.

I myself have experienced an instance of this, which not only in a psychological, but also in a medical point of view appears to me of the utmost importance. I saw, in the full use of my senses, and (after I had got the better of the fright which at first seized me, and the disagreeable sensation which it caused) even in the greatest composure of mind, for almost two months constantly, and involuntarily, a number of human and other apparitions; – nay, I even heard their voices; – yet after all, this was nothing but the consequence of nervous debility, or irritation, or some unusual state of the animal system.

The publication of the case in the Journal of Practical Medicine, by Professor Hufeland of Jena, is the cause of my now communicating it to the Academy. When I had the pleasure of spending a few happy days with that gentleman last summer, at Pyrmont, I related to him this curious incident.

But as it is probable he might not distinctly remember that which I had told altogether accidentally, perhaps indeed not very circumstantially, some considerable errors have been admitted into his narrative. In such a case, however, it is more necessary than in any other, to observe every thing with accuracy, and to relate it with fidelity and distinctness. I shall therefore pass over nothing which I remember with any degree of certainty. Several incidents connected with the apparitions seem to me of great importance; though we might be apt to regard them in a secondary point of view; for we cannot determine of what consequence even a circumstance of the most trivial nature may be, if at a future period (in case more experiments of a like nature are ascertained) some suppositions or conclusions can be made respecting the origin of such phantoms, or on some law of the association of ideas according to which they are modified or follow one another. I was also, which is seldom the case, in a situation to make observations on myself. I took down therefore in a few words what was most important, and recounted it immediately to several persons. My memory, which is extremely retentive, has besides treasured up the most minute circumstances; the more on that account, as this story has very often proved the subject of my impartial consideration, not only with regard to my own particular situation, but also in respect to its many psychological consequences. Its truth will, I hope, require no further assurance on my part, since a member of this academy (Mr. Selle) is an unexceptionable witness of it, having, as my physician, received a daily account of all that happened to me.

It would be extremely improper in an assembly like the present to speak much of myself; it can only be excusable in this particular case, where it serves to throw greater light on scientific investigation. I must request permission therefore to notice several particulars of my situation previous to my seeing the phantoms, as those incidents may have greatly affected the state of my body and mind during that time.

In the last ten months of the year 1790, I underwent several very severe trials, which greatly agitated me. From the month of September in particular, repeated shocks of misfortune had befallen me, which produced the deepest sorrow. It had been usual for me to lose blood by venesection twice a year. This was done once on the 9th of July 1790, but towards the close of the year it was omitted. In 1783 I had been suddenly seized with a violent giddiness, which the physician imputed to an obstruction in the small muscles of the *abdomen*, proceeding from too intense an application to study, and my sedentary manner of life for many years. These complaints were removed by a three years cure, and the rigid observance of a strict diet during that time. In the first stage of the malady the application of leeches to the *anus* had been particularly effective, and this remedy I had from that time regularly applied twice or thrice a year, whenever I felt congestion in the head. It was on the 1st of

March 1790 that the leeches had been last applied; the bleeding therefore and the clearing of the minuter blood-vessels by leeches had, in
1790 been less frequently observed than usual. A circumstance too that
could not tend to benefit my deplorable situation was, that from
September I had been continually engaged in business which required
the severest exertion, and which, from frequent interruptions, was
rendered still more burdensome and distressing.

In the first two months of the year 1791, I was much affected in my
mind by several incidents of a very disagreeable nature; and on the 24th
of February a circumstance occurred which irritated me extremely. At
ten o'clock in the forenoon my wife and another person came to console
me; I was in a violent perturbation of mind, owing to a series of incidents
which had altogether wounded my moral feelings, and from which I saw
no possibility of relief; when suddenly I observed at the distance of ten
paces from me a figure, – the figure of a deceased person. I pointed at it,
and asked my wife whether she did not see it. She saw nothing, but being
much alarmed, endeavoured to compose me, and sent for the physician.
The figure remained some seven or eight minutes, and at length
I became a little more calm; and as I was extremely exhausted, I soon
afterwards feel into a troubled kind of slumber, which lasted for half an
hour. The vision was ascribed to the great agitation of mind in which
I had been, and it was supposed I should have nothing more to apprehend from that cause; but the violent affection had put my nerves into
some unnatural state, from this arose further consequences, which
require a more detailed description.

In the afternoon, a little after four o'clock, the figure which I had seen
in the morning again appeared. I was alone when this happened; a
circumstance which, as may be easily conceived, could not be very
agreeable. I went therefore to the apartment of my wife, to whom
I related it, but thither also the figure pursued me. Sometimes it was
present, sometimes it vanished, but it was always the same standing
figure. A little after six o'clock several stalking figures also appeared;
but they had no connection with the standing figure. I can assign no
other reason for this apparition than that, though much composed in my
mind, I had not been able so soon entirely to forget the cause of such
deep and distressing vexation, and had reflected on the consequences of
it, in order, if possible, to avoid them; and that this happened three hours
after dinner, at the time when the digestion just begins.

At length I became more composed with respect to the disagreeable
incident which had given rise to the first apparition; but though
I had used very excellent medicines, and found myself in other respects
perfectly well, yet the apparitions did not diminish, but on the

contrary rather increased in number, and were transformed in the most extraordinary manner.

After I had recovered from the first impression of terror, I never felt myself particularly agitated by these apparitions, as I considered them to be what they really were, the extraordinary consequences of indisposition; on the contrary, I endeavoured as much as possible to preserve my composure of mind, that I might remain distinctly conscious of what passed within me. I observed these phantoms with great accuracy, and very often reflected on my previous thoughts, with a view to discover some law in the association of ideas, by which exactly these or other figures might present themselves to the imagination. – Sometimes I thought I had made a discovery, especially in the latter period of my visions; but on the whole I could trace no connexion which the various figures that thus appeared and disappeared to my sight had, either with my state of mind, or with my employment, and the other thoughts which engaged my attention. After frequent accurate observations on the subject, having fairly proved and maturely considered it, I could form no other conclusion on the cause and consequence of such apparitions than that, when the nervous system is weak and at the same time too much excited, or rather deranged, similar figures may appear in such a manner as if they were actually seen and heard; for these visions in my case were not the consequence of any known law of reason, of the imagination, or of the otherwise usual association of ideas; and such also is the case with other men, as far as we can reason from the few examples we know.

The origin of the individual pictures which present themselves to us, must undoubtedly be sought for in the structure of that organization by which we think; but this will always remain no less inexplicable to us than the origin of those powers by which consciousness and fancy are made to exist.

The figure of the deceased person never appeared to me after the first dreadful day; but several other figures showed themselves afterwards very distinctly; sometimes such as I knew, mostly, however, of persons I did not know, and amongst those known to me, were the semblances of both living and deceased persons, but mostly the former; and I made the observation that acquaintance with whom I daily conversed never appeared to me as phantasms; it was always such as were at a distance. When these apparitions had continued some weeks, and I could regard them with the greatest composure, I afterwards endeavoured, at my own pleasure to call forth phantoms of several acquaintance, whom I for that reason represented to my imagination in the most lively manner, but in vain. For however accurately I pictured in my mind the figures of such persons, I never once could succeed in my desire of seeing them *externally*; though I had some short time before seen them as phantoms, and they had perhaps afterwards unexpectedly presented themselves to me in the same manner. The phantasms appeared to me in every case involuntarily, as if they had been presented externally, like the phenomena in nature, though they certainly had their origin internally; and at the same time I was always able to distinguish with the greatest precision phantasms from phenomena. Indeed, I never once erred in this, as I was in general perfectly calm and self-collected on the occasion. I knew extremely well, when it only appeared to me that the door was opened, and a phantom entered, and when the door really was opened and any person came in.

It is also to be noted, that these figures appeared to me at all times, and under the most different circumstances, equally distinct and clear. Whether I was alone, or in company, by broad day-light equally as in the night time, in my own as well as in my neighbour's house; yet when I was at another person's house, they were less frequent, and when I walked the public street they very seldom appeared. When I shut my eyes sometimes the figures disappeared, sometimes they remained even after I had closed them, if they vanished in the former case, on opening my eyes again, nearly the same figures appeared which I had seen before.

I sometimes conversed with my physician and my wife, concerning the phantasms which at the time hovered around me; for in general the forms appeared oftener in motion that at rest. They did not always continue present – they frequently left me altogether, and again appeared for a short or longer space of time, singly or more at once; but, in general, several appeared together. For the most part I saw human figures of both sexes; they commonly passed to and fro as if they had no connection with each other, like people at a fair where all is bustle; sometimes they appeared to have business with one another. Once or twice I saw amongst them persons on horseback, and dogs and birds; these figures all appeared to me in their natural size, as distinctly as if they had existed in real life, with the several tints on the uncovered parts of the body, and with all the different kinds and colours of clothes. But I think, however, that the colours were somewhat *paler* than they are in nature.

None of the figures had any distinguishing characteristick, they were neither terrible, ludicrous, nor repulsive; most of them were ordinary in their appearance, – some were even agreeable.

On the whole, the longer I continued in this state, the more did the number of phantasms increase, and the apparitions became more frequent. About four weeks afterwards I began to hear them speak; sometimes the phantasms spoke with one another; but for the most part they addressed themselves to me; these speeches were in general short, and never contained any thing disagreeable. Intelligent and respected friends often appeared to me, who endeavoured to console me in my grief, which still left deep traces on my mind. This speaking I heard most frequently when I was alone; though I sometimes heard it in company, intermixed with the conversation of real persons; frequently in single phrases only, but sometimes even in connected discourse.

Though at this time I enjoyed rather a good state of health both in body and mind, and had become so very familiar with these phantasms, that at last they did not excite the least disagreeable emotion, but on the contrary afforded me frequent subjects for amusement and mirth; yet as the disorder sensibly increased, and the figures appeared to me for whole days together, and even during the night, if I happened to be awake, I had recourse to several medicines and was at last again obliged to have recourse to the application of leeches to the anus.

This was performed on the 20th of April at eleven o'clock in the forenoon. I was alone with the surgeon, but during the operation, the room swarmed with human forms of every description, which crowded fast one on another; this continued till half past four o'clock, exactly the time when the digestion commences. I then observed that the figures began to move more slowly; soon afterwards the colours became gradually paler; every seven minutes they lost more and more of their intensity, without any alteration in the distinct figure of the apparitions. At about half past six o'clock all the figures were entirely white, and moved very little; yet the forms appeared perfectly distinct; by degrees they became visibly less plain, without decreasing in number, as had often formerly been the case. The figures did not move off, neither did they vanish which also had usually happened on other occasions. In this instance they dissolved immediately into air; of some even whole pieces remained for a length of time, which also by degrees were lost to the eye. At about eight o'clock there did not remain a vestige of any of them, and I have never since experienced any appearance of the same kind. Twice or thrice since that time I have felt a propensity, if I may be so allowed to express myself, or a sensation as if I saw something which in a moment again was gone. I was even surprised by this sensation whilst writing the present account, having, in order to render it more accurate, perused the papers of 1791, and recalled to my memory all the circumstances of that time. So little are we sometimes, even in the greatest composure of mind, masters of our imagination.

This is an exact narrative of the apparitions which I observed during the disordered state of my nerves: and I shall now add a few observations, partly with the intention of explaining their origin from other observations made on myself, and partly with a view of pointing out at last some distant psychological consequences, which might be deduced from this remarkable case.

Experience shows that we may, in various manners, imagine that we see figures, and even hear them when they do not really exist.

1st.   And commonly this may happen in dreams. – The manner of dreaming is different in every individual, and probably depends on the joint effects of the powers of the intellect, and those by which the impressions of the senses are received, and these are modified by the state of the system at each particular time. I have myself made some remarkable observations on the nature of my dreams, and compared them with some observations on that subject which have been communicated to me by others.

2nd.   In every degree of mental derangement till absolute insanity.

3rd.   In fevers of the brain, which for a short time, or at certain intermitting periods, occasion a delirium.

4th.   By the mere power of imagination without any fever, when in other respects the judgement is perfectly sound. In this case it is very difficult to discover the truth, unless we combine an accurate habit of observation with the most impartial scrutiny.

Instances are too frequent in which we are imposed upon, not by the imagination, but by the delusion of the judgement. How many are there, who prefer the marvellous and assume an air of importance, when they have an opportunity of relating wonderful things of themselves. – How few are there who endeavour to divest themselves of prejudice, or to check their imagination; and still fewer are they who are accurate in their observations, especially in such as relate to themselves; even those who have sufficient firmness to adhere strictly to the truth form an inconsiderable number. Hence it is, that when a person relates any strange incident, he either detracts or magnifies, and will even fancy that he has verified some facts, which he has invented only at the moment that he relates them. This last is the case with a class of men who obstinately persist in their own opinions, and frequently assert more than they can support, merely with a view to maintain what they have once advanced. All the above mentioned circumstances seem to have coincided in the celebrated visions of Emanuel Swedenborg. He delighted in speculation and mystical theology; he had formed a system for himself in which ghosts were necessary, and it was his primary view to establish this wonderful system. It is possible that he may have seen phantasms, the more so as he studied much, and was a great eater. But in order to appear a prodigy to the world, he embellished his visions on

which he wrote voluminous treatises, by creating new images in con-
formity with his own system.

Lastly, those who are most conversant with the marvellous, give but a
very indistinct idea of their visions. This I have found in conversation with
persons who in other respects were very worthy characters, but who were
great admirers of what are termed occult sciences, which they cultivated
to such a degree, that to give you a notion of it here would seem preposte-
rous. I have frequently discoursed on spirits, and the seeing of spirits, with
a person who ranked very high in the school of secret wisdom, but who
was otherwise a man of very limited capacity, and rather ignorant in all
those sciences which enlighten the mind. This person told me amongst
other things that he should feel very unhappy, were he not continually in
company with spirits. As I have always taken a pleasure in the clear
development of human opinions, however absurd they may appear,
I was desirous to learn in what manner he saw the spirits, and how he
came into company with them? – But here he would not allow of the
appearance of any corporeal forms; he assured me that spirits were only to
be seen with the eye of the spirit: he then added in a very serious tone, 'Just
as the human soul is *Naephaefch*, or a branch taken off the tree, so are all
spirits branched off from the supreme spirit, as it in the astringent motion
compressed its being.' On nearer enquiry I could easily perceive that he
entertained a confused notion of the cabalistick ontology of Spinoza, and
that he imagined all the powers in nature to be spirits. What he meant to
say therefore, was neither more nor less than that he should feel unhappy,
did he live in a world where nature was perfectly inanimate; if he could not
think that every thing around him was in the continual and mutual *exercise*
of its powers. In this belief then he peopled all space with spirits, nearly
in the same manner as the ancient mythology peopled the woods with
Dryads and Hamadryads. Indeed, every thing properly considered, the
opinion of my cabalist is not quite so very absurd as you may suppose; for
in reality, the word *power* is with the philosopher only that which the X is to
the mathematician; and, if I be not altogether mistaken, the mathematician can with his X, bring more clear truths to light, than the philosopher
by the word *power*. If a given power cannot be rendered subservient
to deduction, so that, like Newton's *calculus*, it shall perfectly accord
with experience; nothing more will be determined or explained by the
mere word power, than by the word spirit; and I doubt much whether the
new judicious Kantian system of Dynamic natural philosophy, which
considers all bodies as mere aggregates of powers, would not rather cut
the gordian knot than unravel it.

It is not very uncommon that by a derangement of the corporeal
powers, even without insanity and inflammatory fevers, apparitions do

strike the eye externally, which are only internally the production of the imagination. The experience of this may teach us a lesson of forbearance, not rashly to consider as impostors those well disposed persons who believe they have seen apparitions. But as manifold experience shows us how far the human imagination can go in the external representation of pictures; it may also admonish those well-disposed persons not to ascribe to their visions any degree of reality, and still less to consider the effects of a disordered system, as proofs that they are haunted by spirits.

The celebrated Justus Moser frequently believed that he saw flowers. Another of my acquaintance sees in like manner, at times, mathematical figures, circles, squares, &c. in different colours. More examples of this kind may perhaps be found in Moretz's Magazine, in Krueger's Experimental Psychology, and in Bonnet's Psychological writings. The hearing of sounds is a case which seldomer occurs. My much-lamented friend Moses Meudeljohn had, in the year 1792, by too intense an application to study, contracted a malady, which also abounded with particular psychological apparitions. For upwards of two years he was incapacitated from doing any thing; he could neither read nor think, and was rendered utterly incapable of supporting any loud noise. If any one talked to him rather in a lively manner, or if he himself happened to be disposed to lively conversation, he fell in the evening into a very alarming species of catalepsy, in which he saw and heard every thing that passed around him, without being able to move a limb. If he had heard any lively conversation during the day, a stentorian voice repeated to him while in the fit, the particular words or syllables that had been pronounced with an imperative accent, or loud emphatic tone, and in such a manner that his ears reverberated.

Seldom as it may happen, that persons believe they see human forms, yet examples of the case are not wanting. A respectable member of this academy, distinguished by his merit in the science of botany, whose truth and credibility are unexceptionable, once saw in this very room in which we are now assembled, the phantasm of the late president Maupertuis. A person of a sound and unprejudiced mind, though not a man of letters, whom I know well, and whose word may be credited, related to me the following case. As he was recovering from a violent nervous fever, being still very weak, he lay one night in bed perfectly conscious that he was awake, when the door seemed to open, and the figure of a woman entered, who advanced to his bed-side. He looked at it for some moments, but as the sight was disagreeable, he turned himself and awakened his wife; on turning again however he found the figure was gone. But out of many cases I have never known an instance like my own, in which any person had for almost two months constantly beheld such visionary forms, and seemed even to have heard them; except it was that of two young ladies, who, as I have been credibly informed, frequently saw appearances of this nature.

I am by no means insensible to a certain feeling which admonishes me of the impropriety of talking so much of myself in an assembly like this; but since I transgress only with a scientific intention, to contribute to the knowledge of the effects of the human imagination, I must endeavour to suppress this feeling. I may look for pardon, I trust, from those who know and respect every thing which tends to enlarge the stock of human knowledge, even if I speak more of myself. For, when I proceed to describe the state of my imagination, and the nature of the apparitions during a previous malady, it will be merely with an intention to show the apparitions which form the subject of this lecture in a less wonderful point of view, and by that means perhaps to contribute in some degree to the illustration of so strange an incident.

I must observe that my imagination possesses in general a great facility in picturing. I have for example sketched in my mind a number of plans for novels and plays; though I have committed very few of them to paper, because I was less solicitous to execute than to invent. I have generally arranged these outlines when, in a cheerful state of mind, I have taken a solitary walk, or when travelling I have sat in my carriage, and could only find employment in myself and my imagination. Constantly and even now do the different persons whom I imagine in the formation of such a plot, present themselves to me in the most lively and distinct manner: their figure, their features, their manner, their dress, and their complexion, are all visible to my fancy. As long as I meditate on a fixed plan, and afterwards carry it into effect, – even when I am often interrupted, and must begin again at different times, all the acting persons continue present in the very same form in which my imagination at first produced them. I find myself frequently in a state betwixt sleeping and waking, in which a number of pictures of every description, often the strangest forms, show themselves, change and vanish. In the year 1778, I was affected with a bilious fever, which, at times, though seldom, became so high as to produce delirium. Every day towards evening, the fever came on, and if I happened to shut my eyes at that time, I could perceive that the cold fit of the fever was beginning even before the sensation of cold was observable. This I knew by the distinct appearance of coloured pictures of less than half their natural size, which looked as if in frames. They were a set of landscapes composed of trees, rocks, and other objects. If I kept my eyes shut, every minute some alteration took place in the representation. Some figures vanished, and others appeared. But if

I opened my eyes all was gone; if I shut them again I had quite a different landscape. This case was therefore entirely different from what occurred afterwards in the year 1791, when the figure remained unchanged during the opening and shutting of the eyes. In the cold fit of the fever I sometimes opened and shut my eyes every second for the purpose of observation, and every time a different picture appeared replete with various objects which had not the least resemblance with those that appeared before. These pictures presented themselves without interruption, as long as the cold fit of the fever lasted. They became fainter as soon as I began to grow warm, and when I was perfectly so, all were gone. When the cold fit of the fever was entirely past, no more pictures appeared; but if on the next day I could again see pictures when my eyes were shut, it was a certain sign that the cold fit was coming on. I must further observe, that when I either think deeply on a subject, or write attentively, particularly when I have exerted myself for some time, a thought frequently offers itself which has no connection with the work before me, and this at times in a manner so very lively, that it seems as if expressed in actual words.

This natural vivacity of imagination renders it less wonderful, that after a violent commotion of the mind, a number of delusive pictures should appear for several weeks in succession. Their leaving me on the application of leeches, shows clearly that some anomaly in the circulation of the blood was connected with the appearance of those phantasms; though it may perhaps be too hasty a conclusion to seek for their cause in that alone. It seems likewise remarkable, that the beginning of the apparitions, after the disturbance in my mind was settled, as well as the alteration which took place when they finally left me, happened exactly at the time when digestion commenced. It is no less remarkable, that the apparitions before they entirely ceased, lost their intensity of colours; and that they did not vanish or change as formerly, but seemed gradually to dissolve into air.

Had I not been able to distinguish phantasms from phenomena, I must have been insane. Had I been fanatic or superstitious, I should have been terrified at my own phantasms, and probably might have been seized with some alarming disorder. Had I been attached to the marvellous, I should have sought to magnify my own importance, by asserting that I had seen spirits; and who could have disputed the facts with me? The year 1791 would perhaps have been the time to have given importance to these apparitions. In this case however, the advantage of sound philosophy, and deliberate observation may be seen. Both prevented me from becoming either a lunatic or an enthusiast; with nerves so strongly excited, and blood so quick in circulation, either misfortune might have easily befallen me. But I considered the phantasms that hovered around me as what they really were, namely, the effects of disease; and made them subservient to my observations, because I consider observation and reflection as the basis of all rational philosophy.

Our modern German philosophers, will not allow that observation ought to be admitted in theoretical philosophy. Hence arose Kant's Transcendental Idealism, which at last degenerated into the gross enthusiastic idealism; which is found in Fichte's writings. This philosopher considers all external objects as our own productions. 'What we consider as things independent of us are,' according to him, 'no more than our own creatures, which we fear, admire and desire; we believe our fate to be dependent on a shadow, which the single breath of a free being might destroy.' These are Mr. Fichte's own words.

The mere picture in the mind, without external experience, would never be sufficient to afford us a convincing proof, whether we saw phenomena or phantasms. The critical philosophers maintain, that knowledge deduced from observation is merely empirick, and therefore not to be depended on; it is perhaps true that nature has assigned us no great certainty than this respecting our ideas. But could we be truly conscious of our grounds of reason, if the appearances called external, which follow laws that do not depend on the representations in our mind, did not continually agree with those representations? Are we possessed of any other criterion? Does not the great theoretical philosopher, when he sees every thing yellow, conclude that his eye is jaundiced; or when every thing appears black to him, that his brain is affected? In these cases he does not trust his imagination or mental powers alone.

I may here apply the consideration of the illusions which I witnessed. I am well aware that no general conclusions can be drawn from a single instance; but still the experience of a single case, if accurately observed and faithfully described, is sufficient to destroy hypotheses which have too long been honoured with the name of systems.

According to Fichte, since during the situation I have above described, I was in other respects in the perfect use of my reason, as well as the persons who were really about me; as the apparitions which I saw, as well as those which are considered as realities, were the one as well as the other, my own productions: – Why then were my creatures of both kinds so essentially different?

My judgement showed me this plainly, by conclusions founded on the previous course of observations. The greatest modern idealists who depend so much on the confusion in which they have involved themselves by the supposed depth of their speculations, will certainly never pretend that both perceptions were of the same nature; since if so, I could not have investigated their difference. But by what means could this be done? I observed that real persons followed in a determinate order, by external laws that do not depend on me, in an order that I myself must continually follow, as was evident from my sense of consciousness. I could also lay hold of the real objects, as well as of myself. Neither of these circumstances was, however, the case with the phantasms; I had always found it so in the constant observation of myself, of the apparitions without me, and in my own consciousness.

The phantasms, as well as the phenomena, no doubt, lay in my mind; but I am necessarily compelled to ascribe to the latter, the same reality which I am obliged to ascribe to myself: viz. something that does not lie in my mind alone; something that also exists without my mind; something independent of my consciousness, which determines the nature of my idea; something which we formerly used to call *the thing itself*, before the critical philosophy so unjustly reprobated this unexceptionable term. On the contrary, however, I could not ascribe this same reality to the illusion; I could form no other conclusion, than that they originated in my internal consciousness alone; in a consciousness which was also disordered, as I might justly conclude from the observations I made on myself. I repeat, that both the phenomena and the phantasms existed in my mind: if I had not been able to distinguish between them, I must have been insane. By what means could I distinguish, if I did not attribute reality to the former; – and that they possessed reality, I inferred from observations to which I am still inclined to give confidence, until Mr Fichte can more clearly convince me that it ought in no case to be depended on.

Bibliography

Manuscript sources

C.D. Broad Papers, Wren Library, Trinity College, Cambridge.
Frank Podmore Papers, Wellcome Institute, London.
Ghost Club Minutes, British Library, London.
Henry Sidgwick Papers, Wren Library, Trinity College, Cambridge.
Society for Psychical Research Archive, University Library, Cambridge.

Printed sources

Abraham, Nicolas, 'Notes on the Phantom: A Complement to Freud's
    Metapsychology', trans. Nicholas Rand, *Critical Inquiry* 13:2 (1987), 287–92.
Adair, Patricia, *The Waking Dream: A Study of Coleridge's Poetry* (London, 1967).
'After Twelve Years', *Light* 14 (27 January 1894), 42.
Alderson, John, *An Essay on Apparitions, in Which Their Appearance Is
    Accounted for by Causes Wholly Independent of Preternatural Agency*
    (London, 1823).
'Alif', 'Religion and Schopenhauer', *Light* 12 (7 May 1892), 221.
Allen, Grant, *Strange Stories* (London, 1884).
Althusser, Louis, *Writings on Psychoanalysis: Freud and Lacan*, trans. Jeffrey
    Mehlman (New York, 1996).
Alvarado, Carlos S., 'Dissociation in Britain During the Late Nineteenth
    Century: The Society for Psychical Research, 1882–1900', *Journal of
    Trauma & Dissociation* 3:2 (2002), 9–33.
    'On the Centenary of Frederic W.H. Myers's *Human Personality and Its
    Survival of Bodily Death*', *Journal of Parapsychology* 68 (2004), 3–43.
    'Psychical Research and Telepathy in Nineteenth-Century Issues of *The
    Times*', *Paranormal Review* 43 (2007), 3–7.
American Psychiatric Association, *Diagnostic and Statistical Manual of Mental
    Disorders*, 4th edn, *DSM-IV-TR* (Washington, DC, 2000).
Amm, Marita, 'Might and Magic, Lust and Language – The Eye as a Metaphor
    in Literature: Notes on the Hierarchy of the Senses', *Documenta
    Ophthalmologica* 101:3 (2000), 223–32.
Andrews, Malcolm, *Charles Dickens and His Performing Selves: Dickens and the
    Public Readings* (Oxford, 2006).

Andriopoulos, Stefan, 'Psychic Television', *Critical Inquiry* 31:3 (2005), 618–37.

Ariès, Philippe, *The Hour of Our Death*, trans. Helen Weaver (London, 1983).

Armstrong, Tim, *Modernism: A Cultural History* (Cambridge, 2005).

Armstrong-Jones, Robert, 'Dreams and Their Interpretation, with Special Application to *Freudism*', *Journal of Mental Science* 63 (1917), 200–25.

Assier, Adolphe d', *Posthumous Humanity: A Study of Phantoms*, trans. Henry S. Olcott (London, 1887).

Auerbach, Nina, *Private Theatricals: The Lives of the Victorians* (Cambridge, MA, and London, 1990).

Bacorski, Hans-Jürgen, 'Dreams That Have Never Been Dreamt at All: Interpreting Dreams in Medieval Literature', trans. Pamela E. Selwyn, *History Workshop Journal* 49 (2000), 95–127.

Ballou, Adin, *An Exposition of Views Respecting the Modern Spirit Manifestations: Together with Phenomenal Statements and Communications* (Liverpool, 1853).

Barkhoff, Jürgen, *Magnetische Fiktionen: Literarisierung des Mesmerismus in der Romantik* (Stuttgart, 1995).

Barrett, William F., *Death-bed Visions: The Psychical Experiences of the Dying* (Wellingborough, 1986).

'An Early Psychical Research Society', *JSPR* 21 (1923–1924), 67–71.

On the Threshold of the Unseen: An Examination of the Phenomena of Spiritualism and of the Evidence for Survival after Death (London, 1917).

Barrett, William F., Edmund Gurney and Frederic W.H. Myers. 'First Report of the Committee on Thought-reading', *PSPR* 1 (1882–1883), 13–34.

'Thought-reading', *Nineteenth Century* 11 (1882), 890–901.

Barrett, William F., Edmund Gurney, Frederic W.H. Myers *et al.*, 'First Report of the Committee on Mesmerism', *PSPR* 1 (1882–1883), 217–29.

Barrett, William F., A.P. Perceval Keep, C.C. Massey *et al.*, 'First Report of the Committee on Haunted Houses', *PSPR* 1 (1882–1883), 101–15.

Barrett, William F., C.C. Massey, W. Stainton Moses *et al.*, 'First Report of the Literary Committee', *PSPR* 1 (1882–1883), 116–55.

'Second Report of the Literary Committee', *PSPR* 2 (1884), 43–55.

'Third Report of the Literary Committee: A Theory of Apparitions. Part I', *PSPR* 2 (1884), 109–36.

'Fourth Report of the Literary Committee: A Theory of Apparitions. Part II', *PSPR* 2 (1884), 157–86.

Barrow, Logie, *Independent Spirits: Spiritualism and English Plebeians, 1850–1910* (London, 1986).

Barthes, Roland, 'Textual Analysis: Poe's "Valdemar"', in *Modern Criticism and Theory: A Reader*, ed. David Lodge, 2nd edn (Harlow, 2000), pp.172–95.

Bartlett, Robert, *The Natural and the Supernatural in the Middle Ages* (Cambridge, 2008).

Basham, Diana, *The Trial of Woman: Feminism and the Occult Sciences in Victorian Literature and Society* (Basingstoke, 1992).

Bath, Jo and John Newton, ' "Sensible Proof of Spirits": Ghost Belief during the Later Seventeenth Century', *Folklore* 117:1 (2006), 1–14.

Baudelaire, Charles, Œuvres complètes II (Paris, 1999).
Bayfield, M.A., Rev., 'Andrew Lang and Psychical Research', PSPR 26 (1912–1913), 419–30.
Beard, George M., 'The Psychology of Spiritism', North American Review 129 (1879), 65–81.
Beer, John, Post-Romantic Consciousness: Dickens to Plath (Basingstoke, 2003).
Bell, Matthew, The German Tradition of Psychology in Literature and Thought, 1700–1840 (Cambridge, 2005).
Bell, Robert, 'Stranger than Fiction', Cornhill Magazine 2 (1860), 211–24.
Bennett, Bridget, ed., Women, Madness and Spiritualism: vol. II, Susan Willis Fletcher (London and New York, 2003).
Bennett, Gillian, 'Ghost and Witch in the Sixteenth and Seventeenth Centuries', Folklore 97:1 (1986), 3–14.
   Traditions of Belief: Women and the Supernatural (Harmondsworth, 1987).
Bentall, R.P., 'The Illusion of Reality: A Review and Integration of Psychological Research on Hallucinations', Psychological Bulletin 107:1 (1990), 82–95.
Bergson, Henri, Creative Evolution, trans. Arthur Mitchell (Lanham, 1984).
   Mind-Energy: Lectures and Essays, trans. H. Wildon Carr (London, 1921).
Berrios, German E., 'Historical Background to Abnormal Psychology', in Adult Abnormal Psychology, ed. Edgar Miller and Peter J. Cooper (Edinburgh, 1988), pp.26–51.
   The History of Mental Symptoms: Descriptive Psychopathology since the Nineteenth Century (Cambridge, 1998).
   'On the Fantastic Apparitions of Vision by Johannes Müller', History of Psychiatry 16:2 (2005), 229–46.
   'Tactile Hallucinations: Conceptual and Historical Aspects', Journal of Neurology, Neurosurgery, and Psychiatry 45:4 (1982), 285–93.
Berrios, German E. and M. Gil, 'Will and Its Disorders: A Conceptual History', History of Psychiatry 6:21 (1995), 87–104.
Beyer, Jürgen, 'On the Transformation of Apparition Stories in Scandinavia and Germany, c.1350–1700', Folklore 110 (1999), 39–47.
Bierce, Ambrose, The Devil's Dictionary (London, 2003).
Binet, Alfred, 'Visual Hallucinations in Hypnotism', Mind 9:35 (1884), 413–15.
Blum, Deborah, Ghost Hunters: William James and the Search for Scientific Proof of Life after Death (London, 2007).
Boakes, Robert, From Darwin to Behaviourism: Psychology and the Minds of Animals (Cambridge, 1984).
Böhme, Hartmut and Gernot Böhme, 'The Battle of Reason with the Imagination', trans. Jane Kneller, in What Is Enlightenment? Eighteenth-century Answers and Twentieth-century Questions, ed. James Schmidt (Berkeley, Los Angeles and London, 1996), pp.426–52.
Bondeson, Jan, Buried Alive: The Terrifying History of Our Most Primal Fear (New York and London, 2001).
Boswell, James, The Life of Samuel Johnson, ed. Christopher Hibbert (Harmondsworth, 1979).

Bowyer, Richard A., 'The Role of the Ghost Story in Medieval Christianity', in *The Folklore of Ghosts*, ed. Hilda R. Ellis Davidson and W.M.S. Russell (Cambridge, 1981), pp.177–92.

Brewster, David, *Letters on Natural Magic, Addressed to Sir Walter Scott, Bart*, 5th edn (London, 1842).

Brierre de Boismont, A., *On Hallucinations: A History and Explanation of Apparitions, Visions, Dreams, Ecstasy, Magnetism, and Somnambulism* (Philadelphia, 1853).

Briggs, Julia, *Night Visitors: The Rise and Fall of the English Ghost Story* (London, 1977).

Broad, C. D., *Religion, Philosophy and Psychical Research* (London, 1953).

Brontë, Charlotte, *Jane Eyre*, ed. Margaret Smith (Oxford, 1980).

Brooke, John Hedley, *Science and Religion: Some Historical Perspectives* (Cambridge, 1991).

Brown, Alan Willard, *The Metaphysical Society: Victorian Minds in Crisis, 1869–1880* (New York, 1947).

Brown, J.H., *Spectropia; or, Surprising Spectral Illusions. Showing Ghosts Everywhere, and of any Colour* (London, 1864).

Brown, Samuel, 'Ghosts and Ghost-seers', *North British Review* 9 (1848), 393–416.

Browne, E. Harold, *An Exposition of the Thirty-nine Articles: Historical and Doctrinal*, 6th edn (London, 1864).

Browning, Robert, *Poetical Works, 1833–1864* (London, 1970).

Buchanan, Robert, *The Origin and Nature of Ghosts, Demons, and Spectral Illusions* (Manchester, 1840).

Burrow, J. W., *Evolution and Society: A Study in Victorian Social Theory* (Cambridge, 1966).

Burwick, Frederick, 'Romantic Drama: From Optics to Illusion', in *Literature and Science: Theory & Practice*, ed. Stuart Peterfreund (Boston, MA, 1990), pp.167–208.

Buse, Peter and Andrew Stott, eds, *Ghosts: Deconstruction, Psychoanalysis, History* (Basingstoke, 1999).

Bush, George, *Mesmer and Swedenborg: Or, the Relation of the Developments of Mesmerism to the Doctrines and Disclosures of Swedenborg*, 2nd edn (New York, 1847).

Bushell, W.D., F.S. Hughes, A.P. Perceval Keep *et al.*, 'Second Report of the Committee on Haunted Houses', *PSPR* 2 (1884), 137–51.

Calkins, Mary W., 'Statistics of Dreams', *American Journal of Psychology* 5:3 (1893), 311–43.

Canguilhem, Georges, *The Normal and the Pathological* (New York, 1989).

Caper, Robert, *Immaterial Facts: Freud's Discovery of Psychic Reality and Klein's Development of His Work* (London and New York, 2000).

Carlyle, Thomas, *Sartor Resartus*, ed. Kerry McSweeney and Peter Sabor (Oxford, 1987).

Carpenter, William B., *Mesmerism, Spiritualism, &c., Historically & Scientifically Considered* (London, 1877).

Principles of Mental Physiology: With Their Applications to the Training and Discipline of the Mind, and the Study of Its Morbid Conditions, 6th edn (London, 1891).

Carrington, Hereward, *Psychical Phenomena and the War*, new edn (New York, 1920).

Carroy, Jacqueline, 'Dreaming Scientists and Scientific Dreamers: Freud as a Reader of French Dream Literature', *Science in Context* 19:1 (2006), 15–35.

Carter, Margaret L., *Specter or Delusion? The Supernatural in Gothic Fiction* (Ann Arbor and London, 1987).

'Case of Spectral Illusion from Suppressed Hemorrhöis', *Edinburgh Medical and Surgical Journal* 26 (1826), 216.

Casey, Edward S., *Imagining: A Phenomenological Study*, 2nd edn (Bloomington, 2000).

Casseres, Benjamin de, 'Ghosts and Their Makers', *New York Times* (10 June 1910), p.L. 13.

Cassirer, Ernst, *Kant's Life and Thought*, trans. James Haden (New Haven and London, 1981).

Castle, Terry, *The Female Thermometer: Eighteenth-century Culture and the Invention of the Uncanny* (New York and Oxford, 1995).

Cavaliero, Glen, *The Supernatural and English Fiction* (Oxford, 1995).

'The Census of Hallucinations', *Light* 14 (29 September 1894), 462.

Cerullo, John J., *The Secularization of the Soul: Psychical Research in Modern Britain* (Philadelphia, 1982).

Chadwick, Owen, *The Secularization of the European Mind in the Nineteenth Century* (Cambridge, 1975).

Chapman, William, *Nocturnal Travels; or, Walks in the Night. Being an Account of Ghosts, Apparitions, Hobgoblins, and Monsters* (London, 1828).

Christian, William A., Jr, *Apparitions in Late Medieval and Renaissance Spain* (Princeton, 1981).

'Circular No. 1', *PSPR* 1 (1882–1883), 294–302.

Cixous, Hélène, 'Fiction and Its Phantasms: A Reading of Freud's *Das Unheimliche* (The "Uncanny")', *New Literary History* 7:3 (1976), 525–48.

Clapton, G.T., 'Baudelaire and Catherine Crowe', *Modern Language Review* 25:3 (1930), 286–305.

Clark, Stuart, *Vanities of the Eye: Vision in Early Modern European Culture* (Oxford, 2007).

Classen, Constance, *The Color of Angels: Cosmology, Gender and the Aesthetic Imagination* (London and New York, 1998).

Clery, E.J., *The Rise of Supernatural Fiction, 1762–1800* (Cambridge, 1995).

Cobbe, Frances Power, 'Unconscious Cerebration: A Psychological Study', *Macmillan's Magazine* 133 (1870), 24–37.

Coffey, Nicole, ' "Every Word of It Is True": The Cultural Significance of the Victorian Ghost Story', MA thesis, 2004, University of Manitoba.

Cole, Michael, *Cultural Psychology: A Once and Future Discipline* (Cambridge, MA, and London, 1996).

Coleridge, Samuel Taylor, *Biographia Literaria*: vol. II, ed. J. Shawcross (London, 1965).

The Friend: vol. I, ed. Barbara E. Rooke (London, 1969).

The Notebooks of Samuel Taylor Coleridge: vol. IV, *1819–1826*, ed. Kathleen Coburn and Merton Christensen (London, 1990).

Collins, H.M. and T. J. Pinch, 'The Construction of the Paranormal: Nothing Unscientific Is Happening', in *On the Margins of Science: The Social Construction of Rejected Knowledge*, ed. Roy Wallis (Keele, 1979), pp.237–70.

Comte, Auguste, *System of Positive Polity*: vol. IV (New York, 1969).

Connor, Steven, 'CP: or, a Few Don'ts by a Cultural Phenomenologist', *Parallax* 5:2 (1999), 17–31.

'The Machine in the Ghost: Spiritualism, Technology and the "Direct Voice"', in *Ghosts: Deconstruction, Psychoanalysis, History*, ed. Peter Buse and Andrew Stott (Basingstoke, 1999), pp.203–25.

Constantine, Stephen, 'Introduction: Empire Migration and Imperial Harmony', in *Emigrants and Empire: British Settlement in the Dominions between the Wars*, ed. Stephen Constantine (Manchester and New York, 1990), pp.1–21.

'Constitution and Rules', *PSPR* 1 (1882–1883), 331–6.

Cook, James W., *The Arts of Deception: Playing with Fraud in the Age of Barnum* (Cambridge, MA, 2001).

Coon, Deborah J., 'Standardizing the Subject: Experimental Psychologists, Introspection, and the Quest for a Technoscientific Ideal', *Technology and Culture* 34:4 (1993), 757–83.

'Testing the Limits of Sense and Science: American Experimental Psychologists Combat Spiritualism, 1880–1920', *American Psychologist* 42:7 (1992), 143–51.

'Correspondence', *JSPR* 4 (1889–1890), 143–51.

Cottom, Daniel, *Abyss of Reason: Cultural Movements, Revelations, and Betrayals* (Oxford, 1991).

Courtney, William L., 'The New Psychology', *Fortnightly Review* 26 (1879), 318–28.

Cox, Michael and R.A. Gilbert, eds, *Victorian Ghost Stories: An Oxford Anthology* (Oxford, 1991).

Crary, Jonathan, *Suspensions of Perception: Attention, Spectacle and Modern Culture* (Cambridge, MA, and London, 2001).

Techniques of the Observer: On Vision and Modernity in the Nineteenth Century (Cambridge, MA, and London, 1990).

Crawley, A.E., *The Idea of the Soul* (London, 1909).

Crookall, Robert, *The Next World – And the Next: Ghostly Garments* (London, 1966).

Crookes, William, *Researches in the Phenomena of Spiritualism* (London, 1874).

Crosland, Newton, *Apparitions: A New Theory* (London, 1856).

Cross, W.R., *The Burned-over District: The Social and Intellectual History of Enthusiastic Religion in Western New York, 1800–1850* (Ithaca, NY, 1950).

Crowe, Catherine, *The Night Side of Nature; or, Ghosts and Ghost-seers* (London, 1850).

Spiritualism, and the Age We Live In (London, 1859).

Crowell, Eugene, *Spiritualism and Insanity* (Boston, MA, 1877).

Cruikshank, George, *A Discovery Concerning Ghosts; with a Rap at the 'Spirit-Rappers' ... Illustrated with Cuts* (London, 1863).

Cumberland, Stuart, *That Other World: Personal Experiences of Mystics and Their Mysticism* (London, 1918).

Dacome, Lucia, ' "To What Purpose Does It Think?": Dreams, Sick Bodies and Confused Minds in the Age of Reason', *History of Psychiatry* 15:4 (2004), 395–416.

Daly, Nicholas, *Modernism, Romance, and the 'Fin de Siècle': Popular Fiction and British Culture, 1880–1914* (Cambridge, 1999).

Darnton, Robert, *Mesmerism and the End of the Enlightenment in France* (Cambridge, MA, 1968).

Daston, Lorraine and Katharine Park, *Wonders and the Order of Nature, 1150–1750* (New York, 1998).

Davenport, Reuben Briggs, *The Death-blow to Spiritualism: Being the True Story of the Fox Sisters, as Revealed by Authority of Margaret Fox Kane and Catherine Fox Jencken* (New York, 1888).

Davies, Owen, *The Haunted: A Social History of Ghosts* (Basingstoke, 2007).

Davis, Colin, '*État présent*: Hauntology, Spectres and Phantoms', *French Studies* 59:3 (2005), 373–9.

Davis, Leonard J., *Factual Fictions: The Origins of the English Novel* (Philadelphia, 1996).

'D.D. Home, His Life and Mission', *JSPR* 4 (1889–1890), 101–36.

Defoe, Daniel, *An Essay on the History and Reality of Apparitions etc.* (London, 1727).

de la Mare, Walter, *Short Stories, 1895–1926*, ed. Giles de la Mare (London, 1996).

Dennett, Daniel C., *Consciousness Explained* (London, 1991).

Denton, William, *The Soul of Things: Psychometric Experiments for Re-living History* (Wellingborough, 1988).

Derrida, Jacques, *Specters of Marx: The State of the Debt, the Work of Mourning, and the New International*, trans. Peggy Kamuf (New York and London, 2006).

Devlin, Judith, *The Superstitious Mind: French Peasants and the Supernatural in the Nineteenth Century* (London, 1987).

Dickens, Charles, *Charles Dickens' Christmas Ghost Stories* (London, 1992).
  The Christmas Books (Ware, 1995).
  Christmas Stories I (London, 1967).
  The Pickwick Papers (Ware, 1993).
  The Uncommercial Traveller and Reprinted Pieces, etc. (London and New York, 1964).

Dickens, Charles, Hesba Stretton, George Augustus Sala *et al.*, *The Haunted House* (London, 2003).

Didion, Joan, *The Year of Magical Thinking* (London, 2006).

Dircks, Henry, *The Ghost! As Produced in the Spectre Drama, Popularly Illustrating the Marvellous Optical Illusions Obtained by the Apparatus Called the Dircksian Phantasmagoria etc.* (London, 1863).

Dixon, Joy, *Divine Feminine: Theosophy and Feminism in England* (Baltimore and London, 2001).

Dolby, R.G.A, 'Reflections on Deviant Science', in *On the Margins of Science: The Social Construction of Rejected Knowledge*, ed. Roy Wallis (Keele, 1979), pp.9–47.

Dowbiggin, Ian, 'Alfred Maury and the Politics of the Unconscious in Nineteenth-century France', *History of Psychiatry* 1:3 (1990), 255–87.

'French Psychiatry and the Search for a Professional Identity: The Société Médico-Psychologique, 1840–1870', *Bulletin for the History of Medicine* 63:3 (1989), 331–55.

Duffy, Bernard J., *Food for Thought: A Treatise on Memory, Dreams and Hallucinations* (London and Dublin, 1944).

During, Simon, *Modern Enchantments: The Cultural Power of Secular Magic* (Cambridge, MA, 2002).

Edgeworth, F.Y., 'The Calculus of Probabilities Applied to Psychical Research I', *PSPR* 3 (1885), 190–9.

'The Calculus of Probabilities Applied to Psychical Research II', *PSPR* 4 (1886–1887), 189–208.

Ellenberger, Henri F., *The Discovery of the Unconscious: The History and Evolution of Dynamic Psychiatry* (New York, 1970).

Elliotson, John, 'More Insanity from Spirit-Rapping Fancies', *Zoist* 12 (1854–1855), 174–80.

Elliott, Charles Wyllys, *Mysteries; or, Glimpses of the Supernatural* (New York, 1852).

Ellis, Havelock, 'On Dreaming of the Dead', *Psychological Review* 2:5 (1895), 458–61.

Emerson, Ralph Waldo, 'Demonology', *North American Review* 124:255 (1877), 179–90.

Engels, Friedrich, *Dialectics of Nature*, trans. Clemens Dutt (Moscow, 1954).

Epperson, Gordon, *The Mind of Edmund Gurney* (London, 1997).

Esquirol, J.E.D., *Mental Maladies: A Treatise on Insanity*, trans. E.K. Hunt (New York and London, 1965).

Evans, Christopher, 'Parapsychology: A History of Research', in *The Oxford Companion to the Mind*, ed. Richard L. Gregory and O.L. Zangwill (Oxford, 1987), pp.584–5.

Farmer, John S., *How to Investigate Spiritualism* (London, 1883).

Fenver, Peter, *Late Kant: Towards Another Law of the Earth* (New York and London, 2003).

Ferriar, John, *An Essay Towards a Theory of Apparitions* (London, 1813).

Ferris, Henry, 'Of the Nightmare', *Dublin University Magazine* 25 (1845), 32–44.

[pseud. 'Irys Herfner'], 'German Ghosts and Ghost-seers', *Dublin University Magazine* 17 (1841), 33–50.

Finucane, Ronald C., *Ghosts: Appearances of the Dead and Cultural Transformation* (Amherst, 1996).

Fischer, Andreas, ' "The Most Disreputable Camera in the World": Spirit Photography in the United Kingdom in the Early Twentieth Century', in *The Perfect Medium: Photography and the Occult*, ed. Clément Chéroux, Andreas Fischer, Pierre Apraxine, Denis Canguilhem and Sophie Schmit (New Haven and London, 2005), pp.72–91.

'F.J.T.', 'Spiritualism in the Carpenter Family', *Light* 1 (January 27, 1881), 27.

Flammarion, Camille, *Death and Its Mystery: At the Moment of Death*, trans. Latrobe Carroll (London, 1922).

Flint, Kate, *The Victorians and the Visual Imagination* (Cambridge, 2000).
Flournoy, Théodore, *Spiritism and Psychology*, trans. Hereward Carrington (London, 1911).
Ford, Jennifer, *Coleridge on Dreaming: Romanticism, Dreams and the Medical Imagination* (Cambridge, 1998).
Forster, T., *Illustrations of the Atmospherical Origin of Epidemic Diseases, and of Its Relation to Their Predisponent Constitutional Causes, Exemplified by Historical Notices and Cases, and on the Twofold Means of Prevention, Mitigation, and Cure, and of the Powerful Influence of Change of Air, as a Principal Remedy*, 2nd edn (London, 1829).
Foucault, Michel, *Madness and Civilization: A History of Insanity in the Age of Reason*, trans. Richard Howard (London, 1989).
Fountain, Averil, 'Visual Hallucinations: A Prevalence Study among Hospice Patients', *Palliative Medicine* 15:1 (2001), 19–25.
Fournier d'Albe, E.E., *New Light on Immortality* (London, 1908).
Freud, Sigmund, *Civilization, Society and Religion: 'Group Psychology', 'Civilization and Its Discontents' and Other Works*, ed. James Strachey (Harmondsworth, 1991).
   The Interpretation of Dreams, ed. James Strachey (London, 1961).
   The Standard Edition of the Complete Psychological Works of Sigmund Freud: vol. XII, *1911–1913: The Case of Schreber, Papers on Technique and Other Works*, ed. James Strachey with Anna Freud (London, 1958).
Fussell, Paul, *The Great War and Modern Memory* (New York and London, 1975).
Gale, Harlow, 'Psychical Research in American Universities', *PSPR* 16 (1897–1898), 583–8.
Galton, Francis, *Inquiries into Human Faculty and Its Development* (Bristol and Tokyo, 1998).
   'Statistics of Mental Imagery', *Mind* 5:19 (1880), 301–18.
Gauld, Alan, *The Founders of Psychical Research* (London, 1968).
   A History of Hypnotism (Cambridge, 1992).
   'Psychical Research in Cambridge from the Seventeenth Century to the Present', *JSPR* 49 (1978), 925–37.
Gay, Susan Elisabeth, *Spiritualistic Sanity: A Reply to Dr. Forbes Winslow's 'Spiritualistic Madness'* (London, 1879).
'General Meeting', *JSPR* 4 (1889–1890), 171–4.
'Ghost Hunting', *Irish Times* (31 May 1884).
Gillis, John R., *A World of Their Own Making: Myth, Ritual, and the Quest for Family Values* (New York, 1996).
Glanvill, Joseph, *Saducismus Triumphatus: or, Full and Plain Evidence Concerning Witches and Apparitions*, 2nd edn (London, 1682).
Goethe, Johann Wolfgang von, *Faust* (London, 1970).
Goffman, Erving, *Frame Analysis: An Essay on the Organization of Experience* (Cambridge, MA, 1974).
Gogarty, Oliver St John, *As I Was Going down Sackville Street* (Dublin, 1994).
Goldfarb, Russell M. and Clare R. Goldfarb, *Spiritualism and Nineteenth-century Letters* (Rutherford, 1978).

Goldstein, Jan, *Console and Classify: The French Psychiatric Profession in the Nineteenth Century* (Chicago and London, 2001).

'The Hysteria Diagnosis and the Politics of Anticlericalism in Late Nineteenth-century France', *Journal of Modern History* 54:2 (1982), 209–39.

Gollin, Rita K., *Nathaniel Hawthorne and the Truth of Dreams* (Baton Rouge and London, 1979).

Goodson, D.W., P. Alderson and R. Rosenthal, 'Clinical Significance of Hallucinations in Psychiatric Disorders: A Study of 116 Hallucinatory Patients', *Archives of General Psychiatry* 24:1 (1971), 76–80.

Goodwin, Sarah Webster and Elisabeth Bronfen, 'Introduction', in *Death and Representation*, ed. Sarah Webster Goodwin and Elisabeth Bronfen (Baltimore and London, 1993), pp.3–25.

Gray, Frank, ed., *Hove Pioneers and the Arrival of Cinema* (Brighton, 1996).

Green, Celia and Charles McCreery, *Apparitions* (London, 1975).

Greenblatt, Stephen, *Hamlet in Purgatory* (Princeton, 2001).

Greene, Carleton, *Death and Sleep: The Idea of Their Analogy Illustrated by Examples . . . with a Brief Discourse upon 'Death and Sleep', and a Memoir of the Late Mrs. Carleton Greene* (London, 1904).

Greg, W. W., 'Hamlet's Hallucination', *Modern Language Review* 12:4 (1917), 393–421.

Gunning, Tom, 'Uncanny Reflections, Modern Illusions: Sighting the Modern Optical Uncanny', in *Uncanny Modernity: Cultural Theories, Modern Anxieties*, ed. Jo Collins and John Jervis (Basingstoke, 2008), pp.68–90.

Gurney, Edmund, 'Hallucinations', *Mind* 10:38 (1885), 161–99.

'Letters on Phantasms: A Reply', *Nineteenth Century* 22 (1887), 522–33.

'Note Relating to Some of the Published Experiments in Thought-Transference', *PSPR* 5 (1888–1889), 269–70.

Tertium Quid: Chapters on Various Disputed Questions, 2 vols (London, 1887).

Gurney, Edmund and Frederic W.H. Myers, 'On Apparitions Occurring Soon after Death', *PSPR* 5 (1888–1889), 403–85.

'Visible Apparitions', *Nineteenth Century* 16 (1884), 68–95, 851–2.

Gurney, Edmund, Frederic W.H. Myers and Frank Podmore, *Phantasms of the Living*, 2 vols (London, 1886).

Habermas, Jürgen, *The Structural Transformation of the Public Sphere: An Inquiry into a Category of Bourgeois Society*, trans. Thomas Burger and Frederick Lawrence (Cambridge, 1989).

Hacking, Ian, *Rewriting the Soul: Multiple Personality and the Sciences of Memory* (Princeton, 1995).

'Telepathy: Origins of Randomization in Experimental Design', *Isis* 79:3 (1988), 427–51.

Hall, G. Stanley, 'Psychological Literature', *American Journal of Psychology* 1:1 (1887), 128–46.

Hall, Trevor H., *The Spiritualists: The Story of Florence Cook and William Crookes* (London, 1962).

The Strange Case of Edmund Gurney (London, 1964).

Halliwell, Martin, *Romantic Science and the Experience of Self: Transatlantic Crosscurrents from William James to Oliver Sacks* (Brookfield, 1999).

Hammond, William A., *Spiritualism and Allied Causes and Conditions of Nervous Derangement* (London, 1876).

Handley, Sasha, *Visions of an Unseen World: Ghost Beliefs and Ghost Stories in Eighteenth-century England* (London, 2007).

Hanks, G.W.C. and N. Cherny, 'Opiod Analgesic Therapy', in *Oxford Textbook of Palliative Medicine*, ed. D. Doyle, G.W.C. Hanks and N. MacDonald, 2nd edn (Oxford, 1998), pp.331–55.

Harris, Ruth, *Murders and Madness: Medicine, Law and Society in the 'Fin de Siècle'* (Oxford, 1989).

Harrison, Jane Ellen, *Reminiscences of a Student's Life* (London, 1925).

Harrison, William H., *Spirits before Our Eyes* (London, 1879).

Hartmann, Eduard von, 'Spiritism', trans. Charles C. Massey, *Light* 5 (22 August 1885), 405–9; (29 August 1885), 417–21; (5 September 1885), 429–32; (12 September 1885), 441–4; (19 September 1885), 453–6; (26 September 1885), 466–9; (3 October 1885), 479–82; (10 October 1885), 491–4.

Harvey, John, 'Revival, Revisions, Visions and Visitations: The Resurgence and Imaging of Supernatural Religion, 1850–1940', *Welsh History Review* 23:2 (2006), 75–98.

Hawthorne, Nathaniel, *The Blithedale Romance* (Harmondsworth, 1986).

   The Letters, 1813–1843, ed. Thomas Woodson, L. Neal Smith and Norman Holmes Pearson (Columbus, 1984).

   Twice-told Tales (London and New York, 1932).

Hayes, Richard, ' "The Night Side of Nature": Henry Ferris, Writing the Dark Gods of Silence', in *Literature and the Supernatural: Essays for the Maynooth Bicentenary*, ed. Brian Cosgrove (Dublin, 1995), pp.42–70.

Haynes, Renée, *The Society for Psychical Research 1882–1982: A History* (London, 1982).

Hayward, Rhodri, 'Demonology, Neurology, and Medicine in Edwardian Britain', *Bulletin of the History of Medicine* 78 (2004), 37–58.

   'Policing Dreams: History and the Moral Uses of the Unconscious', *History Workshop Journal* 49 (2000), 142–60.

Hazelgrove, Jenny, *Spiritualism and British Society between the Wars* (Manchester, 2000).

Hearnshaw, L.S., *A Short History of British Psychology 1840–1940* (London, 1964).

Hedge, Frederic H., 'Ghost-seeing', *North American Review* 133:298 (1881), 286–302.

Hellenbach, Lazar, 'The Hallucination of the "Unconscious" ', trans. 'V', *Light* 5 (17 December 1885), 590–2.

Henkin, David M., *The Postal Age: The Emergence of Modern Communications in Nineteenth-century America* (Chicago and London, 2006).

Henson, Louise, ' "Half Believing, Half Incredulous": Elizabeth Gaskell, Superstition and the Victorian Mind', *Nineteenth-century Contexts* 24:3 (2002), 251–69.

   ' "In the Natural Course of Physical Things": Ghosts and Science in Charles Dickens's *All the Year Round*', in *Culture and Science in the Nineteenth Century: Media*, ed. Louise Henson, Geoffrey Cantor, Gowan Dawson *et al.* (Aldershot, 2004), pp.113–24.

Heraeus, Stefanie, 'Artists and the Dream in Nineteenth-century Paris: Towards a Prehistory of Surrealism', trans. Deborah Laurie Cohen, *History Workshop Journal* 48 (1999), 151–68.

Herman, Daniel, 'Whose Knocking? Spiritualism as Entertainment and Therapy in Nineteenth-century San Francisco', *American Nineteenth-century History* 7:3 (2006), 417–42.

Herschel, John F.W., *Familiar Lectures on Scientific Subjects* (New York and London, 1866).

Hervey de Saint-Denys, Marie Jean-Léon, *Dreams and How to Guide Them*, trans. Nicholas Fry (London, 1982).

Hibbert, Samuel, *Sketches of a Philosophy of Apparitions; or, an Attempt to Trace Such Illusions to Their Physical Causes*, 2nd edn (Edinburgh, 1825).

Hiebert, Erwin N., 'The Transformation of Physics', in *Fin de Siècle and Its Legacy*, ed. Mikuláš Teich and Roy Porter (Cambridge, 1990), pp.235–53.

Hillman, Robert G., 'A Scientific Study of Mystery: The Role of the Medical and Popular Press in the Nancy–Salpêtrière Controversy in Hypnotism', *Bulletin of the History of Medicine* 39:2 (1965), 163–82.

Hobbes, Thomas, *Leviathan*, ed. Richard Tuck (Cambridge, 1991).

Hodges, H.A., *The Philosophy of Wilhelm Dilthey* (London, 1952).

Hodgson, Richard and S.J. Davey, 'The Possibilities of Mal-observation and Lapse of Memory from a Practical Point of View', *PSPR* 4 (1886–1887), 381–495.

Hogan, R. Edward and Kitti Kaiboriboon, 'The "Dreamy State": John Hughlings-Jackson's Ideas of Epilepsy and Consciousness', *American Journal of Psychiatry* 160:10 (2003), 1740–7.

Holland, Jeanne, 'Scraps, Stamps, and Cutouts: Emily Dickinson's Domestic Technologies of Publication', in *Cultural Artifacts and the Production of Meaning: The Page, the Image, and the Body*, ed. Margaret J.M. Ezell and Katherine O'Brien O'Keeffe (Ann Arbor, MI, 1994), pp.139–81.

Holland, Michael, ed., *The Blanchot Reader* (Oxford, 1995).

Houdini, Harry, *A Magician among the Spirits* (New York, 1924).

House, Madeline, Graham Storey, Kathleen Tillotson and Angus Easson, eds, *The Letters of Charles Dickens*: vol. VII, 1853–1855 (Oxford, 1993).

Houston, Gail Turley, *From Dickens to Dracula: Gothic, Economics, and Victorian Fiction* (Cambridge, 2005).

'How Many Senses Have You Got?', *The Times* (30 October 1886), 9.

Howitt, William, *The History of the Supernatural in All Ages and Nations and in All Churches Christian and Pagan: Demonstrating a Universal Faith*: vol. I (London, 1863).

Hubbell, G.G., *Fact and Fancy in Spiritualism, Theosophy and Psychical Research* (Cincinnati, 1901).

Hughes, H. Stuart, *Consciousness and Society: The Reorientation of European Social Thought, 1890–1930* (London, 1959).

Hulisch, A., 'Can a Spirit, of Its Own Self, See Another Spirit?', *Light* 8 (17 November 1888), 569–70.

Hume, David, *Enquiries Concerning Human Understanding and Concerning the Principles of Morals*, ed. L.A. Selby-Bigge, 3rd edn (Oxford, 1975).

Humm, Maggie, *Modernist Women and Visual Cultures: Virginia Woolf, Vanessa Bell, Photography and Cinema* (Edinburgh, 2002).

Hunter, Michael, 'The Problem of "Atheism" in Early Modern England', *Transactions of the Royal Historical Society* 35 (1985), 135–57.

Hutton, R.H., ' "The Metaphysical Society": A Reminiscence', *Nineteenth Century* 18 (1885), 177–96.

Hyde, H. Montgomery, *Henry James at Home* (London, 1969).

Hynes, Samuel, *The Edwardian Turn of Mind* (London, 1968).

Ibsen, Henrik, *A Doll's House; Ghosts*, trans. William Archer (New York, 1911).

Illich, Ivan, *Limits to Medicine: Medical Nemesis: The Expropriation of Health* (London, 1976).

Inglis, Brian, *Natural and Supernatural: A History of the Paranormal from Earliest Times to 1914* (London, 1977).

Innes, A. Taylor, 'The Psychical Society's Ghosts: A Challenge Renewed', *Nineteenth Century* 30 (1891), 764–76.

'Where Are the Letters?', *Nineteenth Century* 22 (1887), 174–94.

Ireland, William W., *The Blot upon the Brain: Studies in History and Psychology*, 2nd edn (Edinburgh, 1893).

Through the Ivory Gate: Studies in Psychology and History (Edinburgh, 1890).

Jacobs, J., 'The Dying of Death', *Fortnightly Review* 72 (1899), 264–9.

Jaffé, Aniela, *An Archetypal Approach to Death Dreams and Ghosts* (Einsiedeln, 1999).

James, Henry, *Ghost Stories of Henry James* (Ware, 2001).

Literary Criticism: French Writers, Other European Writers, The Prefaces to the New York Edition, ed. Leon Edel and Mark Wilson (New York, 1984).

James, Tony, *Dream, Creativity and Madness in Nineteenth-century France* (Oxford, 1995).

James, William, 'The Congress of Physiological Psychology at Paris', *Mind* 14:56 (1889), 614–16.

Essays in Psychical Research (Cambridge, MA, and London, 1986).

The Will to Believe, and Other Essays in Popular Psychology (New York, 1898).

Writings 1902–1910 (New York, 1987).

Jarvis, T.M., *Accredited Ghost Stories* (London, 1823).

Jaspers, Karl, *General Psychopathology*, trans. J. Hoenig and Marian W. Hamilton (Manchester, 1963).

Jay, Martin, *Downcast Eyes: The Denigration of Vision in Twentieth-century French Thought* (Berkeley and London, 1993).

Jaynes, Julian, *The Origins of Consciousness in the Breakdown of the Bicameral Mind* (London, 1993).

Johnson, John, 'Henry Maudsley on Swedenborg's Messianic Psychosis', *British Journal of Psychiatry* 165:5 (1994), 690–1.

Johnston, Sarah Iles, *Restless Dead: Encounters between the Living and the Dead in Ancient Greece* (Berkeley and London, 1999).

Jolly, Martyn, *Faces of the Living Dead: The Belief in Spirit Photography* (London, 2006).

Jones, Ann Rosalind and Peter Stallybrass, *Renaissance Clothing and the Materials of Memory* (Cambridge, 2000).

Jones, Chris B., *Radical Sensibility: Literature and Ideas in the 1790s* (London, 1993).

Jones, Ernest, *Sigmund Freud: Life and Work*: vol. I (London, 1953).

Joyce, James, 'The Dead', in *The Oxford Book of Irish Short Stories*, ed. William Trevor (Oxford, 2001), pp.228–66.

Ulysses, ed. Danis Rose (London, 1998).

Jung, Carl Gustav, *Memories, Dreams, Reflections*, trans. Richard Winston and Clara Winston (London, 1963).

Modern Man in Search of a Soul, trans. W.S. Dell and Cary F. Baynes (London, 1984).

Psychology and the Occult (London, 1987).

The Symbolic Life: Miscellaneous Writings, trans. R.F.C. Hull (London, 1977).

Jung-Stilling, Johann Heinrich, *Theory of Pneumatology, in Reply to the Question, What Ought to Be Believed or Disbelieved Concerning Presentiments, Visions, and Apparitions, According to Nature, Reason, and Scripture*, trans. Samuel Jackson (London, 1834).

Kant, Immanuel, *Theoretical Philosophy, 1755–1770*, trans. David Walford and Ralf Meerbote (Cambridge, 1992).

Kaplan, Fred, *Dickens and Mesmerism: The Hidden Springs of Fiction* (Princeton, 1975).

Kardec, Allan, *Experimental Spiritism*, trans. Emma A. Wood (New York, 1970).

Keats, John, *The Major Works: Including Endymion, the Odes and Selected Letters*, ed. Elizabeth Cook (Oxford, 2001).

Kelly, Edward F., Emily Williams Kelly, Adam Crabtree *et al.*, eds, *Irreducible Mind: Toward a Psychology for the 21st Century* (Lanham, 2006).

Kirkland, Winifred, *The New Death* (Boston, MA, and New York, 1918).

Kittler, Friedrich A., *Gramophone, Film, Typewriter*, trans. Geoffrey Winthrop-Young and Michael Wutz (Stanford, 1999).

Kollar, Rene, *Searching for Raymond: Anglicanism, Spiritualism, and Bereavement between the Two World Wars* (Lanham, 2000).

Kontou, Tatiana, 'Ventriloquising the Dead: Representations of Victorian Spiritualism and Psychical Research in Selected Nineteenth- and Late Twentieth-century Fiction', DPhil thesis, 2006, University of Sussex.

Koslofsky, Craig M., *The Reformation of the Dead: Death and Ritual in Early Modern Germany, 1450–1700* (Basingstoke, 2000).

Kottler, Malcolm Jay, 'Alfred Russel Wallace, the Origin of Man, and Spiritualism', *Isis* 65:2 (1974), 144–92.

Kroll, Jerome and Bernard Bachrach, 'Visions and Psychopathology in the Middle Ages', *Journal of Nervous and Mental Disease* 170:1 (1982), 41–9.

Kselman, Thomas, *Death and the Afterlife in Modern France* (Princeton, 1993).

Kuch, Peter, ' "Laying the Ghosts"? – W.B. Yeats's Lecture on Ghosts and Dreams', in *Yeats Annual No.5*, ed. Warwick Gould (London, 1987), pp.114–35.

Kuhn, Thomas, *The Structure of Scientific Revolutions*, 3rd edn (Chicago and London, 1996).

Lamb, Geoffrey, *Victorian Magic* (London, 1976).

Lamont, Peter, *The First Psychic: The Peculiar Mystery of a Notorious Victorian Wizard* (London, 2005).

'Magician as Conjurer: A Frame Analysis of Victorian Mediums', *Early Popular Visual Culture* 4:1 (2006), 21–33.

'Spiritualism and a Mid-Victorian Crisis of Evidence', *The Historical Journal* 47:4 (2004), 897–920.

Lamont, Peter and Richard Wiseman, *Magic in Theory: An Introduction to the Theoretical and Psychological Elements of Conjuring* (Bristol, 1999).

Landy, Joshua and Michael Sale, eds, *The Re-enchantment of the World: Secular Magic in a Rational Age* (Stanford, 2009).

Lang, Andrew, *The Book of Dreams and Ghosts* (Hollywood, 1972).

Cock Lane and Common-sense (London, 1894).

'The Comparative Study of Ghost Stories', *Nineteenth Century* 17 (1885), 623–32.

The Early Sociology of Religion: vol. IV, *The Making of Religion*, ed. Bryan S. Turner (London, 1997).

'Mr F. Podmore's "Studies in Psychical Research" ', *PSPR* 13 (1897–1898), 604–9.

Laqueur, Thomas, 'Why the Margins Matter: Occultism and the Making of Modernity', *Modern Intellectual History* 3:1 (2006), 111–35.

La Rochefoucauld, François de, *Maxims*, trans. Leonard Tancock (Harmondsworth, 1959).

Latour, Bruno, *Science in Action: How to Follow Scientists and Engineers through Society* (Cambridge, MA, 1987).

Lavater, Ludwig, *Of Ghosts and Spirits Walking by Night, 1572*, ed. J. Dover Wilson and May Yardley (Oxford, 1929).

Lavie, Peretz and J. Allan Hobson, 'Origin of Dreams: Anticipation of Modern Theories in the Philosophy and Physiology of the Eighteenth and Nineteenth Centuries', *Psychological Bulletin* 100:2 (1986), 229–40.

Lay, Wilfrid, *Man's Unconscious Spirit: The Psychoanalysis of Spiritism* (New York, 1921).

Leadbeater, Charles W., *The Astral Plane: Its Scenery, Inhabitants and Phenomena* (London, 1895).

Leahey, Thomas Hardy and Grace Evans Leahey, *Psychology's Occult Doubles: Psychology and the Problem of Pseudoscience* (Chicago, 1983).

LeBlanc, André Robert, 'On Hypnosis, Simulation, and Faith in the Problem of Post-Hypnotic Suggestion in France, 1884–1896', PhD thesis, 2000, University of Toronto.

'Lecture by Professor Barrett', *Freeman's Journal* (26 March 1909).

Le Fanu, Joseph Sheridan, *Best Ghost Stories* (Toronto, 1964).

Lélut, Louis Francisque, *L'Amulette de Pascal, pour servir à l'histoire des hallucinations* (Paris, 1846).

Du démon de Socrate, Spécimen d'une application de la science psychologique à celle de l'histoire (Paris, 1836).

'Leo', 'How Spirits are Clothed', *Light* 9 (1 June 1889), 268–9.

Leopardi, Giacomo, *Thoughts; and, The Broom*, trans. J.G. Nichols (London, 2002).

Leudar, Ivan and Wes Sharrock, 'The Cases of John Bunyan, Part 1. Taine and Royce', *History of Psychiatry* 13:51 (2002), 247–65.

'The Cases of John Bunyan, Part 2. James and Janet', *History of Psychiatry* 13:52 (2002), 401–17.

Levine, George, *Dying to Know: Scientific Epistemology and Narrative in Victorian England* (Chicago and London, 2002).

Lewes, George Henry, 'Dickens in Relation to Criticism', *Fortnightly Review* 11 (1872), 141–54.

'Seeing Is Believing', *Blackwood's Magazine* 88 (1860), 381–95.

Liester, Mitchell B., 'Toward a New Definition of Hallucination', *American Journal of Orthopsychiatry* 68:2 (1998), 305–12.

Linton, Eliza Lynn, 'Our Illusions', *Fortnightly Review* 49 (1891), 584–97.

Littré, Émile, 'Un fragment de médecine rétrospective', *Philosophie positive* 5 (1869), 103–20.

Llinás, R.R. and D. Paré, 'Of Dreaming and Wakefulness', *Neuroscience* 44:3 (1991), 521–35.

Lodge, Oliver, 'Memorial to Mr. Myers at Cheltenham', *JSPR* 13 (1907–1908), 148–52.

'In Memory of F.W.H. Myers', *PSPR* 16 (1901–1903), 1–12.

Loe, Thomas, 'The Strange Modernism of Le Fanu's "Green Tea"', in *That Other World: The Supernatural and the Fantastic in Irish Literature and Its Contexts*: vol. I, ed. Bruce Stewart (Gerrards Cross, 1998), pp.293–306.

Luckhurst, Roger, *The Invention of Telepathy, 1870–1901* (Oxford, 2002).

Machen, Arthur, 'Ghosts and Dreams', *Literature* 5 (19 August 1899), 167–9.

Mackay, Charles, *Memoirs of Extraordinary Popular Delusions and the Madness of Crowds* (London, 1869).

Macnish, Robert, *The Philosophy of Sleep* (Glasgow, 1830); 3rd edn (Glasgow, 1845).

Mahowald, Mark W., Sharon R. Woods and Carlos H. Schenck, 'Sleeping Dreams, Waking Hallucinations, and the Central Nervous System', *Dreaming* 8:2 (1998), 89–102.

Mandler, Peter, Alex Owen, Seth Koven and Susan Pedersen, 'Cultural Histories of the Old and the New: Rereading the Work of Janet Oppenheim', *Victorian Studies* 41:1 (1997), 69–105.

Maple, Eric, *The Realm of Ghosts* (London, 1964).

Marshall, Peter, *Beliefs and the Dead in Reformation England* (Oxford, 2002).

Mother Leakey and the Bishop: A Ghost Story (Oxford, 2007).

Martin, Lillien J., 'Ghosts and the Projection of Visual Images', *American Journal of Psychology* 26:3 (1915), 251–7.

Marx, Karl and Friedrich Engels, *The German Ideology. Part One, with Selections from Parts Two and Three, Together with Marx's 'Introduction to a Critique of Political Economy'*, ed. C.J. Arthur (London, 1970).

Massey, C.C., 'The Possibilities of Mal-observation in Relation to Evidence for the Phenomena of Spiritualism', *PSPR* 4 (1886–1887), 75–99.

Matlock, Jann, 'Ghostly Politics', *Diacritics* 30:3 (2000), 53–71.

Maudsley, Henry, *Body and Mind: An Inquiry into their Connection and Mutual Influences, Specifically in Reference to Mental Disorders* (New York, 1871).

'Emanuel Swedenborg', *Journal of Mental Science* 15 (1869), 169–96.

'Hallucinations of the Senses', *Fortnightly Review* 24 (1878), 370–86.

Maudsley, Henry *Natural Causes and Supernatural Seemings* (London, 1886).
The Physiology and Pathology of the Mind (New York, 1867).
Mauskopf, Seymour H., 'Marginal Science', in *Companion to the History of Modern Science*, ed. R.C. Olby, G.N. Cantor, J.R.R. Christie and M.J.S. Hodge (London, 1990), pp.869–85.
Mauskopf, Seymour H. and Michael R. McVaugh, *The Elusive Science: Origins of Experimental Psychical Research* (Baltimore and London, 1980).
Maxwell-Stuart, P.G., *Ghosts: A History of Phantoms, Ghouls, and Other Spirits of the Dead* (Stroud, 2006).
Mayo, Herbert, *On the Truths Contained in Popular Superstitions with an Account of Mesmerism* (Edinburgh and London, 1851).
McCorristine, Shane, 'Last Nights in Paris: Exploring Lautréamont's Surreal City', *The History Review* 15 (2005), 115–35.
McDougall, William, *Body and Mind: A History and a Defense of Animism* (London, 1911).
McGarry, Molly, *Ghosts of Futures Past: Spiritualism and the Cultural Politics of Nineteenth-century America* (Berkeley and London, 2008).
Méheust, Bertrand, *Somnambulisme et médiumnité*: vol. I, *Le Défi du magnétisme* (Paris, 1999).
Somnambulisme et médiumnité: vol. II, *Le Choc des sciences psychiques* (Paris, 1999).
Melechi, Antonio, *Servants of the Supernatural: The Night Side of the Victorian Mind* (London, 2008).
'Mental Epidemics', *Fraser's Magazine for Town & Country* 65 (1862), 490–505.
Micale, Mark S., ed., *The Mind of Modernism: Medicine, Psychology, and the Cultural Arts in Europe and America, 1880–1940* (Stanford, 2004).
Middleton, Jessie Adelaide, *Another Grey Ghost Book: With a Chapter on Prophetic Dreams and a Note on Vampires* (London, 1915).
Mill, John Stuart, *Collected Works of John Stuart Mill*: vol. VII, ed. J.M. Robson (London, 1973–1974).
Monleon, José B., '1848: The Assault on Reason', in *The Horror Reader*, ed. Ken Gelder (London and New York, 2000), pp.20–8.
Montenon, Corinne, 'Materialisation Phenomena in British and French Spiritualism and Psychical Research, c.1870–1920', PhD thesis, 2004, University of Birmingham.
Morrissey, Susan K., 'Drinking to Death: Suicide, Vodka and Religious Burial in Russia', *Past and Present* 186 (2005), 117–46.
Mort, Frank, *Dangerous Sexualities: Medico-moral Politics in England since 1850*, 2nd edn (London and New York, 2000).
Mott, R.H., I.F. Small and J. Anderson, 'Comparative Study of Hallucinations', *Archives of General Psychiatry* 12 (1965), 595–601.
Mourgue, Raoul, 'Étude-critique sur l'évolution des idées relatives à la nature des hallucinations vraies', doctoral thesis, Paris, 1919.
Munthe, Axel, *The Story of San Michele* (London, 1991).
'M.W.G.', 'Clothes Spooks', *Light* 10 (29 November 1890), 572.
Myers, Arthur T., 'International Congress of Experimental Psychology', *PSPR* 6 (1889–1890), 171–82.

Myers, Frederic W.H., 'A Defence of Phantasms of the Dead', *PSPR* 6 (1889–1890), 314–57.

'The Drift of Psychical Research', *National Review* 24 (1894), 190–209.

Human Personality and Its Survival of Bodily Death (New York, 1909).

'In Memory of Henry Sidgwick', *PSPR* 15 (1900–1901), 452–63.

'Multiplex Personality', *Nineteenth Century* 20 (1886), 648–66.

'On Recognised Apparitions Occurring More Than a Year after Death', *PSPR* 6 (1889–1890), 13–65.

'Presidential Address', *PSPR* 15 (1900–1901), 110–27.

'Professor Pierre Janet's "Automatisme psychologique" ', *PSPR* 6 (1889–1890), 186–99.

'Resolute Credulity', *PSPR* 10 (1895), 213–43.

'The Right Hon. W.E. Gladstone', *JSPR* 8 (1897–1898), 260.

'Science and a Future Life', *Nineteenth Century* 29 (1891), 628–47.

'The Subliminal Consciousness', *PSPR* 9 (1893–1894), 3–128.

'The Work of Edmund Gurney in Experimental Psychology', *PSPR* 5 (1888–1889), 359–73.

Myers, Rollo, 'Edmund Gurney's "The Power of Sound" ', *Music and Letters* 53 (1972), 36–42.

Nadis, Fred, *Wonder Shows: Performing Science, Magic, and Religion in America* (New Brunswick and London, 2005).

Nancy, Jean-Luc, *The Inoperative Community*, ed. Peter Connor, trans. Peter Connor, Lisa Garbus, Michael Holland and Simona Sawhney (Minneapolis and London, 1990).

Nelson, Geoffrey K., *Spiritualism and Society* (London, 1969).

Nicholson, William, 'Narrative and Explanation of the Appearance of Phantoms and Other Figures in the Exhibition of the Phantasmagoria, with Remarks on the Philosophical Use of Common Occurrences', *Journal of Natural Philosophy, Chemistry and the Arts* 1 (1802), 147–50.

Nicol, Fraser, 'The Founders of the S.P.R.', *PSPR* 55 (1966–1972), 341–67.

Nicolai, Christoph Friedrich, 'A Memoir on the Appearance of Spectres or Phantoms Occasioned by Disease, with Psychological Remarks. Read by Nicolai to the Royal Society of Berlin, on the 28th of February, 1799', *Journal of Natural Philosophy, Chemistry and the Arts* 6 (1803), 161–79.

Nietzsche, Friedrich, *Human, All Too Human*, trans. Marion Faber and Stephen Lehmann (London, 1994).

Noakes, Richard, 'The "Bridge Which Is between Physical and Psychical Research": William Fletcher Barrett, Sensitive Flames, and Spiritualism', *History of Science* 42 (2004), 419–64.

Nordau, Max, *Degeneration* (Lincoln, NE, and London, 1993).

'Notes', *Mind* 13:49 (1888), 149–50.

Noyes, Ralph. 'The Other Side of Plato's Wall', in *Ghosts: Deconstruction, Psychoanalysis, History*, ed. Peter Buse and Andrew Stott (Basingstoke, 1999), pp.244–62.

'Objects of the Society', *PSPR* 1 (1882–1883), 3–7.

O'Byrne, F.D., *Reichenbach's Letters on Od and Magnetism (1852). Published for the First Time in English, with Extracts from His Other Works, so as to Make a Complete Presentation of the Odic Theory* (London, 1926).
O'Donnell, John M., *The Origins of Behaviorism: American Psychology, 1870–1920* (New York and London, 1985).
Ogden, Daniel, *Magic, Witchcraft, and Ghosts in the Greek and Roman Worlds: A Sourcebook* (Oxford, 2002).
Ollier, Charles, *Fallacy of Ghosts, Dreams, and Omens; With Stories of Witchcraft, Life-In-Death, and Monomania* (London, 1848).
Oman, Charles, 'The Old Oxford Phasmatological Society', *JSPR* 33 (1946), 208–17.
Oppenheim, Janet, *The Other World: Spiritualism and Psychical Research in England, 1850–1914* (Cambridge, 1985).
  'Shattered Nerves': Doctors, Patients, and Depression in Victorian England (New York and Oxford, 1991).
Ostry, Elaine, *Social Dreaming: Dickens and the Fairy Tale* (New York and London, 2002).
Otis, Laura, 'The Metaphoric Circuit: Organic and Technological Communication in the Nineteenth Century', *Journal of the History of Ideas* 63:1 (2002), 105–28.
Owen, Alex, *The Darkened Room: Women, Power and Spiritualism in Late Nineteenth-century England* (London, 1989).
  The Place of Enchantment: British Occultism and the Culture of the Modern (Chicago and London, 2004).
Owen, Robert Dale, *Footfalls on the Boundary of Another World: With Narrative Illustrations* (London, 1860).
Palfreman, Jon, 'Between Scepticism and Credulity: A Study of Victorian Scientific Attitudes to Modern Spiritualism', in *On the Margin of Science: The Social Construction of Rejected Knowledge*, ed. Roy Wallis (Keele, 1979), pp.201–36.
Panek, Richard, *The Invisible Century: Einstein, Freud, and the Search for Hidden Universes* (London, 2004).
Parish, Edmund, *Hallucinations and Illusions: A Study of the Fallacies of Perception* (London, 1897).
Past Feelings Renovated; or, Ideas Occasioned by the Perusal of Dr. Hibbert's 'Philosophy of Apparitions' Written with the View of Countering Any Sentiments Approaching Materialism, Which That Work, However Unintentional on the Part of the Author, May Have a Tendency to Produce (London, 1828).
Paterson, Robert, 'An Account of Several Cases of Spectral Illusions, with Observations on the Phenomena and on the States of Bodily Indisposition in which They Occur', *Edinburgh Medical and Surgical Journal* 59 (1843), 77–102.
Pearsall, Ronald, *The Table-Rappers: The Victorians and the Occult* (Stroud, 2004).
Pease, Edward R., *The History of the Fabian Society* (London, 1916).
Peirce, Charles S., 'Telepathy and Perception', in *Collected Papers of Charles Sanders Peirce*: vol. VII, *Science and Philosophy*; vol. VIII, *Reviews,*

Correspondence, and Bibliography, ed. Arthur W. Burks (Cambridge, MA, 1966), pp.359–97.

Writings of Charles S. Peirce: A Chronological Edition: vol. VI, *1886–1890*, ed. Nathan Houser and Peirce Edition Project (Bloomington, 2000).

Pels, Peter, 'Spirits of Modernity: Alfred Wallace, Edward Tylor, and the Visual Politics of Fact', in *Magic and Modernity: Interfaces of Revelation and Concealment*, ed. Birgit Meyer and Peter Pels (Stanford, 2003), pp.241–71.

Penny, A.J., 'Ready-made Clothes', *Light* 7 (3 September 1887), 411–12.

Pepper, John Henry, *The True History of the Ghost; and All about Metempsychosis* (London, 1890).

Perky, Cheves West, 'An Experimental Study of Imagination', *American Journal of Psychology* 21:3 (1910), 422–52.

Perry, Seamus, *Coleridge and the Uses of Division* (Cambridge, 1999).

Peters, Uwe Henrik, *Studies in German Romantic Psychiatry: Justinus Kerner as a Psychiatric Practitioner, E.T.A. Hoffmann as a Psychiatric Theorist* (London, 1990).

Petroski, Karen, ' "The Ghost of an Idea": Dickens's Uses of Phantasmagoria, 1842–44', *Dickens Quarterly* 16:2 (1999), 71–93.

Phillips, Forbes and R. Thurston Hopkins, *War and the Weird* (London, 1916).

'Philosophius', *Ghosts and Their Modern Worshippers* (London, 1892).

Pick, Daniel, *Faces of Degeneration: A European Disorder, c.1848–c.1918* (Cambridge, 1989).

Pick, Daniel with Lyndal Roper, eds, *Dreams and History: The Interpretation of Dreams from Ancient Greece to Modern Psychoanalysis* (London, 2004).

Plato, *Theaetetus; Sophist*, trans. Harold North Fowler (London, 1921).

Podmore, Frank, *Apparitions and Thought-transference: An Examination of the Evidence for Telepathy* (New York, 1915).

Modern Spiritualism: A History and Criticism, 2 vols (London, 1902).

The Naturalisation of the Supernatural (New York and London, 1908).

'Phantasms of the Dead from Another Point of View', *PSPR* 6 (1889–1890), 227–313.

Studies in Psychical Research (London, 1897).

Porter, Roy, *The Greatest Benefit to Mankind: A Medical History of Humanity from Antiquity to the Present* (London, 1999).

Madmen: A Social History of Madhouses, Mad-Doctors and Lunatics (Stroud, 2006).

Porter, Roy and Helen Nicholson, eds, *Women, Madness and Spiritualism*: vol. I, *Georgina Weldon and Louisa Lowe* (London and New York, 2003).

Preliminary Report of the Commission Appointed by the University of Pennsylvania to Investigate Modern Spiritualism (Philadelphia, 1887).

'Psychical Research', in *The Fin de Siècle: A Reader in Cultural History, c.1880–1900*, ed. Sally Ledger and Roger Luckhurst (Oxford, 2000), pp.278–80.

'Psychical Research', *Lancet* (22 December 1883), 1104.

Quinney, Laura, 'Wordsworth's Ghosts and the Model of the Mind', *European Romantic Review* 9:2 (1998), 293–301.

Rabaté, Jean-Michel, *The Ghosts of Modernity* (Gainesville, 1996).

Rabinow, Paul, ed., *The Foucault Reader* (Harmondsworth, 1986).

Radcliffe, John Netten, *Fiends, Ghosts, and Sprites: Including an Account of the Origin and Nature of Belief in the Supernatural* (London, 1854).

Randi, James, *Flim-Flam!: Psychics, ESP, Unicorns, and Other Delusions* (Buffalo, 1982).

Raverat, Gwen, *Period Piece: A Cambridge Childhood* (London, 1960).

Redgrove, H. Stanley and I.M.L. Redgrove, *Joseph Glanvill and Psychical Research in the Seventeenth Century* (London, 1921).

Report on Spiritualism, of the Committee of the London Dialectical Society, Together with the Evidence, Oral and Written, and a Selection from the Correspondence (London, 1873).

Richards, Graham, 'Britain on the Couch: The Popularization of Psychoanalysis in Britain 1918–1940', *Science in Context* 13:2 (2000), 183–230.

'Edward Cox, the Psychological Society of Great Britain (1875–1879) and the Meanings of an Institutional Failure', in *Psychology in Britain: Historical Essays and Personal Reflections*, ed. G.C. Bunn, A.D. Lovie and G.D. Richards (Leicester, 2001), pp.35–53.

Richet, Charles, *Thirty Years of Psychical Research: Being a Treatise in Metapsychics*, trans. Stanley de Brath (London, 1923).

Roffe, Alfred, *An Essay upon the Ghost-belief of Shakespeare* (London, 1851).

Rogers, Edmund Dawson, 'Origin of the Society for Psychical Research', *Light* 13 (September 1893), 429–30.

Rogers, Edward Coit, *Philosophy of Mysterious Agents, Human and Mundane, etc.* (Boston, MA, 1856).

Ross, Dorothy, *G. Stanley Hall: The Psychologist as Prophet* (Chicago and London, 1972).

ed., *Modernist Impulses in the Human Sciences, 1870–1930* (Baltimore, 1994).

Roth, Michael S., ed., *Rediscovering History: Culture, Politics, and the Psyche* (Stanford, 1994).

Rothblatt, Sheldon, *The Revolution of the Dons: Cambridge and Society in Victorian England* (London, 1968).

Royce, Josiah, 'Hallucination of Memory and "Telepathy"', *Mind* 13:50 (1888), 244–8.

Ruskin, John, *Modern Painters*: vol. III (Boston, MA, 1890).

Russell, Claire, 'The Environment of Ghosts', in *The Folklore of Ghosts*, ed. Hilda R. Ellis Davidson and W.M.S. Russell (Bury St Edmunds, 1981), pp.109–37.

Rylance, Rick, *Victorian Psychology and British Culture, 1850–1880* (Oxford, 2000).

'A Sadducean Bias', *Light* 16 (25 April 1896), 198.

Salter, Helen de G., 'Impressions of Some Early Workers in the S.P.R.', *Journal of Parapsychology* 14:1 (1950), 24–36.

Sarbin, Theodore R., 'The Concept of Hallucination', *Journal of Personality* 35 (1967), 359–80.

Sarbin, Theodore R. and Joseph B. Juhasz, 'The Historical Background of the Concept of Hallucination', *History of the Behavioural Sciences* 3 (1967), 339–58.

Scarry, Elaine, 'On Vivacity: The Difference between Daydreaming and Imagining-under-Authorial-Institution', *Representations* 52 (1995), 1–26.

Schiller, F. C. S., *Humanism: Philosophical Essays* (New York, 1969).

Schiller, Friedrich von, *Aesthetical and Philosophical Essays, the Ghost-seer, and the Sport of Destiny*: vol. V (Boston, MA, 1902).

Schmitt, Jean-Claude, *Ghosts in the Middle Ages: The Living and the Dead in Medieval Society*, trans. Teresa Lavender Fagan (Chicago, 1998).

Schönfeld, Martin, *The Philosophy of the Young Kant: The Precritical Project* (Oxford, 2000).

Schopenhauer, Arthur, *Parerga and Paralipomena: Short Philosophical Essays*: vol. I, trans. E.F.J. Payne (Oxford, 1974).

The World as Will and Idea: vol. I, trans. J. Kemp and R. B. Haldane (London, 1964).

Schultz, Bart, *Henry Sidgwick, Eye of the Universe: An Intellectual Biography* (Cambridge, 2004).

Schwartz, Sophie, 'A Historical Loop of One Hundred Years: Similarities between Nineteenth Century and Contemporary Dream Research', *Dreaming* 10:1 (2000), 55–66.

Scott, Walter, *Letters on Demonology and Witchcraft* (London, 1884).

'Novels of Ernest Theodore Hoffmann', in *Critical and Miscellaneous Essays*: vol. II (Philadelphia, 1841).

Seashore, Carl E., 'Measurements of Illusions and Hallucinations in Normal Life', in *Studies from the Yale Psychological Laboratory*: vol.III, ed. Edward W. Scripture (1895), pp.1–67.

Seltzer, Mark, *Bodies and Machines* (New York and London, 1992).

'The Postal Unconscious', *The Henry James Review* 21 (2000), 197–206.

Selwyn, Pamela E., *Everyday Life in the German Book Trade: Friedrich Nicolai as Bookseller and Publisher in the Age of Enlightenment, 1750–1810* (University Park, 2000).

Shakespeare, William, *The Complete Works of William Shakespeare* (London, 1966).

Shapin, Steven, *The Scientific Revolution* (Chicago, 1996).

Sharp, Lynn L., *Secular Spirituality: Reincarnation and Spiritism in Nineteenth-century France* (Lanham, 2006).

Shell, Susan Meld, *The Embodiment of Reason: Kant on Spirit, Generation, and Community* (Chicago and London, 1996).

Sheppard, E.A., *Henry James and 'The Turn of the Screw'* (Auckland and London, 1974).

Shorter, Edward, *A History of Psychiatry: From the Era of the Asylum to the Age of Prozac* (New York, 1997).

Sidgwick, Arthur and Eleanor M. Sidgwick, *Henry Sidgwick: A Memoir* (London, 1906).

Sidgwick, Eleanor M., 'Notes on the Evidence, Collected by the Society, for Phantasms of the Dead', *PSPR* 3 (1885), 69–150.

'Phantasms of the Living: An Examination and Analysis of Cases of Telepathy between Living Persons Printed in the "Journal" of the Society for Psychical Research since the Publication of the Book "Phantasms of the Living", by Gurney, Myers, and Podmore, in 1886', *PSPR* 33 (1923), 23–429.

'*Zur Kritik des Telepathischen Beweis Matériels*. By Edmund Parish. Leipzig. 1897', *PSPR* 13 (1897–1898), 589–601.

Sidgwick, Henry, 'Address by the President on the Census of Hallucinations',
    PSPR 6 (1889–1890), 7–12.
'Address by the President. Second Address on the Census of Hallucinations',
    PSPR 6 (1889–1890), 407–28.
'The Canons of Evidence in Psychical Research', *PSPR* 6 (1889–1890), 1–6.
The Methods of Ethics, 2nd edn (London, 1877).
'Note on Mr. Massey's Paper', *PSPR* 4 (1886–1887), 99–110.
'President's Address', *PSPR* 1 (1882–1883), 7–12.
'President's Address', *PSPR* 2 (1884), 152–6.
'President's Address', *PSPR* 5 (1888–1889), 271–8.
Sidgwick, Henry, Alice Johnson, Frederic W.H. Myers, Frank Podmore and
    Eleanor M. Sidgwick, 'Report on the Census of Hallucinations', *PSPR* 10
    (1894), 25–423.
Simmel, Georg, *The Sociology of Georg Simmel*, ed. Kurt H. Wolff (New York and
    London, 1950).
Simon, Robert I., 'Great Paths Cross: Freud and James at Clark University,
    1909', *American Journal of Psychiatry* 124:6 (1967), 831–4.
Simpson, Jacqueline, 'Ghosts', in *Encyclopedia of Death and Dying*, ed. Glennys
    Howarth and Oliver Leaman (London and New York, 2001), pp. 207–9.
Simpson, Jeffrey E., 'Thoreau "Dreaming Awake and Asleep"', *Modern
    Language Studies* 14:3 (1984), 54–62.
Škodlar, B., M.Z. Dernovsek and M. Kocmur, 'Psychopathology of
    Schizophrenia in Ljubljana (Slovenia) from 1881 to 2000: Changes in the
    Content of Delusions in Schizophrenic Patients Related to Various
    Sociopolitical, Technical and Scientific Changes', *International Journal of
    Social Psychiatry* 54:2 (2008), 101–11.
Skultans, Vieda, 'Mediums, Controls and Eminent Men', in *Women's Religious
    Experience*, ed. Pat Holden (London, 1983), pp.15–26.
Slade, Peter D. and Richard P. Bentall, *Sensory Deception: A Scientific Analysis of
    Hallucination* (London and Sydney, 1988).
Smajic, Srdjan, 'The Trouble with Ghost-seeing: Vision, Ideology, and Genre in
    the Victorian Ghost Story', *English Literary History* 70:4 (2003), 1107–35.
Smith, Adam, *The Theory of Moral Sentiments*, ed. D.D. Raphael and A.L.
    Macfie (Oxford, 1976).
Soussloff, Catherine M., 'The Turn to Visual Culture: On Visual Culture and
    Techniques of the Observer', *Visual Anthropology Review* 12:1 (1996), 77–83.
Spinoza, Baruch, *The Ethics and Selected Letters*, trans. Samuel Shirley
    (Indianapolis, 1982).
'Spookical Research', *Saturday Review of Politics, Literature, Science, and Art* 62
    (1886), 648–50.
'Spooks and Their Friends', *Saturday Review of Politics, Literature, Science, and
    Art* 62 (1886), 750–1.
'The S.P.R. and the C.A.S.', *Light* 3 (3 February 1883), 54.
Sprinker, Michael, ed., *Ghostly Demarcations: A Symposium on Jacques Derrida's
    'Specters of Marx'* (London, 1999).
Stafford, Barbara Maria, *Artful Science: Enlightenment, Entertainment and the
    Eclipse of Visual Education* (Cambridge, MA, and London, 1994).

Body Criticism: Imaging the Unseen in Enlightenment Art and Medicine (Cambridge, MA, and London, 1991).

Starr, George, 'Why Defoe Probably Did not Write *The Apparition of Mrs. Veal*', *Eighteenth-century Fiction* 15:3–4 (2003), 421–50.

Stead, W. T., 'The Census of Ghosts', *Borderland: A Quarterly Review and Index* 1 (1894), 498–505.

'Wanted, a Census of Ghosts!', *The Review of Reviews* 4 (1891), 257–8.

Steen, Robert Hunter, 'Hallucinations in the Sane', *Journal of Mental Science* 63 (1917), 328–46.

Stirner, Max, *The Ego and Its Own*, trans. Steven Byington (London, 1982).

Stocking, George W., Jr, 'Animism in Theory and Practice: E.B. Tylor's Unpublished "Notes on 'Spiritualism'," ', *Man* 6:1 (1971), 88–104.

Stolow, Jeremy, 'Techno-religious Imaginaries: On the Spiritual Telegraph and the Circum-Atlantic World of the Nineteenth Century', in *Institute on Globalization and the Human Condition Working Paper Series*, ed. William Coleman (Hamilton, ON, 2006).

Stone, G. W., *An Exposition of Views Respecting the Principal Facts, Causes, and Peculiarities Involved in Spirit Manifestations, together with Interesting Phenomenal Statements and Communications* (London, 1852).

Strange, Julie-Marie, *Death, Grief and Poverty in Britain, 1870–1914* (Cambridge, 2005).

Strindberg, August, *Inferno; and from an Occult Diary*, trans. Mary Sandbach (Harmondsworth, 1979).

Stronks, G. J., 'The Significance of Balthasar Bekker's *The Enchanted World*', in *Witchcraft in the Netherlands from the Fourteenth to the Twentieth Century*, ed. Marijke Gijswijt and Willem Frijhoff, trans. Rachel M.J. van der Wilden-Fall (Rotterdam, 1991), pp.149–56.

Struve, Heinrich von, *Hamlet: Eine Charakterstudie* (Weimar, 1876).

Swedenborg, Emanuel, *Heaven and Hell*, trans. George F. Dole (New York, 1990).

Sword, Helen, *Ghostwriting Modernism* (London and Ithaca, NY, 2002).

Symonds, John Addington, *Sleep and Dreams; Two Lectures Delivered at the Bristol Literary and Philosophical Institution* (London, 1851).

Taillepied, Noel, *A Treatise of Ghosts etc.*, trans. Montague Summers (London, 1933).

Taine, Hippolyte, *On Intelligence*, trans. T.D. Haye (London, 1871).

Taylor, Eugene, 'Oh Those Fabulous James Boys!', *Psychology Today* 28:2 (1995), 56–66.

Taylor, Jenny Bourne and Sally Shuttleworth, eds, *Embodied Selves: An Anthology of Psychological Texts, 1830–1890* (Oxford and New York, 1998).

Tennyson, Alfred, Lord, *The Complete Works* (London, 1905).

Thomas, Keith, *Religion and the Decline of Magic: Studies in Popular Beliefs in Sixteenth- and Seventeenth-Century England* (London, 1971).

Thurschwell, Pamela, *Literature, Technology, and Magical Thinking, 1880–1920* (Cambridge, 2001).

Treitel, Corinna, *A Science of the Soul: Occultism and the Genesis of the German Modern* (Baltimore and London, 2004).

Troland, Leonard T., 'The Freudian Psychology and Psychical Research', *Journal of Abnormal Psychology* 8:6 (1914), 405–28.

Turner, Frank Miller, *Between Science and Religion: The Reaction to Scientific Naturalism in Late Victorian England* (New Haven and London, 1974).

'Public Science in Britain, 1880–1919', *Isis* 71:4 (1980), 589–608.

Twain, Mark, 'Mental Telegraphy', in *Literature and Science in the Nineteenth Century: An Anthology*, ed. Laura Otis (Oxford, 2002), pp.99–103.

Tylor, Edward B., *Primitive Culture: Researches into the Development of Mythology, Philosophy, Religion, Art, and Custom*: vol. I, 2nd edn (London, 1873).

Tyndall, John, *Fragments of Science*: vol. II, 6th edn (New York, 1905).

Tyrrell, G.N.M., *Apparitions*, rev. edn (London, 1953).

Vande Kemp, Hendrika, 'Psycho-spiritual Dreams in the Nineteenth Century, Part I: Dreams of Death', *Journal of Psychology and Theology* 22:2 (1994), 97–108.

'Psycho-spiritual Dreams in the Nineteenth Century, Part II: Metaphysics and Immortality', *Journal of Psychology and Theology* 22:2 (1994), 109–19.

Van Eeden, Frederick, 'A Study of Dreams', *PSPR* 26 (1912–1913), 431–61.

Van Ruler, Han, 'Minds, Forms, and Spirits: The Nature of Cartesian Disenchantment', *Journal of the History of Ideas* 61:3 (2000), 381–95.

Venn, John, *The Logic of Chance: An Essay on the Foundations and Province of the Theory of Probability, with Especial Reference to its Logical Bearings and Its Application to Moral and Social Science, and to Statistics*, 3rd edn (London and New York, 1888).

Vernant, Jean-Pierre, *Myth and Thought among the Greeks* (London, 1983).

Vincent, David, 'The Decline of the Oral Tradition in Popular Culture', in *Popular Culture and Custom in Nineteenth-century England*, ed. Robert D. Storch (London and New York, 1982), pp.20–47.

Viollet, Marcel, *Spiritism and Insanity* (London, 1910).

Wagner, Richard, *Beethoven*, trans. Edward Dannreuther (London, 1880).

Walker, Mary, 'Between Fiction and Madness: The Relationship of Women to the Supernatural in Late Victorian Britain', in *That Gentle Strength: Historical Perspectives on Women in Christianity*, ed. Lynda L. Coon, Katherine J. Haldane and Elisabeth W. Sommer (Charlottesville, 1990), pp.230–42.

Walkowitz, Judith R., 'Science and the Seance: Transgressions of Gender and Genre in Late Victorian London', *Representations* 22 (1988), 3–29.

Wallace, Alfred Russel, *On Miracles and Modern Spiritualism* (London, 2000).

'The Psychological Curiosities of Scepticism. A Reply to Dr. Carpenter', *Fraser's Magazine for Town & Country* 16 (1877), 694–706.

Walton, James, 'On the Attribution of "Mrs. Veal"', *Notes and Queries* 54:1 (2007), 60–2.

Warner, Marina, *Phantasmagoria: Spirit Visions, Metaphors, and Media into the Twenty-first Century* (Oxford, 2006).

Weatherly, Lionel A. and J.N. Maskelyne, *The Supernatural? With Chapter on Oriental Magic, Spiritualism, and Theosophy* (London, 2000).

Weaver, Zofia, 'Daniel Dunglas Home Revisited – Evidence Old and New: An Essay Review of *Knock, Knock, Knock! Who's There?*', *JSPR* 72 (2008), 222–30.

Weed, Sarah C., Florence M. Hallam and Emma D. Phinney, 'A Study of the Dream-consciousness', *American Journal of Psychology* 7:3 (1896), 405–11.

Weightman, Mary, *The Friendly Monitor; or, Dialogues for Youth Against the Fear of Ghosts, and Other Irrational Apprehensions etc.* (London, 1791).

Weissberg, Liliane, *Geistersprache: Philosophischer und Literarischer Diskurs im Späten Achtzehnten Jahrhundert* (Würzburg, 1990).

Wells, H.G. 'Peculiarities of Psychical Research', *Nature* (6 December 1894), 121–2.

Weninger, Francis Xavier, *Protestantism and Infidelity: An Appeal to Candid Americans*, 10th edn (New York, 1865).

West, D. J., 'A Mass-Observation Questionnaire on Hallucinations', *JSPR* 34 (1948), 187–95.

'What Is a Spook?', *Saturday Review of Politics, Literature, Science, and Art* 62 (1886), 773.

Whiting, Lilian, 'Do Spirits See Material Objects?', *Light* 17 (31 July 1897), 368–9.

Wigan, Arthur L., *A New View of Insanity. The Duality of the Mind etc.* (London, 1844).

Wilkinson, Alan, *The Church of England and the First World War* (London, 1978).

Wilkinson, Lynn R., *The Dream of an Absolute Language: Emanuel Swedenborg and French Literary Culture* (New York, 1996).

Williams, Charles, *Spiritualism and Insanity: An Essay Describing the Disastrous Consequences to the Mental Health, Which Are Apt to Result from a Pursuit of the Study of Spiritualism* (London, 1910).

Williams, John Peregrine, 'The Making of Victorian Psychical Research: An Intellectual Elite's Approach to the Spiritual World', PhD thesis, 1984, University of Cambridge.

Wilson, Neil, *Shadows in the Attic: A Guide to British Supernatural Fiction, 1820–1950* (Boston Spa and London, 2000).

Winkelman, Michael, 'Spirits as Human Nature and the Fundamental Structures of Consciousness', in *From Shaman to Scientist: Essays on Humanity's Search for Spirits*, ed. James Houran (Lanham, 2004), pp.59–96.

Winslow, L. S. Forbes, *'Spiritualistic Madness'* (London, 1876).

Winter, Alison, *Mesmerized: Powers of Mind in Victorian Britain* (Chicago and London, 1998).

Winter, Jay, *Sites of Memory, Sites of Mourning: The Great War in European Cultural History* (Cambridge, 1995).

Wolffram, Heather, 'Parapsychology on the Couch: The Psychology of Occult Belief in Germany, c.1870–1939', *Journal of the History of the Behavioral Sciences* 42:3 (2006), 237–60.

Wolfreys, Julian, *Victorian Hauntings: Spectrality, Gothic, the Uncanny and Literature* (Basingstoke, 2002).

Wundt, Wilhelm, *Lectures on Human and Animal Psychology*, trans. J.E. Creighton and E. B. Titchener (London, 1901).

'X', 'The Telepathic Theory', *Light* 5 (14 March 1885), 121–2.

'X.P.', 'Believers and Disbelievers; or, Who are the Fools?', *Zoist* 4 (1846–1847), 435–47.

Zerffi, Gustavus George, *Dreams and Ghosts. A Lecture Delivered before the Sunday Lecture Society, on Sunday Afternoon, 7th February, 1875* (London, 1875).

Spiritualism and Animal Magnetism (London, 1873).

Index

Abraham, Nicolas 159, 161
American Psychical Institute and
    Laboratory 227
American Society for Psychical Research
    112, 167, 170, 196
Andrews, Malcolm 135
angels 39, 67, 68
animal magnetism 9, 66, 71
animism 20, 82
anthropology 20, 82, 128, 135
Ariès, Philippe 155
Aristotle 6
Assier, Adolphe d' 95
atheism 43, 51, 220

Baillarger, Jules 55, 194
Balcon, Michael 188
Balfour, Arthur 104, 111, 175
Ballou, Adin 109
Barrett, William Fletcher 109, 110, 112,
    114, 115, 139, 151, 152
Barthes, Roland 158
Bath, Jo 29
Baudelaire, Charles 219
Beard, George M. 221
behaviourism 211, 212, 216
Bekker, Balthasar 29
Bergson, Henri 104, 160, 190
Bierce, Ambrose 91
Binet, Alfred 194
Blackburn, Douglas 116, 169, 189
Blake, William 88
Blavatsky, Helena 164, 165–6
Böhme, Gernot 36
Böhme, Hartmut 36
Bowyer, Richard A. 27
Breton, André 219
Brewster, David 33, 49
Brierre de Boismont, Alexandre 55–7, 60, 89
Briggs, Julia 65
British College of Psychic Science 227
Brontë, Charlotte 11

Brown, Annie 201
Brown, J.H. 47–8
Brown, Samuel 195
Browning, Robert 15, 108
Buchanan, Robert 48
Bulwer-Lytton, Edward 14
Burton, Richard Francis 104
Buss, Robert W. 63
Butler, Samuel 140

Carlyle, Thomas 92
Carpenter, William B. 78, 205, 207
Carrington, Hereward 223, 227
Castle, Terry 33, 35
Cerullo, John 213
Chapman, William 47
Charcot, Jean-Martin 196
Cixous, Hélène 3
clairvoyance 71, 74, 99, 177, 183
Clark, Stuart 31
Clerke, Kate M. 178–9
Cock Lane ghost 8
Coffin, Walter H. 114
Coleridge, Samuel Taylor 17, 37, 56, 79
communication networks 3, 11, 105,
    115, 148–9
communion of saints 157
community of sensation 22, 69, 135–8,
    145, 147, 150, 160–2, 167, 176,
    178, 190, 212
Comte, Auguste 113
Cook, Florence 15, 76, 108, 109
Cottingley fairies 224
Cottom, Daniel 4, 13
Cox, Edward William 'Serjeant' 103
Cox, Michael 17
Crawley, A.E. 84
Creery Sisters 116, 169, 171–2, 189
Crookes, William 15, 76, 104, 108, 109
Crosland, Newton 95
Crowe, Catherine 10–11, 12, 13, 15
Cruikshank, George 90

Darwin, Frank 105
Darwinism 22, 128
Davies, Owen 4, 8
death 3–4, 39, 115, 138, 153–6, 159, 160,
    161, 177, 179, 195, 223–4
  bereavement 49, 93, 148, 149, 155, 224
  compacts 148, 150
  of the other 3, 147, 148, 151, 155, 168
  of the self 160
Defoe, Daniel 8, 17, 31
de la Mare, Walter 222
Denton, William 96–7
Derrida, Jacques 5, 19
Dickens, Charles 6, 13–14, 17, 19, 35,
    88, 135
  A Christmas Carol 61–3, 65
Dickinson, Emily 133, 134
Dilthey, Wilhelm 8
Dodge, Raymond 211–12
Dolby, R.G.A. 190
Doyle, Arthur Conan 104, 187, 223, 224
dreams 160, 192
  of the dead 73, 150, 160–1, 161–2, 179
  and hallucinations 63, 72–3, 161
  theories of 3, 37–40, 50, 57
Drelincourt, Charles 18

Eglinton, William 115
Eliot, George 60, 140
Ellenberger, Henri 10
Ellis, Havelock 204
Engels, Friedrich 218
Enlightenment, the 11, 19, 31–3, 43,
    46, 48, 59, 68, 77, 91, 119,
    130, 216, 218
Esquirol, J.E.D. 20, 53–5, 62, 193
evangelicalism 79
Ey, Henri 55

factionality 10, 14, 16–18, 19, 106,
    223, 227
Faraday, Michael 13
Fata Morgana 52
Ferriar, John 39, 44, 45, 51, 52, 56
Flournoy, Théodore 187, 213
Ford, Jennifer 37
Foucault, Michel 11
Fournier d'Albe, E.E. 151, 223
Fox sisters 12, 66
Freud, Sigmund 39, 57, 104,
    213–14, 223

Galton, Francis 20, 84–7, 88, 198
Gaskell, Elizabeth 14
Gauld, Alan 104, 189

Ghost Club 103
Ghost Society 103
ghost stories (fiction) 13, 14, 16–19, 20,
    35–6, 60, 61–5, 123, 136–7, 223
ghosts
  in the bedroom 63, 144, 158, 174,
    178–9, 205
  and Catholicism 30, 57
  of a child 125
  and clothes 21, 45, 69, 73, 90–100
  crisis-apparition 1, 2, 74, 137–8, 140,
    143, 145–9, 149–51, 153–6, 162,
    167, 169, 195, 199, 200, 208, 227
  as a double 81
  as dreams 3, 19, 23, 40, 45, 65, 69,
    75, 208–9
  as entertainment 47
  forebodings of 158–9
  medieval 27
  phantasms of the dead 22, 99, 130, 134,
    138, 172, 181, 183, 187, 199
  and Protestantism 17, 28, 156, 157–8
  purposeless 3, 126, 173, 180
  of the self 143–5, 150, 222
  testimony of 44, 117–18, 119–24, 130,
    163, 165, 174
  traditional 1, 2, 4, 45, 91, 121, 122, 123,
    154, 159, 173, 175, 179, 199, 227
  and vision 6–8, 32, 42, 44, 45, 46, 48,
    49, 52, 76, 88, 90
Gilbert, R.A. 17
Gladstone, William E. 104, 105
Glanvill, Joseph 30, 220
Goethe, Johann Wolfgang von 81
Goya, Francisco de 37, 64
Grose, Francis 45
Gurney, Edmund 98, 99, 111, 114, 115,
    116, 119, 123, 127, 128, 131, 133,
    135, 139, 140–1, 146, 152, 153–4,
    158, 161–2, 163, 164, 165, 166–7,
    169–70, 171, 172, 174, 175, 176–7,
    178–9, 181, 185, 186, 187, 188,
    189, 193, 194, 195, 198, 199,
    202, 203

Hall, G. Stanley 112, 168–70
hallucination 2, 3, 20, 21, 32, 33, 39, 42,
    45, 52–7, 61–5, 68, 69, 74, 75, 76,
    80–2, 84, 87, 88–9, 90, 91, 97–8,
    100, 117, 119, 124, 190, 215–17
  of an artist 118–19
  definition of 32, 52, 79–80, 88
  as dream 40, 50, 53, 54–5, 59, 63,
    69–70, 82, 83, 91, 92, 98, 202–9,
    210, 216–17

of memory 167, 168
moral cause of 56
origin of 46, 53, 55, 193–4, 199
theory of 46, 117
    French 53–60, 81
Hauffe, Friederike 10, 71
haunted house 114, 117, 118, 123, 172–4,
    175, 176, 222
Hawthorne, Nathaniel 35, 65, 149
    'The Haunted Mind' 63–5
Haynes, Renée 186
Hearnshaw, L.S. 185
Hervey de Saint-Denys, Marie-Jean-Léon
    57, 58–9, 216
Hibbert, Samuel 44–5, 56, 86
Hodgson, Richard 115, 166, 187, 188, 191
Hoffmann, E.T.A. 10, 37
Holland, Henry 50
Home, Daniel Dunglas 15, 76, 108,
    109, 207
Homer 1
Honywood, Mrs 208
Hopkins, R. Thurston 223
Howitt, William 219
Hume, David 69, 129
hypnotism 79, 98, 115, 135, 141, 170, 179,
    182, 183, 194, 196, 207

Ibsen, Henrik 220
Innes, A. Taylor 163–4, 165, 167, 170
Institut métapsychique international 227
International Congress of Experimental
    Psychology 196–7, 210
Ireland, William W. 89–90

James VI and I 29
James, Henry 1, 2, 3, 9, 124, 137, 227
    'The Friends of the Friends' 1–2
James, William 9, 14, 104, 112, 116, 131,
    137, 141, 182–3, 187, 190, 196,
    197, 211, 213–14, 227
Janet, Pierre 59, 196, 213
Joan of Arc 89
Johnson, Samuel 31
Joyce, James 6, 220
Jung, Carl Gustav 15, 104, 156, 214–15
Jung-Stilling, Johann Heinrich 7, 10

Kant, Immanuel 20, 36, 66–70, 71, 74, 75,
    124, 164, 192, 216, 218, 221
Kardec, Allan 11, 93
Keats, John 35
Kerner, Justinus 10
Keulemans, J.G. 125
Kirkland, Winifred 223

Kollar, Rene 157
Kuhn, Thomas 170

Lamont, Peter 16
Lang, Andrew 98, 106, 206, 208–9
Latour, Bruno 211
Lautréamont, Comte de 219
Le Fanu, Joseph Sheridan 18, 35
Lélut, L.F. 89
Leonardo da Vinci 219
Leopardi, Giacomo 219
Lewes, George Henry 76–7, 88
Lewis, Angelo ('Professor Hoffmann') 77
Llinás, R.R. 216
Locke, John 6
Lodge, Oliver 133, 164, 186, 187, 223
London Dialectical Society 14, 208
London Society for the Prevention of
    Premature Burial 154
Luckhurst, Roger 105, 120, 121, 142, 189
Luther, Martin 28, 39, 56, 89

MacAlpine, William 137
Machen, Arthur 223
Macnish, Robert 49
magic 12
Martin, Lillien J. 87–8
Marx, Karl 218
Maudsley, Henry 79–81, 89
Maury, Alfred 57–8, 59–60, 60,
    203, 216
McDougall, William 104
Mesmer, Anton 122
mesmerism 9, 13, 22, 71, 78, 80, 110, 114,
    115, 122, 135, 136, 144, 182
Mill, John Stuart 132–3
Moses, William Stainton 104, 143–4, 145
Most Haunted 1
Muhammad 89
Müller, Johannes 50
Myers, A.T. 196
Myers, Frederic W.H. 21, 22, 98–9, 104,
    105, 106, 107–8, 110, 111, 114,
    115, 116, 119, 128, 134, 137, 139,
    140, 141, 145, 146, 172, 174, 176,
    177–8, 179–80, 181–8, 190, 196,
    210, 213
    *Human Personality and Its Survival of
    Bodily Death* 22, 114, 182, 187, 190

Nancy, Jean-Luc 151
National Laboratory of Psychical
    Research 227
Newton, Isaac 186
Newton, John 29

Nicol, Fraser 141
Nicolai, Christoph Friedrich 40–3, 50, 60, 63, 69, 78, 88, 97, 193
Nietzsche, Friedrich 137

Oliphant, Margaret 223
Ollier, Charles 75
Oppenheim, Janet 5, 185

parapsychology 212, 227
Paré, D. 216
Parish, Edmund 203–6
Pascal, Blaise 89
Paterson, Robert 48–9
Peabody, Sophia 149
Peirce, Charles S. 123, 166–7, 169, 170
phantasmagoria 5, 20, 33–5, 56, 86
Phasmatological Society 103
Philipstahl, Paul de 33, 34
Phillips, Forbes 223
Pinel, Philippe 20, 53
Podmore, Frank 98, 99–100, 114, 115, 139, 141, 172, 174, 180–1, 181–2, 185, 187, 188, 206–8
Porter, Roy 54
Price, Harry 227
psychical research 5, 22, 40, 80, 105, 108, 109–10, 114, 121, 127, 128, 129, 132, 135, 141, 142, 143, 161, 182, 183, 184, 185, 188, 192, 193, 197, 211–12, 214, 223, 227
(see also Society for Psychical Research)
Cambridge 104
psychoanalysis 213–15, 216
Psychological Society of Great Britain 103–4
psychology 5
crowd 56
experimental 23, 84–8, 90, 105, 128, 168, 169, 170, 203, 210, 211, 212
romantic 9–10, 182–3, 185
psychometry 96–7
psychopathology 3, 20, 31, 42, 49, 52, 54, 68, 69, 75, 163, 192
(see also hallucination)
purgatory 27, 28, 156

Quinney, Laura 35

Rabaté, Jean-Michel 221
Raverat, Gwen 105
Rayleigh, Lord (John William Strutt) 176
Reichenbach phenomena 114, 115
Reformation 28, 57

Rhine, J.B. 227
Ribot, Germain Theodore 196
Richet, Charles 104, 132, 196
Rimbaud, Arthur 219
Robertson, C. Lockhart 114
Roffe, Alfred 93
Rogers, Edmund Dawson 110
Rogers, Edward Coit 219–20
Rousseau, Jean-Jacques 69
Royal Society (London) 30
Royal Society of Berlin 40
Royce, Josiah 112, 167–8, 170, 204
Ruskin, John 145

Scarborough, Dorothy 17
Scarry, Elaine 221
scepticism (towards religion) 3, 23, 29–30, 43, 51–2, 89, 105–6, 107, 109, 156, 181
Schiller, F.C.S. 227
Schiller, Friedrich von 35, 219, 220
The Ghost-seer 35–6, 219
Schönfeld, Martin 67
Schopenhauer, Arthur 20, 40, 66, 70–5, 92, 154, 208
Schwartz, Sophie 216
scientific naturalism 15, 21, 23, 71, 80, 100, 108, 121, 128, 136, 139, 140, 143, 147, 170, 171, 186, 188, 214
Scot, Reginald 29
Scott, Walter 49
séance 12, 15, 16, 77, 81, 82, 156, 207
Seashore, Carl E. 87
Seybert Commission Report 170
Shakespeare, William 8, 88, 93
Hamlet 8, 19, 30, 93, 95, 228
Shapin, Steven 53
Shell, Susan Meld 70
Showers, Mary 108
Sidgwick, Eleanor M. 99, 111, 131, 175–6, 187, 196, 197, 201
Sidgwick, Henry 106–8, 109, 110, 111, 117, 128, 133, 140, 141, 142, 171, 181, 186, 188, 191, 196, 197, 201, 207, 210
'Sidgwick Group' 106, 110–11, 175, 183, 184, 186, 187, 188, 189
Simmel, Georg 121
Slade, Henry 108
Smith, Adam 160
Smith, George A. 116, 169, 188–9
Smith, J.P. 201–2
Société exégétique et philanthropique 9
Société médico-psychologique 59

Society for Psychical Research (SPR) 13,
      21–3, 52, 74, 98, 104, 111, 139–91,
      192–217, 222, 227
   Census of Hallucinations 23, 195–206,
      210, 212
   committees 114
   concept of hallucination 23, 105,
      192–215, 216
   foundation 110
   membership 104, 111, 121–2, 129
   Phantasms of the Living 22, 23, 114, 133,
      139–51, 152–72, 175, 176–8, 181,
      183, 187, 190, 195, 199, 202, 204, 210
      criticisms of 162–72
   rules 129
   terminology 115, 117, 118, 124,
      135, 139
Society for the Study of Supernormal
      Pictures 224
Socrates 89
soul 22, 27, 29, 30, 39, 69, 82, 90, 91,
      95, 123, 145, 155, 156, 158, 160,
      173, 178, 182, 183, 184, 185, 186,
      188, 213
spectral illusions theory 20, 41–2, 43–53, 54,
      62–3, 66, 77, 78, 119, 127, 193, 218
   cases of 40, 46, 47–9
Spectre of the Broken 44, 52
Spinoza, Baruch 218
spirit photography 16, 187, 224
spiritualism 4, 5, 9, 11, 12–16, 20–1, 30,
      43, 51, 65, 66, 68, 69, 75–84, 90–8,
      100, 103, 104, 105, 108, 109, 112,
      113, 115, 126, 140, 148, 154, 155,
      157, 158, 170, 174, 175, 176, 181,
      182, 183, 184, 185, 187–8, 199,
      206, 207, 219, 223–4
      (*see also* séance)
   and Society for Psychical Research 105,
      112, 115, 121
   British National Alliance of Spiritualists
      110
Stead, W.T. 15, 106
Stevenson, Robert Louis 104
Stewart, Balfour 115
Stirner, Max 219, 221
Strange, Julie-Marie 224
Stuart, Rosa 223
suicide 2, 59, 118

surrealism 219
Swedenborg, Emanuel 6, 9, 66, 67–70, 89

Taillepied, Noel 29
Taine, Hippolyte 59–60, 61, 84, 86
telegraphy 1, 3, 11, 148, 149, 152
      (*see also* communication networks)
telepathy 23, 99, 106, 112, 116, 117,
      120, 121, 122, 126, 132, 135,
      138, 143, 145, 146, 147, 148,
      151, 152, 153, 154, 162–3, 164,
      165, 168, 169–70, 171, 172,
      174, 175, 178, 180, 181, 182,
      183, 185, 188, 189, 190, 197,
      199–200, 203, 207, 208, 210,
      212, 213, 216, 218
Tennyson, Alfred, Lord 104, 112
Theosophical Society 165, 175
   and Society for Psychical Research
      115, 165–6
theosophy 121, 188
thought-transference 106, 109, 115,
      116–17, 118, 126, 127, 138, 141,
      143, 145, 146, 149, 150, 153, 171,
      188 (*see also* telepathy)
Turner, Frank Miller 128
Tylor, Edward B. 20, 82–4, 214
Tyndall, John 13, 185

Vande Kemp, Hendrika 160
Viollet, Marcel 81
Voltaire (François-Marie Arouet) 32

Wagner, Richard 88
Wallace, Alfred Russel 77
Watson, John B. 211
Weber, Max 218
Wedgwood, Hensleigh 114
Wells, H.G. 122
Williams, J.P. 128, 132
willing game 115, 116
Wilson, Neil 10
Winter, Alison 135
witchcraft 29, 43, 66, 83, 142
Wolfreys, Julian 17
Wordsworth, William 35
Wyld, George 114

Yeats, William Butler 207, 222

For EU product safety concerns, contact us at Calle de José Abascal, 56–1°,
28003 Madrid, Spain or eugpsr@cambridge.org.

www.ingramcontent.com/pod-product-compliance
Ingram Content Group UK Ltd.
Pitfield, Milton Keynes, MK11 3LW, UK
UKHW020336140625

459647UK00018B/2164